The Materiality of the Past

The Materiality of the Past

History and Representation in Sikh Tradition

ANNE MURPHY

OXFORD
UNIVERSITY PRESS

OXFORD

UNIVERSITY PRESS

Oxford University Press is a department of the University of Oxford.
It furthers the University's objective of excellence in research,
scholarship, and education by publishing worldwide.

Oxford   New York
Auckland   Cape Town   Dar es Salaam   Hong Kong   Karachi
Kuala Lumpur   Madrid   Melbourne   Mexico City   Nairobi
New Delhi   Shanghai   Taipei   Toronto

With offices in
Argentina   Austria   Brazil   Chile   Czech Republic   France   Greece
Guatemala   Hungary   Italy   Japan   Poland   Portugal   Singapore
South Korea   Switzerland   Thailand   Turkey   Ukraine   Vietnam

Oxford is a registered trade mark of Oxford University Press
in the UK and certain other countries.

Published in the United States of America by
Oxford University Press
198 Madison Avenue, New York, NY 10016

Library of Congress Cataloging-in-Publication Data
Murphy, Anne, 1967–
The materiality of the past : history and representation in Sikh tradition / Anne Murphy.
pages   cm
Includes bibliographical references and index.
ISBN 978-0-19-991627-6 (hardcover : alk. paper)—ISBN 978-0-19-991629-0 (pbk. : alk. paper)
1. Sikhism—Historiography. 2. Sikhs—Historiography.
3. Punjab (India)—Historiography. I. Title.
BL2017.6.M87   2012
294.609—dc23   2012006856

1 3 5 7 9 8 6 4 2

Printed in the United States of America
on acid-free paper

For Aidan,
who made it all make sense

Contents

Acknowledgments

THIS BOOK HAS grown out of my own experience of the material life of the past. After my father's death when I was nine years old, I would periodically seek out on our shelves the old books in which he had inscribed his name: David A. Murphy. They brought me great comfort. These were days that seem impossible today: before cameras and video were so common, before cell phones and their tiny cameras made images a part of our every moment. We had few photographs of my father. He had once wanted to be a scholar (but he never finished his Ph.D.); his field would have been English literature. As I grew up, it seemed that the one real thing I had as a connection to him were those signatures of his, marking the books he read. I did not think these books embodied him. They could not bring him back. Somehow, though, they kept him alive. It is fitting that this experience of memory culminates in a book, a history, my own answer to those memories with which I grew up.

I have incurred many debts in the writing of this book, and have many people to thank. This is so with any work, but perhaps more so in this case than in others. It is often said that it takes a village to raise a child, and this is true. It also takes many people to help a book come into being. I have many people to thank, for helping me to do both.

This book took its first form as a doctoral dissertation. I was extremely fortunate to benefit from the rich intellectual environment at Columbia University, where attention to South Asian languages and history accompanied a commitment to postcolonial critique and engagement with the politics of the present. My advisor, J. S. Hawley, was a careful and supportive guide, and my intellectual development was shaped profoundly by Nicholas Dirks and Partha Chatterjee. Rachel McDermott and Elizabeth Castelli also contributed in unique ways to the creation of an ideal and stimulating scholarly environment. I received generous support from the Department of Religion and other entities at Columbia (such as the Southern Asian Institute, which offered a vibrant location for the study of South Asia, and the wonderful Undergraduate Writing Program). The graduate student community at Columbia was a rich source of intellectual and personal sustenance—particularly Christian Novetzke and Varuni Bhatia (and her husband Sharmadeep Basu), who have continued to act as important interlocutors and friends. My early work at the University of Washington (with Michael Shapiro, Richard Salomon, Alan Entwistle [may he rest in peace], and Heidi Pauwels) provided excellent grounding that has taken me far.

My doctoral research was funded by a Fulbright-Hays dissertation research grant, allowing me to undertake research in India, Scotland, and England in 2002. The National Institute for Punjab Studies provided affiliation during my stay, and Rishi Singh of that institution provided friendly help. Manjit Singh Bedi and his family welcomed me in Phagwara and in England. The families I visited in Malwa, and the Manager of the Takhat Damdama Sahib, were very hospitable; the Bhai Rupa family and particularly Bhai Buta Singh, who has stayed in touch all these years, were particularly so; and we were well taken care of by the Sandhus of Faridkot, with whom my former student Amrinder Sandhu arranged for us to stay in 2007. The staff at various institutions has been extremely helpful: the Nehru Memorial Museum, the National Archives in Delhi, Punjabi University Library, the Punjab State Archives in Patiala and in Chandigarh (in particular, in 2009–10), and the India Office Library in London. Many people in Birmingham also helped me, particularly Bhai Mohinder Singh and the staff at The Guru Nanak Nishkam Sevak Jatha as well as the staff at the Birmingham Sikh Association. In Scotland, I received valuable help at the National Library and the city archives. Susan Stronge of the Victoria and Albert Museum provided guidance and access. My time in London in 2002 was made far easier and more enjoyable by the wonderful facilities at Goodenough College, which provided me with housing. New York University provided an Eastern Consortium Tuition Fellowship for Persian in the summer of 2003, and the Pluralism Project of Harvard University provided me with essential support for research in California in the same summer.

This book would not have been possible without postdoctoral research support. My research fund at New School University enabled a supplementary research trip in December 2004–January 2005 that allowed me to reconnect with my work and investigate archives for future work, and a similar "start-up" grant at the University of British Columbia, several other grants—and even more crucially, a flexible teaching schedule in my first two years that allowed me to go to India in the falls of 2006 and 2007, and a research leave granted in 2009–10—supported visits to India and England in support of this book and other projects. All this was made possible by the committed support of my Department Heads, J. Ross King and Peter Nosco. To them I owe great thanks. A 2005 summer grant from the British Academy/American Philosophical Society allowed for more extensive investigation in the India Office Library collections. A Senior Research Fellowship with the American Institute of Indian Studies in 2009–10 allowed for research on a related topic; results from this research are found in partial form in chapter 5. The grant allowed me to hire Behnaz Alipour Kaskari as a Research Assistant, enhancing my work with the Khalsa Darbar Records. To her I owe thanks as well. Finally, a Canadian Social Sciences and Humanities Research Council grant in 2010–11 allowed me to undertake related research that at times is reflected in subtle ways in this work.

I have given papers with material from this book in countless places, including Columbia University; The New School for Social Research; Panjab University (Chandigarh), University of Michigan's Graduate Student Symposium in 2011; the annual meetings of the American Academy of Religion, the Association for Asian Studies, and the American Historical Association; the Museum of Vancouver, and others. Participation in the *Modernity, Diversity and the Public Sphere: Negotiating Religious Identities in 18th–20th Century India* workshop in Erfurt, Germany in 2010 was extremely valuable intellectually and provided wonderful feedback; thanks to Vasudha Dalmia and Martin Fuchs for the invitation. Related material has been published in *History and Theory, Early Modern Women: An Interdisciplinary Journal*, the *Journal of the American Academy of Religion*, and *Sikh Formations: Religion, Culture, Theory.* Thank you to contributors to the related edited volume, *Time, History and the Religious Imaginary in South Asia* (Routledge, 2011), which explores similar themes across religious and linguistic communities, and particularly to Rajeev Kinra for sharing his always exciting ongoing work and Purnima Dhavan, whose essay appears in the volume and has always been generous with her ideas and work; the many footnotes to her work in this book attest to the ways her work intersects with mine. The conferences and workshops organized by Arvind Singh Mandair first at Hofstra and now at Michigan have provided sounding boards for this and other work. Thank you is also due in large measure to Oxford University Press and Cynthia Read for their careful work in publishing the book, and to colleagues who have read all or part of it, including colleagues at the New School (Laura Liu, Paul Ross, and others), UBC (Adheesh Sathaye, Katherine Hacker, Christina Laffin, and in particular Pushkar Sohoni), and elsewhere (particularly Bali Sahota at UC Santa Cruz and Nikky-Guninder Kaur Singh of Colby College), and of course the anonymous reviewers who gave such helpful comments on the submitted manuscript. Thank you to Rivka Israel for editing the manuscript and completing the Index; Julie Vig and Raghavendra Rao, who provided essential help in the final stages of preparing the book for publication, and to Raghavendra for the illustrations he made; and Peder Gedda, whose nascent research helped to enrich my discussion of *rahit* here. Thank you also to Roopinder Singh of the Tribune and Bhai Sikandar Singh of Bagrian for friendship, interest, and for the use of the cover image;

thanks also to Bhai Sahib for access to court records related to the settlement of property at Bagrian.

A small grant from The Sikh Cultural Society based in Richmond Hill Queens allowed me to study in Punjab in the summer of 1998; I later came to know Harpreet Singh Toor, who has been very active in the Society, as a respected friend. His brother Bally and wife Jasdeep gave me a generous welcome in Punjab when I was doing dissertation research; I cannot express the importance of this kind of support, particularly to a woman working on her own in India. They later welcomed us back, when my son Aidan was small. Work with Constance Buchanan and the Ford Foundation, for whom I worked as a Research Consultant from 1998 to 2000, shaped my thinking early on in my Columbia career. My work has also been shaped by work at the Seattle Art Museum, Metropolitan Museum of Art, Japanese American National Museum, and Asia Society, with whom I worked over the years. Artist and educator Frederic Wong helped form my early thinking on museums, through thoughtful conversation and debate. Since moving to Vancouver in 2006, I have had the pleasure of shared intellectual and literary interests with a wide range of people, including: Manpreet Dhillon, Mo Dhaliwal, and Naveen Girn of the Vancouver International Bhangra Celebration; Mohan Gill and others of the Punjabi Kendri Lekhak Sabha; my colleagues Sukhwant Hundal, Katherine Hacker, Pushkar Sohoni, Adheesh Sathaye, and Renisa Mawani; writers Ajmer Rode, Brajinder Dhillon, and many others. My wonderful students at the New School and UBC—particularly Julie Vig, Peder Gedda, Parvinder Dhaliwal, Ranbir Johal, Jasmine Sandher, and Amrinder Sandhu—have provided a source of intellectual vitality and growth, and promise for the future.

Friends and childcare providers have made this work thinkable for a scholar who is a mother: first and foremost among them, Jasdeep and Mandeep Tatla, and Darshan Uncle (Darshan Singh Tatla), who gave us a home in Punjab and a place to find respite, speak Punjabi, and garden; Rana and Aruti Nayar, who helped me in innumerable ways during an extended stay in Chandigarh in 2009–10, and Professor Raghbir Singh, who gave Aidan and I not just a place to live in Chandigarh, but also a home, and who inspired Aidan to learn Punjabi; Madge Huntington in New York, whose apartment door was always open; Art and Onagh Currie for some emergency babysitting at crucial times; Jillian Bartlett, who captured my tiny son's heart in 2003–4; Mahua Bose, who was the ideal roommate in Delhi; Birgit Depperman and Stefan Gaezle for love and friendship (and logistical support at times) in Vancouver and during two trips to Germany; Happy Montessori School in Port Washington, which provided essential care for Aidan in the fall of 2007 and Creative Minds in Vancouver, which was supportive, flexible, and saved me several times; of course "Miss Clarisse," whose in-home daycare provided a home-like setting for Aidan in a time of great changes; and recently Mery Yeny Saavedra Flores and Jennifer Jeraldine Benito Saavedra, mother and daughter, who saved the day at the end. My colleagues at UBC—particularly, when I first came, Stefania Burk, Christina Laffin, Ted Slingerland, and Kate Swatek—were helpful and welcoming, to me as an individual and as a parent, and the staff in the Department of Asian Studies has been tirelessly supportive and always fun. As a single parent (which I was until recently), I cannot emphasize the importance of such support. Indeed, at times it has seemed to me in these past years that there is a fragile, unseen web made of outstretched arms (of women, mostly, with some men) who make it possible to have a child and do something like write a book.

This book is written with many in mind: my father of course, who passed away more than thirty years ago; Robert F. Murphy, my father's eldest brother and former professor of anthropology at Columbia University, who passed away in 1991—the one scholar of our family; and Bridget Murphy, my great-aunt who lived in Limerick, Ireland, until her passing in 2010 and always made Ireland a true home. My mother worked very hard, under difficult circumstances, to provide me with an education. To her, I offer sincere thanks and respect; my interest in religion finds its source in her. I write this also with joyful celebration of the love of my partner Raghavendra Rao and our young son, Kabir David. They have brought us a joy we never imagined possible. But, above all, this book is dedicated to my son Aidan, who came into the world as I was writing the dissertation out of which it grew. He has been with me every step of the way. Aidan, you made writing this possible. Somehow, because of all of these people, I imagined I might write this book. It is in their honor that I have made the attempt. Its flaws, of course, are mine alone.

Notes on Transliteration and Related Conventions

I DO NOT use diacritics for names of persons, places, and institutions, and for words commonly known in English contexts, such as languages, castes, and other important words, such as "Sikh," "Khalsa," and "Guru Granth Sahib." I do however use diacritics for such words when quoting from and transliterating a full passage of text. I also use them for the titles of books in Punjabi. If my sources utilize diacritics, I present them as they have implemented them; if they do not, these are not used within the quotations. This has created differences: for example, while I transliterate the term *"rahit,"* W.H. McLeod chooses to use "Rahit." This difference is maintained, in deference to the two different approaches.

I adhere to the conventions of pronunciation used in modern Indo-Aryan languages; that is, for example, I drop the inherent "a" at the end of the name that in Sanskrit would be read as "Shiva." I have adopted the diacritic marks generally utilized for Punjabi, with one exception: I do not distinguish the use of nasalization (ṅ, or ṁ before labials), from full "na" when it is used internally in a word in a conjunct after the first occurrence of the word. Many such words have a normative status within Sikh usage in English today, so diacritics are intrusive (for example, panth). (Since in Punjabi conjunct letters are not used, one does not see full "na" in a conjunct with a consonant. We can therefore read any intermedial "n" prior to a consonant as a nasalization). For "Singh" I opt not to use diacritcs until the word itself is discussed. I have also utilized the single "ca" for what in English would most accurately be rendered as "cha," allowing me to avoid the use of "chha" for the aspirated form. I have rendered transliterated Persian words included here in keeping with the above conventions, for the sake of consistency, while allowing for the specifics of Persian.

I have where possible listed the references for published sources in Punjabi in the India Office Library/British Library; these are indicated in the notes with the notation "IOL." The notation IOR for Indian Office Records is utilized for sources of that type. I have given full information for the Khalsa Darbar Records at the Punjab State Archives in Chandigarh; the volumes in question are located as a set at the end of the chronologically ordered records.

The Materiality of the Past

I

Introduction

THE FORMS OF MEMORY AND HISTORY

IN APRIL 2008, Sotheby's auction house in London withdrew an object from sale, following protests in India. The piece—an eighteenth-century steel armor plate—had been offered for sale on behalf of an unnamed owner. It was described by Sotheby's as being similar to one that had formerly belonged to Guru Gobind Singh, the Tenth Guru of the Sikh tradition. Estimated at the time to be worth over 10,000 pounds, the item was described as "a rare 18th-century Sikh steel armour plate from North West India/Pakistan" and is said to have featured a verse of the Tenth Guru called the "Akal Ustat," which describes the nature of God. Although Sotheby's later argued that the plate had not actually belonged to the Guru—and that they therefore did not "deem the piece to be a relic of the Guru"—in the original auction catalog they had noted its similarity to a set of plates in the collection of the royal family of Patiala, a former princely state in Punjab, which was said to have been gifted to the family by the Guru himself, and that "the existence of this plate . . . suggests that the Guru commissioned more than one set."[1] Controversy then erupted, causing an important Sikh official to argue that "the Central Sikh Museum" in Amritsar, India, "is the right place for such treasures."[2]

This is not the first time that objects belonging to (or possibly, in the Sotheby's case, reminiscent of those belonging to) the Guru have caused controversy in the complicated postcolonial relationship between India and England.

---

1. Amit Roy, "Sotheby's Pulls Sikh Armour Auction," April 8, 2008, http://www.telegraphin dia.com/1080408/jsp/nation/story_9107735.jsp (accessed June 16, 2008). The "Akal Ustat" is found at the opening of the Dasam Granth, a text attributed to the Tenth Guru.

2. Arifa Akbar, "Sikh Protests Stop Sotheby's Auction of 'Religious Relic,'" http://www.independent.co.uk/news/uk/this-britain/sikh-protests-stop-sothebys-auction-of-religious-relic-806323.html (accessed June 16, 2008). The official was Avtar Singh Makkar, the President of the Shiromani Gurdwara Parbandhak Committee (SGPC). See below for more on this organization.

Another example is the repatriation in 1966 of objects that were the property of the Tenth Guru. These possessions of the Tenth Guru had been housed in the imperial collection or *toshākhānā* of the independent state founded by Maharaja Ranjit Singh centered at Lahore, in what is now Pakistani Punjab. In 1849, the East India Company annexed the state and the imperial treasury came into British hands. At the time, the Earl and later Marquess of Dalhousie, then Governor-General, perceived a dangerous relationship between these objects and Sikh sovereignty. He therefore advised the Court of Directors of the East India Company that "it would not be politic . . . to permit any Sikh institution to obtain possession . . . of these sacred and warlike symbols of a warlike faith." The objects thereafter became part of his private collection and remained in the United Kingdom until they were sought by the Indian High Commission for return to India in 1966.[3] More recently, one of the items prized by the Maharaja, the *kalgī* or turban ornament of the Tenth Guru, which has been sought multiple times in the past, is said to have been found and returned to India, although the claim is controversial.[4]

We can call these objects "relics," as Sotheby's does, and in so doing evoke a larger set of materials and practices in other world religions. There is good reason for doing so. Consider a similar set of objects belonging to the Sixth Guru, Hargobind, which traveled abroad from India in 2007. The objects—including a robe, letters, and a turban—visited Vancouver, British Columbia, to take part in the annual Vaisakhi parade here, in celebration of the spring festival associated with the founding of the Khalsa, an orthodox form of being Sikh founded in 1699 by Guru Gobind Singh. Such objects were described by an article in a major local newspaper, *The Vancouver Sun*, as "a symbol of reverence and belief," and Mrignayan Singh, a resident of Surrey—a Vancouver suburb with a large Sikh population—described them as "a live proof of [the] existence of something that we believe in." As such, the objects hold "an emotional significance for the community," and "it is a blessing to be a witness first hand."[5] In 2008 and 2010, another group of objects came to Vancouver, from the village of Bhai Rupa in India. Those objects attest to the close relationship of the family of Bhai Rup Chand, the founder of the village, and subsequent generations with the Gurus; in Vancouver,

3. Copy of letter included in Archer Papers, IOL Mss. Eur F236/215. India Office Library, British Library, United Kingdom. For more on this case, see: Anne Murphy, "The Guru's Weapons," *Journal of the American Academy of Religion* 77, 2 (June 2009): 1–30.

4. See: Anne Murphy, "March 1849 Lahore, Punjab, India," *Victorian Review* 36, 1 (Spring 2010): 21–26.

5. Anupreet Sandhu Bhamra, "Vaisakhi Parade to Feature Float with Holy Articles," *Vancouver Sun*, Saturday, April 14, 2007, p. B7.

they allowed local Sikhs to "connect to the past" and experience it directly (see figure 1.1).[6]

These brief examples demonstrate the rich meanings of Sikh objects. They function as "relics" in the sense identified by Buddhist Studies scholar Kevin Trainor, as "a technology of remembrance and representation," with a continuing religious and historical significance for the Sikh community.[7] Through such objects, the past is experienced and proved, and history narrated and performed for a trans-national religious community, within religious settings as well as cultural, artistic, and political ones. They refer to the memory of the ten Sikh Gurus, from the first, Guru Nanak (1469–1539), to the final embodied human Guru, Gobind Singh (1666–1708), and of other important persons revered by the community of Sikhs. As such, they act as links with, or memorial technologies to recuperate, the past. In this capacity, they are related to another form of materializing the Sikh past: the gurdwara. This is the congregational site of the Sikh community, where members come together to worship. The term *gurdwārā* means literally "doorway to the Guru," and is the link to, and place of the experience of, the Guru. Today, the Guru is represented not in human form, but in the form of the canon of the Sikh tradition, the Guru Granth Sahib. This name indicates its status: *sāhib* is an honorific term, and *grańth* means text.[8] This status of the text as Guru was established at the

---

6. Interviews were conducted with those involved in bringing the objects to Vancouver, and with several members of the *sańgat* or community who came to view the images, November 12–13, 2008, at the Dasmesh Darbar Gurdwara in Surrey, BC. These objects also visited Fresno, California, previously, as have others; see conclusion, and "Sacred Trust: Followers of the Sikh Faith flock to Fresno to View Centuries-old Relics on Loan from India," *The Fresno Bee*, February 21, 2000, A1. The cover image of this book hails from the Bhai Rupa collection. For more on the village and the collection, see Bhayee Sikandar Singh and Roopinder Singh *Sikh Heritage: Ethos and Relics* (New Delhi: Rupa & Co, 2012), 117 ff.

7. Kevin Trainor, *Relics, Ritual, and Representation in Buddhism: Rematerializing the Sri Lankan Theravada Tradition* (New York: Cambridge University Press, 1997), 26. The term "relic" was utilized, for example, by the National Institute of Punjab Studies in recent publications that have highlighted object traditions: Mohinder Singh, *Anandpur* and *The Golden Temple*; Mohinder Singh and Rishi Singh, *Maharaja Ranjit Singh* (all three New Delhi: UBS in association with National Institute of Panjab Studies, 2002). See also Bhayee Sikandar Singh and Roopinder Singh, *Sikh Heritage*. See further discussion of the term and its meanings in chapter 2.

8. This text is also referred to as the Adi Granth in some contexts; at other times Adi Granth and Guru Granth Sahib are used to denote different versions of the text. For those who use the terms for different texts, Adi Granth refers to the first compilation of the text, the Kartarpur Pothi, in 1604, and Guru Granth Sahib to the later version that was canonized as the living Guru at the beginning of the eighteenth century. For others, Adi Granth is a general synonym for the Guru Granth Sahib. Important works on the text and the history of its formation include: Pashaura Singh, *The Guru Granth Sahib: Canon, Meaning and Authority* (New Delhi: Oxford University Press, 2000) and *Life and Work of Guru Arjan: History, Memory, and Biography in the Sikh Tradition* (New Delhi, India: Oxford University Press, 2006); Gurinder

FIGURE 1.1 Objects from the village of Bhai Rupa, with Bhai Buta Singh, in Vancouver in 2010. Bhai Buta Singh belongs to the family in possession of these objects, and accompanies the objects to public displays around India and the world. Photograph by Anne Murphy.

death of the Tenth Guru, when the office of the Guru was transferred to the sacred scripture. This text is thus now the living presence of the Guru of the Sikh tradition, and the gurdwara is the place where this Guru-text is experienced, and the connection is made between Guru—as principle and as text—and followers.

Indeed, the very name "Sikh" connotes this relationship: "Sikh" is related to the Punjabi verb *sikhnā*, to learn, and can be seen as a derivative of the Sanskrit term *shishyā*, or student. The name defines the relationship to, and memory of, the Guru. Guru Nanak founded the community and a lineage of human "embodied" teachers that endured into the beginning of the eighteenth century, when Guru Gobind Singh died in 1708. This community has grown and changed over the centuries since the time of the human Gurus, and with reference to the living Guru as text, to form the global community that exists today. It has spread out from South Asia—with particularly strong communities in the United Kingdom and Canada—but has retained strong ties to Punjab, the center of the Gurus and

Singh Mann, *The Goindval Pothis: The Earliest Extant Source of the Sikh Canon* (Cambridge, MA: Department of Sanskrit and Indian Studies, Harvard University and Harvard University Press, 1996), and *The Making of Sikh Scripture* (Oxford: Oxford University Press, 2001).

the home of most Sikhs, through a latticework of memory-making cultural forms.[9] Some of these forms are tied to the landscape of Punjab, such as some gurdwaras; others are less so. All contribute to the continuing and evolving presence of the Sikh community, simultaneously looking to the past and looking forward. The ways in which the relationship has been forged between place as territory and the historical representation of the Sikh past, and how objects come to operate in a different register, comprise the central concern of this book.

History and the Formation of the Sikh Community

"Historical memory," cultural theorist Andreas Huyssen has noted about our current moment, is "not what it used to be."[10] Just as it has changed in its forms and methods in the West, historical representation has a long and complicated past in Sikh sources as well, in both popular and more formal spheres. Indeed, a Sikh interest in history has been most noted by scholars and other observers within the discourse associated with the separatist movement of the 1980s and '90s, which sought an independent Sikh state in Punjab under the name "Khalistan." This is what we might expect, in relation to the larger field of what constitutes history; "history was the mise-en-scène of modernity,"[11] Huyssen also notes, and the production of the nation—that quintessentially modern political form—was anchored within it. As anthropologist Veena Das and others noted when the Khalistan movement was at its height, the very modern struggle for an independent Sikh nation-state has been "framed in a language which immediately places it in the context of modern nation states," and at the same time has been "represented as a continuation of a series of struggles that Sikhs have historically had to wage in order to preserve their identity."[12] In the course of the struggle, a

9. On postcolonial and contemporary forms of memory making in relation to the gurdwara, see: Anne Murphy, "The Gurdwara Landscape and the Territory of Sikh Pasts," in *Negotiating Identity amongst the Religious Minorities of Asia*, ed. Avrum Ehrlich (Leiden: Brill, forthcoming).

10. Andreas Huyssen, *Present Pasts: Urban Palimpsests and the Politics of Memory* (Stanford, CA: Stanford University Press, 2003), 1.

11. Huyssen, *Present Pasts*, 1.

12. Veena Das, *Critical Events: An Anthropological Perspective on Contemporary India* (Delhi: Oxford University Press, 1995), 121. See also: Brian Keith Axel, *The Nation's Tortured Body: Violence, Representation, and the Formation of a Sikh "Diaspora"* (Durham, NC: Duke University Press, 2001); Robin Jeffrey, "Grappling with the Past: Sikh Politicians and the Past," *Pacific Affairs* 60 (1987); Mark Juergensmeyer, "The Logic of Religious Violence," *Journal of Strategic Studies* 10 (1987); Harjot Oberoi, "Sikh Fundamentalism: Translating History into Theory," in *Fundamentalisms and the State: Remaking Polities, Economies, and Militance*, ed. Martin E. Marty and Scott Appleby (Chicago: University of Chicago Press, 1993).

"normative model of Khalistani historiographical discourse," in the words of
Brian Axel, was established.[13] The production of Sikh history has thus been
mobilized for the political present in the last twenty-five years particularly
within a nationalist frame, and in both academic and popular discourse, Khalistani and nationalist representations of the past have received almost singular
attention, to the exclusion of other modes. The Sikh case is not unusual in this
regard; history has provided the locus for national and religious imaginaries in
South Asia more generally in the modern period, and was a primary means for
the emergence of the nation in the nationalist and post-Independence periods.[14]
Indeed, as we will see, claims to historicity have been determined by conflicting
notions of history, identity, and rights (property and civil) within colonial and
postcolonial contexts, and are deeply embedded within contemporary power
struggles.[15]

Yet, the Sikh engagement with historical representation is not a solely
modern concern, just as history has a longer past in South Asia more generally.
The previously widespread assumption that historical representation did not
exist in precolonial South Asia has been successfully challenged in recent years
by a range of scholars. These scholars built upon the early work of Romila
Thapar, and later Nicholas Dirks, who called for appreciation of the ways in
which the past is constructed within "indigenous" texts "in terms and categories that are consonant with the particular modes of 'historical' understanding posited by the texts and traditions themselves."[16] The engagement
with the past as a locus for forms of social and community formation thus has

---

13. Brian Keith Axel, "Diasporic Sublime: Sikh Martyrs, Internet Mediations, and the
Question of the Unimaginable," *Sikh Formations: Religion, Culture, Theory* 1, 1 (2005):
127–154, see p. 129.

14. For discussion of history in relation to the nation, see chapter 4.

15. Veena Das makes a similar argument: *Critical Events*, 42, as do several of the authors in
Sarvepalli Gopal, ed., *Anatomy of a Confrontation: The Babri-Masjid-Ramjanmabhumi Issue*
(New Delhi: Viking Penguin Books India, 1991). New modes of historicity have shaped reli-
gious communities in profound ways; see, for example, Philip Lutgendorf, "The Quest for the
Legendary Tulsidas," in *According to Tradition: Hagiographical Writing in India*, ed. Winand
M. Callewaert and Rupert Snell, 65–85 (Wiesbaden: Harrassowitz Verlag, 1994), 76ff.

16. Nicholas B. Dirks, *The Hollow Crown: Ethnohistory of an Indian Kingdom* (Cambridge:
Cambridge University Press, 1987), 57. Romila Thapar, "Society and Historical Consciousness:
The *Itihasa-Purana* Tradition," in *Interpreting Early India* 1992 [1986] (Delhi and New York:
Oxford University Press, 1992), 137–73; Romila Thapar, "Time as a Metaphor of History: Early
India," in *History and Beyond* (Delhi: Oxford University Press, 2000). I have contributed to
this discussion with reference to the Sikh tradition in "History in the Sikh Past," *History and
Theory* 46, 3 (October 2007): 345–65. See the references cited there for more on the larger
debate on historiography in South Asia.

a longer existence than a solely modernist account of history's past in South Asia can encompass. This book builds upon such insights into the past place of historiography in South Asia to explore the formation of the Sikh community through the commemoration of the past and the construction of a historical consciousness out of a range of memorial forms. Here we explore the social and religious transformations enabled by the production of the past as history, out of memory, as we consider the representations themselves that produce these effects.[17]

Descriptions of the Sikh tradition—both scholarly and popular—generally do not emphasize material expressions of the Sikh past, for various reasons. Indeed, according to mainstream Sikh thought, divinity is beyond representation; as a result, all forms of representation within religious contexts are treated with caution. One will generally not find anthropomorphic representations, therefore, within the central sanctum of a gurdwara, where the sacred canon is housed and displayed, and the congregation gathers to experience and participate in the recitation and celebration of the Word, as represented in the Sikh sacred scripture, the Guru Granth Sahib. Representations of the Gurus and Sikh heroes and martyrs, however, are quite common in other parts of gurdwara (such as in the *langar* hall, where the community gathers to eat together) and are the staple of the increasingly common "Sikh Museum," a type of museum usually associated with a gurdwara but generally kept separate from it. (The Central Sikh Museum, mentioned earlier, is located in the complex of the Golden Temple, one of Sikhism's holiest shrines, but is outside the gurdwara itself.) Within the museum associated with Sis Ganj, a major Sikh gurdwara in Old Delhi, a sign instructs visitors on the correct way to interact with the images contained there:

> The Sikh religious principles and practice permit the painting of portraits of the Gurus and depicting the events concerning Sikh history in paintings. But the garlanding of the portraits of the Gurus, offering worship of [and] touching the feet of the Guru as shown in the paintings is not allowed. Every Sikh should avoid doing so. To indulge in such practices is to go against the basic tenets of Sikhism.[18]

---

17. Thus we address Norbert Peabody's concern that we understand not just that representations of the past differ, but "the different processes of social and political transformation that are built upon those pasts" (Norbert Peabody, *Hindu Kingship and Polity in Precolonial India* [Cambridge: Cambridge University Press, 2003], 9).

18. This was on view in the museum associated with the Sis Ganj Gurdwara in 2002 and 2006.

Such concern over the status of anthropomorphic images, indeed, led to the decision to eschew such representations in the new Khalsa Heritage Centre, which opened in Anandpur, Punjab, in the end of 2011.[19]

Yet, while controversial, material and visual forms of transmission have accompanied the textual forms that are so important in Sikh tradition and have, due to their centrality, received extensive treatment in the past. Images of the Gurus have received some attention, albeit with the constraint indicated above, regarding their religious meaning.[20] They serve as the core of the museological representation that is in some senses a primary articulation point for Sikh public representation in the postcolonial period, both in India and abroad: the first Sikh museum in Leicester, England, was officially recognized by the British state in 2002, and numerous exhibitions have taken place on the Sikh tradition in the United Kingdom and the United States of America in the last ten years, such as at the Smithsonian Institution in Washington DC, the Asian Art Museum of San Francisco, and elsewhere.[21] Objects, on the other hand, are notable for their relative absence within scholarly literature about the Sikhs, even though they sometimes accompany images in museological contexts—but only at times. Sikh historical objects were, for example, excluded from the Khalsa Heritage Centre in India, precisely because of their importance: their presence would have, in the words of Director George Jacob, turned the museum into a "shrine."[22] They are however ubiquitous, referred to within the Sikh historiographical literature

---

19. George Jacob (Director, Khalsa Heritage Centre), lecture and conversation, University of British Columbia, November 2, 2011. On the center, see Anne-Colombe Launois (Sat Kaur) "The Khalsa Heritage Complex: A Museum for a Community?" in *New Insights into Sikh Art*, ed. Kavita Singh, 134–45 (Mumbai: Marg Publications, 2003), and brief discussion in Saloni Mathur, *India By Design: Colonial History and Cultural Display* (Berkeley: University of California Press, 2007), 169.

20. The classic work on this is W. H. McLeod, *Popular Sikh Art* (Oxford: Oxford University Press, 1991). See also Kerry Brown, ed., *Sikh Art and Literature* (London: Routledge, 1999).

21. See conclusion for further discussion, and Anne Murphy, "Museums and the Making of Sikh History," unpublished paper delivered in panel "Whose Museum? The Collection and Consumption of History, Nation and Community," Annual Meeting of the Association for Asian Studies (San Diego, CA, March 2004); Anne Murphy, "The Politics of Possibility and the Commemoration of Trauma," unpublished paper delivered at "After 1984?" conference (Berkeley, CA, September 12–13, 2009). See also: Lisa Allen-Agostini, "In the Sikh Spirit at the Smithsonian," *Washington Post*, Monday, August 13, 2001, C08; Cotter, Holland, "Wonders of Sikh Spirituality Come Alive." *New York Times*, September 18, 2006 http://www.nytimes.com/2006/09/18/arts/design/18sikh.html?ex=1316232000&en=2acdf712f34e9724&ei=5088&partner=rssnyt&emc=rss (accessed April 5, 2007); "Lahore Museum to Set up Sikh Gallery," *The Hindu*, May 17, 2004, online edition: http://www.thehindu.com/2004/05/17/stories/2004051702162000.htm (accessed June 1, 2004).

22. George Jacob, lecture and conversation, November 2, 2011.

associated with the tradition from the eighteenth century on. They also hold a particular importance in relation to sacred sites, the places associated with events and persons in the Sikh past.

Objects relate to the Gurus and others in various ways. The gifts of the Guru are, for instance, collected and displayed in the small village of Phaphare Bhai Ki in southwestern Punjab. Here these objects—weapons and clothing belonging to the Tenth Guru, such as a *kaṭār* or dagger with a wide handle, and a pair of shoes— attest to the long relationship of the village and the family of a village patriarch, Bhai Bahilo, and his descendants with the Gurus.[23] The Bhais of Bagrian also hold objects that attest to the relationship of their family with the Gurus; they too are descended from the patriarch Rup Chand, of Bhai Rupa (referred to earlier). The Sixth Guru presented a ladle and other gifts to the family in conjunction with a mandate to provide *langar* (a charitable open kitchen) for the community; the Bhais of Bagrian are renowned for their commitment to this promise. The Bhais then came to act as the primary religious authorities for the princely states of eastern Punjab, who also were seen to derive their right to rule from the Guru.[24] The materiality of the past has thus operated in the formation of the Sikh community through various means: by gifting, by use, and as a kind of proof of the past that attests to the authority of the Guru and his followers. Objects function to express relationships, past events, cultural heritage, and even (as the Governor-General of the East India Company feared in 1849) sovereignty. As we see with objects on tour in California and British Columbia, they also travel.[25] As Carol Breckenridge has noted, it is now a commonplace that objects undergo a metamorphosis when they are collected; such changes are inherent to the changing nature of the object.[26]

23. Gurpreet Kaur Dhillon, *Shrī Gurū Gobind Singh jī dī bakshish gur-vastāṇ dā itihās* (Punjabi) (New Delhi: Manpreet Prakashan, 1999). The *kaṭār* it generally worn tucked into the waist.

24. On the Bhais of Bagrian, see: Harjot Oberoi, "Brotherhood of the Pure: The Poetics and Politics of Cultural Transgression," *Modern Asian Studies* 26, 1 (1992): 157–97, see 164ff.; W. L. Conran and H. D. Craik, *Chiefs and Families of Note in the Punjab: A Revised edition of "The Punjab Chiefs" by Sir Lepel Griffin and of "Chiefs and Families of Note in the Punjab" by Colonel Charles F. Massy*, vol. 1 [Lahore: Civil and Military Gazette Press, 1909], 183–88; Bhayee Sikandar Singh and Roopinder Singh, *Sikh Heritage*.

25. Relics that travel thus demonstrate the way "things-in-motion" reflect their social and political context; see Arjun Appadurai, "Introduction: Commodities and the Politics of Value" in *The Social Life of Things: Commodities in Cultural Perspective*, 3–63 (Cambridge: Cambridge University Press, 1986), 6.

26. Carol Breckenridge, "The Aesthetics and Politics of Colonial Collecting: India at World Fairs," *Comparative Studies in History and Society* 31 (1989): 196. On the complex and changing nature of the object, despite its apparent stability, see Bill Brown, "Thing Theory" *Critical Theory* 28 (Autumn 2001): 1–22.

This book describes this historical process: how the Sikh community has produced itself through the representation of the past, and how the *media* of representation—in this case, the object and site—have acted to constitute the community in multiple terms. It is through means of transmission both textual and material that the past is made present and, simultaneously, the community created through the representation and mediated experience of the remembered past. For this reason, I explore textual representations with reference to materiality, as part of a single conceptual field.[27] This book, which focuses on the changing historical constitution of the community through the life of objects and sacred sites, is meant to augment, not replace, the textually defined narratives that have dominated understandings of the formation of the Sikh community. Indeed, it will be argued that the material and the textual are allied in the Sikh context, and should not be seen in oppositional terms. Attention to material and visual representation therefore may in fact dispel concerns (rather than raise them) regarding such practices, once they are placed in the broader context of cultural memory production and a Sikh historical imperative.[28] Further, our understanding of material practices, in this case, relies upon textual representations. The concern here, therefore, is not with the authenticity of objects in isolation, but with the larger historical imagination they represent.[29]

The Book and its Approach

This work began with an interest in Sikh object culture today and how it operates in the Sikh imagination and experience of the past, in the present and historically. This led to exploration of the representation of the past in the Sikh tradition in general terms, as well as closer study of the intimate relationship between the historical object and historical site, and the way the two also operate *differently* over time in their representation and embodiment of the past. The book is an account, historical in scope, of how and why this is the case, in relation to a broader investigation of the representation of the past in Sikh tradition. It thus takes as its starting point the diverse and sometimes contrasting forms that the

---

27. For discussion of a similar relationship between text and materiality, see Finbarr B. Flood *Objects of Translation: Material Culture and Medieval "Hindu-Muslim" Encounter* (Princeton: Princeton University Press, 2009), 9–12, 14.

28. Thus the argument here is not that such objects function as *murtī*s or images in the sense seen in Hindu temples.

29. The issue of authenticity has been raised: Bajinder Pal Singh, "Punjab Body to Get Sikh Relics Authenticated," *Indian Express*, July 14, 2000. http://www.indianexpress.com/ie/daily/20000714/ina14015.html (accessed March 1, 2004).

representation of the past takes within Sikh contexts today, particularly as material object and sacred site, and attempts to sketch a history and the underlying logic of these representational practices. That historical account begins in 1708, the year of the death of Guru Gobind Singh, and also (most importantly, for our purposes) a date suggested for the first historiographical text written about the Tenth Guru and the community, by the author Sainapati.[30] It ends with the official recognition in 1925 of a managing body for Sikh gurdwaras, the Shiromani Gurdwara Parband-hak Committee or SGPC, which enshrined a particular notion of what it means to be Sikh in relation to Sikh religious sites and their history and plays a crucial role in the modern formation of a Sikh historical sensibility. Although much more happens after 1925 that must inform understanding of Sikh object and site cultures today, the book examines this pivotal transition period of the eighteenth to early twentieth century because this is when foundational changes occurred. The goal in exploring the past in relation to the present is to analyze the ways in which the memorial practices and forms of historical representation associated with the Sikh tradition have been transformed within changing circumstances from the early modern through the colonial modern periods, and at the same time suggest how these practices and representations are manifest in our present moment.

We start with today, here and in the second and concluding chapters, where aspects of the continuing life of material representation in the Sikh tradition in the present are described and analyzed with reference to a Sikh historical imagi-nary explicated in the intervening chapters. There we see that materiality within Sikh tradition is not a series of anomalies, nor simply equivalent to similar phe-nomena in other religions, but instead part of a larger cohesive approach to the representation of the community's history and the life of the past in the present. Objects and sites constitute this past in the present to take part in a broader his-torical imaginary, through which the Sikh community is produced through its living relationship to the past. The materiality of Sikh subject formation is also clearly seen in the case of the markers of the Khalsa, the *panj kakkar* or "Five Ks": the *kes* (hair), *kanghā* (comb), *kirpān* (dagger), *karā* (steel bracelet) and *kaccha* (undergarment). The Five Ks can be seen as the generalized marker of the Guru, producing the community in memory of the Guru and on the path or *panth* (the term also used for the community) the Guru explicated.[31] Chapter 2 also ad-dresses the central question of the relationship between history and memory in relation to the representations examined.

---

30. On the dating of Sainapati's text, see chapter 3, footnote 55.

31. As noted, following occurrences of this word will dispense with diacritics.

The two main sections of the book that follow the second chapter describe the history of present practices. Section 1 explores how the past was conceived and represented in the 150 years from the time of the end of living human Guruship at the beginning of the eighteenth century—which inaugurated a new relationship to the past—to the end of the nineteenth century, after the annexation of the Lahore state of Maharaja Ranjit Singh by the British East India Company in 1849. In addition to heralding a period of new historiographical production, the eighteenth century is of key importance within Sikh tradition itself, for it comprises the crucial period of transition from the period of human Guruship to the primacy of the *representation* of the Guru through text—a transition from personal charismatic leadership to a textualized one, in which memory constitutes the presence of the Guru, an absence in body but a presence in performed and living Word. This memory is mobilized toward the production of a history: the history of the community, as a living embodiment of the past. Several eighteenth- and early nineteenth-century texts are examined to describe Sikh interest in the representation of the past in this time. Consideration of the period of colonial transition in historical representation follows. This predates the formal institution of British rule in Punjab, for it was in the early decades of the nineteenth century that Punjabi and Sikh historiography came under the direct influence of British forms of historical writing in tandem with an increasing British presence in political terms. The book traces the impact of such influence on the representation of the past through analysis of the first Sikh novel and related literature, with attention to broader orientations toward the writing of history in the subcontinent. In this way, the final part of the first section shows the particular salience of the representation of the past in a developing British-Sikh discourse that reflects broader discourses over history, religion, and nation taking place across the subcontinent.

The history of the Sikh community was a concern before the onset of British rule, and indeed—as section 1 demonstrates—the telling of this history was itself a project in the production of the community and its enduring presence across the temporal disjuncture that constitutes the narration of that which is past. The Sikh historical imaginary comes to be configured in the colonial context, however, in relation to a particularly territorialized notion of the Sikh community, as described in section 2. In this section we explore the understanding of the "soil" of the Sikh past—the landscape that represents Sikh history—in both precolonial and colonial terms, expanding on and providing greater historical depth to early observations on this theme by Harjot Oberoi.[32] The specific ways in which

---

32. Harjot Oberoi, "From Punjab to 'Khalistan': Territoriality and Metacommentary." *Pacific Affairs* 60, 1 (1987): 26 41; Oberoi sees Sikh territoriality as emerging in response to the

the relationship of the Sikh community to land and history was configured in the colonial period, with reference to precolonial practices, are the concern of chapter 5. Investigation of precolonial imperial court records reveals how Sikh religious sites were managed in the court of the last independent rulers of Punjab, Maharaja Ranjit Singh and his successors, and the attendant understanding of ownership that underpinned management practices. These practices are then compared with colonial period discourse and practice. We see in section 1 that concerns for the past were reconstituted in the nineteenth century in relation to increasing British power, such that, as Purnima Dhavan has noted, "the recording of Sikh history and its careful presentation to the British was . . . an essential part of statecraft in the princely states of Punjab."[33] This was perhaps even more the case within the parts of Punjab under direct East India Company rule, and after 1858, Crown rule. In section 2, we see how the establishment of property regimes in colonial Punjab impacted how religious sites were configured as property, leading to a territorialization of the Sikh historical consciousness in the shape of the gurdwara, and impacting an overall Sikh orientation to the past by 1925. The way the gurdwara came to be administered under British rule in relation to a legislatively and juridically defined and exclusive religious "identity" impacted how religious sites were imagined, and a particular notion of Sikh territory was substantialized.

We see that at this juncture the logic of representation shared between object and site breaks down, and the two come to embody very different relationships to the writing of Sikh history, even as they both remain a part of the experience of the past by the community. Objects come to lose some of their prominence, as the drive for the articulation of Sikh territory prevails, and the logic of the religious site vis-à-vis the state and the community articulated in the precolonial period—such as under Maharaja Ranjit Singh—changes. Objects thus come to be marginalized among representations of the Sikh past, and the Sikh historical landscape in territorialized terms is the material form that has dominated in the representation of the Sikh past since the beginning of the twentieth century.

Pakistan movement; see pp. 36–37 and following. He also focuses on the idea of Punjab, whereas my interest lies in the landscape of the Sikh past, which is not coterminous with Punjab (indeed, consideration of the wide range of Guru Nanak's travels compels a broader view of the geography of the tradition); Verne Dusenbery has made similar observations (Verne Dusenbery, *Sikhs at Large: Religion, Culture, and Politics in Global Perspective* [Oxford: Oxford University Press, 2008], 99). Recent efforts to imagine a Sikh landscape in relation to Punjab lie outside the scope of this book (but were a concern of Oberoi, in "From Punjab to 'Khalistan'"; see also Axel, *The Nation's Tortured Body*).

33. Purnima Dhavan, "Rehabilitating the Sikh 'Marauder': Changing Colonial Perspectives of Sikhs, 1765–1840," unpublished paper delivered at the Association for Asian Studies meeting (New York, March 2003), 8. I thank Dhavan for providing me access to her early work.

As technologies of memory and authority, material objects and sites do both continue today to contribute to the constitution of the Sikh community in relation to the representation, recollection, and substantiation of the past, as is shown in chapter 2. The object and the gurdwara, in their continuing significance, however, can be seen to embody two alternative perspectives toward the past and present: a de-territorialized one and a territorialized one. The conclusion discusses these two modes in the postcolonial period, as the object and place have been transformed in their representative import yet again, in relation to both an Indian audience and a diasporic one. These representational practices suggest compelling possibilities and intersections in the constitution of the Sikh community in transnational and national modes, partially through a "museumizing" imagination that reflects a colonial genealogy but cannot be limited to it. This hybrid and postcolonial imagination creatively engages with the museum as a form of colonial knowledge, to create something else. The operation of objects in a de-territorialized diasporic mode in the postcolonial period suggests how objects function in a unique way in our global present.

The Territory of the Sikh Past

This exploration of the representation of Sikh history in object and the gurdwara, in how they both coincide and how they come to differ, does not only attend to questions of historiography and its forms. The strong relationship of the articulation of Sikh history to the mapping of Sikh territory suggests that more is at stake in such representations than mere formal differences in kind. Attention to generally neglected representational practices such as those expressed in material culture provides a unique view of the community's self-imagination in a de-territorialized diasporic and fluid environment. Such a rethinking of the nature of territory in relation to sovereignty was suggested early on by Arjun Appadurai, and more specifically for the Sikh community within the recent work of Giorgio Shani.[34] A territorialized imagination of the Sikh community and its past has dominated within Khalistani visions of the Sikh present (a vision that still holds potent force in some diasporic locations)—so early dismissal of the potency of such an imagination

---

34. Arjun Appadurai, *Modernity at Large: Cultural Dimensions of Globalization* (Minneapolis: University of Minnesota Press, 1996), 49ff. See also Arjun Appadurai, "Sovereignty Without Territoriality: Notes for a Postnational Geography," in *The Geography of Identity*, ed. Patricia Yeager (Ann Arbor: University of Michigan, 1996), 40–58. On the territorialization of the Sikh community, see Giorgio Shani, *Sikh Nationalism and Identity in a Global Age* (London: Routlege, 2008), 84 and elsewhere.

were premature. But it is accompanied by other ways of constructing the community's history.[35] Objects in some senses deny territory, and produce new Sikh localities—or "re-territorializations"—through their travel and their dynamic representation of the past in the present.[36] In general, Shani argues that the Sikh community provides an example where "the sovereignty of the territorialized nation-state over the religious community as established in the aftermath of the Peace of Westphalia in 1648 can no longer be assumed in our 'global age,'" such that "Sikh *diasporic* narratives do not attempt to place territorial limits on the sovereignty of the *quam* [or nation] . . . [because] the contemporary phase of globalization has effectively de-territorialized *sovereignty*."[37] Even sites associated with the Sikh past—the "soil" of that past—are not necessarily the *territory* of the past; as Appadurai points out, "'soil' needs to be distinguished from territory . . . while soil is a matter of a spatialized and originary discourse of belonging, territory is concerned with integrity, surveyability, policing, and subsistence."[38] The soil of this past has complex relationships with territorialization. While this book will suggest how processes of territorialization and de-territorialization relate to Sikh representations today, its focus will be the historical formation of these two ways of understanding the past within the Sikh tradition, further strengthening the arguments of Shani and others about the current moment, but without privileging recent political engagement with Sikh territory as a central theme.

There is of course a politics of this discussion, as is true of any attempt to account for the history of our present—in this case, the history of representations of the Sikh past.[39] Discussion of the historical production of Sikh territoriality within such representations can seem to support the idea of Khalistan—that is, the quest for an independent Sikh state within South Asia—and might seem to give such territoriality a powerful prehistory. This exploration can also, conversely,

---

35. The resurgence in 2007 and following of a very territorially conceived Khalistani rhetoric in British Columbia, Canada, provides evidence that Appadurai was premature in declaring that "states are the only major players in the global scene that really need the idea of territorially based sovereignty" in 1996 ("Sovereignty Without Territory," 49), arguing that the Khalistani example is a "different" sort of national imaginary (50). Shani also notes that rhetoric on the demise of the nation-state was premature (*Sikh Nationalism*, 9).

36. Appadurai, "Sovereignty Without Territoriality," 54.

37. Shani, *Sikh Nationalism*, 16 (first quote), 156 (second quote).

38. Appadurai, "Sovereignty Without Territoriality," 46–47.

39. Michel Foucault's conception of the "history of the present" guides this work; see Michel Foucault, *Discipline and Punish: The Birth of the Prison*, 2nd ed., trans. Alan Sheridan (Westminster, MD: Vintage Books, 1995 [1977]), 31; and for discussion, Michael Roth, "Foucault's 'History of the Present'" *History and Theory* 20, 1 (Feb. 1981): 32–46.

be seen to advocate a de-territorialized imagination of the Sikh *panth* in contra-distinction to a Khalistani orientation. It would be a mistake, however, to adhere too closely to a political application of the arguments presented here, and to interpret a history of our present simply in service of a particular set of present politics. Even though concerns about the present guide this discussion, no histor-ical account such as this one can provide the answer to a current political issue, such as the quest by some Sikhs for political independence within India, the res-olution of very specific political and material concerns regarding the relationship between the state of Punjab and the Indian federal government, and/or the status of religious minorities in the postcolonial Indian state. The history of our present does enable understanding of how our time has come into being, but it necessi-tates no *particular* politics. As David Scott has noted in a discussion of Sinhala nationalism, debate over the relative verisimilitude of claims about the past, upon which identity claims in the present are founded, is largely ill-chosen as a tool against nationalist and exclusionary ideology in the present. That is to say, we do not gain much by claiming the existence or nonexistence of histories or identities in the past, and the existence of historical consciousness in the past does not, regardless, historically justify violence in the present based—even if tenuously— on such historical claims. It is most important, he argues, instead, to deny "a natural or necessary link between past identities and the legitimacy of present political claims."[40] I caution, therefore, *against* a simplistic reading of politics in the cultural history explored here, regarding the territorialized and de-territorialized imaginaries of the Sikh community or *panth* and how they are sub-stantialized. This book does explicate the historical resources that de-territorialized and diasporic modes of engagement described by Shani and Verne Dusenbery draw upon, and of how a territorialized vision of the past has been produced within the Sikh *panth* or community as a part of its broader self-imagination with reference to the past.[41] In the end, however, neither are the grievances that animate the Khalistan movement resolved, nor is such a movement *neces-sitated*, by any cultural history.

To understand the power of the past and its representation in the modern context, however, an analysis of its role in historical terms is crucial, for it is only by understanding the multivalent and evolving nature of the representation of the past that we may open a broader and less constrained discursive field among dif-ferent visions of it. This is why this study focuses not on Sikh representations of

40. David Scott, *Refashioning Futures: Criticism after Postcoloniality* (Princeton, NJ: Prince-ton University Press, 1999), 103.

41. See Dusenbery, *Sikhs at Large*, 99–100, 110–11, 129–30, and elsewhere.

violence in the past—which have received all too much attention in the past—but on representations of the past in broader terms that have accompanied the commemoration of violence in the Sikh past.[42] Such an examination enables us to approach an answer to Scott's question of "so what?" in his discussion of historiographical interventions in the Sri Lanka conflict. Instead of focusing on historical narrative itself, we can change the question of "what was the past?" into "how and why was the past imagined?" to get at what is important about the reconstruction and representation of the past at different moments, in the present and in the past.[43] The concern of this book, therefore, is not so much with the Sikh past itself, but with the forms of its representation, why they have taken such forms, what they continue to be, and what they have produced. As I will suggest in the conclusion, a further question—regarding what they *might* be—proceeds from this inquiry.

---

42. Brian Axel's *The Nation's Tortured Body* provides an example of an analysis of representations of violence, with limited attention to other representational forms in the community.

43. Scott, *Refashioning Futures*, 93–105.

2

Sikh Materialities

THE SIKH PAST is made material and experienced in the present through objects and sites. Such objects are found in gurdwaras and private homes throughout the Punjab and Sikh diaspora, and consist of a wide range of types: clothing, shoes, chariots, and weapons (see figure 2.1). All are associated with the ten Sikh Gurus, martyrs, or other revered persons. Weapons are the most commonly found. Such weapons are, for example, collected and displayed at the center of Takhat Keshgarh Sahib in Anandpur, one of the five Takhats (literally "throne" or "seat,") which collectively have an authoritative status in the community and in the administrative structure of the SGPC, or Shiromani Gurdwara Parbandhak Committee. Weapons are also described orally—who used them, when, and why—to an audience every evening in the most prominent of the five Takhats, the Akal Takhat, across from the Darbar Sahib or Golden Temple, and at Nanded, the Takhat associated with the death of the Tenth Guru, in Maharashtra (see figure 2.2). Weapons are collected at smaller sites and in private hands and are often displayed next to the Guru Granth Sahib or in special locked cases in the central congregational hall of a gurdwara. There are, however, many other types of "sacred objects."

There is no one term for these objects in Punjabi: while they are called "relics" in English by some scholars, they are described as *itihāsik vastūāṅ* ("historical objects") and *shastar vastar* ("weapons and clothes") in Punjabi texts from the late nineteenth and early twentieth century, in which lists of them were compiled.[1] All are most commonly described as being *itihāsik* (historical). This term links objects to sites that commemorate the lives and activities of the Gurus. Thus, while the gurdwara in general understanding is any site where the Sikh sacred scripture, the Adi Granth or Guru Granth Sahib, lies in state, a special understanding of the *itihāsik* gurdwara was brought into being in *administrative* terms in the 1920s in the wake of the Gurdwara Reform Movement, when Sikhs came into direct conflict with the colonial state over the control of Sikh sites. These sites were officially designated as Sikh Gurdwaras versus non-Sikh "Deras"

---

1. These texts, which I call "gurdwara guides," are discussed in chapter 7.

FIGURE 2.1 Objects at Manji Sahib in Kiratpur: cloth embroidered by the daughter of the Sixth Guru, and the *topī* or hat of Guru Nanak. Photograph by Anne Murphy. July 1999.

FIGURE 2.2 Here the historical weapons kept at the Takhat are described to those in attendance in Nanded, Maharashtra. Photography by Anne Murphy. April 2002.

(as the alternative term came to be fixed) after 1925, when the SGPC was officially recognized as the managing body for gurdwaras proven to be historically linked with Sikh tradition. This designation of one term that is generally used for both objects and sites reflects the conceptual order that links them: both the historical site and object represent relationships in time to the Gurus, and experience of and respect for them constitute a way of participating in the community in relation to the past.

The Idea of the "Relic"

I am not the first to express an interest in the "lives," to use Richard Davis's term, of a set of objects, and to attempt to understand their multiple meanings.[2] Davis has done so for Hindu religious images by examining the different contexts for viewing these objects and how these contexts shape interpretation. He identifies two "frames" that constitute the act of looking: the frame of the location of the object and the interpretational frame that constructs the viewer, something "global" and "diffuse," "an outlook on the cosmos, on divinity, on human life and its possibilities, and on the role of images in a world so constituted."[3] As Davis demonstrates, a Hindu object can be all of these things: deity, loot from a rival kingdom, a way of expressing and enacting power, an example of a period in an art-historical timeline, and/or a masterwork of world art. Davis uses the term "dispensation" to describe the "historically grounded and socially shared understandings of the systems . . . by which things are ordered and administered," in an attempt to outline the meanings of images inside and outside of the originary semantic structures that created them.[4]

Sikh object practices are parallel to similar traditions in other religions, serving as technologies of memory that in the Sri Lankan context, in Kevin Trainor's words, "act as a basic strategy through which the followers of the Theravada tradition in Sri Lanka have forged a sense of the unbroken continuity of that tradition over more than two millennia."[5] The use of the term "relic" gestures toward this connection among religious traditions, a reference to, as Gregory Schopen has noted, "something left behind."[6] Relics are generally defined as "the

2. Richard Davis, *Lives of Indian Images* (Princeton, NJ: Princeton University Press, 1997).

3. Davis, *Lives*, 10. See also Robert Sharf, "On the Allure of Buddhist Relics," *Representations* 66 (1999): 76–99, see p. 89.

4. Davis, *Lives*, 10.

5. Trainor, *Relics*, 26–27.

6. Gregory Schopen, "Relic" in *Critical Terms for Religious Studies*, ed. Mark Taylor, 256–68 (Chicago: University of Chicago Press, 1998), 256.

venerated remains of venerable persons," as well as "objects that they once owned and, by extension, things that were once in physical contact with them."[7] Two aspects of the "relic" are thus described: bodily remains and "objects of use" that are associated with the remembered person. The power of both body and object is said to derive from principles of "contagious magic," by which a part of a person's body or an object associated with her/him can stand for the whole person.[8] While almost all relic objects in Sikh tradition are those used or gifted by the Gurus, both types of relics are common in the relic traditions of Christianity and Buddhism.[9] The normative Buddhist tradition since approximately the fifth century CE has recognized different classes of relics that are revered and stand in some relation to the Buddha or holy person: corporeal relics, relics of use, and commemorative relics.[10] In Christianity, non-bodily or "associative" relics[11] (or, as I have called them, "objects of use") have a significant role alongside bodily remains, particularly in the memorialization of angels and persons assumed bodily into heaven, such as Jesus and his mother Mary.[12] Christian traditions also feature the veneration of weapons said to have been used in the Crusades and

7. Mircea Eliade, ed., *The Encyclopedia of Religion* (New York: Macmillan Publishing Company, 1987), 275. Schopen's definition cited in footnote 6 deals primarily with bodily remains; a broader definition is more useful here.

8. See the more in-depth discussion in Sharf, "On the Allure of Buddhist Relics," and below, footnote 90.

9. The hair of Guru Amardas (in Goindwal, Punjab) represents one rare example of a bodily relic in Sikh tradition. On bodily remains in the Christian tradition, see, for example, Patrick J. Geary, *Furta Sacra: Thefts of Relics in the Central Middle Ages* (Princeton, NJ: Princeton University Press, 1978); Geary, *Living with the Dead in the Middle Ages* (Ithaca, NY: Cornell University Press, 1994); Geary, *Phantoms of Remembrance: Memory and Oblivion at the End of the First Millennium* (Princeton NJ: Princeton University Press, 1994). On Buddhism, see Richard Davis, ed. *Images, Miracles, and Authority in Asian Religious Traditions* (Boulder, CO: Westview Press, 1998); David Germano and Kevin Trainor, eds. *Embodying the Dharma: Buddhist Relic Veneration in Asia* (Albany: State University of New York Press, 2004); Gregory Schopen, *Bones, Stones and Buddhist Monks: Collected Papers on the Archaeology, Epigraphy and Texts of Monastic Buddhism in India* (Honolulu: University of Hawaii Press, 1997); Trainor, *Relics*. To my knowledge, significant work has not been done on the contrasts and connections between object-relics and bodily ones, in either tradition; Trainor points out the distinctions, but does not explore them in depth (Trainor, *Relics*, 30).

10. See below and Trainor, *Relics*, 30, 89.

11. See A. T. Lucas, "The Social Role of Relics and Reliquaries in Ancient Ireland," *Journal for the Royal Society of Antiquities of Ireland* 116 (1986): 5–37.

12. For example, see Annemarie Weyl Carr, "Threads of Authority: The Virgin Mary's Veil in the Middle Ages," in *Robes and Honor: The Medieval World of Investiture*, ed. Stewart Gordon, 59–93 (New York: Palgrave, 2001). The Eucharist, indeed, acts as a kind of relic for Jesus; see Geary, *Living with the Dead*, 185.

objects associated with saints, such as bells, staffs, and books. In both, the relic "is or has virtue, grace, benevolence, and life."[13]

There are thus numerous forms of this kind of object, the "relic." Through such objects, a relationship is established between a physical mode of representation and that which is remembered and/or experienced through it. This is usually a person; this is a defining feature of the relic, its link to persons. This relationship between the remembered and the representation is worked out in various ways. An object might embody the remembered, a kind of living presence, as Gregory Schopen has shown is the case for relics in early Buddhism.[14] It might act as a memorial device, as we most often see in Islamic traditions or in Buddhist relic traditions that are commemorative. The relic can provide a bridge with the past, a relationship with a presence that is absent, reflecting the role of memory in its most essential sense.[15] In other cases, it represents a relationship with absence itself.[16] Its relationship with the image is complicated, in some ways parallel to it, in other ways quite distinct, in the way it not only stands in for but also in some cases contains a past presence that continues.[17] Such material forms accompany

---

13. Schopen, "Relic," 262.

14. Schopen, *Bones*.

15. See Paul Ricoeur, *Memory, History, Forgetting*, trans. Kathleen Blamey and David Pellauer (Chicago: University of Chicago Press, 2004), particularly chapter 1 and 230–33.

16. On the idea of absence and the worship of images in the Jain tradition, see John Cort, *Framing the Jina: Narratives of Icons and Idols in Jain History* (New York, Oxford University Press, 2009), 63–66. The idea of absence in the Buddhist tradition is, according to some theorists, multiple—not just about temporal absence, as in all representations of that which is past, but also in the sense of the absence of self. John Strong asserts this position (John Strong "Buddhist Relics in Comparative Perspective: Beyond the Parralels" in *Embodying the Dharma: Buddhist Relic Veneration in Asia*, ed. David Germano and Kevin Trainor, 27–49. (Albany, NY: State University of New York Press, 2004), 32; see also John Strong, *Relics of the Buddha*. (Princeton, NJ: Princeton University Press, 2004).). Yet Robert Sharf notes that while the idea of denotation of absence is in keeping with Buddhist scriptural injunctions, it is unsupported by the evidence at large (Sharf, "On the Allure of Buddhist Relics," 78. See also Robert H. Sharf, "Introduction" in *Living Images: Japanese Buddhist Icons in Context* ed. Robert H. Sharf and Elizabeth Horton Sharf (Stanford: Stanford University Press, 2001).). Sharf notes that doctrines related to the multiple existences and forms of the body (*kaya*) of the Buddha fundamentally address the ontological connundra created by the presence/representation problem (Sharf, "Allure," 85ff.; see also Schopen, *Bones*, 278). The work of Gregory Schopen, cited above, asserts the need to cease privileging textual understandings of the tradition over the material record, and the profound impact that embrace of the material side of Buddhist religiosity has on our understanding of the tradition in historical terms.

17. For a compelling discussion of the status of the relic in relation to the image in the context of Buddhism, see: Vidya Dehejia, "Aniconism and the Multivalence of Emblems," *Ars Orientalis* 21 (1991): 45–66; Susan Huntington, "Early Buddhist Art and the Theory of Aniconism," *Art Journal* 49, 4 (1990): 401–8; and Susan Huntington "Aniconism and the Multivalence of Emblems: Another Look." *Ars Orientalis* 22 (1991): 111–56.

the memorial representations we are accustomed to finding in word and text. In Sikh tradition, the representations of the past embodied in textual historiography are supported by the evidence that the relic and site provide, as part of a single historiographical project (as will be shown in chapters 3 and 4). Relics in this context act as objects of memory, and the means for the construction of the history of the community.

Material Representation in South Asian Religions

The Sikh object takes its place among a wide range of object-related representational traditions in South Asian religions, with divergent understandings of the ontological status of the representation. The *murti*—the devotional image central to much (but not all) Hindu religious practice—represents the most prominent example of the visual and material at the center of religious practice, embracing the idea of embodiment central to many Buddhist and medieval Christian approaches to the relic.[18] Sometimes radically different and sometimes allied approaches to material and visual representation are discerned at various points in the development of the related religions of South Asia—Jainism, Buddhism, what we now designate with the single term "Hinduism"—from the middle of the first millennium of the Common Era through the fifteenth century, many associated with the development of temples and other institutions associated with worship.[19] Representation through material forms and visual images has also been debated in these traditions,

---

18. I am simplifying this discussion of religious images in Hindu contexts considerably; see Davis, *Lives* for fuller discussion. On the *murti* vs. the *svarūp*, see Norbert Peabody, "In Whose Turban Does the Lord Reside? The Objectification of Charisma and the Fetishism of Objects in the Hindu Kingdom of Kota," *Comparative Study in Society and History* 33, 4 (1991): 726–754, see 739ff. For more on the connections between Christian and Buddhist understandings of relics, see Schopen, "Relic."

19. The term "Hinduism" here is in quotes for reasons that are, by now, quite well-known in both academic and popular circles: that the notion of a singular "great" tradition of Hinduism is a product of the nineteenth century, and in its modern form was a product of colonial codification of the non-Muslim and non-Christian religious practices of the subcontinent. Not all agree on this; for three different views see, for instance, Heinrich von Stietencron, "Religious Configurations in Pre-Muslim India and the Concept of Hinduism," in *Representing Hinduism: The Construction of Religious Traditions and National Identity*, ed. Vasudha Dalmia and H. von Stietencron, 51–81 (Thousand Oaks, CA: Sage Publications, 1995); J. S. Hawley, "Naming Hinduism," *Wilson Quarterly* 15, 3 (1991): 20–34; and David Lorenzen, "Who Invented Hinduism," *Comparative Studies in Society and History* 41 (1999): 630–59. Brian Pennington's book, *Was Hinduism Invented? Britons, Indians, and the Colonial Construction of Religion* (New York: Oxford University Press, 2005) provides a comprehensive account of the debate. It is clear, regardless, that the term "Hindu" was ambiguous in its reference in the pre-colonial period (as indeed it has proved to be since), and that its functioning as an overarching category was rare and partial. This is important to keep in mind when considering the Sikh

throughout the period of their use.[20] After the consolidation of centralized powers in the north and Deccan under rulers from Central and West Asia, which helped support the spread of Islam as a significant cultural and religious force, such image and relic traditions continued alongside Islamic approaches to representation in regional kingdoms and imperial formations alike, exhibiting instances of both conflict and accommodation between differing approaches and with local as well as new supra-local patronage. The devotional cult of Krishna, for example, represents an image-oriented tradition that flourished in the Mughal period, with patrons from across northern India from a range of social positions, and strong Rajput and Mughal patronage.[21] Islamic representational norms generally have eschewed anthropomorphic representation of the divine, such as characterized the Krishna tradition, providing at times the grounds for conflict.[22] Other kinds of material practices, however, do exist in Islamic contexts. Relics and sites for example are

---

tradition, since most debates regarding the relationship between Hinduism and Sikhism assume a clarity in what represents "Hinduism" (and, therefore, the relationship of Sikhism to it) that does not exist in the period of formation of the Sikh tradition. Indeed, it is when Hinduism comes to be clearly defined in the nineteenth century that many Sikhs make an effort to distinguish Sikhism from it.

20. Gerard Colas, "The Competing Hermeneutics of Image Worship in Hinduism (Fifth to Eleventh Century AD)," in *Images in Asian Religions: Texts and Contexts*, ed. Phyllis Granoff and Koichi Shinohara (Vancouver: UBC Press. 2004); Richard Davis. "Indian Image-Worship and Its Discontents," in *Representation in Religion: Studies in Honor of Moshe Barasch*, ed. Jan Assmann and Albert J. Baumgarten, 107–32 (Leiden: Brill, 2001); Phyllis Granoff, "Images and Their Ritual Use in Medieval India: Hesitations and Contradictions," in *Images in Asian Religions: Texts and Contexts*, ed. Phyllis Granoff and Koichi Shinohara, 19–55 (Vancouver: UBC Press, 2004). On debate in Jain image traditions, see Cort, *Framing the Jina*, overall and particularly chapter 5.

21. On the success of the *Puṣṭimārg* community in the Mughal period, see Shandip Saha: "The Movement of Bhakti along a North-West Axis: Tracing the History of the Puṣṭimārg between the Sixteenth and Nineteenth Centuries," *International Journal of Hindu Studies* 11, 3 (Dec. 2007): 299–318. On the rise of Braj literature in this context, "at this conjuncture of Vaishnava fervor with Rajput and Mughal patronage of the Braj built environment," see Allison Busch *Poetry of Kings: The Classical Hindi Literature of Mughal India* (New York: Oxford University Press, 2011), 7.

22. Contrary to popular representations of Islam as absolutely intolerant of images, however, Richard Eaton has shown that the characterization of Muslim rulers as engaging in wholesale destruction of South Asian religious images and temples is unsupported by the historical record. See Richard M. Eaton, "Temple Desecration and Indo-Muslim States," in *Essays on Islam and Indian History*, 94–132 (New Delhi: Oxford University Press, 2000); on the idea and practice of "idolatry" in the Ghurid and Ghaznavid periods, see also Flood *Objects of Translation*, 27–37. The formulation of Islam as inherently hostile to the image overall is also problematic with reference to the historical record; see Oleg Grabar, "From the Icon to Aniconism: Islam and the Image" in *Museum International* 55, 2 (2003): 46–53.

common in association with Sufi and other charismatic leaders: a site dedicated to Baba Farid in Faridkot, Punjab (India), features a tree branch, now covered in green cloth and part of it enclosed in a case, that was touched by the Baba. Devotees of diverse religious backgrounds present offerings to it (see figure 2.3).[23] One might also add to the category of "relic" representation the practice of Tazia processions in places such as Lucknow, in which models of important tombs in the Shi'i tradition, such as that of Imam 'Ali, are displayed in procession. These objects do not purport to be originals, but represent the absent original to the devoted. These objects-as-copies themselves then come to be revered.

A distinction is made in South Asian religions regarding the representation of divinity as being "without qualities" (*nirguṇ*), or "with qualities" (*saguṇ* or *sarguṇ*): the former posits a vision of a formless, indescribable God, while the latter defines a vision of divinity that is made of the material (*guṇ*) of our world.[24] In North India—relevant to any discussion of Sikh forms of representation—the sixteenth-century poet-saint Ravidas, for example, sang of the divine as a formless, unknowable *nirguṇ* Lord. This transcendent God could not be known through a physical form.[25] The Islamic understanding of God can be framed in such terms. An alternative view of God, in literal terms, was held by the poet-saint Surdas. He extolled the very physical virtues of the boy-god Krishna, an incarnation, or *avatār*, of the great God Vishnu. Surdas's Krishna was a celebration of the senses in every way: in the beauty of his eyes, the lilting tune of his flute, and the dark luster of his skin.[26] The distinction between these two stances should not however be overdrawn, however, since the use of this binary distinction as a defining feature of devotional orientations and practices was not prevalent until later, and there is much interplay between the two modes.[27] Thus, for the blind

---

23. Salt is left at the site for the healing of skin diseases. The author visited on May 1, 2002. On Farid's shrine in Pakpattan, see Richard M. Eaton, "The Political and Religious Authority of the Shrine of Baba Farid," in *Moral Conduct and Authority: The Place of* Adab *in South Asian Islam*, ed. Barbara Metcalfe (Berkeley: University of California Press, 1984), 262–84.

24. In keeping with the conventions of modern Indo-Aryan languages, terms here and throughout lose the inherent final "a." These terms are *nirguṇa* and *saguṇa* in Sanskrit.

25. See Winand M. Callewaert and Peter G. Friedlander, *The Life and Works of Raidas* (New Delhi: Manohar, 1992), and J. S. Hawley, *Songs of the Saints of India*, text and notes by John Stratton Hawley, translations by J. S. Hawley and Mark Juergensmeyer (New York: Oxford University Press, 1988).

26. See J. S. Hawley, *Krishna, The Butter Thief* (Princeton, NJ: Princeton University Press, 1983) and *Surdas: Poet, Singer, Saint* (Seattle: University of Washington Press, 1984).

27. See J. S. Hawley, "The Nirgun/Sagun Distinction in Early Manuscript Anthologies of Hindu Devotion," in *Bhakti Religion in North India: Community Identity and Political Action*,

FIGURE 2.3 Baba Farid is said to have touched this tree. Salt and other offerings are given at the site, and it is associated with the curing of skin diseases. Photograph by Anne Murphy. May 2002.

Surdas, his "vision" of a beautiful child God was in actuality an inner, formless one, while divinity infuses the visual, material world in *nirguṇ* traditions, as well. Both approaches to God persist today in modern-day Hinduism. Adherents of the Arya Samaj, a reformist school founded in the nineteenth century that was particularly influential in Punjab, generally eschew reliance upon images in worship, while those who follow what they call Sanatan Dharm (the "eternal religion") assert the validity of images as a means of worshipping and interacting with the divine.[28]

Sikh traditions are generally located firmly within the *nirguṇ* stream, involving a rejection of the image as the focus of devotion and a vision of God as

ed. David N. Lorenzen (Albany: State University of New York Press, 1995), 160–80 on the relevance of this category in the premodern period. As Christian Novetzke has noted, this "division of the *guṇas* marks tendencies in expression, not battle-lines of debate." (Christian Novetzke *History, Bhakti, and Public Memory: Namdev in Religious and Secular Traditions* [Ranikhet: Permanent Black, 2009; first published, New York: Columbia University Press, 2008], 61).

28. See Vasudha Dalmia, *The Nationalization of Hindu Traditions: Bharatendu Harischandra and Nineteenth-Century Banaras* (Delhi: Oxford University Press, 1999). As Philip Lutgendorf has noted, in the context of nineteenth-century North India, the use of the term "Sanatan" constituted "a self-conscious affirmation of religious conservatism in a perceivably pluralistic

beyond human perception and description. Yet if the distinction between the two is contingent and often illusory in general, this is particularly so in the Sikh tradition, where the Gurus used the play between *sargun* and *nirgun* as a way to destabilize conventional ways of knowing in the most fundamental terms. Thus, as Arvind Mandair rightly argues, "for Nanak these two opposing terms are also the same: *nirgun āp sargun bī ohī* ("being absent the same One is also fully present," or "the one detached is the same as the one involved"). So 'God' is beyond, yet 'God' actualizes himself through the relation of equivalence, and therefore substitutability, between all names and things."[29] *Nirgun*, then, infuses *sargun*, and vice versa. We must pause therefore before disregarding as adulteration materiality in *nirgun* contexts, such as at the Kabir Chaura Maṭh and Ravidas Janam Sthan (birthplace) in Benares, which both feature relics of their respective poet-saints, Kabir and Ravidas, whose vision of the divine falls reflects a *nirgun* orientation.[30] This is also the case with the infusion of meaning and an experience of the past in the landscape. As Diana Eck has noted, in speaking of the Hindu mythological landscape in India, "the land bears the traces of the gods and the footprints of the heroes. Every place has its story, and conversely, every story in the vast storehouse of myth and legend has its place."[31] But, while

---

context" (Philip Lutgendorf, *The Life of a Text: Performing the Ramcaritmanas of Tulsidas* [Berkeley: University of California Press, 1991], 363). See the articles by Vasudha Dalmia and M. Horstmann in Vasudha Dalmia and Heinrich von Stietencron, eds., *Representing Hinduism: The Construction of Religious Traditions and National Identity* (Thousand Oaks, CA: Sage Publications, 1995). On aspects of the Sanatan Dharm debate with the Arya Samaj, see Kenneth Jones, *Arya Dharm: Hindu Consciousness in Nineteenth-Century Punjab* (Berkeley: University of California Press, 1976).

29. Arvind-pal Singh Mandair, *Religion and the Specter of the West: Sikhism, India, Postcoloniality, and the Politics of Translation* (New York: Columbia University Press, 2009), 376. The citation from the Guru Granth Sahib is found on p. 287 of the standard text (pagination for the scripture is consistent among published versions).

30. The shoe-making equipment of Ravidas, a cobbler, is found at the Janam Sthan. We can treat such material religious forms as later Vaishnava accretions, given the Vaishnava interests evinced by adherents in the Kabir tradition today, but as argued here, this need not be the only way to understand such traditions. See the following works by David Lorenzen: "The Kabir Panth: Heretics to Hindus," in *Religious Change and Cultural Domination*, ed. by David Lorenzen, 151–71 (Mexico: El Collegio de Mexico, 1981); "The Kabir Panth and Social Protest," in *The Sants: Studies in a Devotional Tradition of India*, ed. Karine Schomer and W. H. McLeod, 281–303 (Berkeley: Berkeley Religious Studies Series and Motilal Banarsidass, 1987); "Traditions of Non-caste Hinduism," *Contributions to Indian Sociology* 21, 2 (July–December 1987): 263–83.

31. Diana Eck, *India: A Sacred Geography* (New York: Harmony Books, 2012), 5, see also 16 and elsewhere.

we might expect the South Indian *bhakti* (devotional) poets to sing in Tamil of the geography of the interaction of their God with the land as a physical experience in a clearly *sagun* mode,[32] in keeping with their general orientation, the landscape carries many more narratives as well. Benares, it must be remembered, is also the city of Kabir and Ravidas, not just the Hindu God, Shiv.

We see in the variety of object practices described briefly here certain tensions: between representation and embodiment—and on a related level, between absence and presence—and the material versus that which is beyond representation. Sikh objects do not partake of "embodiment," distinguishing them from the *murti* and the Buddhist embodied image, although both of these examples also offer a kind of complexity that denies an easy absolute distinction. The conceptual category that most fundamentally "enlivens" sacred Sikh objects, and their interpretation, is the narrative representation of the past in relation to the constitution of the Sikh community, and the participation of these objects and the sites that are related to them as forms of evidence in the narrative construction of the past.[33] Memory is substantialized through the object and site, and a connection established and attested to through them. The Sikh community is produced through this living process of remembrance, the history that is constituted out of this memory. This of course is by its nature a political process, but so are all "relic" and other object traditions, as well as any idea of a sacred landscape. Indeed, it is the social context of relic traditions that connects them most across traditions. One can make fruitful comparisons between the social lives of Sikh objects, therefore, and the authorizing function of Vallabhite sacred statues that are directly linked to political and religious power in western India, even if the ontological status of these objects differs significantly.[34] In a more recent example, we see how relics act as vehicles for modern identitarian claims: in March 2002, a Bharata Janata Party (BJP) Member of Parliament in India claimed that the sacred hair of the Prophet Muhammad housed at the Hazratbal shrine in Kashmir—one of the most famous Muslim relics in India today—was actually that of a Hindu holy man and needed to be returned to the Hindu community. Violence and a court case followed, providing a direct parallel between this relic case and that of the mosque in Ayodhya destroyed by Hindu nationalists

---

32. Indira V. Peterson, *Poems to Siva: The Hymns of the Tamil Saints* (Princeton, NJ: Princeton University Press, 1989).

33. See Anne Murphy "Materializing Sikh Pasts," in *Sikh Formations: Religion, Culture, Theory* 1, 2 (December 2005): 175–200.

34. Peabody, "In Whose Turban."

in the attempt to complete a Hindu landscape (see below).[35] As Bill Brown has noted, "however materially stable objects may seem, they are, let us say, different things in different scenes."[36] Power, ownership, and community are therefore crucial to the constitution of relic and object traditions, as well as the experience of a sacred landscape, and also invite the possibility of conflicting and changing interpretations.

The Sikh Gurdwara and the Itihāsik *(Historical)*

The gurdwara took central stage in the early formation of the Sikh community, in direct reference to its name—the doorway to the Guru (or under the related designation *dharamshāla*). Early mentions of the "doorway to the Guru" do not necessarily reflect the institutional sense of the term as it later develops: Guru Nanak spoke of *sacu sālāhī dhaṅnu gurduāru*: "That blessed doorway to the Guru, where there is praise of Truth" and the Third Guru, Amardas, spoke of coming before the Guru—"*devaṇ vāle kai hathi dāti hai gurū duārai pāi*": "The gift is in the hands of the giver. It is received at the doorway to the Guru."[37] As Gurinder Singh Mann has noted, the idea of the Guru as pilgrimage center developed into "the belief that the Guru 'sanctifies' the spot where he sits and Sikhs should aspire 'to rub their forehead with its dust.'"[38] The site of access to the Guru was thus foundational to the growing community around him, in a spiritual as well as institutional sense, and the reverence for the site of the Guru came to be extended to those that were related to the Guru in the past—and were remembered in early histories and other texts. These sites grew in their institutional formality during the period of the Sikh Gurus and after, particularly with the acquisition of political power by Sikhs in the late eighteenth century. Examples include the founding of a gurdwara in memory of the deaths of the sons of the

---

35. "MP faces trial in relic row," BBC website, March 15, 2002, http://news.bbc.co.uk/1/hi/world/south_asia/1874462.stm (accessed May 29, 2005; Zafarul-Islam Khan, "Katiyar claim sets Kashmir Valley aflame," 2005, http://www.milligazette.com/dailyupdate/200203/20020314a.htm (accessed May 29, 2005); "Protests over BJP MP's remarks on Hazratbal," http://www.tribuneindia.com/2002/20020314/j&k.htm#1 (accessed May 29, 2005).

36. Bill Brown, "Thing Theory." *Critical Theory* 28 (Autumn 2001): 1–22, see p. 9.

37. See Guru Granth Sahib, p. 153 (first quotation); p. 33 (second quotation). The term *duārā* is utilized commonly to indicate the means to an end or a goal, such as *mokh duārā*, the doorway to moksha or liberation. See also generic use of *dharamsāl* (for example) in Japji Sahib, stanza 34.

38. Gurinder Singh Mann, "Sources for the Study of Guru Gobind Singh's Life and Times," *Journal of Punjab Studies* 15, 1–2 (2008): 229–84, see p. 231. See also Balwant Singh Dhillon, "Dharamsala: An Early Sikh Religious Centre," in *On Gurdwara Legislation*, ed. Kharak Singh, 36–48 (Chandigarh: Institute of Sikh Studies, 1996), 37.

FIGURE 2.4 Important sites highlighted in this book. Artist: Raghavendra Rao K.V.

Tenth Guru, Fateh Singh and Zoravar Singh, in 1710, and the commemorative sites founded by Baghel Singh in the 1780s.[39] The landscape of Punjab (and beyond) today is populated by such *itihāsik* or "historical" gurdwaras associated with the Sikh Gurus (see figure 2.4). The materialization of history thus takes place in site as well as object: the marking of memory on a sacred landscape in relation to a specifically Sikh historical imaginary accompanies the history being marked out through object and described in text.

We can see the way the Sikh past is made present in the example of Takhat Sri Damdama Sahib. In the southwest of Indian Punjab, near the city of Bathinda, the Takhat stands on the soil of Sikh memory.[40] Damdama Sahib is said to commemorate a visit by the Ninth Guru, Tegh Bahadur, and an extended visit in 1705 by Guru Gobind Singh. The Tenth Guru traveled in the region and was welcomed by the village *caudhurī* (headman) Bhai Dalla Singh, who served the Guru and was a major devotee. Here Guru Gobind Singh regrouped after devastating battles fought in the early years of the eighteenth century, when a growing Sikh challenge to both Mughal authority and other local rulers—particularly small polities in the Punjab Hills—had

---

39. On the former, see Mann, "Sources for the Study," 234. On Baghel Singh, see the beginning of chapter 5.

40. This site is discussed briefly in Murphy, "Gurdwara Landscape."

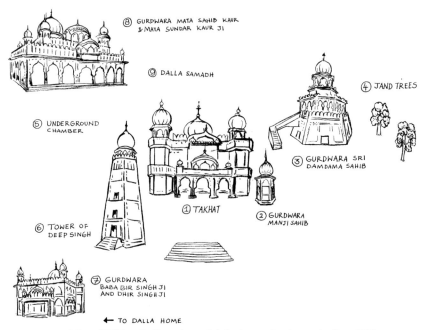

FIGURE 2.5 Map of Takhat Sri Damdama Sahib. Artist: Raghavendra Rao K.V.

brought about the loss of the Sikh center of Anandpur, where the Khalsa had been founded.[41] The Sikh *panth* or community, after its founding by Guru Nanak, had thrived under the direction of the nine subsequent Gurus, and as early as the seventeenth century had begun to be perceived as a powerful force by, and possible threat to, local authorities. By the eighteenth century, this dynamic had advanced further, and it was in this context that Guru Gobind Singh came into conflict with Mughal and other local powers, leading to his stay at Damdama Sahib. The period of his stay there was one of recovery and rest (as reflected in the name of the site: *dam leṇā* is to take rest in Punjabi). As Guru Gobind Singh took rest, he visited local families, enhancing the nascent influence of this still growing religious community in the region; the community was already well established in the central (Majha) region of Punjab, but not in this region, known as Malwa. Guru Gobind Singh was the last living Guru to build his following this way; as has been mentioned, he ended the period of human Guruship and invested the authority of the Guru in the sacred canon, the Guru Granth Sahib, before his death in 1708.[42]

Damdama Sahib is a testament to the Sikh past, inscribed in land and building (see figure 2.5). The site acts as a map of the past in the present, with

_____

41. See discussion in chapter 3.

42. This is why we must distinguish between the human Gurus and the Guru as a continuing principle and experience within the text, although the continuum between them must also be emphasized.

the attribution of historical significance to particular buildings—even when
they do not date from the time they are said to refer to—and in relation to the
historical objects displayed at the center of the Takhat itself. Like every *itihāsik*
or "historical" gurdwara, Damdama Sahib exemplifies the way a site participates in and allows for the experience of the past. First and foremost, are references to the past presence of the Gurus—here, primarily Tegh Bahadur and
Gobind Singh—at the main Takhat buildings, 1, 2, and 3 on the map, but also
the trees on the site (4), where the Tenth Guru is said to have tied his horse.
This reference to the past presence of a Guru is the constitutive marker of
itihāsik gurdwaras, and ultimately the justification for their management and
control under the SGPC, as will be explored at length in section 2 of this book.
Several other heroes—such as the famous martyr, Baba Deep Singh (5 and 6),
two lesser known followers of the Guru, Bir Singh and Dhir Singh (7), and the
wives of the Guru (8)—are commemorated at the site in multiple ways.[43] The
village headman Dalla also occupies a prominent place within the historical
geography of the site, through the *samādh* or grave marker of Dalla himself (9),
as well as through prominent signs that link the Dalla family home (*havelī*)
with the Takhat complex. As visitors move through the site, clockwise, visiting
smaller buildings after having been to the central buildings, they experience
these memorials to persons who are said to have visited this site in the past.
Damdama Sahib as a site is also multivalent in the histories it references.
While it is constituted by the inscription of Sikh history onto place, it also
participates in the transfiguration of *other* spaces into Sikh space; it is called,
for example, "Guru Ki Kashi," naming it as a site of learning equivalent to

---

43. According to tradition, Baba Deep Singh was appointed the first *jathedar*, or
leader, of the Takhat at the time of Guru Gobind Singh and is credited with creating
copies of the Adi Granth. He is famous for going to Amritsar to protect the Golden
Temple from desecration. He is said to have been beheaded en route, but was so determined to reach his destination and protect it that he carried his head the remainder of
the way into the city; see Louis Fenech, *Martyrdom in the Sikh Tradition: Playing the
"Game of Love"* (Delhi: Oxford University Press, 2000). See also Murphy, "Gurdwara
Landscape." The two followers—Bir Singh and Dhir Singh—were said to have volun-
teered to act as targets for the Guru when he was demonstrating to the headman Dalla
the level of bravery of his men; the father and son pair fought for the right to risk their
lives for the Guru. Bhai Mani Singh is also said to have finished the final version of the
Guru Granth Sahib at Damdama Sahib; he came to Talwandi Sabo with the wives of the
Guru, Mata Sundar Kaur and Mata Sahib Kaur, who are also remembered prominently
at the site.

Benares/Kashi/Varanasi, in Uttar Pradesh.[44] Such a renaming inscribes the old onto the new, to gain the authority of the old, but also to circumscribe its power; it also expresses the multiplicity and replication that characterizes a broader sacred geography of India.[45]

Objects that relate to the persons commemorated at Damdama Sahib are kept within the main gurdwara itself: Baba Deep Singh's sword; Guru Gobind Singh's sword; a seal with the sign of the Takhat; a gun; and a mirror (see figure 2.6).[46] The gun is said to have been made by a resident of Lahore, Bhai Udday Singh, who gave it to the Guru as a gift. Tradition holds that it was fired by Guru Gobind Singh himself, to demonstrate the loyalty of his followers, Bir and Dhir Singh, who fought for the right to stand as targets for the Guru.[47] The mirror was given to Guru Gobind Singh by the community (*saṅgat*) in Delhi. The Guru is said to have blessed the mirror, saying that anyone who comes with love (*prem nāl*) and sits looking into it for three days, reciting Ardas and eating chickpeas (*chole de dāne*), will be cured of facial paralysis or a similar type of facial ailment.[48] The story of the mirror and other objects is narrated daily to devotees at the site.

The Damdama Sahib complex is not unusual in the way it maps events and people onto place. The Golden Temple or Darbar Sahib in Amritsar, for example, provides a similar mapping of the past onto the sacred site. Traversing the *parikramā* or circumference of the Darbar Sahib, one encounters numerous places

44. This description of Damdama Sahib as Kashi is found in the mid to late eighteenth century text discussed in chapter 3, Kuir Singh, *Gurbilās Pātshāhī Das*, ed. Shamsher Singh Ashok, introduction by Fauja Singh (Patiala, Punjab: Publications Bureau, Punjabi University, 1999), 213 (which also features a general description of the historical geography of the site). See also (discussed in chapter 4) Attar Singh, ed. and trans., "The Travels of Guru Tegh Bahadur Singh and Guru Gobind Singh," *The Panjab Past and Present* IX, 1 (1975), 22, 29, 31, 66, 67; see also references in the pamphlet *Sankhep Itihās: Shrī Damdamā Gurū kī Kāshī* (Talwandi Sabo, Bathinda: Manager, Takhat Sri Damdama Sahib (Guru Kashi), no date). Such transfiguration happens elsewhere, such as at the nearby site of the battle of Mehiraj, which is called the Guru's Kurukshetra.

45. For a parallel process with respect to Constantinople as the "new Rome," see J. Z. Smith, *To Take Place: Toward Theory in Ritual* (Chicago: University of Chicago Press, 1987), 75. On the multiple Kashis in Indian sacred geography, see Eck, *India: A Sacred Geography*, 3.

46. The seal was used to attest a *hukamnāmā* or order of authority from the end of the nineteenth century (Balwant Singh, *Shrī Damdamā Gurū Kī Kāshī* (Bathinda: Giani Kaur Singh Sahitya Shastri Sadan, 1995?), 73).

47. Balwant Singh, *Shrī Damdamā*, 71. Related in detail in an interview with Bharpur Singh, manager of the Takhat in 2002.

48. Interview, Bhai Mann Singh, the Damdama Sahib Takhat's head *granthī* or textual specialist, March 2002.

FIGURE 2.6 Historical objects kept within Takhat Sri Damdama Sahib. These are described orally to visitors by staff at the site. Photograph by Anne Murphy. March 2002.

associated with Gurus and saints: for instance the place where the Fourth Guru, Ramdas, supervised the construction of the sacred tank, a bathing place associated with healing. Like every such gurdwara and Takhat, such sites can be seen as *lieux de mémoire* (sites of memory), as defined by Pierre Nora.[49] The objects and sites under consideration here too provide evidence and experience of the past, a bridge between past and present. They are then transformed into historical objects that attest to or provide evidence of a narration of the past. Relationships with the Guru are attested to and made manifest; objects associated with historical narrations of the Sikh past articulate and substantiate these narratives, written and oral. Through sites like Damdama Sahib and others, it is a larger historical

49. Pierre Nora, ed., *Realms of Memory: Rethinking the French Past* (New York: Columbia University Press, 1996). Ricoeur provides a useful overview of Nora's work in *Memory, History, Forgetting*, 401–11. Nora draws upon and extends work on social and collective memory; see the foundational work of Maurice Halbwachs, *On Collective Memory*, ed., trans., and intro. by Lewis A. Coser (Chicago: University of Chicago Press, 1992). For a very useful overview of scholarship on "collective memory" and particularly an overview of scholarship on the relationship between memory and history, see Jeffrey Olick and Joyce Robbins, "Social Memory Studies: From 'Collective Memory' to the Historical Sociology of Mnemonic Practices." *Annual Review of Sociology* 24 (1998): 105–40, particularly 110ff.

narrative of the Sikh community and its Gurus that takes shape: a set of public engagements with the historical object and site transforms the memory of the past into the experience of the religious present in the form of the history of the community.[50] In general terms, a gurdwara is defined as any place where the Guru (now in the form of the canonical text, the Adi Granth or Guru Granth Sahib) is present. It is the public location for the meeting of the two central authorities of the community: *granth* (text) and *panth* (community). Yet, as a historical or *itihāsik* gurdwara, Damdama Sahib is associated with the history of the Sikh community, not just the presence of the sacred text; this is the basis for its inclusion within the management structure of the SGPC, which was founded to manage gurdwaras that are proven to be historically Sikh.

The inscription of history onto this site involves the mapping of two modes of recuperation of the past: of *event* and *presence*. Objects and buildings represent the past presence of people, as well as events they are associated with; these two work in concert to provide evidence and experience of a narrative of the past—a history—that the sites participate in, with striking consistency, within a wide range of written and oral sources.[51] The presence being commemorated is, it must be emphasized, a *past* presence; the continued presence of the Guru or his disciples is not foregrounded, even in relation to the miracles sometimes associated with the mirror, for example. The continued or living "presence" such as is central in some Buddhist and Christian relic traditions is not therefore operating here; the continuing, experienced presence of the Guru is reserved for the text itself, the performance of the Word, and the community organized around that text. The Sikh historical site and objects instead are animated by the experience of the past that they bring into the present. The scripture in a sense operates in an entirely different register, part of a continually performed and experienced present. The community is thus created at the intersection of these two temporal registers: with reference to the past marked out in place, object, and narrative and brought by them into the present, and in an always unfolding now, in relation to the Word.

The objects at the center of Damdama Sahib represent relationships that constitute the community of the Guru. Their presence marks the space of the gurdwara

---

50. Novetzke's description of the public enactment of *bhaktī* or devotion, and the formation of publics through *bhaktī*, is allied with my sense here (Novetzke, *History, Bhakti, and Public Memory*, 13ff.).

51. Narratives associated with the Dalla family, are, however, less consistent (see discussion below).

with the narratives of this community-in-formation. That presence—the presence of the community that continues—is the one that lives in the present through the narration such objects and places participate in.[52] Thus, each place becomes a stage of the narration of this community: the place of its articulation, its lived and experienced aspect; and each object represents a relationship: a past relationship with the Guru and a continuing relationship of community constituted through the Guru. In this way, the past as memory and the past as a continuing presence become simultaneous—as Veena Das observed within Khalistani narratives, which collapsed distinctions between past and present and located current conflicts as continuations of the past. The temporal integration that Das highlights therefore relates to a larger imperative within Sikh tradition, tied to the experience of the Word in the continuous present and the narration of the past as history, out of memory.

The process by which site and object come together is vividly demonstrated today in another example, Gurdwara Bhattha Sahib, near Kotla Nihang Khan[53] (see figure 2.7). This gurdwara provides what I will call a "tale of discovery" that is important for understanding the category of the *itihāsik* gurdwara more generally—a narrative of the site's founding in relation to the discovery of its history. The historical nature of this site is not only attested to by the objects on display here, but also by the the earth itself, as a historical object; below the main altar at the center of the gurdwara are the footprints of Guru Gobind Singh's horse, preserved in clay: the earth as relic. Located at the back of the building, where *kīrtan* (singing of the contents of the Adi Granth, a central practice at a gurdwara), *pāṭh* (recitation or reading of the sacred text), and other activities take place, are Guru Gobind Singh's sword (*shrī sāhib*) and his *kaṭār* or dagger. His shield is held at another gurdwara,[54] but was originally gifted by the Guru to the family of Nihang Khan (for whom the village that stood here was named) along with the weapons at Bhattha Sahib.

Every *itihāsik* gurdwara, like this one, features a historical account that justifies the special relationship of the site to the Guru (usually utilizing various types of proof), and the subsequent designation of the place as *itihāsik*. This narrative is articulated in multiple ways at each site: on boards on display at sites, in pamphlets

---

52. Compare with the argument put forward in Anne Murphy, "History in the Sikh Past," and as discussed in chapter 3.

53. See Gurmukh Singh, *Historical Sikh Shrines* (Amritsar: Singh Brothers, 1995), 165 and the published introduction to the site distributed there: *Gurdwārā Srī Bhaṭṭhā Sāhib* (in Punjabi) (Amritsar: SGPC, n.d.), 6.

54. That site is associated with Bachitar Singh's martyrdom. *Gurdwārā Srī Bhaṭṭhā Sāhib*, 6.

FIGURE 2.7 The clay that is said to have been touched by the horse of the Guru is displayed prominently at Bhattha Sahib. Photograph by Anne Murphy. March 2002.

distributed on site, and in oral accounts given by gurdwara staff. This narrative provides the evidence of this site as a part of a larger category of the historical, and the administrative controls this entails, within the SGPC. According to the accounts given by the staff at Bhattha Sahib,[55] laborers were working with hot fire in a kiln (*bhaṭṭhā*) that belonged to Nihang Khan, an Afghan, when the Guru arrived there with his followers. The Guru asked for a place to rest, and the workers mockingly told him to rest in the fire. The fire turned cold with the touch of the Guru's horse, preserving the signs of the horse's hooves in three separate locations in the hardened clay that now stands at the center of the gurdwara. The followers of the Guru then started to do *pāṭh* (recitation of the sacred text) at this place. Nihang Khan came to be devoted to the Tenth Guru and the Guru presented him with the weapons that are today housed at the site, in honor of his loyalty.[56] Some years later, fleeing Anandpur, Guru Gobind Singh came to Nihang Khan's house and Khan protected him.[57]

---

55. And corroborated by other sources, such as Gurmukh Singh, *Historical Sikh Shrines*.

56. The order in which these events took place is represented differently in the oral accounts received on March 8, 2002 and in the published description in *Gurdwārā Srī Bhaṭṭhā Sāhib*.

57. According to narratives provided at the site and in other sources, a devotee of the Guru, Bachitar Singh, had been injured and Nihang Khan tried to save him but was unable to. Nihang

This site was not always recognized as an *itihāsik* site. According to gurdwara staff, people used to come here to have *darshan* (sacred viewing) and light lamps, but there was no formal gurdwara or religious site here until relatively recently. Baba Juun[58] Singh, who lived in a village around five kilometers away, had a dream telling him to come to this place. He abandoned his home and built a small hut on the site.[59] He started doing *sevā* or service, clearing the site, and digging—slowly, it is said, the *bhaṭṭhā* came out of the ground, a kind of gift from the past: "When we love someone," staff at the site said, "we give them things that we care about so that they will remember us, so they will never be sad." Juun Singh learned the story of the Guru's connection with the place from local people who revered the site: the site had power, and all wishes requested at the site were fulfilled. As a staff member of the gurdwara put it: "If it were not for people like him [Juun Singh], our history would be hidden." When the descendants of Nihang Khan left at Partition, they presented the weapons they owned to the gurdwara.[60] Juun Singh passed away in 1995, and Harbans Singh of the Delhi-based Kar Seva organization soon afterward took over the development of the site.[61]

The past is made manifest and is experienced through the historical site. Such material forms do not occupy the central locus of Sikh practice and community formation: this location is occupied by the sacred scripture and its performance in congregational settings. At the same time, they accompany this central practice and define the community as a community of memory of the Guru, a living product of the narration of the past as history.

Itihāsik *Objects*

If you were to follow the arrow in the lower left corner of the map of Takhat Damdama Sahib, you would find the Dalla family house, not far from Damdama Sahib (see figure 2.8). The home is clearly marked as a *part* of the visitor's experience at the Takhat—signs indicate how to get to the house from there. Yet, it is a private

---

Khan performed the last rites for him as required according to Sikh custom. This is a recurrent motif, the performance of *sanskars* or rites according to *another* community's standards, such as at Meheraj in Malwa. Nihang Khan's daughter, Mumtaz Khan, is then said to have accepted the Guru as her "true" (but unconsummated) husband, as a result of his being hidden with her. (See Gurmukh Singh, *Historical Sikh Shrines*, 165, and *Gurdwārā Srī Bhaṭṭhā Sāhib*).

58. Or Jiwan.

59. The exact date of this was hazy in the oral accounts given, but it appears to have been in the early twentieth century, when activism around the control of gurdwaras was at its height; see chapter 5.

60. This is corroborated in Gurmukh Singh, *Historical Sikh Shrines*.

61. *Gurdwārā Srī Bhaṭṭhā Sāhib*, 6–7. See also Murphy, "Gurdwara Landscape," on this organization.

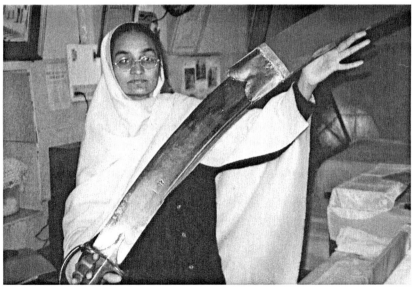

FIGURE 2.8 A member of the Dalla family displays a sword from the collection; instructions in Punjabi direct viewers on correct behavior and attitude. Photographs by Anne Murphy. January 2005.

home, not a part of the SGPC-managed institutional site. The range of objects that constitute the relic type—text, clothing, weapon—can be seen in this collection. The objects are held in a private home, but the discipline enforced is that generally associated with the museum.[62] The extension of such behavior from the museum to the private home takes on a particular salience in South Asia, where the discipline of museum behavior/participation has always been partial in its enactment, as Tapati Guha-Thakurta has noted.[63] As we saw at the museum in Old Delhi, an array of rules governs viewing in this location as well. At the large, traditional entrance—like most households in Malwa, adorned with neem leaves for protection and to promote the auspicious—are large signs in Punjabi, saying "this is a home, not a gurdwara." The signboards note appropriate behavior: shoes, sunglasses, and cloth that restrains the beard should be removed;[64] visitors should not ring the bell at the entrance more than once or twice; the owners of the premises are not responsible for belongings left in cars and so these should be locked; and people should not be in a rush while having *darshan* (viewing) of the holy *shastar vastar* (weapons and clothes) of the Guru. It is strictly forbidden to offer money at the site or to give the distributed *parshād* or blessed food to a dog (thereby doing it disrespect). Viewers are told that they should not try to touch the sacred weapons and clothes of the Guru. Visitors gather in the courtyard of the site, and receive *darshan* of the objects in formal presentations by female family members.[65] The room is dominated by a large painting of Guru Gobind Singh. All the objects are stored away, and some are not brought out for viewing at all; photographs of some of them—including a *hukamnāmā*, or order of the Guru—are on display.[66] The Guru Granth Sahib is located at the center of the room.

---

62. On the museum and the disciplining of public behavior, see Tony Bennett, *The Birth of the Museum: History, Theory, Politics* (London: Routledge, 1995); also Tony Bennett, "The Exhibitionary Complex" and Carol Duncan, "From the Princely Gallery to the Public Art Museum: The Louvre Museum and the National Gallery, London," both in *Representing the Nation: A Reader. Histories, Heritage and Museums*, ed. David Boswell and Jessica Evans (New York: Routledge, 1999), 332–61 and 304–31.

63. See Tapati Guha-Thakurta, *Monuments, Objects, Histories: Institutions of Art in Colonial and Postcolonial India* (New Delhi: Permanent Black, 2004), 43, 45, 79. See also Gyan Prakash, *Another Reason: Science and the Imagination of Modern India* (Princeton, NJ: Princeton University Press, 1999).

64. A fine cloth band is often used to restrain the beard among *keshdhārī* Sikhs, but is not considered by most to be orthodox.

65. The Dalla family displays their belongings from 7 AM to 5 PM every day, after making *kaṛāh parshād*, the standard type of offering given in Sikh gurdwaras, composed of sugar, ghee or clarified butter, and wheat flour. I describe a visit in 2002, but have visited the site at other times as well (2005, 2007), with similar experiences.

66. See discussion of *hukamnāme* in chapter 3.

The objects were first displayed at the decision of Shamsher Singh, a member of the Legislative Assembly for the alliance of princely states called PEPSU, formed after independence in 1947; these states were eventually merged into the state of Punjab in the 1950s. The "special summary of the loving faith and devotion of Dalla Singh," distributed by the family to visitors at the site, was written by local Nirmala scholar Balwant Singh.[67] As is common in the discourse of object possession, the relationship of the family to the Gurus is first defined: "Dalla Singh's ancestors had converted to Sikhism at the hand of Guru Hargobind. At the age of four or five, Dalla Singh had *darshan* of Guru Tegh Bahadur, and received his blessing."[68] Dalla served the Tenth Guru faithfully, and exchanged gifts with the Guru and his wife. These objects form the collection now in the possession of the family. The display and respect given to the objects at the Dalla household is said to continue an earlier tradition of honoring them; Dalla himself was said to have performed *pūjā* or worship of these objects with utmost respect.[69] Within the narratives produced and distributed at the site, both orally and in print, the objects stand for the devotion of the family to the Guru and attest to a strong relationship with the Guru. They also demonstrate the importance of Dalla family locally and the spread of Sikhism in the region.[70] In the Dalla family context, the miraculous nature of the objects is downplayed, while elements of this are retained at the Takhat; in both cases, objects are treated as *historical*—they

67. Balwant Singh, *Bhāī Dallā Siṅgh* (no publication information given). Balwant Singh is responsible for a large number of texts about the Malwa region, as well as histories of the Nirmala *panth*, of which he is a member. The Nirmalas, a small group within the larger Sikh *panth*, have traditionally served a scholarly function in the tradition, with a somewhat controversial status due to puranic influences sometimes evident in their work.

68. Balwant Singh, *Bhāī Dallā Siṅgh*, 1. The Dalla lineage had close ties with Mughal authority in the making of its own regional position in Malwa, and the first grant was made to the family after the assistance it gave to Babur at the battle of Panipat in 1525. Akbar (1556–1605) granted the family patriarch the title of *caudhurī*. See Balwant Singh, *Bhāī Dallā Siṅgh*.

69. Balwant Singh, *Bhāī Dallā Siṅgh*, 2.

70. It is not surprising, therefore, that Dalla's *samādh* or funerary marker is included in the Damdama Takhat complex. However, this is not unproblematic: the location of the *samādh* within the central precinct of the gurdwara is not mentioned in the Takhat literature examined, and the head *granthī* of the Takhat said Dalla's pride led him to want his *samādh* there. Thus, as this comment indicates, the role of the Dalla family is remembered differently in non-family sources (both printed and interviews at the Takhat). See *Sankhep Itihās*, distributed at the site; and Balwant Singh, *Shrī Damdamā*. Dalla is also associated with the stories of Bir and Dhir Singh, as the Guru requested volunteers as a way to humble Dalla's pride after he bragged that his troops were superior to the Guru's.

are authentically of and document a past.[71] They are valuable, worthy of preservation and protection, as evidence of a set of relationships with the Guru and his family.

The objects of Sikh pasts contribute to the formation of those pasts into a narrative order.[72] We might call these objects of memory, in the terms Pierre Nora has defined, where in our experience of modernity "memory" is of a fundamentally different order than "history."[73] The difference between history and memory is seen by him and numerous others as absolute and hierarchical: memory precedes history. History represents a rupture from the past that is alienated and coercive; memory is an experience of the past that is lived, full, and alive, undistorted and non-rationalized. Yet, if history is determined by larger social and political forces, then so too is memory; neither exists in a pure space outside of the contestation of power, since *both* are socially constructed.[74] There is a sense of alienation within the construction of the past as history—a separation between past and present that allows the narrativization of that past—but such a separation constitutes memory as well, as does the constructive force of narrative.[75] History and memory both act to bridge the now and the then, and recuperate the loss between. The two are thus intimately intertwined.

History in the Sikh context builds upon the nascent narration of the past as memory in individual, personal terms to create another entity as the subject of

71. The miraculous nature of other objects has been a source of controversy. For example, "Clarify stand on Ganga Sagar, SGPC told" December 19, 2004, http://www.tribuneindia.com/2004/20041219/punjab1.htm (accessed April 23, 2005). See discussion of the Ganga Sagar in the concluding chapter.

72. See Hayden White, *Content of the Form: Narrative Discourse and Historical Representation* (Baltimore: John Hopkins University Press, 1987).

73. Nora, *Realms of Memory*, 19–20. There is a large literature on the distinction between history and memory, and it relates to a broader polemic regarding the nature of "history"; see Paul Connerton, *How Societies Remember* (Cambridge: Cambridge University Press, 1989) and Halbwachs, *On Collective Memory*. For more on the idea of history as resulting from absolute rupture, advocating a more presentist approach, see Constantin Fasolt, *The Limits of History* (Chicago: University of Chicago Press, 2004). See the discussion of the problems with this position in Murphy, "Materializing Sikh Pasts." For a similar critique of Nora, see Olick and Robbins, "Social Memory Studies," 121ff.

74. For a related critique of an absolute distinction between memory and history, see Geary, *Phantoms of Remembrance*, 10ff.

75. See Michel de Certeau, *The Writing of History*, trans. Tom Conley (New York: Columbia University Press, 1988), 3ff. and 34ff.

history: the community.[76] Memory becomes history when it is fully narrativized as the past in relation to a subject outside of that memory, outside of that intimate relation that is memory itself. Thus, while Paul Ricoeur concedes that collective memory is the "soil in which historiography is rooted," it is also the case that history distances itself, moves out of memory.[77] Memory thus fuels history, constitutes it; even as the two are distinct, they are linked. As Jacques Le Goff put it, "just as the past is not history but the object of history, so memory is not history, but both one of its objects and an elementary level of its development."[78] Indeed, Patrick Hutton has argued that history as a discipline should be seen as a modern example of the "art of memory" that proliferated in medieval Europe and that it exists in multiple forms in multiple cultures:[79] it is a particular kind of cultivated memory, and it takes different forms. Modern Western historiography is only one of these.

The objects and sites examined here may be seen as one kind of technology designed to bridge the gap between past and present, to bring memory into history, as they are organized and presented to constitute the Sikh community through the representation of the past. At the center of that memory is the Guru. The remembering and calling into narrative of a range of persons (Gurus and related honored persons) and relationships (particularly with the Guru) produces the community around the Guru, the followers who call themselves "Sikh." The nature of the narrative constructed differs depending upon the person/institution telling—and authorizing—it, and thus the meaning of the objects is constituted differently over time. At Damdama Sahib today, for example, an institutionalized history is articulated around object and site through the rituals and speech of officials there, and the signs and publications provided. It is the SGPC, the central official organizing body of historical Sikh gurdwaras, that ties these narrations

---

76. On the multiple forms that totalizing master-narratives can take, see Inden and Ali in: Ronald Inden, Jonathan Walters, and Daud Ali, eds., *Querying the Medieval: Texts and the History of Practices in South Asia* (Oxford: Oxford University Press, 2000), 62, 179. On narrative and history, see White, *Content of the Form*; for a critique of White's position, see A. Dirk Moses, "Hayden White, Traumatic Nationalism, and the Public Role of History," *History and Theory* 44, 3 (2005): 311–32; and "The Public Relevance of Historical Studies: A Rejoinder to Hayden White," *History and Theory* 44, 3 (2005): 339–347.

77. Ricoeur, *Memory, History, Forgetting*, 135ff, see p. 69 for quotation.

78. Jacques Le Goff, *History and Memory*, trans. Steven Rendall and Elizabeth Claman (1977, reprint, New York: Columbia University Press, 1988), 129.

79. Patrick H. Hutton, *History as an Art of Memory* (Hanover, NH: University Press of New England, 1993), chapter 1 in particular. On history and memory as addressing separation or loss, see 166–68.

and sites together to create a history that has been linked to the landscape of Punjab. There are, and have been, other possible narrators of such histories, and therefore other possible histories, as we will explore in the chapters that follow. What
the object and site do, their agency, therefore, is determined within this field. As
is shown in the analysis of the court records of Maharaja Ranjit Singh in chapter
5, sites were authorized in different ways in the precolonial and colonial periods.
The historical process by which the SGPC came into being as the narrator of the
Sikh history found in *itihāsik* gurdwaras is described in chapters 6 and 7. The authorizing function of the state and/or similar institutions, therefore, determines
whose past is on display at a given site, and how a community is configured in
relation to it. This may indicate the difference between the Sikh case and other
allied traditions in South Asia, such as that of Namdev, for which Christian
Novetzke has argued memory "is the site of continuity with the historical subject,
whereas history is the source of disassociation from the past."[80] Sikh interest in the
past is imbued with memory, but calls it to an order that is also more than memory,
authorized in different ways by different narrators of the past. For this reason,
perhaps, the historical has been a contested terrain in Sikh contexts, more so than
in others.[81]

The collection of Dalla Singh and the construction of Takhat Sri Damdama
Sahib provide contemporary examples of how objects and sites have functioned
as historical evidence of a past that constitutes the community. Descriptions
within recent historiography focus on the forms of Dalla's service to the Guru,
and the closeness of their relationship is made clear in the gifts that were
exchanged between them. He is said to have performed service with absolute
faithfulness and selflessness, as required by the ideal of *nishkām sevā* or "selfless
service."[82] He challenged the authority of the Mughal representative at the local
center of Sirhind, with whom the Guru had already been in serious conflict:
when a letter came asking that the Guru be handed over to authorities, Dalla is
said to have replied: "The Guru is my life; who gives his own life to someone
else?"[83] This relationship took other forms: Dalla Singh took *amrit* or formal

---

80. Novetzke, *History, Bhakti, and Public Memory*, 73.

81. Anne Murphy, "Introductory essay" in *Time, History, and the Religious Imaginary in South Asia*, ed. Anne Murphy, 1–11 (New York: Routledge, 2011), 7.

82. For more on the concept of *nishkām sevā*, or service without the expectation of reward, in Sikh traditions, see Anne Murphy, "Mobilizing *Seva* ('Service'): Modes of Sikh Diasporic Action," in *South Asians in Diaspora: Religions and Histories*, ed. Knut Jacobsen and Pratap Kumar (Leiden: Brill, 2004), 337–72. This is repeatedly emphasized in the text: Balwant Singh, *Bhāī Dallā Siṅgh*, 2.

83. Balwant Singh, *Bhāī Dallā Siṅgh*, 2.

initiation into the order of the Khalsa, as prepared by the Guru, and was of central importance in the promotion of the Takhat as a holy place: "He did not think that this place was a normal hillock, but that it had become holy with the feet of the Guru, and accepted it as a great holy place."[84] *Sevā* thus is a central mode that defines the relationship of members of the community and the Guru, and is attested to through material representations of such service. The objects at the Dalla household, Damdama Sahib, and elsewhere reflect a range of relationships among givers and receivers, between those remembered and those remembering. They also reflect—as Marcel Mauss demonstrated in his early exploration of *The Gift*—a range of different meanings: economic, religious, and political, within a complex accounting of the relationships enacted and substantialized in the social setting of the exchange. These objects are not commodities, because of their limited and specific exchange life and their intimate relation to the persons engaged in the giving and receiving.[85] They are valued for being "terminal," in Arjun Appadurai's use of the term, as objects which are *not* exchanged further.[86] The meaning of objects is thus found in the close connections between givers and receivers, objects and places, the community and the remembrance of the Guru.

In Balwant Singh's history of the family, descriptions are provided of the gifts provided by Dalla to the Guru: "a horse, a heavy shawl, and 100 rupees . . ." and to his wife "a very good Tiur [a gift set consisting of three garments]."[87] The Guru reciprocated, giving Dalla "a *kirpān* [dagger], a *ḍhāl* [shield], 2,000 pairs of inlaid bracelets and an apron."[88] Such objects—and the site itself—represent the relationship between Dalla and the Guru. This use of the object to substantiate and represent relationships is not new: the form of Dalla's gifts to the Guru follows

84. Balwant Singh, *Bhāī Dallā Singh*, 3.

85. Marcel Mauss, *The Gift: Forms and Functions of Exchange in Archaic Societies* (New York: W. W. Norton, 1967). A useful discussion of the significance of Mauss in the Indian context is found in Jonathan Parry "The Gift, The Indian Gift, and the 'Indian Gift'" in *Man* 21, 3 (1986): 453–73.

86. Arjun Appadurai, "Introduction: Commodities and the Politics of Value," in *The Social Life of Things: Commodities in Cultural Perspective*, ed. Arjun Appadurai (Cambridge: Cambridge University Press, 1986), 23. To clarify further the relationship of the present work to that encompassed in Appadurai's volume, I am interested primarily in the social history of these objects, rather than the cultural biography of particular objects (Appadurai, "Introduction," 34; see also I. Kopytoff's article in the same volume, "The Cultural Biography of Things: Commoditization as Process"). I am in addition consciously not pursuing issues related to authenticity in relation to these objects, on which see Appadurai, "Introduction," 45ff.

87. Balwant Singh, *Bhāī Dallā Singh*, 1.

88. Balwant Singh, *Bhāī Dallā Singh*, 2.

traditional forms of *khil'at*, royal gifting traditions.[89] Objects exchanged through *khil'at* established a client-patron relationship, granting the blessing (*baraka*) or essence of the giver to the receiver.[90] In Finbarr Flood's words, such objects functioned as "an incarnated sign of sovereign authority."[91] The practice, with Central Asian origins and a sphere of influence that extended from Europe to China, became common in South Asia with the advent of Central Asian and Persianate rule, although it was a Muslim practice neither in origin nor in ongoing use. It was commonly practiced among many non-Muslim rulers in South Asia, alongside Muslim ones; it was also used in religious contexts, such as among Sufis.[92] As Gail Minault notes, *khil'at* took its place among a range of rituals that, within the context of the Mughal court, symbolized "the grant of patronage and protection, on the one hand, and clientage and service, on the other," linking "imperial authority to divine authority, the source of all earthly power."[93] The exchange of turbans was also commonly practiced in eighteenth century Punjab as a means for expressing political and social equivalence and collaboration among Sikh

89. Stewart Gordon, ed., *Robes and Honor: The Medieval World of Investiture* (New York: Palgrave, 2001) and *Robes of Honour: Khil'at in Pre-Colonial and Colonial India* (New Delhi: Oxford University Press, 2003). On *khil'at* and its role in the Sikh tradition, see Louis E. Fenech *The Darbar of the Sikh Gurus: The Court of God in the World of Men* (New Delhi: Oxford University Press, 2008), 64ff. Not all of the objects related to the Gurus reflect the kind of exchange involved in *khil'at*, however, as will be discussed.

90. Stewart Gordon, "Introduction: Ibn Battuta and a Region of Robing," in *Robes of Honour: Khil'at in Pre-Colonial and Colonial India*, ed. Stewart Gordon, 1–30 (New Delhi: Oxford University Press, 2003), 12–13. See also Flood *Objects of Translation*, 82–83. Mauss's formulation of the gift relies on just such a sense of the giving of the essence of the person in the gift (see discussion in Parry, "The Gift, The Indian Gift, and the 'Indian Gift,'" 456–59). Such a sensibility does inform the Sikh object, to a degree, but should not be construed as being equivalent to the notion of embodiment that operates fully in Buddhist and medieval Christian understandings of the relic. The Sikh case may indeed corroborate Parry's findings that gifting where reciprocity is involved—such as we can construe in the Sikh case, where the gift of the Guru is matched by the gift of the *sevā* of the devotee—does not involve the transfer of "spirit" through the gift (Parry, "The Gift, The Indian Gift, and the "Indian Gift," 463; see also Jonathan Parry *Death in Banaras* [Cambridge: Cambridge University Press, 1994], 134). On the other hand, the gift of the Guru might also be conceived of as another way of being "united with the Guru's substance," or the incorporation of "the natural substance and moral code for conduct of the Sikh Guru," which Verne Dusenbery suggests is the Punjabi understanding of the basis for being Sikh (*Sikhs at Large*, 19).

91. Flood, *Objects of Translation*, 76.

92. Gordon, "Introduction," 1, and Stewart Gordon "Conclusions," in *Robes of Honour: Khil'at in Pre-Colonial and Colonial India*, ed. Stewart Gordon, 140–46 (New Delhi: Oxford University Press, 2003), 140.

93. Gail Minault, "The Emperor's Old Clothes: Robing and Sovereignty in Late Mughal and Early British India," in *Robes of Honour: Khil'at in Pre-Colonial and Colonial India*, ed. Stewart Gordon, 125–39 (New Delhi: Oxford University Press, p. 126, 2003), 126.

chiefs, as well as in broader terms among other martial groups.[94] Such material forms of authority building were enthusiastically perpetuated by the British through the system of honors utilized in formal durbars or court settings, exemplified in Punjab by the "Public Viceregal Durbar" held at Lahore in October 1864; a list was published in Lepel Griffin's work, in which "Chiefs and Native Gentlemen" of Punjab were listed with their level of *khil'at.*[95]

The gift has a central role in other South Asian contexts in the articulation of power, both within and outside the Mughal court. Although Nicholas Dirks's work deals with southern India, which takes us far from the locus of Sikh object traditions, his observations regarding the role of the gift in constituting authority support findings in the Sikh case. For Dirks, gifting practices invested authority in the king. Relationships between the king and his subjects were fundamentally constituted by gifts, Dirks argues, which were "basic to statecraft" in precolonial South India.[96] The gifts granted by the king—in various forms, as land or as object— provided a means for participation in the sovereignty of the king, demonstrated publicly a relationship between sovereign and subject, and represented a part of the king to the recipient, much as was the case with the gifted object in *khil'at.*[97] Such articulations of kingly power need not, however, make irrelevant religious claims to power as articulated through the gift. Norbert Peabody has noted the role of gifts in the articulation of authority in western Indian kingdom of Kota, where gifts were made and received by kings but also made and received by the Vallabha Goswamis. In this case, the relationships articulated through the gift express "rival constructions of the principles underlying the social order," and it was a "contested matter as to both who was subordinating whom and what the gift fundamentally meant."[98] Kingly as well as other forms of authority were thus expressed.

For this reason we cannot simply differentiate exchanges as "religious" or "nonreligious." Dirks has observed that the form of the relations articulated in

---

94. Purnima Dhavan, *When Sparrows Became Hawks: The Making of the Sikh Warrior Tradition, 1699–1799* (New York: Oxford University Press, 2011), 142–43. See also Bernard Cohn, *Colonialism and Its Forms of Knowledge: The British in India* (Princeton, NJ: Princeton University Press), 115–16.

95. Lepel H. Griffin, *The Panjab Chiefs: Historical and Biographical Notices of the Principal Families in the Territories Under the Panjab Government* (Lahore: T.C. McCarthy-Chronicle Press, 1865), v–lvii. See Cohn, *Colonialism,* 117ff.

96. Dirks, *Hollow Crown,* 129, 130ff. See also the relevance of these arguments to his more recent work: Nicholas Dirks, *Castes of Mind: Colonialism and the Making of Modern India* (Princeton, NJ: Princeton University Press, 2001), 63ff.

97. See also Ali in Inden, Walters, and Ali, eds., *Querying the Medieval,* 205.

98. Peabody, "In Whose Turban," 747.

the royal gift bore resemblance to those established in *pūjā* or worship, which Dirks calls "the root political metaphor," but were political in nature and were established in recognition of service by subordinate to superior.[99] This is not to say that there was not a ritual character involved: "[g]ifts were public acts of kingship and established relations, however variable, between the grantor and the grantee. On the one hand, ritual was a pervasive political fact; on the other, politics was permeated by ritual forms."[100] Just as the power of the king was articulated alongside other forms of power through the gift, religious and nonreligious modes of engagement were intermingled in such practices. This is also revealed in Sudipta Sen's work on the construction of history in Indo-Persianate contexts in North India. In this case, interaction with the emperor was performed in religious modes, particularly but not exclusively in relation to the Mughal emperor Akbar. In such a context, particular importance was granted to the remembering of interactions with the emperor within historical accounts: "it is no surprise," Sen notes, "that the memory of imperial association added transcendental significance to the past, particularly among a heterogeneous nobility which was not necessarily bound by the same religious sensibility."[101]

These multiple associations of power, sovereignty, and the representation of the past in both religious and nonreligious modes must shape our understanding of the object in the Sikh case. We are thus not speaking simply of the "religious" nature of the Sikh object as enlivened by divine presence, but its role within a complex system of exchange, and community- and authority-building processes, as Bernard Cohn has generally observed for the social role of clothing.[102] In terms of state formation, material practices worked to constitute authority: indeed, one way in which the sovereignty of the Mughal state was circumscribed by the British in the nineteenth century was by denying the right to grant *khil'at*.[103] In the context of statecraft, gifting was essentially tied to the establishment and continuation of sovereignty, but sovereignty took multiple forms. In the Sikh context, such gifts by the Guru reflect both politics in relation to state formation

---

99. Dirks, *Hollow Crown*, 47. Puja as a root metaphor for political relations does not mean that all politics were religious: "the deity was not so much the paradigmatic sovereign as worship was the paradigmatic exchange" (289).

100. Dirks, *Hollow Crown*, 129.

101. Sudipta Sen, "Imperial Orders of the Past: The Semantics of History and Time in the Medieval Indo-Persianate Culture of North India," in *Invoking the Past: The Uses of History in South Asia*, ed. Daud Ali, 231–57 (New Delhi: Oxford University Press), 250.

102. Cohn, *Colonialism*, 114.

103. Sudipta Sen, *Distant Sovereignty: National Imperialism and the Origins of British India* (New York: Routledge, 2002), xiii.

and the politics of community building in more general terms, as was true in Sufi contexts. These gifts themselves then became part of claims to sovereignty, such as with the weapons of the Guru collected (for instance) in the *toshākhānā* of Maharaja Ranjit Singh, and those utilized in the coronation ceremonies of the princely states of East Punjab, the Phulkian states.[104] The honors granted in this way were traditionally collected and displayed for posterity, and were common among families of different social backgrounds and statuses, ways of substantializing client-patron relationships and internal familial hierarchies and relationships.[105] Such practices can be seen even today across Punjab. This is what is attested to within Sikh historical objects and sites—the Guru's giving of a gift to Dalla is evidence of that relationship and allows for the remembering of it. This was a common way for the Gurus to maintain and strengthen ties among their followers, to establish and demonstrate authority.[106] This is not to say that objects in general do not contain other characteristics that contribute to their value within the cultural economy of exchange—in some traditions, the idea of embodiment *is* central—but to argue that the primary idiom engaged in the Sikh case is one of authority- and community-building, rather than the intrinsic nature of the object in containing or representing the essence of the user or the divine.[107]

The power of objects to contain and substantiate authority links those objects revered as gifts and those revered for their use by the Gurus: through use, the substance and power of a person is attached to an object, attesting to that person's authority. Not all revered objects in Sikh tradition thus obtain their value within the process of exchange. Objects Guru Nanak used to ply his trade in Sultanpur Lodhi (where he was in charge of the civil supplies store), for example, are held with reverence at a gurdwara there.[108] Objects also express family relationships. Thus even objects that are not the product of exchange with the Guru can carry

---

104. On the Guru's weapons that were held in the *toshākhānā*, see Murphy, "The Guru's Weapons." On the use of the Guru's sword in coronation, see Bhai Sikander Singh and Roopinder Singh, *Sikh Heritage: Ethos and Relics*, 136. See further discussion in chapter 3.

105. Cohn, *Colonialism*, 119–20.

106. See Fenech, *Darbar of the Sikh Gurus*, 103.

107. Compare Cohn and Bayly in this regard: C. A. Bayly, "The Origins of Swadeshi (Home Industry): Cloth and Indian Society, 1700–1930," in *The Social Life of Things: Commodities in Cultural Perspective*, ed. Arjun Appadurai (Cambridge: Cambridge University Press, 1986), 285–321. Bayly's concerns are in some ways parallel to Cohn's, but he de-emphasizes the political nature of cloth and its exchange, and in particular does not explore the importance of *khil'at* (Bayly, 292). He focuses more on the "consumption preferences" of the Mughal court (Bayly, 300ff.).

108. See Murphy, "Materializing Sikh Pasts."

the power of authority, as they are passed on within a family or at a site and therefore attest to the authority of that family or site. This is particularly demonstrated with the Bedi family, associated with Dera Baba Nanak, the city built by Sri Chand, the son of Guru Nanak, in honor of his father, near Gurdaspur. A gurdwara here, Sri Chola Sahib, is the location of the *cholā* or apron of Guru Nanak, which is widely revered (see figure 2.9). The *cholā* of Guru Nanak is displayed every year at a *melā* (festival) that commemorates its return to the family's possession, 350 years ago; members of the family are also looked to with reverence, for being within the lineage of the Guru.[109] As this example demonstrates, *persons* act as a source of authority, in similar terms and in some senses as an extension of the relic, authorized in relation to the Guru. Personal charismatic authority exists in general terms in Sikh contexts—leaders such as the now-deceased Harbhajan Singh Yogi in the United States and Mohinder Singh of the Guru Nanak Nishkam Seva Jatha in Birmingham, England, demonstrate that individual leaders do retain importance within the tradition, even without blood ties to the Gurus.[110] As will be discussed in the chapters that follow, historically within Sikh tradition there have been ways of understanding the role of personal connections and blood relations that do not allow for the *automatic* attribution of authority, while still accepting the role of personal authority and blood lineage. What matters here is that lineage connection to the Guru has in the past constituted, and continues to constitute, its own form of authority building, because of the historical connection to the Guru that is thus expressed.

Dera Baba Nanak is not alone in being both an object site and a site connected by lineage to the Gurus. The Sodhis at Kartarpur (the family that holds the Kartarpur Pothi, the precanonical version of the Adi Granth compiled in 1604) and the Bhalla family (part of which is located at Pinjore, and holds volumes of the Goindwal Pothi, an earlier version) provide other examples: these families genealogically connected to the Gurus collect both text and objects, and

---

109. Three families now hold the apron jointly. They are the all the direct descendants of Guru Nanak. See the literature published by Bedi at Dera Baba Nanak, such as *Sākhī Srī Cholā Sāhib Jī* (obtained June 2002 from Manjit Singh Bedi in Leeds, England).

110. See, for example, Darshan Singh Tatla, "Nurturing the Faithful: The Role of the Sant Among Britain's Sikhs," *Religion* 22 (1992): 349–74.

FIGURE 2.9 Main display at the Chola Sahib festival in March of 2002. Photography by Anne Murphy. March 2002.

occasionally make them available for public viewing.[111] As will be discussed in chapter 7, the Sodhis in particular have been criticized for their possession of the 1604 version of the scripture. Such examples allow us to see how a text can serve as object within the tradition, outside of and alongside the function of the text as Word, which fulfills its *primary* function.[112] I have noted that the objects of memory we have seen so far interact in complex ways with the memorialization strategies found within textual traditions. This is not, however, only the case in relation to the *content* of texts, in the ways in which memories are encoded in word, story, and performance, as in the hagiographical literature of the *janam-sākhī*s, which describe the life and travels of the first Sikh Guru, Guru Nanak,[113] and later historiography, examined in the following chapters. Object culture also

---

111. There are various branches of the Sodhi family; the main centers are at Kartarpur and at Una in Himachal Pradesh.

112. Mann notes the usefulness of considering the text as an artifact, as well (Mann, "Sources for the Study," 235).

113. See W. H. McLeod, *The Evolution of the Sikh Community* (New Delhi: Oxford University Press, 1976), 20–36, and W. H. McLeod, *Early Sikh Tradition: A Study of the Janam-sakhis* (Oxford: Oxford University Press, 1980).

relates in complex ways to the development of the Adi Granth, the Sikh sacred scripture, as an object itself. The category of the Sikh relic object therefore can include text, as well as in the more conventional sense of "object."

G. S. Mann's reconstruction of the history of the Adi Granth demonstrates the ways in which the construction and preservation of the sacred text has been implicated in disputes over succession and authority.[114] According to Mann, the text was first written down during Guru Nanak's lifetime, sometime in the beginning of the sixteenth century. The actual text from this period is not available, nor are any full identical copies in existence; there is, however, some limited evidence that attests to its existence.[115] This *pothī* or text, known as the Harsahai Pothi in honor of the place where it later came to rest, was used as the basis for the Goindwal Pothi of the late sixteenth century.[116] The Goindwal Pothi remained in the hands of the descendants of the Third Guru, Amardas, while the Fourth Guru, Ramdas, who left Goindwal to found a new city—the city of Ramdaspur, or Amritsar—took possession of the Harsahai Pothi. This *pothī* later came into the possession of his son, Prithi Chand, who did not accept the Guruship of the Fifth Guru, Arjan. His followers, known as the *mīṇās*, challenged Arjan's authority and remained outside of the mainstream Sikh *panth* until much later, when they joined the Khalsa. Guru Arjan compiled the Kartarpur Pothi in 1604, which became the basis for the later canonical text of the Guru Granth Sahib.[117]

Although this is a simplified reconstruction of the complex early history of the Adi Granth, the 1604 version of the canon, and the Sri Guru Granth Sahib, the final canonical version of the scripture, it will suffice for the present discussion. The development of the canon was, in short, characterized by the preservation of alternative and developing versions of the sacred text within individual family traditions. This process certainly relates to the importance of the recording

---

114. Gurinder Singh Mann, *The Making of Sikh Scripture* (Oxford: Oxford University Press, 2001).

115. Mention is made of this text in Tara Singh Narotam, *Shrī Gurū Tīrth Sangraih* (Kankhal: Sri Nirmal Pancaeti Akhara, 1971 [1883]), 289. IOL 14162.n.7 (2). See the discussion in Mann, *Making of Sikh Scripture*. The author viewed photographs, said to be of this text, in the summer of 1998, in Chandigarh.

116. Two volumes of the Goindval Pothis are still extant; one is held at Pinjore. See Gurinder Singh Mann, *The Goindval Pothis: The Earliest Extant Source of the Sikh Canon* (Cambridge, MA: Department of Sanskrit and Indian Studies, Harvard University and Harvard University Press, 1996).

117. On the history of the text, see also Pashaura Singh, *The Guru Granth Sahib: Canon, Meaning and Authority* (New Delhi: Oxford University Press, 2000).

and propagation of the *bāni* or sacred Word, which stands at the center of Sikh tradition from its inception.[118] Versions of the canon, therefore, are testament to the primary importance of the sacred Word. The relationship between *possession* of the text and authority, however, is another key element in the story of the early scripture, as the text was passed down from Guru to Guru, and within families. The possession of the text seems to have been associated with the claim to Guru-ship, and thus the text on a material level acted as an object of authority. Many of the cities associated with the early Sikh tradition (Kartarpur, Khadur, Goindwal, Amritsar) were founded and then came to be contested because of tensions arising from dissent over the right to Guruship. The text as an object and in recording the words of the designated Gurus was an important part of the asser-tion of authority and succession to the seat of Guruship within the early Sikh *panth*. The treatment of the text, beyond its *primary* role as a mediating interface for the sacred Word, thus reflects the larger category of relic that has been pro-posed. As I have said before, this object-role for the text is *secondary* to its role as the vehicle for the Word, which is *not* material. This must be emphasized. Indeed, the text as a physical object only derives its value from the primacy of this sacred Word. The object-nature of the text itself is, however, of interest, in how it extends our understanding of the function of the canon in social terms. Thus the scripture has functioned on multiple levels: most importantly, in containing the Word that describes the revelation of God received by Guru Nanak and the other Gurus and which stands at the center of the Sikh religious and experiential system; but also as an object of possession, and therefore authority, for those vying for power and position within the religious community; in memory of the tradition's teachers, as the hymns were recorded according to author, even as all signed their names in the name of Nanak; and as an object of ritual, tied to all of these prior roles. Along these latter lines, Mann describes the ways that the book was integrated into inauguration and other ceremonies within the early tradition: the book as a physical presence was authorizing.[119] In this mode, the text acts as Word and as object, and thus shares much with the object as a possession, outside of and alongside its primary role as the embodied Word. Here again we see how the multiple temporal orders of Sikh religiosity—the connection to the past, and the performance of the present—are linked.

---

118. This is debated. Compare, for example, Harjot Oberoi, *The Construction of Religious Boundaries: Culture, Identity, and Diversity in the Sikh Tradition* (New Delhi: Oxford Univer-sity Press, 1994) with Mann, *Goindwal* and J. S. Grewal, *Historical Perspectives on Sikh Identity* (Patiala: Punjabi University, 1997).

119. Mann, *Making of Sikh Scripture*.

The Objects of Community: The Markers of the Khalsa

The Five Ks, the markers that are worn to signify membership in the Khalsa, provide another example of how Sikh materiality functions to produce the community. The order of the Khalsa defies easy definition: it comprises, in some senses, an
ideal, a definition of what is a full and authentic Sikh—to be dressed, as Pashaura
Singh has described it, "in the word of God."[120] Founded by Guru Gobind Singh in
1699 at Anandpur, the Khalsa in its most essential sense provided a binding link
between the community and the Guru, and among community members.[121] The
term *khālsā* literally means "pure," but also relates to a term in Mughal land-revenue
administration, *khālisā*, which refers to lands held by the emperor, the revenue of
which went directly into the treasury of the imperial state. This was an appropriate
term for this new vision of being Sikh, for the formation of this community of
Sikhs entailed the abrogation of a formerly important office within the Sikh *panth*,
the office of the *masaṅds*, who had represented the Guru's interests within the small
congregations of Sikhs spread across Punjab and beyond. Khalsa members were
brought into direct relation with the Guru—and after the Tenth Guru's death, with
the sacred text—through an initiation ceremony known as *khaṅḍe-dī-pahul*, or the
initiation of the sword, involving the taking of *amrit* or nectar stirred with the
sword. This use of the sword is significant, for the order of the Khalsa had strong
military connotations as well. It is from the formation of the Khalsa that Sikhs
came to be known by the names "*Siṅgh*" (literally "lion," a name associated with
kingship in northwestern India, for men) and "*Kaur*" (or princess, for women).[122]

The historical formation of the insignia of the *Khalsa* as a set—the *kes* (uncut
hair), *kaṅghā* (comb), *kirpān* (dagger or sword), *kaṛā* (steel bracelet), and *kaccha*
(undergarment)—is complicated. Our understanding of the history—and also
the present role—of the insignia of the Khalsa relies upon a particular genre of
literature: the *rahit* texts. The *rahit* is generally credited with the explication of
the requirements for a Khalsa Sikh, the shaping of the material form of Sikh identity in the form of the Five Ks in the present as well as the past. W. H. McLeod
defined this literature as "the code of discipline which all members of the Khalsa
must vow to observe."[123] But it is also much more than a code of conduct: "it

---

120. Pashaura Singh "Formulation of the Convention of the Five Ks: A Focus on the Evolution of the Khalsa Rahit," *International Journal of Punjab Studies* 6, 2 (1999): 155–69, see p. 155.

121. The year of the founding of the Khalsa has been called into question by Mann, "Sources
for the Study," 249ff.

122. For a historical account of the formation and development of the Khalsa and its ethos, see
Dhavan, *When Sparrows Became Hawks*.

123. Chaupa Singh, *The Chaupa Singh Rahit Nāmā*, trans., ed. W. H. McLeod (Dunedin: University of Otago Press, 1987), 9.

involves belief and also a perspective," a way of understanding being Sikh at particular historical moments.[124] The *rahit* texts—a total of twenty-one have been suggested by W. H. McLeod as representing the genre—evolved from the eighteenth to the nineteenth century, without one clearly primary articulation of the code emerging in this period; all are attributed to contemporaries of the Guru and are thought to derive from or reflect the pronouncements of the Tenth Guru.[125] A number of twentieth-century versions of the *rahit* exist, drawing upon and developing further existing early forms. These represent the effort to systematize the codes presented in the different versions, as well as bring them into line with the evolving orthodoxy associated with the Singh Sabha, the reform movement that defined the contours of modern Sikhism in the late nineteenth to early twentieth century.[126] There was a version developed and published as *Gurmat Prakāsh Bhāg Sanskār* in 1915, which never gained wide acceptance; a much more widely accepted version developed by the SGPC was published in 1950 under the name *Sikh Rahit Maryādā*. An English version—with subtle differences—was published in 1971 in the United Kingdom as *Rehat Maryada: A Guide to the Sikh Way of Life*.[127]

Although there are indications within the historical record that something of the *rahit* did in fact exist at the time of Guru Gobind Singh (1666–1708), there is no single document from this period that directly tells us what that code looked like.[128] There is also much work that remains to be done on early manuscripts of the *rahit* tradition.[129] According to McLeod, the existing evidence in the record of the eighteenth century "does not indicate that Guru Gobind Singh uttered a Rahit which was opposed to the traditional version that we have today or that it was inconsistent with it. It does, however, suggest that he announced a considerably simpler one."[130]

---

124. W. H. McLeod, *Sikhs of the Khalsa: A History of the Khalsa Rahit* (New Delhi: Oxford University Press, 2003), 3. For Harjot Oberoi, this literature "helped distinguish Khalsa Sikhs from the rest of Punjabi society" (*Construction*, 67).

125. McLeod, *Sikhs of the Khalsa*, 14.

126. See discussion of the Singh Sabha movement in chapters 4 and 6.

127. For details on the range of texts related to *rahit*, see McLeod, *Sikhs of the Khalsa*. See also: W. H. McLeod "The Problem of the Panjabi Rahit-namas," in *Exploring Sikhism: Aspects of Sikh Identity, Culture and Thought*, 103–25 (New Delhi: Oxford University Press, 2000).

128. The 1718 dating of the *Tankhāhnāmā,* the purportedly earliest text known, as a copy, as Purnima Dhavan notes, suggests a tradition contemporary to the Tenth Guru; see below.

129. McLeod's work has been foundational but problematic; new work is required on early manuscripts. The forthcoming doctoral work of Peder Gedda promises to shed significant light on early *rahit* traditions.

130. McLeod, *Sikhs of the Khalsa*, 48.

McLeod has offered readings of earlier Sikh works—such as the Guru Granth Sahib—as "proto-Rahit" in an effort to create continuity for the *rahit* through Sikh tradition. In doing so, he argues that the lack of one central definitive textual version of the *rahit* in the early period need not be taken to mean that the *rahit* of today is unrelated to earlier formulations and, indeed, earlier senses of Sikh behavior and identity: "The fact that the Rahit testifies to an ongoing evolution quite rightly implies continuity, a continuity which can easily be traced throughout the entire history of the Khalsa."[131] McLeod argues that "it can thus be assumed that an early version of the Rahit would have been enunciated during the lifetime of the Guru."[132] At the same time, he avers that "only a portion of the Rahit dates from the time of Guru Gobind Singh" and that it "evolved according to the conditions of the time, producing significantly different patterns as the circumstances of the Sikh Panth changed."[133] G. S. Mann has also argued for another kind of "proto-*rahit*" from earlier than the time of Guru Gobind Singh, making connections between the *rahit* and a set of prescriptions that appeared within manuscripts by 1600; he also argues for generally earlier dating to the *rahit* texts that do exist, and that they might have been composed prior to the generally accepted date for the formation of the Khalsa, with which they are associated.[134]

An exemplary text related from the early period is Sainapati's *Gur Sobhā*, generally accepted to be from 1711 but more plausibly dated to 1708 or soon after, given that reference to post-1708 events is absent.[135] It provides an account of the Guru's life but also describes elements that would later become consistent within *rahit* traditions.[136] Like all early texts, however, it does not mention the Five Ks as such.[137] Maintenance of uncut hair is specifically mentioned, as is initiation and the

---

131. Chaupa Singh, *Chaupa Singh Rahit Nāmā*, 9.

132. Chaupa Singh, *Chaupa Singh Rahit Nāmā*, 14.

133. McLeod, *Sikhs of the Khalsa*, 6.

134. Mann, "Sources for the Study," 249ff. Like Mann, Fenech also notes the use of the term Khalsa before 1699 (Fenech, *Darbar of the Sikh Gurus*, 88).

135. See footnote 55 in chapter 3.

136. See Ganda Singh, "Importance of Hair and Turban," in *Sikh Forms and Symbols*, ed. Mohinder Singh (New Delhi: Manohar, 2000), 39–44 and Murphy "History in the Sikh Past."

137. See Ganda Singh, "Importance." Interestingly, in the same volume Trilochan Singh claims that the 5Ks are mentioned in the Sarabloh Granth while J. S. Neki concedes that only three of the five are mentioned (see Mohinder Singh, ed., *Sikh Forms and Symbols*, 45 and 85; see also McLeod, *Sikhs of the Khalsa*, 207).

title "Singh." Arms figure prominently in the account, and the Khalsa is seen as the inheritor of the Guru's authority.[138] Early examples of the *rahit* include the *Tankhāhnāmā*, attributed probably spuriously to Nand Lal Goya, that is dated from 1718–19 but represents a copy of an earlier manuscript; another version called *Sākhī Rahit Kī*, also attributed to a Nand Lal, from approximately the 1730s; and the *Chaupa Singh Rahitnāmā* with its Nand Lal component, described in greater detail in the next chapter, from the middle of the century.[139] These versions of the *rahit* feature considerable variation, but McLeod notes several features that are consistent among the existing early versions of the *rahit* that do exist: a sense of deepening problems and ultimate triumph of the community; a set of behavioral injunctions meant to distinguish the Sikhs from other religious communities, with a clear sense that the Sikh community saw itself in conflict with Muslims; and, within several versions, the declaration of a Vaishnava savior in relation to the triumph of the community.[140] Significantly, for the purposes of this discussion, they do not define the Five Ks as a clear set, although features of what a Singh should wear are indicated and prominence is given to the five weapons.[141] Indeed, as Pashaura Singh has rightly noted, the number five has broad significance in South Asian traditions in general, and in Sikh tradition in specific; early on, however, the five was indicated for weapons.[142] The first explicit listing of the Five Ks as we know them today is given in 1881, in Gian Singh's *Tavārīkh Gurū Khālsā*.[143] Thus, "prior to the establishment of the Singh Sabha there is no reference to the Five Ks nor of

138. See Murphy, "History in the Sikh Past," and McLeod, *Sikhs of the Khalsa*, 60–61.

139. McLeod, *Sikhs of the Khalsa*, 68–70 on *Tankhāhnāmā*; 70 on Chaupa Singh's *Rahitnāmā* and *Sakhi Rahit Ki*. Also on the *Tankhāhnāmā* (apparently also called the *Nasīhatnāmā*), see Jeevan Deol, "Eighteenth-Century Khalsa Identity: Discourse, Praxis, and Narrative," in *Sikh Religion, Culture, and Ethnicity*, ed. Christopher Shackle, Gurharpal Singh, and Arvind-pal Singh Mandair (Surrey: Curzon Press, 2001); Fenech *Darbar of the Sikh Gurus*, 264 fn. 140, 291, fn. 40; Dhavan *When Sparrows Became Hawks*, 66. Strangely, Deol relies upon a published version of the text, which features unclear provenance, "supplemented" by the manuscript version of the text in Guru Nanak Dev University library (mss. 770; he also mentions but does not elaborate on mss. 29). See p. 45, fn. 27.

140. McLeod, "Problem of the Panjabi Rahit-namas," 115–16.

141. See the explication of the sources in McLeod, *Sikhs of the Khalsa*, 204–13. Pashaura Singh argues for the "presence" of the five Ks in the eighteenth century, although "they were not defined as such" (see "Formulation," 162). He argues here also that the Singh Sabha may have promoted the five religious symbols instead of five weapons in response to the banning of weapons by the British in colonial Punjab.

142. Pashaura Singh "Formulation." 156ff.

143. McLeod, *Sikhs of the Khalsa*, 208.

their inclusion in the Rahit,"[144] and their formation as a set was not clear until the nineteenth century.

The life of the objects of the Khalsa or Five Ks has thus been dynamic, and this is no less the case in the present than in the past. They have been in recent years at the center of battles by Sikhs for the right to express their religious identity in multiple contexts. An awareness of such contexts must inform our understanding of the symbol and the object in Sikh history and in contemporary representations; the present of this history inevitably shapes our representation of the past. As Simeran Man Singh Gell notes, the keeping of the *kes* or hair for many boys in Britain is a source of "enduring taunts" and "memorable playground scuffles."[145] Gell argues that for such boys and for most others in Britain, Sikhism is reduced on some levels to a "look."[146] But she also shows how it is much more than that, since adoption of the external markers of being Sikh is commonly seen as something one endures when young, eschews when making a career for oneself, and adopts with confidence again later in life when security is achieved.

Nikky-Guninder Kaur Singh has rightly noted that the Ks are both sign and symbol, identifying the wearer and also moving the wearer to "participate in a deeper universal reality."[147] They are, as she has observed, a "way of cultivating the self," "concerned with forming an ethical citizen situated within an active social, political, and religious world."[148] The practice of the "Sikh look" is complicated by geography, and by social location and stage in life, and the wearing of the Five Ks is both determined by, and determines, the forms of self-formation available within them. Any discussion of the Five Ks must account for the varying subject positions thus enabled by the self-formation that the Ks contribute to and represent. As Valerie Stoker has noted, legal conflicts over the status of the *kirpān* or dagger in Québec, Canada, allowed Sikhs in the province and in the country overall to articulate their own interpretation of the *kirpān* within the frames set

---

144. McLeod, *Sikhs of the Khalsa*, 212.

145. Simeran Man Singh Gell, "The Origins of the Sikh 'Look': From Guru Gobind to Dalip Singh," *History & Anthropology* 10, 1 (1996): 37–84, see 38. This discussion of the torment suffered by boys for keeping long hair addresses to an extent Nikky-Guninder Kaur Singh's consternation that long hair is seen as fundamentally male in its association with the formation of the Khalsa, instead of being associated with women as well. As this passage suggests, it is the anomaly that long hair constitutes in male contexts that makes long hair as a Khalsa emblem so marked for males. See discussion below.

146. Gell, "Sikh Look," 38.

147. Nikky-Guninder Kaur Singh, *The Birth of the Khalsa: A Feminist Re-Memory of Sikh Identity* (Albany: State University of New York Press, 2005), 98.

148. Nikky-Guninder Kaur Singh, *Birth of the Khalsa*, 98.

by progressive Québec Francophone interests and general Canadian discourses regarding inclusivity and tolerance.[149] Such representations are not created ex nihilo and thus are not "new," but do reflect the particularities of specific state and community formations in distinctive national contexts.[150] The meaning of these markers therefore changes: alongside their life as symbols of the Khalsa, they also are made meaningful within multicultural politics, debates over the right to religious expression, and within the changing personal circumstances of those who hold them.[151]

It is the symbolic meaning of these objects of the Khalsa that is central to their life today, among interpreters both within and outside of the Sikh community.[152] Most academic discussions of the symbolic nature of the Five Ks draw heavily upon the work of J. P. S. Uberoi, who saw them as a set of structural oppositions that define power (such as the power of *kes* or uncut hair) and that which controls it (in the case of *kes*, the *kaṅghā* or comb).[153] Gell extends this interpretation to see the structural oppositions Uberoi outlines as rendering the Sikh both recognizable and unrecognizable: "the 'look' gives individuality to every Sikh only insofar as he personifies a community … [but] the idiosyncratic form of individual bodies is negated by assuming an image of striking uniformity."[154] The image here functions in the formation of the Sikh

---

149. Valerie Stoker, "Zero Tolerance? Sikh Swords, School Safety, and Secularism in Québec," *Journal of the American Academy of Religion* 75, 4 (December 2007): 814–39.

150. Sarah V. Wayland, "Religious Expression in Public Schools: *Kirpans* in Canada, *Hijab* in France," *Ethnic & Racial Studies* 20, 3 (July 1997): 544–60; for a discussion of how national context has shaped the articulation of difference in more general terms, see Verne Dusenbery, "The Poetics and Politics of Recognition: Diasporan Sikhs in Pluralist Polities," *American Ethnologist* 24, 4 (November 1997): 738–62.

151. Vinay Lal, "Sikh Kirpans in California Schools: The Social Construction of Symbols, the Cultural Politics of Identity, and the Limits of Multiculturalism," *Amerasia Journal* 22, 1 (1996): 57–90.

152. See Nikky-Guninder Kaur Singh, *Birth of the Khalsa* for a general account of the dominant interpretations of each K.

153. J. P. S. Uberoi, "The Five Symbols of Sikhism," in *Perspectives on Guru Nanak*, ed. Harbans Singh (Patiala: Punjabi University, 1975), 502–13. The long hair or *kes* represents the spiritual power of the renunciate, well known throughout Indian religious traditions, but unlike that of the *sādhū* or Hindu holy man, the Sikh religious person's hair is well kept—and controlled—by the *kaṅghā*, or comb, another of the Five K's. The *kirpān* (sword or dagger) represents the military might of the Sikh soldier, and the *karā* or steel bracelet the containment of that power. The *kaccha* or undergarment Uberoi sees in opposition to the male sexual marker—the male sexual marker as a source of sexual energy and action, and the *kaccha* as containing this.

154. Gell, "Sikh Look," 60. Gell's further discussion of the Sikh "look" as a negation of Asianness in the British context is of real interest, but is not relevant here (64).

subject in negation, representing a community that is set apart. For others, the materiality of the body underlies engagement with the markers of the Khalsa.[155] It is from this overall embrace of the materiality of the body in dynamic relation to the spirit, that the embrace of the markers of the Khalsa devolves. In Kaur Singh's estimation, this radical acceptance of the body, of the human in all its forms, is fundamentally disruptive of gendered hierarchies, which view sexual difference as absolute and determinist. In Kaur Singh's "re-memory" of the Khalsa's founding and the symbolism of the Five Ks, Guru Gobind Singh "intended them to have revolutionary consequences for the wearer" in countering gender hierarchy; her reading of the symbolic value of the Five Ks thus emphasizes the articulation of "synchronicity," not opposition, for example, in the case of the *kes* and *kaṅghā*.[156] Thus she contends that "we need to remind ourselves again and again that the five K's are symbols of sexual equality, and continually struggle to overturn their construction as symbols of phallogocentric subjectivity and spirituality."[157]

The Five Ks therefore are symbolically charged and subject to wide interpretation. Most recent engagements with the symbolic nature of the Five Ks, however, do not see themselves as explicating their symbology in the present or near-present, but instead as addressing their symbolic meaning as a set at their traditionally understood time of founding, with the formation of the Khalsa.[158] Yet such interpretations do not address the textual history of their prescription, which does not allow them to be seen as a set so easily, in historical terms. This disjuncture invites another level of interpretation of these objects that does not require them to function fully as a set, in line with the concerns of this book overall and the history of materiality that it describes. To do so, we can begin with the simple observation that these objects serve both an individual purpose and have a corporate life, "as aids," in the words of Teja Singh "to the preservation of the corporate life of the community."[159] If we consider the Five Ks outside of the symbolic mode most interpreters focus on (and which relies upon a historically unsupported sense of these as a set), and place them instead

155. Trilochan Singh, "Turban and Sword of the Sikhs," in *Sikh Forms and Symbols*, ed. Mohinder Singh, 45–55 New Delhi: Manohar, 2000, 45.

156. Nikky-Guninder Kaur Singh, *Birth of the Khalsa*, 103 for first quotation, 115 for discussion of "synchronicity."

157. Nikky-Guninder Kaur Singh, *Birth of the Khalsa*, 134.

158. Most of those writing about the Khalsa markers in Mohinder Singh, ed., *Sikh Forms and Symbols* emphasize this nature of the objects.

159. Teja Singh, "Sikh Symbols," 21.

within a larger history of materiality in the Sikh community, it is possible to understand them in a new light. We can see them, in both historical and contemporary
terms, as generalized objects of memory, objects that animate a memorial relation to
the Guru, and in their narration produce the history of this community in intimate,
personal relation to the Guru. If so, they may not just signify "through historical vi-
cissitudes, the distinctive identity and collective aspirations of the Sikh people," as
Neki argues, but also, as he alludes, act as "keepsakes of the tenth Guru who sacrificed all that was his for the Khalsa."[160] Such generalized bodily practices and clothing
act in the formation and experience of memory as a kind of performance, as described
by Paul Connerton.[161]

By reading these insignia as the generalization of the imaginary that informs
the production of the historical object and site, we can understand the Five Ks in
dynamic interchange with other forms of memory production. This does not in
any way deny their symbolic power, and the multivalency (and the evolving symbolic nature) of this power. The materiality of the Five Ks and their role as instances of memory production only expand their place in the formation of the Sikh
panth as a community of memory. These objects act as a generalized *khil'at*, or gift
of the Guru to every member of the community—clothing, jewelry, weapon, personal object—to constitute relationships of the community with the Guru, and
among community members. This is in essence what the Khalsa is about. The addition of uncut hair makes entirely bodily this remembrance of the Guru—assuredly
with the added valences regarding power and reverence for the whole body that
Uberoi's and others' interpretations highlight. We can see these as an extension of
the memory-making and substantiation discussed thus far, the transformation of
the body into a memorial process—a natural, biological extension of *khil'at*—and
an essential part of the narration of the community and its formation through the
rahit and other literatures of the period into history, a history of a community with
reference to the Guru.

I have engaged at length with the Five Ks because they offer an aspect of Sikh
materiality that is ubiquitous today but is often perceived as anomalous and singular,
outside of more standard characterizations of the core aspects of Sikh tradition—an
emphasis on interiority, corporate worship, openness to all—and are usually seen
solely in symbolic terms. The idea of the Khalsa markers as mnemonic technology in

---

160. J. S. Neki, "The Five Sikh Symbols," in *Sikh Forms and Symbols,* ed. Mohinder Singh,
85–88 (New Delhi: Manohar, 2000), 88.

161. Paul Connerton, *How Societies Remember* (Cambridge: Cambridge University Press,
1989).

relation to the construction of the history of the community can thus be considered a crucial neglected aspect of the meanings of these material characteristics of being Sikh. The nature of the 5 Ks as objects of memory is central to the constitution of the community through the narration of its past, and its experience of the past *as Sikh*, as the next chapter demonstrates.

Conclusion

Texts as physical manifestations of the Word of the Guru; objects used or gifted by the Guru; sites associated with the Guru in a Sikh historical landscape; the markers of the Khalsa, available for all members of the community—these represent different modalities of the material representation of the Sikh community in relation to the past, each contributing to the construction and experience of a Sikh historical imaginary. Multiple modes can be present in a single instance: objects of exchange articulate and substantiate authority; they also create a relationship with the Gurus who have possessed them. They act, therefore, along the lines Trainor has articulated for Buddhist relics, as "technologies of remembrance" or "objects of memory." The histories that enliven these objects provide a frame for them, within which they are made meaningful.

Gregory Schopen suggested decades ago that it is necessary to construct an archeology of religion, focusing on materiality in relation to, and not to the exclusion of, texts.[162] An archeology of Sikhism is indeed necessary, in order to make present a broad range of practices and features that have not fit into conventional solely text-centered representations of the tradition.[163] This archeology, once performed, however, leads us in directions different from those found in Schopen's work, and need not be prurient, as Robert Sharf has argued much interest in object culture and relics is.[164] Instead of constituting the continued presence of the Guru in the world within a culture of embodiment, Sikh objects participate in the construction of a narrative of the past presence of the Guru in the world and of both past and *continuing* relationships with the Guru in the form of the community, with reference to the ongoing experience of the Guru-text. In this sense the central concern of textual historical representation is a

---

162. Schopen, *Bones*, 114–47. Such a concern for materiality in religion informed the founding of the journal *Material Religion* in 2005; see the editorial statement, *Material Religion* 1, 1 (March 2005): 4–8.

163. As noted earlier, the intention of this work is to *augment* the text-centered narrative, not replace it.

164. Sharf, "On the Allure of Buddhist Relics," 80.

parallel one. The construction of the community in relation to the memory of the Guru, and the constitution of that community as a continuing presence in the world through the production of its history, is accomplished through object and literary text alike. It has been central to this tradition since the early eighteenth century, at the end of the period of human Guruship.

The materiality of Sikh subject formation is clearly seen in the case of the markers of the Khalsa, which I have connected here to broader material practices. It should come as no surprise that it is in the time of the Singh Sabha movement, when multiple institutions and individuals in Punjab are clarifying the definition of being Sikh, that the Five Ks take shape as a comprehensive set of markers of the Khalsa. This is also a period within which Sikh memorial practices take a more formal and comprehensive form in relation to the writing of Sikh history. I have suggested that there is a life of the image and the object within Sikh tradition that is not a series of anomalies, nor simply equivalent to Hindu practices. Instead, Sikh materiality exists as part of a larger approach to the memorial, as the material representation of the relationships and authority that constitute the community and its living past. The Five Ks can be seen as the generalized marker of the Guru producing the community in memory of the Guru and on the path or *panth* (the term used for the community) the Guru explicated. In exploring the nature of representation within object and site, the form of material representation in the Sikh case must be considered in relation to nonreligious forms of materialization, as well, and cannot be relegated to "the religious" in simplistic terms. The parallels between these practices and the multivalent secular and religious practices of *khil'at* demonstrate this.

We also must remember the particularity of the histories we explore. The politics of the historicality of place has been particularly toxic in the last three decades in India with reference to the alleged birthplace of the Hindu deity Ram in Ayodhya. The Babri Masjid was destroyed by Hindu *kārsevak*s in 1992 because it was said to have been built on the temple that commemorated the birthplace of Ram. The site has remained a source of contest, a vivid expression of the uneasy position of Muslims (and any religious minority) today in the state of India.[165] It would be wrong to assume simple equivalence between this case and the Sikh interest in the history of the tradition located in place; it would also be a mistake to read the long history of the marking of the Indian landscape with a sacred geography tied to the representation of the past as only a modern and communalized concern.[166] Each instance of a sense of historicity with reference to a particular

---

165. See brief discussion in chapter 5.

166. Eck, *India: A Sacred Geography*, 5–6.

location is a product of its own history and a particular politics. Not all replicate the politics visible in case of the Babri Masjid. At the same time, however, we must remain attentive to the exclusions and inclusions accomplished by such interests in the historicality of place. Such a particular history will be explored in the remainder of this book, where we see the specific ways the Sikh past is mapped onto territory, and how objects of the past constitute a different way of representing the Sikh past.

From here we will trace the representation of the past in Sikh contexts through the eighteenth century, towards the achievement of sovereignty by Maharaja Ranjit Singh at the end of the century, and the achievement of smaller sovereign polities under other Sikh rulers earlier in that period, until annexation by the East India Company in 1849. In the British period, we will see that the logic of representation of object and site ultimately breaks down, and the two come to embody very different relationships to the writing of Sikh history. Yet, the two are tied: as embodiments of Sikh memory, and a crucial part of the experience of the past by the community they produce, and the history that narrates that community in the world.

The Past in the Sikh Imagination

3

Writing the Community

LITERARY SOURCES FROM THE
EIGHTEENTH CENTURY

HISTORICAL OBJECTS ARE made meaningful in relation to the narratives
that they represent and substantiate, the literary historiography that animates the
past's more material form. The material of Sikh history, therefore, only makes
sense as part of a larger historiogaphical project that we can recuperate mainly
in its literary forms. In the two chapters of this section, we explore precolonial
and early colonial period literary representations of the past to reconstruct how
history has been imagined and represented in Sikh terms.[1] By understanding the
representation of the past in Sikh tradition in literary terms, we come to understand what is at stake in the representation of the past as object and as site, and
how they participate in a larger historical imaginary. My concern here is not the
relative historical value of the texts under examination—that is, the question of
whether or not these texts can function as accurate historical documents that
contribute to the reconstruction of the period and region they hail from or address.[2] This is how these texts have generally been read, and they are indeed important sources for a historical reconstruction of Punjab and the formation of
the Sikh community in the eighteenth and nineteenth centuries. My interest lies
instead in how the texts themselves understand and construct the past, through
memory and into history. We will see that textual representations and material
ones participate together in a shared articulation of the community of the Gurus
through the represented past.

---

1. Parts of this chapter draw upon Anne Murphy, "History in the Sikh Past."

2. As Ganda Singh (the editor of the published version I rely upon) points out in his introduction to Sainapati's text, there are places where Sainapati's text provides "historical
information," and places where it does not: see Sainapati, *Kavi Sainapati Racit Sri Gur
Sobhā*, ed. Ganda Singh (1967, reprint Patiala: Publications Bureau, Punjabi University,
1988), 7ff.

Forms of historical representation in South Asia have received significant attention in recent scholarly literature, refuting the conventional colonial formulation that the writing of history did not truly arise in intellectual traditions of the region until the introduction of European historiography during the colonial period, with some debate over whether or not the presence of Islamic intellectual traditions introduced a form of historiography.[3] Arguments regarding the role of history within South Asian traditions have taken a number of different but related forms in recent debate; most are as centrally concerned with the political location of history as with its form and content.[4] For example, within the work of Ranajit Guha, the quest for a South Asian historical imagination represents a call to action to recover a historiography outside of the state by looking at alternative genres and forms of literature for a real "world history," a "historicality" that is distinct from history-as-state.[5] V. Narayana Rao and his colleagues take an allied approach: to demonstrate that the "assertion ('History is a post-Renaissance Western genre') can only be sustained by willfully ignoring a vast body of materials available from South Asia."[6] They thus separate "history" from a distinct historiographical genre— arguing that history is "not a matter of strict adherence to formal characteristics and types"—and a particular set of modern political relations.[7] At the same time, they demonstrate a deep connection between historical representation and state-formation.

These inquiries into the category of "history" in South Asia represent an attempt to "provincialize," as Dipesh Chakrabarty has suggested is necessary,

---

3. For discussion, see Dirks, *The Hollow Crown*, 55; Romila Thapar, "Time as a Metaphor of History," 3ff. Such a formulation informs diverse work, from Marx to Dumont, as well as that of more recent theorists: see Richard King, *Orientalism and Religion: Post-colonial Theory, India and the Mystic East* (New York: Routledge, 1999) and Ashis Nandy, "History's Forgotten Doubles," *History and Theory* 34, 2 (1995): 44–66.

4. I draw out the connections among these efforts, rather than the distinctions. Velcheru Narayana Rao, David Schulman, and Sanjay Subrahmanyam, *Textures of Time: Writing History in South India, 1600–1800* (Delhi: Permanent Black, 2001), 12ff., for example, distinguish their efforts from Dirks' "ethnohistory," but the overall aims, if not the vocabulary used to describe them, are parallel.

5. Ranajit Guha, *History at the Limit of World-History* (New York: Columbia University Press, 2002), 5. Guha's efforts thus seek to stop "history" in South Asia, in Chakrabarty's words, from looking "like yet another episode in the universal and . . . the ultimately victorious . . . march of citizenship, of the nation-state, and of themes of human emancipation spelled out in the course of the European Enlightenment and after" (Dipesh Chakrabarty, *Provincializing Europe: Postcolonial Thought and Historical Difference*, [Princeton, NJ: Princeton University Press], 39).

6. Narayana Rao et al., *Textures of Time*, xi.

7. Ibid., 3.

European historiography within a wider field, and to challenge the idea that history is a single genre that reflects a finite set of modern political and social relations.[8] The role of history within the Sikh discursive context I explore here thus can take its place alongside the examples I have mentioned: another regionally and culturally specific case of a transition in the making of history in early modern South Asia.[9] Reconstructing such a historical vision is valuable in and of itself as a part of a more general effort, identified by Daud Ali, to construct "a history of conceptions of the past, or a history of *regimes of historicity*, in South Asia" that is not simply identical to European forms.[10] But in the Sikh case, it does more than this: reconstruction of a Sikh historical consciousness allows us to understand how the representation of the past has contributed to the construction of the Sikh community, in religious and other terms. It also allows us to understand the material representations that exist in relation to this larger ideology.

Literary Representations of the Sikh Past

The workings of the representation of the past in the Sikh case have been shaped and transformed at various junctures—by changing power dynamics in eighteenth-century Punjab, by the colonial presence, and most recently by the diasporic experience. This changing nature of the historical is, indeed, also not unique—such changeability is characteristic of all historiographical traditions, South Asian, European, and otherwise. Examination of the formation of Sikh historical representations—material and literary—in the eighteenth century reveals that in the Sikh case the narration of the past as history was a means for the constitution of the community around the memory of the Guru, and that this past was substantiated both materially and textually in the eighteenth and early nineteenth centuries, a period of turbulence and uncertainty in Punjab as

---

8. Chakrabarty, *Provincializing Europe*.

9. This time period, parallels that explored by Narayana Rao and his colleagues. (Narayana Rao et al., *Textures of Time*, 129; see also 264).

10. Daud Ali, ed., *Invoking the Past: The Uses of History in South Asia* (New Delhi: Oxford University Press, 1999), 4. This is allied with the historical anthropological approach recently outlined by Eric Hirsch and Charles Stewart, which seeks to pursue "ethnographies of historicity" to take account of a broader sense of historicality, rather than the narrow confines of history. See Eric Hirsch and Charles Stewart, "Ethnographies of Historicity: An Introduction," *History & Anthropology* 16, 3 (2005): 261–74. There are no easy coincidences or correspondences here between Indian and European forms of historical thinking; see: Sheldon Pollock, "Mimamsa and the Problem of History in Traditional India," *Journal of the American Oriental Society* 109 [1989]: 603–10.

successor claims to sovereignty rose while Mughal power waned. Later, in the nineteenth century, a colonial historical sense came into being that shaped forms of Sikh historical representation, particularly in Punjabi, in new ways.

The literary history of North India in general is the result of a complex interplay between western Asian and southern Asian intellectual legacies and literary traditions, and this is particularly so for Sikh intellectual production—located (for the most part) in Punjab, at a meeting point in northwestern India that has seen intensive interaction with cultures to the west.[11] Sources from the region that are relevant to Sikh literary and religious cultural production exist in three major languages: Punjabi and other modern Indo-Aryan languages (such as Braj, a vernacular literary language prominent across North India that was "newly ascendant" at the turn of the sixteenth century), utilized in the Guru Granth Sahib, Dasam Granth (attributed to the Tenth Guru), and the *janam-sākhīs*; Persian (the literature of history, commerce and court—in the Mughal court and beyond—as well as part of the Dasam Granth); and, later, English.[12] Indeed, many of the Gurus' compositions in both the Guru Granth Sahib and Dasam Granth are influenced by or in Braj, which Allison Busch has called "a highly versatile poetic idiom that appealed to many," from Vaishnava devotional poets to Mughal patrons, without whom "Braj literature would never have attained the status it came to enjoy."[13] Muzaffar Alam has shown that Persian traditions were well established in literary and administrative terms in the region by the eleventh century, when Lahore was known as "Little Ghazna," clearly linking Punjab with political centers to the west.[14] After Persian was formally designated as the language of administration in the time of the emperor Akbar, it came to dominate the courts of the Mughal administrators of the *sūbā* or province, just as it would in the later courts of the Sikh

---

11. Of particular interest on this interaction, besides works cited elsewhere, are Sen, *Invoking the past*, 231–57; Farina Mir, "Genre and Devotion in Punjabi Popular Narratives: Rethinking Cultural and Religious Syncretism," *Comparative Studies in Society and History* 48, 3 (2006): 727–58.

12. Busch, *Poetry of Kings*, 6. Urdu was particularly important in the colonial period, when it was the official language of the province, but was not the major language used for Sikh cultural production. Punjabi in the Shahmukhi or Perso-Arabic script, however, was very common for vernacular publishing in that period by Sikhs and others. See Farina Mir, *The Social Space of Language: Vernacular Culture in British Colonial Punjab* (Berkeley: University of California Press, 2010). There was also a wealth of oral literature in the precolonial period, reflecting the great linguistic diversity of the Punjabi linguistic region, to which we do not now have access (see Fenech, *Martyrdom in the Sikh Tradition*, 135ff. for relevant discussion).

13. Busch, *Poetry of Kings*, 7, 19.

14. Muzaffar Alam, "The Culture and Politics of Persian in Precolonial Hindustan," in *Literary Cultures in History: Reconstructions from South Asia*, ed. Sheldon Pollock (New Delhi: Oxford University Press, 2003), 133.

rulers of the post-Mughal Punjab.[15] Guru Gobind Singh, it must be recalled, also wrote in Persian—his famous appeal for justice to the Mughal emperor, the *Zafar Nāmā* (which is contained in the Dasam Granth) is a well-known example. Other referents for Sikh cultural production were located solidly within the Sanskrit and vernacular linguistic realm. Thus we see that Punjab exhibits the dynamic described by Narayana Rao and colleagues for vernaculars in relation to Persian in other parts of India, where we see "complementarity," "synergy," and "complex overlap," rather than competition.[16] As Louis Fenech has well noted, there was some discomfort with the use of Persian within Sikh discursive contexts; this does not mean, however, that Persian was not influential, nor that Persian compositions were not honored (such compositions were thus integrated into Sikh contexts in the Gurmukhi script, rather than in the Shahmukhi/Perso-Arabic script).[17] The same was indeed true of texts written in Braj; generally written in the Devanagari script, Braj literature in Sikh contexts was usually written in Gurmukhi, the script associated with the Sikh scripture.

The Dasam Granth exemplifies the linguistic dynamic of the period. This diverse collection is attributed to the Tenth Guru but probably represents the literary production of his court, or *darbār*.[18] The compilation featured great diversity in its early manuscript forms and reflects a wide range of religious and cultural influences, including Persian sections (reproduced in Gurmukhi) and parts drawing on Persianate courtly idioms, and at the same time showing strong affinities with puranic sources, as Jeevan Deol and Robin Rinehart, among others, have explored.[19] Sikh historical literature was therefore born within a

---

15. On Akbar's declaration of Persian as the Mughal language of administration, see Muzaffar Alam and Sanjay Subrahmanyam *Writing the Mughal World: Studies on Culture and Politics* (New York: Columbia University Press, 2012), 313, 427; see chapters 7 and 9 on the use of Persian by scribes of a range of social backgrounds.

16. Narayana Rao, et al., *Textures of Time*, 225–26.

17. Fenech, Darbar of the Sikh Gurus, 241–45.

18. Although it shared authority with the Guru Granth Sahib—particularly at sites associated with the Tenth Guru—the Dasam Granth did not occupy the same general authoritative status as the Guru Granth Sahib. See: Fenech, *Darbar of the Sikh Gurus*, 148ff.; Robin Rinehart, "Strategies for Interpreting the Dasam Granth," in *Sikhism and History*, ed. Pashaura Singh and N. Gerald Barrier, 135–50 (New Delhi: Oxford University Press, 2004); Robin Rinehart, *Debating the Dasam Granth* (New York: Oxford University Press and the American Academy of Religion, 2011).

19. Deol, "Eighteenth-Century Khalsa Identity"; Rinehart, *Debating the Dasam Granth*. Fenech also describes the connections between the Dasam Granth and puranic and other South Asian literary sources, but emphasizes the courtly aspects of the collection (Fenech, *Darbar of the Sikh Gurus*, 158ff.). On the different contents of eighteenth-century Dasam Granth manuscripts, see Deol, "Eighteenth-Century Khalsa Identity," 32 and Mann, "Sources for the Study" 255.

centuries-old Persianized intellectual and political milieu and refers to diverse literary forms—both courtly and religious—in both Braj and Persian. The courtly nature of Sikh literature took shape early in the tradition, according to Fenech, who highlights how the "grammar" of the Mughal court shaped Sikh "rituals, symbols, and ceremonies" overall, in all linguistic registers. This is not surprising; as Busch notes, "[c]ourtliness in India was in part an imitative behavior, which is to say that courts responded to what other courts were doing, particularly those that were higher in status."[20] Fenech also argues that "at the centre of the Sikh court was the one true spiritual king of the universe," rather than a temporal sovereign.[21] This court, therefore, was not necessarily a fully political one. Deol and Rinehart have argued that the Dasam Granth exhibits a "new Sikh conception of the role of the leader with both spiritual and worldly responsibilities," in the words of Rinehart, and that "the Khalsa notion of *dharam* [right conduct] valorizes ideas of rule and political sovereignty in a way that classical definitions and others contemporary to the Khalsa do not," constituting an "unusual if not unique" orientation in the period, according to Deol.[22] As will be discussed, such a formulation requires further qualification, in relation not only to the courtly literature of the period, as Rinehart and Fenech have pursued, but also with reference to other "religious" community formations and associated contexts for literary production in the period. The use of Braj is significant in this regard, as it relates to both Vaishnava devotional literatures and their institutional contexts, as well as to courtly ones—which were deeply tied.[23] There were complex reasons for language choices: in the case of Braj, Allison Busch highlights the possible reasons that authors in the Mughal court might choose Braj over Sanskrit, such as a desire for accessibility, to allow for the "admixture of Perso-Arabic vocabulary in a manner forbidden to the more sanctified, and

---

20. Busch, *Poetry of Kings*, 169.

21. Fenech, *Darbar of the Sikh Gurus*, 10 for first quotation, 23 for second. Although Fenech makes a clear distinction between the court as such and the state (page 24), his work presents arguments for the location of both spiritual and temporal power in the Guru's court, on which see pages 57–58, 60, 65–66, 104–5, 133, 149–50, 162–63, 286. Ultimately he notes that direct control by the Guru was located only in Anandpur (271 n. 180).

22. Rinehart, *Debating the Dasam Granth*, 10 (for quotation) and 160; Deol, "Eighteenth-Century Khalsa Identity," 40. Where appropriate, I opt for Punjabi spellings, so *dharam* for *dharm* or *dharma*.

23. Allison Busch, "The Anxiety of Innovation: The Practice of Literary Science in the Hindi/*Riti* Tradition," *Comparative Studies of South Asia, Africa, and the Middle East* 24, 2 (2004): 45–59, see 51. On the role of Rajput courts in Braj literary production, see Busch, *Poetry of Kings*, chapter 5, and for an excellent analysis of the intersection of *bhakti* (devotional) and *riti* (classical Hindi courtly) poetry, see Heidi R. M. Pauwels, "Romancing Radha: Nagaridas' Royal Appropriations of Bhakti Themes," *South Asia Research* 25, 1 (2005): 55–78.

linguistically sanctimonious, realm of Sanskrit," or possibly because of the particular sensibilities evoked by Braj that might afford "access to emotive and in some cases feminine registers of expression not as readily available in Persian."[24] As we will see, our conceptualization of the *darbār* or "court" is impoverished if we only see it as statist: a more accurate translation for *darbār* might be "gathering" or "audience," a translation that recognizes it as a form of social and cultural organization that existed outside the strictly political sense of the "court."[25] Regardless, the courtly orientations gestured toward earlier in Sikh tradition (with the complex valences noted) were certainly further enhanced—and took on more temporal features, in a more conventional "courtly" fashion—with the acquisition of political power by leaders of Sikh *misal*s or kinship-based militias that banded together to organize resistance, engage in raids in the countryside, and consolidate local control in the early to mid eighteenth century.[26]

The writing of histories in Persian, Punjabi, and Braj (and often a combination of the latter two, or a Punjabi-ized version of Persian) came to occupy an important place in Sikh centers of power in the late eighteenth century.[27] The establishment of an imperial presence under Ranjit Singh provided a source of patronage for historical production, as did the courts of Sikh rulers of smaller states in the eastern Punjab who resisted absorption into Ranjit Singh's kingdom. As Purnima Dhavan has shown, "Persian historical production in these courts" was part of a "diplomatic counter-offensive to maintain their autonomy from the encroachments of Ranjit Singh and the East India Company."[28] The acquisition of sovereignty inflected the historical sense of the time, as well as courtly collecting and other memorial practices. Historical representations in Punjab were thus produced in relation to various

---

24. Allison Busch, "Hidden in Plain View: Brajbhasha Poets at the Mughal Court," *Modern Asian Studies* 44, 2 (2010): 267–309; see 290 for first quotation, 303 for second. On accessibility, see Busch, *Poetry of Kings*, 146–47; on the greater versatility of Braj, see 90, 94, 183. See Fenech, *Darbar of the Sikh Gurus*, 238ff. on issues regarding language and script choice with reference primarily to the Nanda Lal material and Persian compositions in the Dasam Granth that are commonly rendered in Sikh contexts in the Gurmukhi script.

25. Busch, "Hidden in Plain View," 294.

26. On this period, see Dhavan, *When Sparrows Became Hawks*; Bhagat Singh, *A History of the Sikh Misals* (Patiala: Publication Bureau, Punjabi University, 1993); and Grewal and Habib, *Sikh History from Persian Sources*.

27. See Dhavan, *When Sparrows Became Hawks* and Purnima Dhavan, "Redemptive Pasts and Imperiled Futures: The Writing of a Sikh History," in *Time, History and the Religious Imaginary in South Asia*, ed. Anne Murphy, 40–54. (New York: Routledge, 2011). Much of the Persian of the records associated with the court of Ranjit Singh examined in chapter 5, for example, feature Persian that exhibits the influence Punjabi verb structures and vocabulary.

28. Dhavan, "Redemptive Pasts" (2011) 40.

literary and linguistic (as well as religious) influences in the eighteenth and early nineteenth centuries, and a complex genealogy is represented by the place of history within Sikh sources, too. Just as the historical sense in South India investigated by Narayana Rao and his colleagues can be said to relate to the introduction of Islamic forms of historical understanding without simplistically attributing all to "Islamic influence"—"one cannot see the 'rise of historiography' in South India as the result of the transplantation of a model derived from the Arabic and Persian histories onto Indian soil"—the same must be said of Sikh forms of historical consciousness.[29] Indeed, Islamic, Hindu, and Sikh traditions in Punjab were all born of a shared milieu, in which history was inscribed in complex ways: as *tārīkh*, or history in the Persianate tradition, and *sākhī*, the biographical sense associated with hagiographical traditions, literally meaning "witnessing."[30]

The texts here examined are representative of a Sikh (rather than Punjabi, or South Asian) perspective on the past in just this sense: they are written about the Sikh Gurus and members of the community of followers of the Gurus.[31] This Sikh historical sensibility is organized around the soteriological teachings of the Gurus and the formation of the community as a central institution of authority in relation to the Guru. The fact that these texts are written in Punjabi and Braj does not in itself mark them as particularly Sikh, since, as has been mentioned, Persian also played important and enduring roles in the formation of the literary imagination of Punjab and of the Sikhs; Braj was a literary language across the north, and was in religious terms indeed most strongly associated with Vaishnavism; and Punjabi was also a language of religious expression in Islamic and Hindu traditions—the Sufi saint Baba Farid, mentioned earlier, is a central figure in the early formation of Punjabi literature.[32] One sees a particularly strong orientation in these sources

---

29. Narayana Rao, et al., *Textures of Time*, 250.

30. History could also be conceived of as "*qissā*"; see Bhai Mihar Singh, *Panjāb dā Raushan Kisā* (Manuscript, dated 1859, IOL Oriental Manuscript Panjabi B41), for an example of such a formulation. Mir has also noted the inclusion of popular *qisse* in a similarly dated Persian historical work, *Cār Bāgh-i-Panjāb* (Mir "Genre and Devotion in Punjabi Popular Narratives," 727–28). See discussion in Purnima Dhavan, "Reading the Texture of History and Memory in Early-Nineteenth-Century Punjab," *Comparative Studies of South Asia, Africa, and the Middle East* 29, 3 (2009): 515–27, see particularly 519–20 and Dhavan, *When Sparrows Became Hawks*, 37, on *sākhī* and *caritrā*. See also Narayana Rao et. al *Textures of Time*, chapter five and particularly 209 ff. on Islamic and Persianate forms of historical representation, and 250 on the need to appreciate developments in Indo-Persian historical representation in India.

31. These texts therefore do not represent the full range of cultural expressions by Sikhs; neither should we assume that those writing about the Sikhs were always Sikh. See Dhavan, "Redemptive Pasts" (2011) and Dhavan, *When Sparrows Became Hawks*.

32. On the dangers of the term "Braj" for its Hinducentric connotations, given the strong Vaishnava associations of the region of Braj, see Busch, *Poetry of Kings*, 9.

towards the reconstruction of the Guru in history, and thus they provide a vision of a Sikh historical imagination among authors and patrons in the period, in intertextual relation to other works.[33] The texts function, I will show, to construct the Sikh community in relation to the memory of the Gurus through historiographical processes that are tied, textual and material/geographic.

I focus in this and the following chapter on texts from the eighteenth and nineteenth centuries that exemplify a developing Sikh historical imaginary: Sainapati's *Gur Sobhā* from the beginning of the eighteenth century, with reference to later eighteenth-century works; Chaupa Singh's *Rahitnāmā* from the middle of the eighteenth century; Bhai Santokh Singh's *Srī Gur Pratāp Sūraj Granth* from 1843, with brief reference to a short text of *sākhīs* from about the 1820s (and reference to a text from the same period by Rattan Singh Bhangu); and the first novel by Bhai Vir Singh, written in 1898.[34] With the exception of Chaupa Singh's *rahit* text, these texts comprise a genre of literature composed from the beginning of the eighteenth century to the twentieth, called *gurbilās*: "the play of the Guru."[35] Chaupa Singh's text represents a primary example of the genre of literature known as *rahitnāme* discussed in the last chapter, which features injunctions regarding behavior, as well as some possibly later narrative components which are reminiscent of the *gurbilās* genre.[36] This range of texts will allow us entry into the production of the Sikh past prior to and then at the beginning of the British colonial intervention, when the terms of the writing of history changed (again). These

---

33. For a compelling discussion of the relationship between Punjabi and Persian sources, see Dhavan, "Redemptive Pasts" (2011).

34. Sainapati, *Gur Sobhā*. Santokh Singh, *Srī Gur Pratāp Sūraj Granth*, ed. Vir Singh (1843; repr., Amritsar: Khalsa Samachar for Bhai Vir Singh Sahitya Sadan, 1961–65). Referred to hereafter as the *Sūraj Granth*; *Sāhib Srī Gurū Teg Bahādar Jī ate Sāhib Srī Gurū Gobind Singh Jī de Malwā Desh Ratan dī Sākhī Pothī*, 2nd ed. (Amritsar: Khalsa Samachar, 1968). Chaupa Singh, *The Chaupa Singh Rahit Nāmā*, trans., ed., and intro. by W. H. McLeod (Dunedin, New Zealand: University of Otago Press, 1987); Bhai Vir Singh, *Sundarī* (New Delhi: Bhai Vir Singh Sahit Sadan, 2003).

35. On the genre and the major texts associated with it, see Fenech, *Martyrdom*, 123ff.; W. H. McLeod, "The Hagiography of the Sikhs," in *According to Tradition: Hagiographical Writing in India*, ed. Winand M. Callewaert and Rupert Snell (Wiesbaden: Harrassowitz Verlag, 1994), 33ff.; W. H. McLeod, ed., *Textual Sources for the Study of Sikhism* (Chicago: University of Chicago Press, 1984), 11ff.; and W. H. McLeod, *Who is a Sikh? The Problem of Sikh Identity* (Oxford: Clarendon Press, 1989), 51. See also see Dhavan, *When Sparrows Became Hawks*, chapter 7 in particular; Murphy, "History in the Sikh Past"; and Murphy, "The *Gurbilas* Literature and the Idea of 'Religion,'" in *The Punjab Reader*, ed. Anshu Malhotra and Farina Mir, 93–115 (New York and New Delhi: Oxford University Press, 2012).

36. See the discussion in W. H. McLeod, introduction to Chaupa Singh, *Rahit Nāmā*, 26–28. *Gurbilās* texts, at the same time, feature aspects of the *rahit*; see, for example, Kuir Singh, *Gurbilās Pātshāhī Das*, 111.

examples of the historiographical literature of Punjab of the eighteenth and nineteenth centuries can only be understood, however, in relation to literary production in Persian, and other new Indo Aryan languages, as well as (later) English. Although it is not comprehensive in its coverage, the material examined here allows entry into the nature of historical representations in Punjabi-language Sikh literature and bridges the gap from the precolonial to the colonial to provide a sense of both the continuities and ruptures that constitute the Sikh historical imagination through the eighteenth and nineteenth centuries.[37]

Sikh Political Ascendance in the Eighteenth Century

The production of literature in this period fundamentally reflects shifting political as well as religious circumstances. The eighteenth century brought great changes for the Sikh community. The community transitioned from a period of direct charismatic leadership, under the careful guidance of the Ten Gurus, to one with the sacred canon as the continuing Guru: Guru Gobind Singh is credited with the decision to discontinue the office of the human Guru and to locate authority from that time forward in the community (*panth*) and sacred canon (*granth*).[38] Even in the face of such changes, continuities were maintained, through the authority of the wife of the Guru; the leadership of the rebel Banda Bahadur and others; and of course core principles and practices of the *panth*: the continuation of the authority of the sacred word (enshrined in the book that is the Guru, the Guru Granth Sahib), the practices of the communal worship, and the establishment and embellishment of particular forms of Sikh identity—particularly those associated with the Khalsa— that were solidified over the first decades of the eighteenth century. Sikh memorial practices, both textual and material, contributed to the continuation and elaboration of the community in the period.

This was also a period of great change across Punjab and the subcontinent in political terms, although it was not necessarily the dramatic upheaval portrayed by earlier historians of the period.[39] With the end of the rule of the Mughal emperor Aurangzeb in 1707, centralized imperial Mughal power began to

---

37. Examination of this range and development calls attention to the ongoing sense of continuity believers perceive in being Sikh; diachronic examination is crucial in relation to the construction of "tradition," in order to understand the changes and continuities that constitute it.

38. The classic study of the life of the Tenth Guru is J. S. Grewal and S. S. Bal, *Guru Gobind Singh: A Biographical Study* (Chandigarh: Panjab Publication Bureau, 1987 [1967]).

39. See Alam, *Crisis of Empire* and Peter Marshall, "Introduction," in *The Eighteenth Century in Indian History: Evolution or Revolution?* ed. Peter Marshall, 1–49 (New Delhi: Oxford University Press, 2003).

fracture at the peripheries, and successor groups began to vie for power.[40] Many of the successor states that arose over the century however continued to pay allegiance to the Mughal center at Delhi, and/or continued many aspects of Mughal administration and culture, even when largely independent. The rise of Sikh states in Punjab in the later part of the eighteenth century, culminating in a large centralized state under Maharaja Ranjit Singh based at Lahore and strong smaller states in the eastern and southern part of Punjab (the so-called Phulkian states of Patiala, Kapurthala, and others, descended from a common ancestor Phul), reflected the Punjabi manifestation of this larger process.[41] Sikhs rose in the eighteenth century in the wake of declining Mughal power and in response to changing economic circumstances. Although some credit the rise of Sikh contestants for power solely to the influence of Sikh ideology, it is clear that circumstances of the time shaped this response, and also that Sikhs were not alone in this process, as Purnima Dhavan's recent work has shown.[42] Loyalties were not solely bounded by religious identity, and accommodation and collaboration characterized relations among Muslim, Hindu, and Sikh contestants for power throughout the period, depending on the balance of power in a particular region and the necessities of the moment, as well as a shared sense of martial honor that was shared among them.[43] The period also saw the rise of non-Sikh groups, many from backgrounds similar to the Jats (who dominated in Sikh mobilization), like the Bhattis, Gujjars, and Manj Rajputs, who had entered the *zamīndār* ranks during Mughal rule and sought independence with the waning of Mughal power, what Dhavan describes as a "more complicated struggle among multiple ethnic groups."[44]

Banda Bahadur, a follower of the Tenth Guru, is credited with leading the first rebellions across Punjab in the early eighteenth century. Although he was

---

40. The classic account of this is Muzaffar Alam, *The Crisis of Empire in Mughal North India: Awadh and the Punjab, 1707–1748* (New Delhi: Oxford University Press, 1986).

41. For a detailed study of the period, and a focus on the articulation of sovereignty among a range of Sikh leaders at the time, see Dhavan, *When Sparrows Became Hawks*, particularly chapter 5 on the Phulkian states; and Bhagat Singh, *History of the Sikh Misals*.

42. For Grewal's characterization of the important role of Sikh ideology, see J. S. Grewal, *The Sikhs of the Punjab* (Cambridge: Cambridge University Press, 1990), 82; and for Chetan Singh on the same, see Chetan Singh, *Region and Empire: Panjab in the Seventeenth Century* (New Delhi: Oxford University Press, 1991), 271ff. Dhavan argues that "historians working within categories of religious rebellion or banditry have attributed a cohesive political or religious ideological motivation to Khalsa Sikhs in the eighteenth century that the surviving historical record does not support" (Dhavan, *When Sparrows Became Hawks*, 141; see also 116 and elsewhere). On the period, see Alam, *Crisis of Empire*, 182–83 in particular, and also his concluding chapter.

43. Dhavan, *When Sparrows Became Hawks*, 141.

44. Dhavan, *When Sparrows Became Hawks*, 48.

not named the next Guru of the community, Bahadur did invoke the authority of the Guru in his campaigns.[45] His orthodoxy as a Sikh is open to question,[46] but nonetheless, by 1710, he had experienced such success that he struck coins in the name of Guru Nanak and Guru Gobind Singh and issued *hukamnāme* under his own seal (rather than the seal of the Guru, showing that he did not see himself in this office). Within a few years, there was dissent within the movement—some Sikhs distanced themselves from Banda and did not accept his authority, reflecting a commitment to what Dhavan calls "the joint sovereignty of the Khalsa as a corporate body and with the evolving notion of *gurū panth*."[47] Still, his military successes continued until 1715, when he and his followers were forced to surrender. Hundreds were executed, including Banda and other leaders. As Dhavan notes, Banda's movement had wide support, at least at first, but his rebellion did not take place in isolation and was accompanied by other rebellious activity, often organized on a kinship basis, as were the Sikhs.[48]

Other former parts of the Mughal Empire achieved independence or near independence—accepting the symbolic authority of the Mughal emperor but acting otherwise independent of it—in the first part of the eighteenth century. The Deccan was essentially independent under the Nizam ul-Mulk Asaf Jah, and the Marathas were recognized as rulers in the west in 1719. They defeated the Nizam nearly twenty years later, extending their control into the Deccan and limiting the Nizam's domain to Hyderabad. In the middle of the century, the weakening of central control in Delhi was exacerbated by the intrusions of Nadir Shah of Persia into Punjab and then into Delhi. Although Nadir Shah reinstated Muhammad Shah, the Mughal emperor who ruled until 1748, he did so at huge financial cost to the Mughal elite, and by formally taking control of all lands west of the Indus, as well as parts of the province of Lahore. The eastern provinces of the empire, too, were all but lost to the Mughal center, falling to Shuja ud-Daula and his successors. The governor of Awadh also exerted his independence of Mughal control in the same period. The Punjab saw political upheaval in this period; the *choṭā ghallūghārā* or "small carnage" took place in the 1740s, when Sikhs were hunted down to avenge the death of a Mughal functionary at Sikh hands.

---

45. In this historical account, I rely heavily here on Grewal, *Sikhs of the Punjab*, and Dhavan, *When Sparrows Became Hawks*. See also Bhagat Singh, *History of the Sikh Misals*.

46. Fenech, *Martyrdom*, 129ff.

47. Dhavan, *When Sparrows Became Hawks*, 56.

48. Dhavan, *When Sparrows Became Hawks*, on fluctuating support for Banda Bahadur, see 53; on kinship, see 55.

By 1757, the Mughal emperor had ceded the province of Lahore to Ahmad Shah Abdali, together with Multan, Kashmir, and the *sarkār* of Sirhind. The Marathas set their sights on Punjab as well; they were defeated by Abdali at Panipat in 1761. Punjab did not remain restful, however, in the hands of Abdali, and conflict with Sikh and other organized militias continued. It was during this period that the *vaḍḍā ghallūghārā* or "great carnage" took place, when thousands of Sikhs were attacked and killed near present-day Ludhiana. By 1765 a coin was struck in Lahore by Sikh *misal* leaders, establishing a sovereign presence that would culminate in the establishment of the kingdom of Lahore under Ranjit Singh of the Sukerchakia *misal*, through military conquest and alliance building with other *misal*s, in 1799.[49] The history of the Phulkian states exemplifies the dynamic of the century and reflects the ways in which new forms of sovereignty were articulated among competing powers. The capital of Patiala was founded by Sardar Alha Singh in 1752.[50] Alha Singh had fought against Ahmad Shah and saw defeat at Barnala; after receiving ransom from Alha Singh, Ahmad Shah granted him the villages around Patiala and bestowed the title of Raja upon him. Alha Singh later joined with other Sikh rebels in attacking Sirhind after Ahmad Shah's return to Afghanistan, and at its destruction brought most of its inhabitants to the growing city of Patiala. In 1812, the British intervened, and the status of the family continued with British support. According to the updated version of the well-known Griffin and Massy descriptions of Punjabi elites, *Chiefs and Families of Note in the Punjab*, after the death of Amar Singh, the grandson of Alha Singh, administration in the state lapsed and "it was necessary for the British Government to intervene authoritatively in the Patiala affairs."[51] In the eighteenth century, however, the rise of states like Patiala signaled a new force in Punjab that had not yet reckoned with growing East India Company power.

---

49. On what he calls the "Sikh interregnum" and the process by which local leaders came to establish the beginnings (and sometimes more) of sovereign control, see Andrew Major, *Return to Empire: Punjab Under the Sikhs and British in the Mid-Nineteenth Century* (New Delhi: Sterling Publishers, 1996), chapter 2. Coins were struck throughout the end of the eighteenth century; see Grewal and Bal, *Guru Gobind Singh*, 173 and n. 36.

50. Alha Singh, a Sidhu Jat Sikh, was the grandson of Phul (the common ancestor of the kings of Patiala, Jind, and Nabha) and son of Rama. According to Griffin and Massy, Sidhu, the progenitor of the family, was a patriarch of the Rajputs of Jaisalmer, and as they note, his "children are thus spread all over the Eastern Punjab; and their blood is the oldest and the bluest in the Province south and east of the Sutlej, save and excepting the chiefs of the Simla Hills." (Conran and Craik, *Chiefs and Families of Note*, 394.) Phul was descended from Baryam, who had been granted the office of revenue collector for the region to the northwest of Delhi by Emperor Babur in 1526. I draw heavily from Conran and Craik in this paragraph. See also Dhavan, *When Warriors Became Hawks*, chapter 5.

51. Conran and Craik, *Chiefs and Families of Note*, 395.

Sainapati's Gur Sobhā *and the* Gurbilās: *a Sikh Vision of the Past and Future*

The period under consideration, therefore, is one in which Sikhs (among others) increasingly sought sovereign rule. It is essential, however, that in considering the textual evidence of the period we do not see later developments—such as the achievement of sovereignty by Ranjit Singh at the end of the eighteenth century—as historically inevitable in earlier moments. Thus, the texts examined here are located at very particular and distinctive points on the road toward the achievement of sovereignty by Sikh leaders, and without a necessary relationship between Sikhness, per se, and state sovereignty. In questioning this equation, we can attempt to understand the multiple Sikh historical imaginaries at work in the eighteenth century that do not presuppose the Sikhs as a "nation" (the preoccupation of much recent discourse, as has been mentioned), nor even the achievement of sovereignty within the kingdoms of the later eighteenth century, and allow for alternative representations of collective representation and organization that are not necessarily statist. Here the notion of the *panth* or "community" takes shape as a Sikh form of collective organization that is not reducible to statist forms of sovereignty. Indeed, the achievement of sovereignty by Sikh leaders was always haunted by this other form of egalitarian, collective sovereignty that did not correspond to the statist sovereignty of Realpolitik.[52]

The first text in question—*Gur Sobhā*, or "Splendor of the Guru," by Sainapati—was produced in the early eighteenth century as the Sikh community transitioned from the period of human Guruship to the articulation of ultimate authority within the sacred canon (the Adi Granth or Guru Granth Sahib) and the community, the paired principles of *granth* (text) and *panth* (community) articulated by Guru Gobind Singh. The *Gur Sobhā* provides a narrative description in poetry of the life of the final living Guru and the formation of the Sikh community in this period. In examining this text, as well as others, I will explicate the multiple visions of the past utilized by the writer. This is not to say that texts like *Gur Sobhā* exhibit the first Sikh interest in the representation of the past. An interest in such representations (with an emphasis on the importance of evidence and witnessing) was evinced from the earliest stages of Sikh tradition: the *Bālā Janam Sākhī*, a popular version of the hagiography of Guru Nanak, opens with a search by Guru Angad for a Sikh who can "tell the story of Guru Nanak," and also tell specifically the date of the Guru's birth.[53] Such

---

52. Dhavan, *When Sparrows Became Hawks*, 97.

53. *Bhāī Bālevālī Janamsākhī* (Amritsar: Bhai Jawahar Singh Kripal Singh and Company, n.d.), 1.

concerns are more fully developed in the eighteenth century, in the forms examined here, but are a continuation rather than an entirely new set of commitments. Indeed, as Dhavan points out, Sainapati's *Gur Sobhā* was itself a *sākhī* in the eyes of its author.[54]

Sainapati's *Gur Sobhā* was written in the first decade of the eighteenth century.[55] The author opens his text by stating its purpose—"to describe the praise of the Guru"[56]—crediting the true Guru for the inspiration and ability to write the text: "Then into the mind of this sinner ... came the compassion of the Guru, and a way was found."[57] The author then defines the date of the creation of the text, the lineage of Sikh Gurus, and then the formation of the *panth*.[58] The past in this text is thereafter chronologically ordered and concerned with specific, narrated events—the Guru within history. However, this text is not only a form of "history" as a biography of the Guru, but also seeks to narrate the Sikh community itself as a historical process. It therefore exhibits a Sikh rationale for the particular kind of historicality, one which we will see is connected to the narration of the past in other forms.

Sainapati's text is generally considered to be a particularly important early example of a genre of literature composed from the beginning of the eighteenth

---

54. See Dhavan, *When Sparrows Became Hawks*, 40 fn. 56.

55. I refer here to Ganda Singh's edited version of *Gur Sobhā*. Purnima Dhavan's suggestion of 1708 for the text's completion is convincing; for an overview of the debate and her rationale, see: Purnima Dhavan, *When Sparrows Became Hawks*, 182 fn. 5 and 6. G. S. Mann argues for the date of 1701 for the initiation of the text (Mann, "Sources for the Study," 252). On the text in general, see Surjit Hans, *A Reconstruction of Sikh History from Sikh Literature* (Jalandhar: ABS Publications, 1988), 245ff. and J. S. Grewal, "Praising the Khalsa: Sainapat's Gursobha," in *The Khalsa: Sikh and non-Sikh Perspectives*, ed. J. S. Grewal (New Delhi: Manohar, 2004), 35–45. The text was first published in print in 1925 by Akali Kaur Singh Ji Nihang. It is composed of twenty chapters and features a range of poetic types.

56. Sainapati, *Gur Sobhā*, 63.

57. Sainapati, *Gur Sobhā*, 64.

58. Sainapati, *Gur Sobhā*, 63–65. Throughout the text, the location and duration of events is emphasized (69 and 74). The author places himself as narrator throughout, in relation to the Guru who inspires the text (as has been noted earlier) but also in relation to events (74). The typical invocation of the Guru at the beginning of a text, followed by a conventional list of the Gurus as accepted by orthodox Sikh tradition, clearly places the text within that tradition. Thus the text positions itself outside of the splinter groups that existed in the eighteenth century and can be seen as a way to stake claims about the orthodox lineage, and therefore the *panth* organized around it. See Grewal, *Sikhs of the Punjab*, 77. This presentation of the lineage of Gurus invites comparison with other traditions, such as Vaishnava representations of devotees and lineage. Such lineages have been discussed by Thapar, Dirks, Narayana Rao et al., and Jonathan Walters in Inden, Walters, and Ali, *Querying the Medieval*. *Gurpranālī*s, another form of lineage text, were written in the eighteenth century and later, reflecting the same kind of historical interest (Deol, "Eighteenth-Century Khalsa Identity," 27–28).

century on, called *gurbilās*: the "sport" or "play" of the Guru.[59] Generally these begin with writings attributed to the Tenth Guru, particularly his *Bacittar Nāṭak*. According to Surjit Hans, who has written extensively on these materials, the *Bacittar Nāṭak* (like all *gurbilās* literature) is singularly concerned with history: "this is a work of nascent history," he writes, "which under the stress of circumstances, is more faithful to the demands of the future than the quiet details of the present."[60] *Gur Sobhā* concentrates on the life of Guru Gobind Singh, although mention is made of his father, Guru Tegh Bahadur;[61] the chronologically driven narration ends with Guru Gobind Singh's death in 1708.[62] Rupert Snell has described the goal of hagiography—which this text might be seen as—to be "to locate the life-stories of its subjects in a sweep of time knowing no boundaries between the contemporary and the ahistorical."[63] Such a description does not hold in this case, however: the past here is chronologically and geographically ordered and located, and concerned with specific, chronologically narrated events—the Guru within history, and the community around the Guru within time and space. The transformations evident within this text stand at religious and political crossroads, reflecting the transition from living Guruship in the beginning of the eighteenth century and the political instability in Punjab as successor groups began to vie for power as Mughal power began to fracture. This process was only beginning at the time of the writing of this text, but the conflicts described reflect the place of the Sikh community in an unstable political field at an early stage of this process. The *gurbilās*, indeed, provides a location for the articulation of a broad range of interests in this dynamic context, as sites of both, in Dhavan's words, "contested history, memory, and loyalty," as well as, later, "an expression of shared historical memory."[64]

---

59. See W. H. McLeod, "Hagiography of the Sikhs," 33ff.; McLeod, ed., *Textual Sources*, 11ff. Texts in the genre are strongly intertextually related. *Bilās* is in this context often translated as "splendor," but the core meaning of *bilās* or *vilās* is as noted. The use of *bilās* in this way parallels the common usage of the term *līlā*, such as in Vaishnava traditions; for uses of the term *līlā* in this text, see Sainapati, *Gur Sobhā*, 69, 77. This usage should not be too strongly associated with Vaishnavism; such terms and concepts were used in a fluid manner within different contexts and should not be seen as particular to one.

60. Hans, *Reconstruction of Sikh History*, 233–34.

61. It follows the Tenth Guru's life through his residency at Anandpur, through numerous battles with kings of the Punjab Hills and with Mughal forces, to his exile from Anandpur and eventual meeting with the Mughal emperor Bahadur Shah. For events of the period, see Grewal, *Sikhs of the Punjab*, 72–79.

62. The Guru died at Nanded, in present-day Maharashtra.

63. Rupert Snell, "Introduction: Themes in Indian Hagiography," in Callewaert and Snell, eds., *According to Tradition*, 1.

64. Dhavan, *When Sparrows Became Hawks*, 153.

In broad structural terms, *Gur Sobhā* features the repeated interweaving of three key narrative modes, within an overarching chronologically driven narrative frame set up within the first chapter of the work. The first major recurring element is the description of the actions of the Guru and events related to his Guruship, which are essential to the maintenance of the overall narrative frame. The events include in particular the armed conflict that accompanied the formation of the Guru's community as a challenge to both smaller polities (mostly in the Punjab Hills) and Mughal political formations in Punjab.[65] The text identifies key individual actors, at the same time that it describes general characters—soldiers, brave and cowardly, strong and weak, as "types." A second recurring element consists of the theological and doctrinal pronouncements of the Guru; at times these pronouncements take on such a central role in the text that they almost—but not quite—overwhelm reference to a particular place and time of utterance. The third major element is the description of interactions between the Guru and his followers and, later, description of these followers. After the first chapter sets up the frame, events in subsequent chapters are related in chronological order, with each chapter focusing on one or two of these three narrative elements.[66] The final two chapters turn primarily to praise of the Guru and a reiteration of his teachings.

The ways in which these different modes—event narration, theological and doctrinal explication, and description of community and followers—are organized reveal how the text conceives the past as a territory within which to locate the Guru in action and idea. The narration of the Guru's actions in the world fully integrates theological and doctrinal concerns with the particular events associated with the Guru. This pattern can be seen, for example, in the description of Guru Gobind Singh at Anandpur, which had been established as the seat of the Guru's authority by the Ninth Guru, Tegh Bahadur. The author emphasizes the location and time of events, such as those at Anandpur associated with the founding of the Khalsa.[67] (Although Sainapati's description of the founding of

---

65. For a general account of the period, see Grewal, *Sikhs of the Punjab*.

66. The chapters up to and including the fourth are short and concise, describing particular events (mainly battles). From the fifth chapter, we see a transition to longer chapters that provide theological/doctrinal content within a weak narrative frame. After the fifth, sixth, and seventh chapters, the overall chronological and event-oriented narrative frame takes over again. Although later chapters provide interludes for both discussion of the community and its members and theological and doctrinal explication, they do so without challenging the strong overall narrative frame of the work until the last two chapters.

67. For examples, see Sainapati, *Gur Sobhā*, 69 and 74.

the Khalsa does not include features key to later portrayals, the account does carefully delineate the context and nature of the event.[68]) Alongside a description of the time and place of action, the words of the Guru are recorded as events and are tied to a larger narration of his actions:

> Now the poet describes Guru Gobind Singh at Anandpur
> With the impassable mountains around, the auspicious place on
>   the bank of the Satluj (1)
> The month of Chet passed and all had gathered for a *mela* [festival
>   gathering] unmatched.
> For the lesson of Vaisakhi the true Guru deliberated (2)
> The *sangat* from all cities [came] for *darshan* ["sacred viewing"]
> He was compassionate and gave *darshan*, that doer and creator
>   of the world (3)
> Gobind Singh was made happy and the *sangat* was made rapturous
> He revealed the Khalsa and lifted up all difficulties (4)
> All the collected community gathered on the bank of the Satluj. . . .[69]

This passage thus provides specific situational information and narrates events as a series of unfolding happenings. The text and community are both constructed around the words of the Guru, as "event," and in relation to a larger narration of the Guru's actions. The teachings of the Guru—in particular, his definition of the Sikh community and the meaning of the "Khalsa"—are also situated within particular events, when the Guru addresses his followers, or when followers engage in dialogue. Indeed, the entire chapter concludes with the frame "Thus the Guru spoke," and in the lines that follow, the injunctions described in the previous lines of the chapter are presented in summation.[70] The event of the Guru's speaking to his followers is remembered, and doctrinal teachings are subsumed structurally within it.

One might separate out these two—the description of a series of battles within a chronological frame, and a series of teachings and injunctions for a religious community—and place them in different "modes," a historical narrative mode and a religious or doctrinal one, as has often been done in the past for distinctions between mythological and historical contents in work on the Puranas, for

68. See the discussion in McLeod, *Who is a Sikh?* 29.

69. Sainapati, *Gur Sobhā*, 78.

70. Sainapati, *Gur Sobhā*, 87.

example.[71] Such a distinction does work here. Regarding the possible "mythic" aspects of Guru Gobind Singh's person—that is, references that relate to a larger mythological tradition as explicated within the Puranas and other texts—it is indeed useful to consider two modes of engagement, one that is historical in concern, and one that provides a mythological background to or an overarching context for this history. Mythological references are peripheral to it.[72] However, the doctrinal and theological concerns in this text are not peripheral and are intertwined significantly. The designation of separate doctrinal/religious and historical modes here would detract from both the inner coherence of the text and the possible meanings of these sections of the text as one piece.

By the later chapters, the reportage of events takes over, and comments on the Khalsa and the Singhs are placed within the overwhelmingly chronological narrative of the story, one that points toward the culmination in chapter 18 with the death of the Guru.[73] That event signals the end of the reportage part of the text, to be replaced by a more general mode of praise and description of the Guru and a further explication of his message:

> I have given the Khalsa my robe;
> The Khalsa is my form, I am near the Khalsa.
> In the beginning and the end, shining in the Khalsa.[74]

The final two chapters (18 and 19) are of a different order from chapters 2–4 and 8–17, and do not constitute the same kind of historical narrative. Their role in the text, however, may be understood in relation to the whole of the work—the

---

71. Narayana Rao et al., *Textures of Time*, provides a recent example, separating mythological and historical content within the historical representations they explore from South India; see, for example, 112. They argue that mythological references can be seen as a foreground for historical content and "are completely distinct from the cosmological and pre-historical sequences that we find in the *puranas* themselves, where the present loses its concrete specificity and is absorbed by the frame—or, one might say, where the present functions as a timeless mode, perhaps 'mythic' but in any case programmed to recur ritually or in other ways" (245). Also see Sen, "Imperial Orders of the Past," 255.

72. Mythological references in other *gurbilās* texts, such as Kuir Singh's late eighteenth/early nineteenth-century text, are common and fundamental to the description of the identity of the Guru. It has been argued that the use of Vaishnava references within Sikh texts reflects a "hybrid" religious culture in which "Hindu" and "Sikh" are not discrete categories. This is the tenor of the argument put forward most famously by Harjot Oberoi regarding the construction of "Sanatan Sikhism," which had strong ties to Hindu traditions and did not articulate a separate Sikh (and, in particular Khalsa) identity (Oberoi, *Construction*). Such enunciations, however, did not necessitate a lack of identity. See below.

73. Sainapati, *Gur Sobhā*, 169.

74. Sainapati, *Gur Sobhā*, 170.

culmination of a description of the Guru's place in the world and a discussion of
the significance of his worldly presence. The above reference to *khil'at*, or ritual
gift-giving of a robe of honor as a way of expressing authority, with its simultaneously political and religious communitarian referents in Islamic as well as
Sikh contexts, contributes to the overall logic that is central to the story Sainapati seeks to tell.[75] As was discussed in the previous chapter, the practice of
khil'at is central in material remembrance of the Guru, and connections to him,
and the materiality of the connection between the Guru and the community,
are expressed eloquently here.

As is clear in these references to the formation of the Tenth Guru's community, the Khalsa, there is more than biography/hagiography at work in this text.
The simultaneously religious and historical nature of the text lies not *only* in the
more obvious sense of the religious—simply in the fact that "God enters into
history with Guru Gobind Singh," as Surjit Hans put it[76]—or in the historicality
of the central figure of the narrative, but in the structure of the narrative of *Gur
Sobhā* overall. In this structure, the theological and the historical narrative are
interlinked. Further, the discursive formation of the *panth* around the Guru is
central to the function of Sainapati's text *as a history*, in keeping with the Guru's
message that hereafter Sikh identity would be formed around *granth* and *panth*.
We can see this particularly in the fifth chapter of the text, which narrates events
associated with the foundation of the Khalsa and the speeches of the Guru that
emphasize the formation of the *panth*: "All the community (*sangat*) from beginning to end is my Khalsa," the Guru declares; "who obeys my order will be a true
Sikh."[77] Both these elements—events and direct speech—work to define the
community in relation to others and with the Guru. For example, the specific
injunctions to "Make the Masands [early community representatives of the Guru]
far from you . . .,"[78] and "Donate to the Guru and do not give into the hands of
others"[79] are directly related to the making of the community and its relationship
with the Guru (the *masand*s were perceived to constitute a challenge to the office
of the Guru at this time, and the role was eradicated at the time of the Tenth
Guru, with the formation of the Khalsa).

75. Gordon, ed., *Robes and Honor: The Medieval World of Investiture* and Gordon *Robes of Honor:* Khil'at *in Pre-Colonial and Colonial India.*

76. Hans, *Reconstruction of Sikh History*, 231.

77. Sainapati, *Gur Sobhā*, 81.

78. Sainapati, *Gur Sobhā*, 79.

79. Sainapati, *Gur Sobhā*, 82.

The formation of the community stands at the center of this text, through the detailing of behavior that is fundamental to the *panth*'s constitution, defining the boundaries of the community in relation to other communities at the time, as well as purifying the community internally.[80] This impulse is exemplified by prohibitions against behaviors that mark particular cultural and religious groups, such as the smoking of tobacco, associated with west Asian and Muslim cultures, and ritual requirements associated with Hindu traditions. Such assertions and injunctions are related by means of particular events, as when the Guru addresses his followers, or when followers engage in dialogue:

> "Abandon the *hukkā* and sing the virtues of Hari!
> If you desire food, partake of the nectar of Hari.
> Abandon the shaving of heads, oh Brother!"
> [The Guru] said this to the Sikhs. (21)
> "Whoever's mother or father dies
> They should not shave their heads
> Gobind is our mother and father. . . ."[81]

Here, the radical nature of Guru Gobind Singh's teachings is expounded fully: the Guru is identified as the mother and father, supplanting the central role of parents, making unnecessary the rites and rituals associated with their deaths. Deol has shown that the central point at issue in this teaching regarding the prohibition of rituals associated with the death of relatives was the avoidance of a Mughal tax on this practice, and as such represented a challenge to Mughal sovereignty.[82] Deol relates this injunction to a larger phenomenon, namely, the creation of what he calls a "metanarrative" derived from the Dasam Granth in which the aspirations of the Khalsa community to define itself as distinct and sovereign were placed within a framework based on puranic myth, defining *dharam* in a mode that is simultaneously religious and political.[83] According to this "grand

---

80. Concern for community is a standard in texts associated with *bhaktī* (devotional) traditions. Some references to community thus are typical of a broader genre (see the use of such references, for example, in Sainapati, *Gur Sobhā*, 83–85 and elsewhere—*sati saṅgat, saṅt sabhā, saṅtjaṇā*). For more discussion of Sainapati and his concern for internal purification, see Dhavan "Redemptive Pasts" (2011), 44.

81. Sainapati, *Gur Sobhā*, 87, 80 for quotation. Hari here refers to God. Although this term is also used in Vaishnava contexts, it does not always carry such connotations and should be construed in a generic sense.

82. Deol, "Eighteenth Century Khalsa Identity," 26–27.

83. Deol, "Eighteenth Century Khalsa Identity," 30ff. See also 38–39. *Dharam* and *dharm* represent Punjabi spellings of the word *dharma*.

narrative," "at the centre of Khalsa self-construction lie the worship of weapons and the perception of partaking in the Guru's mission to reestablish dharma, a mission that is itself embedded in a wider cosmological cycle of battles against evil that extends back into mythical time."[84] At the same time, the Khalsa redefined *dharam* and brought political as well as religious content to it.

Within the sweep of the literature of the period, Deol's characterization has much in its favor: without a doubt there are aspects of both political and religious ideologies at work here.[85] The use of *khil'at*, in both material and metaphorical terms, exemplifies this, as does the worship of weapons that Deol highlights. The *Shastarnāmmālā* in the Dasam Granth provides the literary apotheosis of this orientation in its praise of weapons and association of them with both worldly and otherworldly power: "You are the arrow, the spear, the hatchet (*tabar*), and the sword (*talwār*) / Who recites your name crosses the fearful ocean."[86] In this text, the naming of weapons constitutes a form of power. God is named as equivalent to the weapon, and to the many forces of the universe (Indra, the Goddess, etc.) that are themselves encompassed by God—indeed, God is the people and God is the ruler: "You are Rama, you are Krishna, and a form of Vishnu / You are all of the people of the whole world and you are lord of the earth."[87] Indeed, at another point the author notes, "All warriors and poets should understand this in their hearts, that there is no difference between the name of the *chakra* [discus] and Vishnu."[88] Sikh tradition has indeed interpreted references to the Goddess in

---

84. Deol, "Eighteenth Century Khalsa Identity," 33.

85. William Pinch's reading of the Vaishnava hagiographical text, the *Bhaktamal of Nabhadas* (of 1600), reveals a similar vision: the construction of a community, in social as well as religious terms, through the intersection of historiographical and religious concerns. His analysis allows us to understand how the past is the ground upon which are constructed multiple and sometimes conflicting notions of community through exclusion and inclusion (William Pinch, "History, Devotion and the Search for Nabhadas of Galta" in Ali, ed., *Invoking the Past*). Pinch's work on the formation of warrior ascetic groups similarly demonstrates the multiple political and social formations that must inform our understanding of Khalsa mobilization. See William Pinch, *Peasants and Monks in British India* (Berkeley: University of California Press, 1996); William Pinch, *Warrior Ascetics and Indian Empires* (Cambridge: Cambridge University Press, 2006) and the early work of Lorenzen on this topic: David Lorenzen, "Warrior Ascetics in Indian History," *Journal of the American Oriental Society* 98, 1 (1978): 70–71.

86. Sri Dasam Granth Sahib Ji Satik (Sri Dasam Granth with Commentary in Modern Punjabi). Commentary by Pandit Narain Singh Ji Giani (Amritsar: Jawahar Singh Kripal Singh and Company, 1992) V. 5, p. 322, L. 4. As Fenech notes, praise of the Guru's sword and other objects associated with courtly power are common (*The Darbar of the Sikh Gurus*, 141). On the *Shastarnāmmālā* in the context of the Dasam Granth, see Rinehart *Debating the Dasam Granth*, 33–34.

87. Sri Dasam Granth, V. 5 p. 324, l. 17.

88. Sri Dasam Granth, V. 5 pp. 343–4, l. 74.

this light, construing the term *bhagautī* (for example) in metaphorial terms as meaning sword, as well as power more generally.[89] The material culture of weapons is thus central to a larger political and religious imperative expressed in *Gur Sobhā* and other texts of the period.

Yet, lest we consider this phenomenon an isolated one, we must remember that the worship of weapons did not stand at the center of only Sikh conceptions and ritual invocations of temporal power. William Pinch's recent work on warrior ascetics in late medieval and early modern South Asia makes this clear. Weapons and the religious power associated with them were thus generally a "part of a shaktiyoga repertoire that centered on harnessing supernormal forces both within and beyond the human body" and were central to the growth of warrior asceticism in the eighteenth and nineteenth century, to the degree that "by 1800 armed ascetics were a familiar and valued component of the military economy of northern India."[90] Such weapons and symbols of war were not only valued when associated with the Guru, even in the Sikh context; the worship of weapons and standards were commonplace in Punjab overall, reflecting the broader presence of arms and warrior culture across the region.[91] As Dirk Kolff has shown, "it is clear that Indian agrarian society was to a large extent an armed society, skilled in the use of arms," in the Mughal period.[92] The powers associated with the gifting of weapons and other kinds of symbolically powerful gifts (such as robes) that were important in Mughal and other economies of exchange lent yet another layer of value upon objects, in both religious and political terms.[93]

Thus, several qualifications need to be introduced to make Deol's characterization fully persuasive. The terms of the social formations at work in the "political," vs. the "religious," require further explication (as William Pinch's work on warrior ascetics makes clear). The sovereignty proclaimed within different Sikh-oriented Punjabi

89. Rinehart *Debating the Dasam Granth*, 107.

90. Pinch *Warrior Ascetics and Indian Empires*, 10 for first quotation; 77 for second. See 70ff. on weapons in general in the period.

91. For just one example of the mention of the worship of military standards in the period of Ranjit Singh, see Indu Banga and J.S. Grewal, eds., *Maharaja Ranjit Singh: The State and Society* (Amritsar: Guru Nanak Dev University, 2001), 184, Document 377.

92. Dirk Kolff, *Naukar, Rajput, and Sepoy: The Ethnohistory of the Military Labour Market in Hindustan, 1450–1850* (Cambridge: Cambridge University Press, 1990), 7. Dhavan contextualizes the Khalsa in the broader military labor market of the period, building on the excellent early work of Kolff and others: Dhavan, *When Sparrows Became Hawks*, 12–13, 75, 126, and throughout.

93. This and the prior paragraph draw on Anne Murphy "The Guru's Weapons."

texts from the eighteenth century does not reflect a single vision. In Sainapati's text, this sovereignty is not singularly territorial and bounded. Deol is certainly correct that Sainapati is centrally concerned with sovereignty over the city of Anandpur and its environs—and certainly the practice of dedicating copper plates to temples, uncovered by G. S. Mann, mirrors the practices of sovereigns in the period.[94] Material practices therefore support the textual assertion of sovereign status at the city. The notion of the *panth* articulated overall in the text, however, is not encompassed by this vision, and the boundaries of the community are dispersed.[95] Even Fenech's extensive and compelling exploration of the court culture of the Gurus, and particularly the Tenth Guru, concedes that the notion of sovereignty at work within courtly formations in the Sikh context is ambiguous. In the end, Fenech suggests that the Guru's interest in direct sovereign control was limited to the city of Anandpur, as suggested above.[96] Thus, in *Gur Sobhā* the community in Delhi is a central concern, particularly in descriptions of the responses of the community to the teachings of the Guru, including those of some high-caste followers unwilling to abandon certain caste customs.[97] The community and its shape are thus being negotiated. Moreover, the sense of this community is not constructed in relation to formation of a Sikh state, and a simple equivalence of the sovereignty of the Guru over the community with state formation is, at the time of Sainapati, untenable. The Sikh imagination of the past, at this particular time in the work of Sainapati, therefore, both is and is not centrally concerned with political sovereignty. Or, rather, the meaning of sovereignty as political is not always clear (and is certainly not fundamentally territorialized or statist).[98] It is evoked in certain senses—the mantle of authority of *khil'at* and the use of the past, as can be found in other communities *both* political and religious—but at the center is the formulation of the community in relation to the Guru. And the community—the subject of history—is not equivalent to the state. Deol's contention that "the Khalsa notion of dharma valorizes ideas of rule and political sovereignty in a way that classical definitions and others contemporary to the Khalsa do not" does not quite capture the de-territorialized sovereignty and communitarian orientation of the

---

94. Mann, "Sources for the Study," 241.

95. Deol, "Eighteenth Century Khalsa Identity," 33–34. There are other aspects of sovereignty expressed, such as authority over local villages, but this is not equated with the Sikh community (Sainapati, *Gur Sobhā*, 116). As Grewal too notes, sovereignty is in question only within larger concerns (Grewal, "Praising the Khalsa," 93).

96. Louis E. Fenech, *The Darbar of the Sikh Gurus: The Court of God in the World of Men* (Delhi: Oxford University Press, 2008), 271, footnote 180. For more on this work and the issue of sovereignty, see Anne Murphy's review in *Indian Historical Review* 36, 1 (2009): 154–58.

97. See Dhavan, *When Sparrows Became Hawks*, 42–43.

98. See Oberoi, "From Punjab to Khalistan," 34.

Khalsa and the community as conceived within Sainapati's text, nor does it account for other modes of social/political organization contemporary with Sikh activity.[99]

The formation of the *panth* and the nature of its sovereignty must be understood in multiple terms, both within the conceits of the political and around other imaginative engagements with community formation. This provides the connection between Sainapati's text and other examples of literature with a Sikh orientation in the eighteenth and early nineteenth centuries: the *rahitnāma* literature, the earliest examples of which hail from the early to mid-eighteenth century, and the later texts of the *gurbilās* genre in the remainder of that century and the early nineteenth century. The *rahit* literature attempts to define Sikh behavior, and through this the formation of the nascent community—it provides a central location for the articulation of the Khalsa Sikh subject—but it is not structured overall as a historical narrative; thus, its form is quite distinct from *Gur Sobhā*. At the same time, the narrative portions of the *rahit* are also deeply tied to the *gurbilās* literature, and aspects of the evolving *rahit* appear in *Gur Sobhā*, has been discussed in chapter 2. *Gur Sobhā* thus acts as a historical account of the Guru's life in the world, but also relates some of the earliest elements of the *rahit* that we have available to us, offering, as McLeod notes, "the first clear impression of what the Guru required of those who were initiated as the first members of the Khalsa order."[100]

Later *gurbilās* texts include Kesar Singh Chibber's mid-eighteenth-century *Baṅsāvalīnāmā Dasāṅ Pātshāhīāṅ kā*, which features an organizational structure (based on the lineage of Gurus) different to that of the *Gur Sobhā*, but is similarly chronologically driven, and Kuir Singh's mid to late eighteenth century *Gurbilās Pātshāhī Das*, which is similar in organization to *Gur Sobhā* but features strong mythological content and a clearer sense, appropriate to its time of composition, of political sovereignty in relation to the Mughal state and other smaller Hindu kings from the Punjab Hills.[101] Texts of this period exhibit great diversity in their approach and interpretation of key issues, such as caste, demonstrating Purnima Dhavan's assertion that "while the narrative content of the recent Sikh past appears to achieve a more concrete narrative by the end of the eighteenth century, the meanings derived from this past occupied a contested terrain as the exegetical

---

99. Deol, "Eighteenth Century Khalsa Identity," 40.

100. W.H. McLeod *Sikhs of the Khalsa: A History of the Khalsa Rahit* (New Delhi: Oxford University Press, 2003), 59.

101. Kuir Singh, *Gurbilās Pātshāhī Das*; Kesar Singh Chibber, *Baṅsāvalīnāmā Dasāṅ Pātshāhīāṅ kā*, ed. Piara Singh Padam (Amritsar: Singh Brothers, 1997). On the dating of these texts, see Hans, *Reconstruction of Sikh History*, 266 and 281, and Dhavan, *When Sparrows Became Hawks*, 182 n. 6) and Murphy "The *Gurbilās* Literature and the Idea of 'Religion.'"

traditions within Sikhism became diverse."[102] Yet, in general terms one can discern in these texts of the late eighteenth and early nineteenth centuries, including the *rahit* literature, a central concern: the articulation of connections between the Guru and the *panth*, and the narration of what constitutes the *panth*. In this way, the narration of the Guru's life and connections to his followers constitutes the means for the formation of the Sikh community. Sainapati's text writes of the Guru's life, but also, in relation to it, of the *panth* gathered around the Guru, of Sikhness, and it does so in multiple modes.

The Past and its Futures

Authors such as Surjit Hans and others have assumed that *Gur Sobhā* and other texts like it represent a Sikh (and therefore, another example of a South Asian) form of history. However, "historicity," rather than "history," may be a more appropriate term, where the former refers to an approach to the past that is not defined by a particular set of assumptions associated with European forms of political order or formations of knowledge. In this conception, "history" is a type of a more generic and possibly universal kind of "historicity." In the words of Eric Hirsch and Charles Stewart, modern historiography relies upon the "naturalized assumption that 'history' belongs to the domain of the past. The past is separate from the present and this separation allows the recognition of history as an object. History is over and done with—gone forever."[103] This is the sense of "history" in the European modern conception, as defined by Dipesh Chakrabarty, Hayden White, and others; history, in Michel de Certeau's words, "is born in effect from the rupture that constitutes a past distinct from its current enterprise."[104] History so defined is constitutive of a historical sense that is distinct from alternative forms of historicity found outside the European and modern.

Gur Sobhā, however, features multiple visions. In its *theological* dimension the notion of the separation of the past and present is of great importance within the text. There *is*, therefore, a theological sense of completeness to the past expressed in the text, a sense of rupture, of the formation of the present in relation to the

---

102. Dhavan "Redemptive Pasts" (2011) 45. On Chibber's work, see J. S. Grewal, "Brahmanizing the Tradition: Chhibber's Bansāvalināma" in *The Khalsa: Sikh and Non-Sikh Perspectives*, ed. J. S. Grewal (New Delhi: Manohar, 2004), 59–101, on caste see 71–72. The fourth chapter of Chibber's text, for example, opens with controversy over caste status within the Sikh community.

103. Hirsch and Stewart, "Ethnographies of Historicity," 263.

104. Michel de Certeau, *The Writing of History*, trans. Tom Conley (New York: Columbia University Press, 1988), 46.

past as *truly past* and no longer present.[105] This sense of rupture is central to the conceit of the text as "religious"—that is, in defining Sikhness as following the Guru, and in defining the community that gathers around him. It is complicated with the death of the Tenth Guru and the transference of Guruship to the *granth* and *panth*. With this, the *panth* is defined in a way opens up a sense of the past that is not over and done with, but rather continues to operate in the present and on into the future. This happens because the Guru transfers the notion of Guruship to the text and to the community: the presence of the Guru continues beyond his death right up to the present and beyond. This initiates a new relationship of the community with its past, a new temporality, and therefore a new historical sense, one in which the past is in one sense gone, and in another, ever-present. The *historical* dimension of *Gur Sobhā* is thus predicated not *just* on the pastness of the Guru, but also on the continuing presence of the community in direct relation to the Guru. Daud Ali has noted that "[j]ust as the nation uses the past to legitimise and valorise its project, so too . . . medieval polities, castes, *bhaktas*, and courts used the past as a legitimising discourse."[106] In the case of *Gur Sobhā*, then, the narration of religious content within a historical narrative provides a means not only for relating the teachings of the Guru by means of certain past events, but for creating the community itself as the continuation of this past into the present. This is the overarching narrative at the center of history.

This theologically inflected historical sense associated with the Tenth Guru is further complicated in literary and other representations that follow in the eighteenth and early nineteenth centuries. In later examples of the *gurbilās* genre, mythological associations of the Guru are further developed, and the Guru is seen to be connected to other religious authorities, particularly but not exclusively Ram; as Kuir Singh writes, some see the Guru and call him Ram, and others see Shankar or Shiva.[107] The final chapter of Kesar Singh Chibber's *Baṅsāvalīnāmā* also features such elements. Its fourteenth chapter is dominated by extensive puranic elements, such as the story of Sukracarya and repeated tellings of the Ramayana; the Guru's families (Bedi, Trehan, Bhalla, and Sodhi) are said to descend from the sons of Dasharatha.[108] These features are interspersed with definitions of being Sikh and

---

105. Purnima Dhavan has also observed this sense of rupture; see her "History, Prophecy, and Power: The Role of Gurbilas Literature in Shaping Khalsa Identity," lecture at the University of Wisconsin Annual Conference on South Asia, October 2005. I thank her for sharing her paper.

106. Ali, ed., *Invoking the Past*, 11; *bhaktā* may be glossed as "devotee."

107. For examples of references to Ram, see Kuir Singh *Gurbilās Pātshāhī Das*, 15, 18–20, 50; the reference to both Ram and Shiva is on 21.

108. Chibber, *Baṅsāvalīnāmā*; on the geneaology of the Gurus, see 241–42; for Sukra, 264–67.

the descriptions of the greatness of the Guru. Such broad references can be seen as positioning the Guru in relation to a larger cosmology, within a vision of the preeminence of the Guru. This is particularly visible in Chibber's text, in which the puranic elements are largely separate from references to the Gurus, except for within the genealogy of the Gurus' families. In this way, Kuir Singh's and Chibber's texts strongly resonate with aspects of the Dasam Granth, which features extensive mythological references; indeed, a bulk of the Dasam Granth is dedicated to the description of the incarnations of Vishnu and praise of the Goddess (as well as other controversial components).[109] Rinehart has cogently argued that "it may be more fruitful to read the Dasam Granth goddess and other 'Hindu' mythological material as indicative of participation in the broad realm of Indian culture— dharma in its broadest sense—rather than looking for a solely religious reading of the text and its topics of concern."[110] Certainly, such references work effectively in articulating forms of temporal power in general terms.[111] They also constitute a shared narrative "sourcebook" upon which many religious traditions drew, just as *qisse* or story traditions in Punjab were available across religious boundaries.[112] Most vividly, these texts demonstrate the diversity of interpretation in the *gurbilās* genre noted by Dhavan, which was in great flux in its content even as historiography became fixed as a significant genre of Sikh self-representation.

In Kuir Singh's text, as I have noted, there are clearly state-oriented articulations of the meanings of sovereignty: the Guru is explicitly called upon to counter repressive state powers, Guru Tegh Bahadur is called the "arm of the Jat" (a caste group prominent among the Sikhs), and the Guru is meant to "destroy the Mlechas" or foreigners, just as he destroys desire and anger in the mind.[113] This vilification of the foreigners or "Turks" is directly related to state power and should not be seen as specifically religious, as has been observed in other texts that articulate the distinction between Mlecha and not.[114] The trappings of the Guru's authority are

---

109. See Rinehart, *Debating the Dasam Granth* for an overview of contents, with an emphasis on their connections to mythological material and description of foundational literature on the text in Punjabi.

110. Rinehart, *Debating the Dasam Granth*, 112.

111. Rinehart, *Debating the Dasam Granth*, 70, 111.

112. Mir, "Genre and Devotion in Punjabi Popular Narratives."

113. See Kuir Singh, *Gurbilās Pātshāhī Das*, 12 and 50.

114. See, for instance, Cynthia Talbot, "Inscribing the Other, Inscribing the Self: Hindu-Muslim Identities in Pre-Colonial India," *Comparative Studies in Society and History* 37, 4 (1995): 692–722. Indeed, distinctions between Muslim and non-Muslim shift in the text. There is not room to explore this further here; see Hans, *Reconstruction of Sikh History* and "Murphy The idea of 'religion,'" for some discussion.

explicitly royal in form, and the vocabulary of state sovereignty runs through the text.[115] As has been noted, this development reflects the ascendancy of sovereignty among the successors to Mughal authority as the eighteenth century progressed. In Kesar Singh Chibber's text, this is similarly described: *pāp kari turkāṅ dā rāj nās hoi gaiā* "Having sinned, the rule of the Turks is destroyed"—and the Sikhs are there to obtain rule in the wake of its demise.[116] The sovereignty of the Guru at the time these two texts were created is therefore imagined as statist, and the sense of rupture complicated. Returning to the theological nature of the historical, however, even in Kuir Singh, a sense of connectedness to the Guru is established through its narration as a past event; the narration of the Guru in the past provides the founding logic of the community. This is the underlying logic of Chibber's *Baṅsāvalīnāmā*, as well, in its final section: to describe the community and establish its relationship to the Guru. Thus, different kinds of Sikhs are described, among assertions of the relationship of the true Sikh to the Guru.[117]

Though the sense of temporal disconnectedness marks the modern European sense of history, this was not always the case. It is well known that historicality—with its sense of the connectedness of past, present, and future—developed in European intellectual traditions in relation to Christian ideologies and the writing of sacral history. This interest in history, of course, was not consistent and singular in orientation. As J. Z. Smith (following on the earlier work of Halbwachs) has artfully shown, concern for history has experienced multiple transformations within Christian traditions: interest in the earthly life of Christ transformed Christianity in the fourth century CE, and then again in the seventeenth century with the rejection of this imagination.[118] Interestingly, these transformations are legible most profoundly through Christian interest in the material grounds of Christ's life: in the sacred landscape of Jerusalem, and in the inscription of the life of Jesus onto space, providing a compelling parallel with Sikh concerns that evolve in this period.[119]

The Christian view of temporality was characterized by a sense that what was occurring now was inextricably linked to what happened then (for example, the

---

115. See, for example, Kuir Singh, *Gurbilās Pātshāhī Das*, chapter 5.

116. Chibber, *Baṅsāvalīnāmā*, 230.

117. For descriptions of different kinds of Sikhs, see Chibber, *Baṅsāvalīnāmā*, 230, and see also 216.

118. Smith, *To Take Place*, 88ff. On Halbwachs and specifically analysis of his work on collective memory in Christianity, see Hutton, *History as an Art of Memory* and Elizabeth Castelli, *Martyrdom and Memory: Early Christian Culture-Making* (New York: Columbia University Press, 2004).

119. See further discussion in the conclusion.

Crucifixion) and what will happen (for example, the Second Coming). The modern notion of "history" ultimately *rejected* the temporalities imagined within the Christian theological sense of historicality. As Reinhart Koselleck has argued, it is only when "Christian eschatology shed its constant expectation of the imminent arrival of doomsday that a temporality could be revealed that would be open for the new and without limit."[120] Modern history, he claimed, involved the transformation of notions of temporality and the future, in tension with Christian-constructed notions of time and futurity.

In this case, Sikh temporalities contain elements of both rupture and continuance that emerge in the eighteenth century and reach in complicated ways into modernity. One can therefore see a *particular* justification for the writing of human history and the living power of remembrance within the Sikh imagination, built upon the *humanization* and collectivization of authority with the transformation of the *panth* in the early eighteenth century, after the death of the last human Guru. This justification does not require a rejection of religious ideologies as being in opposition to human-derived notions of temporality. The human community, indeed, becomes the *locus* of history: the sovereign narrative produced through the articulation of history. We might see this in Weberian terms, as aspects of the routinization or institutionalization of charisma, the institution built upon the leader who is gone; such routinization encourages the writing of this charisma as past in relation to the present of the community.[121] One can see Christian historiography in such a vein; but the differences in theological and soteriological terms between Christian and Sikh notions of temporality and futurity demand that we not assume the same articulation of secularity and religiosity in the formation of a historical sense in these different contexts, nor oppose them to modern forms of historical imagination in the same way.[122] A Sikh historical orientation in the formation of the community is not centered on otherworldly soteriology; it locates the subject of history within a social formation: the community, in multiple terms. This speaks to the way in which historical representation constitutes a fundamental constituting principle of the community: that which refers to the past and produces the present. There is no doubt that the Sikh concern for the past through the eighteenth century was fundamentally

120. Reinhart Koselleck, *Futures Past: On the Semantics of Historical Time* (Cambridge, MA and London: MIT Press, 1985), 241.

121. Max Weber, *On Charisma and Institution Building: Selected Papers*, ed. S. N. Eisenstadt (Chicago: University of Chicago Press, 1968).

122. I cannot address the issue of the secular here, but the formation of a kind of secular space in the writing of the past as history is a central concern of any who seeks to understand the history of historiography in South Asia. See Inden et al., eds., *Querying the Medieval*.

shaped by the redefinition of sovereign relations within a post-Mughal Punjab, building upon the broader, preexisting, non-statist, theologically driven orientation that can be seen in *Gur Sobhā*. Different social formations of the *panth* with regard to caste in particular shaped the conception of the community as well. The narration of the past produces the community of the Guru, however, no matter how that community is described.

The Rahitnāme *and the Materiality of Community Boundaries*

In Sainapati's text, the narration of the past is fundamentally tied to the text's overall theological and doctrinal interests. The author locates authority in name, date, and site and concerns himself repeatedly in the text with the boundaries of the Sikh community, and with the behavior that is associated with belonging to this community. Such stipulations are, within fifty years, explicated more fully in what is called the *rahitnāme* literature.[123] The *Rahitnāmā* of Chaupa Singh Chibber, dated to between 1740 and 1765, shows how a document that sets out, quite explicitly, to define a Sikh, does so in relation to history. This form of history is expressed through categories of evidence: those traces of the Gurus that remain, through blood lineage, place, and object. McLeod notes that the historical value of the Chaupa Singh *Rahitnāmā* is of questionable quality, as is true of Kesar Singh's *Bansāvalīnāmā*, another product of the Chibber clan from later in the eighteenth century.[124] As McLeod notes, the texts are most useful not so much for the history they present, but for their portrayal of their contemporary present. In keeping with such a sentiment, we will examine aspects of this text, utilizing my translations of the Punjabi original he provides (with reference to another printed version of this text), to understand how elements of the past are represented, and what these representations tell us as a whole about the perception of the past within the text.

I have noted earlier that the representation of the past is fundamentally linked to the articulation of authority, around which the community is formed. What are the forms of authority highlighted in this text and how are connections established? The ultimate authority for the text is the Guru: as McLeod puts it, "one must observe the Rahit because the Guru has decreed it. Submission to the Guru is the only means of liberation for the Sikh and if the Guru ordains the Rahit his

---

123. See Deol, "Eighteenth-Century Khalsa Identity," 35ff.; McLeod, *Textual Sources*, 71–86 and "Introduction" in Chaupa Singh *Rahit Nāmā*. See discussion in chapter 2.

124. Both, in his view, are "informed by family bias and extensively based on hearsay"; yet, both offer verifiable historical content; thus, "it would be rash to read them uncritically; and it would be unjust to dismiss them out of hand." (McLeod, introduction to Chaupa Singh, *Rahit Nāmā*, 18).

loyal disciple has no choice by to obey. . . ."[125] The text bears resemblance to Sain-apati's in this and other fundamental approaches, such as in its exaltation of the Guru and its location of authority within him. One important feature of the text—and an element that has supported suspicions that it is biased and not an objective record of the Guru's injunctions—is the central place given to the Chib-ber family (and Brahmins in general).[126] This is clearly seen, for example, in the following lines: "The words were spoken, 'Call the Chibber Sikhs.' Sahib Chand and Dharam Chand both came and were present. The words were spoken 'You must do the work of the Guru.' They replied, 'Oh Protector of the poor, we are not worthy of this.' [The Guru replied,] 'Your elders have always been in the Guru's service."[127] After this, the Guru then relates the history of the Chibber Brahmins' relationships with prior Gurus. Earlier, it is written that Brahmins in general are deserving of honor: "[a]ny Sikh of the Guru who is a Brahmin should receive twice the service. There will be double the reward."[128]

The text, therefore, is constructed as a part of a claim to a particularly close and authorizing relationship with the Guru—"a record unparalleled for its faithful service to the Gurus and this record demands recognition."[129] In this sense, it functions as an authorizing object, much like the objects described in the last chapter: a narrative means to stake a claim in relation to the Gurus. Other aspects of authority delineated in the text are clearly behavioral. Beyond the fun-damental ground of the Guru and the personal/familial interests of the Chibber clan, it is through appropriate behavior that the status of a *gursikh* (or Sikh de-voted to the Guru) is attested to, and through these means then one can identify

---

125. McLeod, introduction to Chaupa Singh, *Rahit Nāmā*, 47.

126. Noted also by McLeod, introduction to Chaupa Singh, *Rahit Nāmā*, 18; and Hans, *Reconstruction of Sikh History*, 281.

127. Chaupa Singh, *Rahit Nāmā*, lines 170–71, p. 81 (for McLeod's translation, see 169). All translations of the Chaupa Singh text are mine, utilizing the Punjabi original provided by McLeod. It must be noted that McLeod clearly states that his published version "is essentially that of the *GNDU* [Guru Nanak Dev University] manuscript," which dates from the middle of the nineteenth century. (For quotation, see McLeod, introduction to Chaupa Singh, *Rahit Nāmā*, 22; for date see p. 21). Notations of alternative readings in the version published by Shamsher Singh 'Ashok' are noted in footnotes (Shamsher Singh 'Ashok'. *Guru Khalse de Rahitname* (Amritsar: Sikh History Research Board, 1979).). McLeod dismisses Ashok's ver-sion (McLeod, introduction to Chaupa Singh, *Rahit Nāmā*, 19). We have reason to believe that Ashok's version is closer to the earlier Sikh Reference Library manuscript (dated to 1765) which was destroyed during Operation Bluestar in 1984 (See McLeod, introduction to Chaupa Singh, *Rahit Nāmā*, 19–20); Peder Gedda's doctoral research along such lines will be revealing. Thank you to Peder Gedda for his assistance and insights into the published versions.

128. Chaupa Singh, *Rahit Nāmā*, line 24, p. 60 (for McLeod's translation, see 151).

129. McLeod, introduction to Chaupa Singh, *Rahit Nāmā*, 18.

and attest to the authority of the Guru. Some of these behavioral injunctions refer to how special persons should be treated. For instance, the author writes that "Whoever is a religious teacher [*jagat dā gurū*][130] of the Guru's teachings will be twice honored."[131] Sikh religious leaders, in general, are thus highlighted as being worthy of respect. Descendants of the Gurus are identified as an important element of authority, alongside general religious leaders: "The residents of a village who neglect any well-known Sikhs, descendants of the Guru, or bearers of *hukamnāmā*s who may visit their village"[132] should thus undergo penance. This treatment is generalized, and respect is extended towards the Guru's descendants, as well as to a range of items and people associated with the Guru:

> A Sikh of the Guru should accept the descendants of the Gurus; places associated with the Gurus should be respected. All who serve the Guru should be respected; the Guru's writings should be accepted. All whom the Master has called his own should be honored. [Even] the Guru's dogs should be respected.[133]

Reverence for the descendants of the Guru, therefore, should be understood within a broader context of what must be revered in association with the Guru—including the *hukamnāme*, or orders of the Guru, as objects in themselves (see discussion below and figure 3.1).[134] It seems that the operative category is "things associated with the Guru, which participate in his authority through this association," not "descendant of the Guru" as an isolated category. This is articulated even more clearly in the translation offered by McLeod of the Prahilad Rai *Rahitnāmā*, which he dates to the same period as Chaupa Singh's text, where the Guru is said to be present in family of the Gurus and "within those commands which I gave in written form."[135] This is further explicated by the criticism within the Chaupa

---

130. McLeod argues this would mean the Guru or any other leader.

131. Chaupa Singh, *Rahit Nāmā*, line 24, p. 60 (for McLeod's translation, see 151). This line does not appear in Ashok.

132. Chaupa Singh, *Rahit Nāmā*, line 413, p. 106 (for McLeod's translation, see p. 181).

133. Chaupa Singh, *Rahit Nāmā*, line 107, p. 70 (for McLeod's translation, see pp. 158–59). In Ashok's version, this line reads: "A Sikh of the Guru should accept the descendants of the Gurus. All whom the Master has called his own should be honored. [Even] the Guru's dogs should be respected." (Translation mine.)

134. This is visible in the possibly earlier Prahlad Rai Rahit Nāmā (dated by McLeod as from the 1730s), where reverence is argued for the famliies of Guru Nanak, Guru Angad and Guru Amardas, and that the Guru is "present within those commands [*hukam*] which I gave in written form" (McLeod, *Sikhs of the Khalsa*, 287–88).

135 McLeod, *Sikhs of the Khalsa*, 287–288. McLeod "hesitantly" dates this text to the 1730s, 71.

FIGURE 3.1 *Hukamnāmā* given to the family at Bhai Rupa, displayed. Photograph by Anne Murphy. April 2002.

Singh text for certain possible behaviors of the descendants of the Guru—according to this author, descendants of the Guru are not automatically to be accepted as authorities. Thus, for example, it condemns "[a]ny in the line of the Gurus who passes on to outsiders [that which was offered at] Ardas."[136] In describing the five reprobate groups with which no Sikh should have dealings, the author notes that this is the case even though some of these groups are related to the Guru: "In the community of the five [reprobate groups] are also members of the Guru's own family. But those who spread slander are wicked. In the same way that flowers, fruit, leaves, and branches emerge from trees, so too do thorns. These [reprobate relatives] are such thorns."[137] Within the text, therefore, relatives of the Guru are not inherently worthy of respect. They are only so to the degree to which they represent and maintain their allegiance to the Guru and his teachings. This reflects, surely, the fact that some relatives of the Guru had overtly challenged the Guru lineage accepted by the mainstream tradition. The principle at work, however, is consistent with a larger category of authority through association that carries forth in relation to place and person alike.

It is often emphasized in discussions of Sikh tradition that there is a strong eschewal of "sacred places" or shrines. Yet, in the Chaupa Singh text, there are clear injunctions to respect the places associated with the Guru and, in particular, places associated with Sikh martyrdom.[138] For example, in a section on who should be censured: "Wherever Sikhs have sacrificed their lives for the Sikh faith should be regarded as places of martyrdom (*shahīd gañj*). Burn a lamp [at such places]"[139] and "If a Sikh of the Guru goes on a pilgrimage [*udāsī*] he/she should see places of the Gurus."[140] This injunction to visit and respect the places associated with the Gurus is accompanied by injunctions to avoid visiting sites associated with other religious groups: "A Sikh of the Guru should not accept the authority of any tomb, shrine, *derā*, mosque, Mullah or Qazi. There is none but

136. Chaupa Singh, *Rahit Nāmā*, line 367, p. 104 (for McLeod's translation, see p. 179). The term translated here as 'foreigners' is *mlech*.

137. Chaupa Singh, *Rahit Nāmā*, line 6, p. 58 (for McLeod's translation, see p. 150).

138. On portrayals of Sikh martyrdom in the period, see Fenech, *Martyrdom*, 63ff.

139. Chaupa Singh, *Rahit Nāmā*, line 474, p. 110 (for McLeod's translation, see p. 184).

140. Chaupa Singh, *Rahit Nāmā*, line 121, p. 72 (for McLeod's translation, see p. 160). Although there are places in the *rahit* where males are clearly addressed, the grammar of this sentence in Punjabi is ambiguous with reference to gender and this translation reflects this. In Ashok's version, the reference to Guru's places does not appear; if this is an authentic version of the earlier manuscript, the omission is significant; we cannot definitively address this issue at this time, except to note that by the nineteenth century respect for such places *was* clearly indicated.

one's own Guru."[141] There is thus a broad category at work among the things to be revered: those objects, places, and people associated with the Guru.[142] This can provide a means for understanding the reverence paid to the sword within the text, as well.[143] Thus: "A Sikh of the Guru should revere and worship [*pūjā kare*] the sword [*sirī sāhib*]. The Guru worshipped [his sword]."[144] Similarly, "A Sikh of the Guru should show respect for the letters of the Gurmukhi alphabet. These should never come beneath one's feet, nor be made into wrapping."[145] Respect is paid to a range of objects and representatives of Sikh authority; none should be seen in isolation. The key to all is the degree to which they represent an "authentic" connection to the Guru, proven (particularly in the case of the descendants of the Guru) by behavior. The worship of weapons must in particular be seen in a larger context as well, as explicated earlier, in relation to the Guru's worship of weapons as described in the *Bacittar Nāṭak*, for example, and in the *Shastarnāmmālā*.[146] Below is a selection from the *Bacittar Nāṭak*, a translation of which was included in a recent commemorative volume for the Guru Gobind Singh Marg. It demonstrates how the text is popularly invoked in the present, in English, with its formal tone and biblical sensibility:

> Sword that smiteth in a flash,
> That scattereth the armies of the wicked
> In the great battlefield;
> O Thou symbol of the brave!
> Thine arm is irresistible, thine brightness shineth forth,
> The blaze of the splendour dazzling like the sun,
> Sword, thou art protector of saints,
> Thou art the scourge of the wicked;

141. Chaupa Singh, *Rahit Nāmā*, line 137, p. 76 (for McLeod's translation, see p. 163). The term *derā* (in this text, spelled *dehurā*) here clearly designates a non-Sikh religious site; this is the term that formally is accepted for such sites in the legislation associated with Gurdwara Reform (see Section 2).

142. Indeed, one can interpret the role of the Guru's wives after the death of the Tenth Guru as extending this concern for those connected to the Guru. Deol, "Eighteenth Century Khalsa Identity," 28.

143. See outline, Chaupa Singh, *Rahit Nāmā*, 40.

144. Chaupa Singh, *Rahit Nāmā*, line 41, p. 63 (for McLeod's translation, see p.153).

145. Chaupa Singh, *Rahit Nāmā*, line 147, p. 78 (for McLeod's translation, see p. 166). Gurmukhi is a syllabary, but for the sake of clarity here, this terminology is used.

146. For discussion of the *Shastarnāmmālā* and the worship of weapons, see Murphy, "The Guru's Weapons." See also Deol, "Eighteenth Century Khalsa Identity."

Scatterer of sinners, I take refuge in thee.
Hail to the Creator, Savior, Sustainer,
Hail to Thee: Sword Supreme.[147]

This brief analysis of the Chaupa Singh *Rahitnāmā*, presented as representative of the genre in a mid-eighteenth-century form, thus defines associations with the Guru through people, places, and things as constituting a claim to authority and reason for reverence. Considered alongside Sainapati's text, which is thought to be from a few decades earlier, we see a concern for past and its narration, and a concern for reverence for those people, places, and things associated with the Guru, which participate in that authority. In Sainapati, it is the community that constitutes this continuing authority, this continuing presence. Importantly, this authority-through-association is not defined by the author in the *rahitnāmā* as absolute. Those descendants of the Guru whose actions are not in keeping with Sikh practice as defined by the author as normative and orthodox are defined as being outside the community, and not worthy of reverence. The category, therefore, relies upon allegiance and behavior.

Conclusions

Sainapati's *Gur Sobhā* and Chaupa Singh's *Rahitnāmā* represent the two major Sikh literary genres of the eighteenth century: *gurbilās* and *rahitnāme*. Texts of this type are fundamentally constituted by memory-making. Like the Chaupa Singh *Rahitnāmā*, the *Baṅsāvalīnāmā* of Kesar Singh Chibber of 1769 constituted a means for articulating and remembering an authorizing relationship with the Guru.[148] Similar texts include the *Mahimā Prakāsh* (1770?) of Sarup Das Bhalla, Sukha Singh's *Gurbilās Daswīn Pātshāhī* (1797), and the already discussed *Gurbilās Pātshāhī Das* by Kuir Singh, of the mid-eighteenth to early nineteenth century. Each of these "remembers" the past in different modes: Kesar Singh Chibber's text has an ambivalent view of Sikh political sovereignty, while Sarup Das Bhalla's work takes Sikh political ascendancy as a given and clearly seeks to justify the authority and status of the Bhalla family in the eyes of the new rulers, and the Khalsa in general.[149] According to Surjit Hans, Sukha Singh's text bears

---

147. *Guru Gobind Singh Marg: The Great Pilgrimage (Mahan Yatra)*. Publication information unavailable.

148. On the relationship of the Chibber family with the Gurus and how this influences Chibber perspectives, see Dhavan, *When Sparrows Become Hawks*, 155.

149. For overview, see Hans, *Reconstruction of Sikh History*, 281–87.

the mark of Udasi influence—the Udasis were followers of Guru Nanak's son Sri Chand, who followed an ascetic path, and Udasi interpretations often displayed Vedantic sensibilities. The text proceeds with a puranic, cosmological under-standing of the historical import of Guru Gobind Singh's work in the world; we have seen, however, that puranic content is typical of the texts of the eighteenth century.[150] Dhavan argues that the diverse content of such *gurbilās* texts reflect their participation in "a mutually enobling love," a set of "complex affective ties of patronage and devotion that had begun to weave disparate groups within Panjabi society into an emotional community devoted to Guru Gobind Singh." In such a context, "the rigid modern categories of religious identity and conversion . . . cannot reconcile the fluid movement of people and ideas among multiple-faith communities with the simultaneous presence of sharp sectarian ideologies within these same communities."[151] Alternative models are required to account for the simultaneous existence of both exclusive and inclusive positions, and the com-plexity of identity in its context-sensitive articulation. Thus, overall the *gurbilās* literature became a means for such "disparate groups . . . to engage with each other," as well as with the memory of the Guru.[152] Similarly, the *rahitnāma* literature defines (among other things) modes of interaction with the past, marked in the present, organized around prescriptions regarding behavior. These prescriptions, too, changed over time, as the distinctions within the community came to be less significant than those with those outside.[153] The quest to retain the memorial con-nection to the Guru, however, was retained.

In this chapter, we have seen how the Sikh community has been produced in discursive terms in relation to the past, and examples of how memory and its forms of representation have been treated. I have argued that a particular mode of historical narration was formed in this period in the Punjabi text of *Gur Sobhā* at a moment within Sikh thought that allowed for a reimagination of the nature of history by means of locating the continuing authority of the Guru in the commu-nity, as articulated in history and as represented through connections to the Guru. Though the later history of "history" in relation to the Sikhs is defined in relation to the transition of political formations in the late Mughal period, and

---

150. Hans, *Reconstruction of Sikh History*, 250–52.

151. Dhavan, *When Sparrows Became Hawks*, 152 for discussion of "mutually enobling love," 150 for second quotation, 151 for third. On ways of thinking through the enunciation of Sikh identity with reference to other religious identities in the pre-modern period, see also Mandair, *Religion and the Specter of the West*, 236.

152. Dhavan, *When Sparrows Became Hawks*, 160.

153. Dhavan, *When Sparrows Became Hawks*, 69.

thus directly in relation to state formation, in *Gur Sobhā* the particular concern is with the disjuncture of the past, the making of a history of the Guru, and *through this* memorial process the production of the community of the Guru as the continuing presence and narration of the past. Historical events (and locations) are a means for the articulation of the Guru's splendor to shine in and through his community. Inden has argued that "[h]istory . . . has always been important for any community that tries to make itself a polity, a complex agent capable of shaping itself and its world."[154] In the Sikh case, the sovereignty of the community around the Guru (and not the sovereignty of the state) is the product of history's narrative imagination.[155]

In Sainapati, the past matters in soteriological terms and is a constituting force in the present in the formation of the community. In the *rahit*, behavior becomes a means of remembrance, and forms of memory-making occupy an important place in the text (alongside others). It is no surprise, then, that the *pañj kakkar*, when they do manifest, take their shape in the *rahit* literature, as another form of memorial technology (as argued in chapter 2). Another set of literary sources demonstrates how memory-making was tied to community-building in the human Guru period and then, in new ways, in the post-Guru period: the *hukamnāme*. This literature consists of letters written to members of the Sikh *sangat* or community, sometimes to entire localities, sometimes to individuals, sometimes to families. The *hukamnāme* evoke the formations of sovereignty—these are the orders of the Guru, to be enacted within his community. Primarily, the documents served two main purposes: to maintain connections between the Gurus and distant Sikh communities and to garner support (sometimes in the form of actions, sometimes in material forms) from these communities for the maintenance of the community as a whole, and for specific purposes (such as supplies or weapons, armed soldiers for fighting, and/or provisions for the maintenance of the *langar* or community kitchen).[156] The text of the *hukamnāme* attests to the relationship constituted by *sevā* or service between the Guru and his community. Through the *hukamnāme* most clearly, for instance, the Guru's relationship with the Bhai Rupa family was articulated and the acts of *sevā* requested and described:

154. Inden et al., eds., *Querying the Medieval*, 4.

155. James Sheehan's exploration of the ways in which sovereignty operates outside of and alongside the operation of the state and nation in Europe is suggestive of the productivity of thinking about multiple forms of sovereignty that are not directly connected (yet) to state-formation in the early modern period in South Asia. James Sheehan, "The Problem of Sovereignty in European History," *American Historical Review* 111, 1 (2006): 1–15.

156. Ganda Singh, *Hukamnāme: Guru Sahiban, Mata Sahiban, Banda Singh and Khalsa Ji de.* 1967[?] Reprint, (Patiala: Publication Board, Panjabi University, 1999), 5 ff.

Bhai Mahir Chand
You should come,
do not stay.
I am very happy with you.
We are your keeper in every way.
You are with me at the fore.[157]

Interestingly, as suggested by the *rahit* citation above, such *hukamnāme* themselves came to act as relics, and even today are collected and displayed by families, such as in Bhai Rupa and with the Dalla family. *Hukamnāme* therefore as *texts* act as a means through which the authority of the Guru was articulated through the key persons to which the letters were addressed; their content attests in a continuing way to the direct relationship between members of the Sikh community and the Guru. Their materiality allows such connectivity to be attested to and directly experienced, proof of a relationship in the past with the Guru, and a continuing relationship with the Guru in the present.

It is in the post-Guru period, in the face of the transfer of the Guru's living authority to text and community, that memorial linkages to the Guru were transformed and emphasized, to bridge the gap brought about by the end of human Guruship. The texts of the eighteenth century in different ways constitute the Sikh *panth* through history, organized around the Guru and in his memory. The concern for history satisfied particular theological and social concerns of the Sikh community in its self-identity formation around the narration of the past in relation to the intervention of the Gurus in the world in that past and the continuing presence of the Guru in the present through the relationships that form the community. The relationships that constitute the community are constructed through various means: the textual production of the past, and the markers of those connections, in material terms. In the next chapter, we turn to later texts that also produce the community through memory-making of the Guru, and the definition of the community as the subject of history. Objects and sites take their place within this larger historical imaginary, evidence of a past, producing a community in the present.

---

157. Ganda Singh, *Hukamnāme*, 126–27: no. 33. The Bhai Rupa family was mentioned in chapter 1.

4

Into the Nineteenth Century

HISTORY AND SOVEREIGNTY

WHAT IS THE continuing significance of narrating the story of the Guru in the past, in relation to a continuously unfolding present? The remembrance of the past in the eighteenth century was marked by dynamic changes: the transition from the period of the embodied Guru to that where the *granth* and *panth* form the centers of the community, and political instability in Punjab that brought chaos and violence, as well as the promise and then achievement of political power by Sikh leaders. Texts of the eighteenth century reflect such changes in diverse ways, shaping the representation of the past in relation to the community's changing form and its political and social makeup. In the nineteenth century, with the establishment of centralized Sikh powers in Punjab under both Maharaja Ranjit Singh and other *misal* leaders, representations of the past take on new forms, influenced not only by historical representation in courtly contexts but also by the historical interests of the British, as increasing contact with the British and the effort to influence East India Company opinion came to shape representation of the community and its past.

This chapter presents sections of two exemplary nineteenth-century texts from prior to the formal institution of colonial rule, and one from the British period, to suggest the transformations that occur in that century in the imagination of the past and its forms of evidence. From the mid-nineteenth century, I will examine Santokh Singh's *Srī Gur Pratāp Sūraj Granth* (hereafter, *Sūraj Granth*), with references to a source text, available in its earliest published form in English as "The Travels of Guru Tegh Bahadur and Guru Gobind Singh" (see below), and (to a lesser extent) Rattan Singh Bhangu's *Prācīn Panth Parkāsh*.[1] These texts reveal how the Guru's interaction in the world is described, how this narration of

---

1. Santokh Singh, *Srī Gur Pratāp Sūraj Granth*, ed. Vir Singh (1843; repr., Amritsar: Khalsa Samachar for Bhai Vir Singh Sahitya Sadan, 1961–65; henceforth cited as *Sūraj Granth*). Rattan Singh Bhangu, *Prācīn Panth Parkāsh*, ed. Vir Singh (1841; repr. New Delhi: Bhai Vir Singh Sahit Sadan, 1993; henceforth cited as *Panth Parkāsh*). See n. 7 on "Travels."

the Guru's life relates to the formation of the community, and how this history is found in its forms of evidence. These two can be seen to represent two poles within the Sikh cultural expressions of the period. The first, Santokh Singh's work, is one that Harjot Oberoi has connected to what he has called "Sanatan Sikhism," an older and hybrid form of Sikhism, in which distinct religious boundaries were fluid and practices multiple. The second, the work of Rattan Singh Bhangu, has been called by W. H. McLeod the "most notable of all Khalsa dissertation," thus expressing a more Khalsa-centric view of being Sikh.[2] I locate the two on a continuum, rather than in opposition. They do however reveal diverse articulations of being Sikh in the period. The third text considered here at length, Bhai Vir Singh's novel *Sundarī* from 1898, will provide entry into how the imagination of the past was rendered after the annexation of Punjab by the British and the concomitant expansion of European and British influence in the region. We focus on the broad historical vision discerned in these texts. Understanding this overall approach to the past is crucial, because it is within this broader historical imagination that the meanings of objects and sites begin to change in the colonial period.

Sikh Historiography in the Nineteenth Century

As has been discussed, Sikhs were prominent among the multiple successor powers to challenge Mughal authorities that rose in the eighteenth century. Ranjit Singh consolidated his rule over the lands to the northwest of the Satluj, particularly after the 1809 Treaty with the British, which brought British East India Company recognition of his sovereignty over Punjab. Principalities that lay on the southern side of the Satluj, the Phulkian states, remained independent of Ranjit Singh's control by accepting a British presence as a counterweight to the Maharaja's power to the west. Ranjit Singh lay claim to Kashmir and Peshawar, and consolidated his rule over areas east of the Indus. After his death in 1839, however, it took only ten years for the orchestration of the British takeover of the kingdom and its integration into British East India territory.

This period is important in literary and historiographical terms in several regards. The rule of Ranjit Singh was characterized by deep interest in Western technologies and forms of knowledge, and the rule of Sikh chiefs in general was highly influenced by interaction with the British East India Company over the

---

2. See Oberoi, *Construction*, 120ff. to see how Santokh Singh fits into Oberoi's larger argument regarding the role of religious specialists in formulating the Sanatan Sikh worldview. On Bhangu, see McLeod, *Textual Sources*, 67.

course of the first half of the nineteenth century. The Punjabi and Sikh imaginative universe was also shaped in relation to Western forms of knowledge, even before the annexation of Punjab by the East India Company in 1849. The writing of history in particular became a central means through which positions were articulated in relation to expanding British power. As Tony Ballantyne has described in some detail, "from the early 1780s, the East India Company built an increasingly dense archive of information on both Punjab itself and on Sikhism."[3] Early accounts of the Sikhs by British and other European observers, gathered through a network of news writers and runners, and reports of merchants and travelers, portrayed the Sikhs as primarily petty marauders.[4] Many of the earliest histories of region were indeed commissioned by the British agents in Delhi and Ludhiana, partially as a way of gaining intelligence about affairs in Punjab and as a way to settle property and inheritance claims in the part of Punjab under East India Company control.[5] This environment spawned both the writing of new texts and the translation of existing ones: Budh Singh's Persian account, *Risāla-e Ahwal-e Nānak Shāh*, was written at the request of his employer, the British resident Major Browne,[6] and the "The Travels of Guru Tegh Bahadur and Guru Gobind Singh" was first published as an English translation in 1876 for the colonial administration of Punjab, dedicated to the Prince of

3. Tony Ballantyne, *Between Colonialism and Diaspora: Sikh Cultural Formations in an Imperial World* (Durham, NC: Duke University Press, 2006), 39.

4. Purnima Dhavan, "Rehabilitating the Sikh 'Marauder': Changing Colonial Perspectives of Sikhs, 1765–1840," unpublished paper delivered at the Association for Asian Studies meeting, New York, March 2003, p. 2. See Ganda Singh, ed., *Early European Accounts of the Sikhs* (Calcutta: Quality Printers and Binders, 1962); Fauja Singh, ed., *Historians and Historiography of the Sikhs* (New Delhi: Oriental Publishers and Distributors, 1978).

5. Dhavan, "Reading the Texture of History and Memory," 515.

6. A translation by Major Browne is available in Ganda Singh, *Early European Accounts*. For discussion, see Ballantyne, *Between Colonialism and Diaspora*, 39ff. See the discussion of Ahmad Shah's *Tārīkh-i-Hind*, also composed for a British diplomat, in the beginning of the nineteenth century (J. S. Grewal, *From Guru Nanak to Maharaja Ranjit Singh* [Amritsar: Department of History, Guru Nanak Dev University, 1982], 107ff.) and of the *Cār Bāgh-i-Pañjāb* by Ganesh Das, written in 1849, soon after the annexation of the kingdom of Lahore to the British Empire, modeled on a medieval Persian chronicle and presented to Richard Temple, the settlement officer of Gujrat (J. S. Grewal and I. Banga, eds. and trans. *Early Nineteenth Century Panjab: From Ganesh Das's Char Bagh-i-Panjab* [Amritsar: Department of History, Guru Nanak University, 1975]; also see Grewal, *From Guru Nanak*, 116ff.). See footnote 30 in chapter 3. A history of Punjab was also composed in the Gurmukhi script for John Beames in 1859. See: Bhai Mihar Singh, *Pañjāb dā Raushan Kisā*. For more on the dynamic environment that influenced historical writing in the Sikh court and under the influence of British East India Company officials, see Dhavan, "Redemptive Pasts" (2011).

Wales.[7] Historical and contemporary accounts were written in English by British observers and also commissioned, primarily in Persian, by British power-brokers—and these Persian accounts were used as the basis for later English-language histories of the Sikhs, such as the well-known version by Joseph Cunningham.[8]

As Jeffrey Diamond shows in his work on the transition from Persian to Urdu in Punjab under the British, the British were very interested in the production of histories of Punjab and particular of the Lahore state, and enlisted the help of Persian court-writers, who produced *tārīkh* (histories) for British use.[9] As Sikh chiefs gained power, they patronized the writing of histories as well, as a "diplomatic counteroffensive to maintain their autonomy from the encroachments of Ranjit Singh and the East India Company."[10] Purnima Dhavan has described "the attempts of Sikh chiefs and intellectuals to modify the negative opinions of the Company's officials, and the selective manner and cultural filters through which the East India Company received these attempts."[11] A range of texts produced in European languages and Persian attest to this. Examples of the *gurbilās* genre, in particular, played a central role in the representation of the Sikhs to the British.[12] At the same time, authors at the time—both within court settings and outside of them—presented a version of "Sikh tradition" that was "the product of more recent historical events in Punjab," reflecting "a local response to the growing corpus of colonial documents and histories from Punjab that were quickly becoming accepted by colonial agents as the official record of rule, and also attempts by the

---

7. Attar Singh, ed. and trans., "The Travels of Guru Tegh Bahadur and Guru Gobind Singh." Translated from the original Gurmukhi (Lahore: Indian Public Opinion Press, 1876). IOL 14162.b.10. Later reprinted as: Attar Singh, ed. and trans., "The Travels of Guru Tegh Bahadur and Guru Gobind Singh" in *The Panjab Past and Present*, ed. Ganda Singh, IX, I, 17 (1975): 17–81; hereafter "Travels" (I refer here to the 1975 version. It was later published in Gurmukhi/Punjabi in its first edition in 1950 and second edition in 1968, the one available to the author: *Sāhib Srī Gurū Teg Bahādar Jī ate Sāhib Srī Gurū Gobind Singh Jī de Mālwā Desh Raṭan dī Sākhī Pothī* (Punjabi). 2nd ed. Amritsar: Khalsa Samachar, 1968).

8. For a comprehensive account of British scholarship on the Sikhs, see Ballantyne, *Between Colonialism and Diaspora*, chapter 2. See also: Dhavan, "Redemptive Pasts" (2011), 40; Dhavan, "Reading the Texture"; Joseph D. Cunningham, *A History of the Sikhs, From the Origin of the Nation to the Battles of the Sutlej* (London: J. Murray, 1849).

9. From an oral presentation of a paper at the Association for Asian Studies meeting in March 2003, New York.

10. Dhavan, "Redemptive Pasts" (2011), 40.

11. Dhavan, "Rehabilitating," 1. See also Dhavan, "Redemptive Pasts" (2011), 46.

12. Dhavan, *When Sparrows Became Hawks*, 165. See below.

more powerful Sikh chiefs to transform their territories into monarchal states."[13] This was true in Punjabi, but also in Persian. Thus texts written in Persian by *munshīs* or clerks to describe the history of the Sikh community integrated the logic and commitments of the *gurbilās* literature, as well as aspects of Persian histories—without their negative views of the Sikhs.[14] As Dhavan notes, "while the Sikh chiefs were ultimately successful in convincing the company to accept them as an elite warrior group, their new-found status within north India could only be expressed within a colonial rubric that greatly constrained and limited the political power that warrior groups had formerly exercised."[15] The writing of history therefore was crucial, but controlled, within transformed power relations under the British.

The Sri Gur Pratāp Sūraj Granth

Sainapati's *Gur Sobhā*, it has been argued, is concerned with the narration of events related to the Guru in the world, alongside doctrinal, theological, and prescriptive injunctions—these are tied modes of narration, which focus on the interaction of the Guru in the world with his devotees and the continuing life of the community in history. The period of the Guru's rest in Malwa, associated with the Damdama Takhat and the family narratives discussed in chapter 2, do not feature prominently in Sainapati's text. Malwa is mentioned, but details regarding the devotees of the Guru in the region are not provided.[16] Individuals and particular community formations are, however, mentioned in other contexts, such as in the sixth chapter, when the responses of members of the community in Delhi are described.[17] Ultimately, Sainapati's text, however, does not revolve around specific tales of devotees—interactions with devotees tend to be generalized and subsumed within the overall chronological/historical narrative.

Bhai Santokh Singh's *Srī Gur Pratāp Sūraj Granth*, however, is structured differently. In the *Sūraj Granth*, we see a reorientation of narrative/historical focus—a transition to a full explication of the Guru's community in detail and an articulation of the authority of the Guru in relation to this community, reminiscent of the

---

13. Dhavan, "Reading the Texture," 517.

14. Dhavan, "Redemptive Pasts" (2011).

15. Dhavan, "Rehabilitating, 1. See also Dhavan *When Sparrows Became Hawks*, 146–47.

16. Sainapati, *Gur Sobha*, 135.

17. Sainapati, *Gur Sobha*, 88ff.

kinds of narrations available within the *janam-sākhī*s.[18] Mythological and cosmological elements are important to the text, particularly in the sections on Guru
Nanak; the tale of the Vaishnava devotee Prahlad is incorporated in the narration
of Guru Nanak's life and travels, as are other stories.[19] Later sections of the text,
which focus on later Gurus and Guru Gobind Singh in particular, include less
mythological material, and follow a more chronologically informed trajectory. We
see, in a sense, the transition from *janam-sākhī* to *gurbilās*, within this one text.
These later sections of the text also differ from Sainapati, however, because of their
particular emphasis on the Guru's followers. The nature of the history being recalled
and represented, therefore, is different from that structured within Sainapati's text,
even when it covers similar historical ground.[20]

Before we consider how this text functions as a history of the community, a
few notes on the author. Bhai Santokh Singh was born in Samvat 1845 (1791 CE)
in the district of Amritsar, the son of Rajdevi and Bhai Deva Singh. He was
apprenticed to a Nirmala scholar of the name Giani Sant Singh, with whom he
remained for fifteen years.[21] From there he went to Burida in Ambala district,
where he began to compose poetry. According to the introduction to his works,
by Rajinder Singh of Bhasha Vibhag, Punjab, in Samvat 1880 (1826 CE) he then
went on a "tour of Punjab" for four years to learn the history of the Sikhs.[22] He
was invited by King Udday Singh of Kaithal to stay there, which he did until his
death in Samvat 1900 (1846 CE). The text under consideration, the *Sūraj Granth*,
was written in 1843 or 1844.[23] According to one of the introductions to the

---

18. Denis Matringe has noted the parallels between some writings of Bhai Vir Singh and the
*janam-sākhī*s, but these correspondences can be seen with other texts as well; see chapter 7.
(Denis Matringe, "The Re-enactment of Guru Nanak's Charisma in an Early-Twentieth-Century
Panjabi Narrative," in *Charisma and Canon: Essays on the Religious History of the Indian Subcontinent*, ed. Vasudha Dalmia et al., [New Delhi: Oxford University Press, 1996], 213).

19. Santokh Singh, *Sūraj Granth*, vol. 3, 700ff. These "mythological" elements have garnered
criticism of the text from the early twentieth century to the present.

20. Santokh Singh, *Sūraj Granth*, vol. 11 and following. The overall scope of the texts is different: Santokh Singh's text covers the history of all ten Sikh Gurus, ending after the death of
Guru Gobind Singh and the immediate actions of his wives and followers.

21. Preface to the first volume of the *Sūraj Granth*, by Rajinder Singh, Director, Bhasha Vibhag (Languages Department, Punjab), 1. Oberoi ties the prominence of Nirmala scholars in the
nineteenth century with the rise of Sanatan Sikhism (Oberoi, *Construction*, 123ff.).

22. This narrative of touring Punjab to experience and understand Sikh history is one iterated
up to the present by many; see below.

23. This was in 1843 according to Pashaura Singh, *Guru Granth Sahib*, 225; 1844 according to
W.H. McLeod, *Who is a Sikh? The Problem of Sikh Identity* (Oxford: Clarendon Press, 1989),
67 and Jeevan Singh Deol, "Non-Canonical Compositions Attributed to the Seventh and
Ninth Sikh Gurus," *Journal of the American Oriental Society* 121, 2 (2001): 197.

text,[24] Udday Singh of Kaithal was a descendant of Bhai Bhagatu—who figures prominently in Santokh Singh's text as well as in Malwa object traditions associated with Chakk Fateh Singhwala, a location that features an extensive collection of objects related to the Guru and the Guru's devotees (see figure 4.1).[25] This and the author's location may account for the strong focus on Malwa in the text, which is particularly in evidence in its fourteenth and final volume that we examine here. It should be noted that this is not a text that has been used a great deal by historians, probably due to its reputation for being "Hinduized"—somewhat unfairly, perhaps, given the prevalence of "mythological" elements within other comparable texts that are referred to more often.

We have already discussed Damdama Sahib and the Dalla family and mentioned the objects related to Bhai Rupa; these object and site traditions are all located in Malwa. The arrival of Guru Gobind Singh in this region of Punjab is related in the fourteenth volume of the *Sūraj Granth*. Several features of the Dalla story that are well known today are featured there:[26] for example, the arrogance of Dalla and his bragging about his soldiers' courage and the story of the two brave volunteers of the Guru.[27] This last section of the *Sūraj Granth* is said to be based in part upon an allegedly earlier text, "The Travels of Guru Tegh Bahadur and Guru Gobind Singh," (mentioned above; "Travels" hereafter).[28] This much smaller text consists largely of a log of the last two Gurus' travels in Malwa, noting locations they stopped at and their interactions with devotees at these places. In this we see a pattern that is replicated in the "gurdwara guides" that proliferate in the late nineteenth and early twentieth centuries (see chapter 7), as well as one that can be seen earlier in the descriptions of Guru Nanak's travels found in

---

24. The first volume is dedicated to introductory material. Several introductions are given for various published editions of the text.

25. The memorial and material traditions associated with Chakk Fateh Singhwala are discussed in Anne Murphy, "Objects, Ethics, and the Gendering of Sikh Memory," *Early Modern Women: An Interdisciplinary Journal* 4 (2009): 161–68.

26. Santokh Singh, *Sūraj Granth*, 6070–71. See also my discussion in chapter 1 on the Dalla family.

27. Santokh Singh, *Sūraj Granth*, 6075.

28. See footnote 7 above. The later Punjabi published version of "Travels" was based on Attar Singh's translation, as well as a Gurmukhi/Punjabi version of the text that was found in 1935 (see introduction in *Sākhī Pothī*). The unnamed editors of the Punjabi text estimated that the original text was written in the 1820s, and utilized the text to check against the *Sūraj Granth* for its second edition; it was said to have been used as a source text for the *Sūraj Granth*. Thanks to Mrs. Devinder Kaur, Librarian at Punjabi University, Patiala, for help in obtaining the Punjabi/Gurmukhi version of this text in June 2002. I use the English version here because it was published significantly prior to the Punjabi version.

FIGURE 4.1 Jasbir Singh, patriarch of the caretaker family at Chakk Fateh Singhwala, with the *tawā* used to make food for the Tenth Guru. Photograph by Anne Murphy. March 2002. The display context for the objects at the site has changed dramatically in the decade since this picture was taken.

the *janam-sākhī*s, what is known as his period of *udāsī*. "Travels" opens with the invocation that the Guru Tegh Bahadur had wandered on the earth for the sake of humanity and that the story of his travels "should be read by pilgrims for their guidance in this vale of tears."[29] The *sākhī*s that follow describe the travels of Guru Tegh Bahadur and Guru Gobind Singh. The story of Dalla as represented in the *Sūraj Granth* is found in a contracted form in this much shorter text, although the story of the two volunteers from the Guru's army—and the relative cowardice of the soldiers of Dalla—as described in literature at the site today is not included.[30] Other aspects of the story are included in both, including the arrival of the Guru's wives and the service that Dalla provided to the Guru.

The gifts given to the Guru by Dalla are described as follows in the *Sūraj Granth*:

> One horse, and one very expensive woolen, embroidered shawl
> and a gift of 100 silver pieces.

29. Attar Singh, ed. and trans., "Travels," 21.

30. The *sākhī*s that relate to the Dalla family are: 78, 87, 89, 91, 101, 102, 109, 112, in Attar Singh, ed. and trans., "Travels."

These he gave these to the Lord, and lowered himself before him.
He was very happy and achieved a contented state of mind. (46)
To the two Mothers, [the wives of the Guru,] he gave two sets of three gifts,
Then there was great auspiciousness upon him.
He gave 50 silver pieces then.
They all became very happy and sipped some water. (47)
Rising, the *Satgurū* [or "True Guru"] arrived at [Dalla's] own dwelling.
All the Singh followers at this time
praised Dalla in many ways.
Doing the service of the Guru he was exuberant. (48)[31]

The narration continues, presenting interactions of the Guru with other prominent
devotees in the region. Interaction between the Guru and the son of Malwa Sikh
community leader Bhai Bhagatu, Dayal Das, is described, for example, including
the latter's refusal to take initiation into the Khalsa; the eventual acceptance of
initiation by his sons is also described.[32] The Guru's time at Damdama[33] is described
in this way, through a long series of interactions with devotees, and with the
Singhs, his followers, in general. The story of his interaction with the female warrior Mai Bhāgo is provided in the midst of these narratives of local devotees: how
she followed the Guru as an ascetic, wandering about without clothing. The Guru
spoke to her, and convinced her to wear clothes.[34] Mai Bhago is famous for fighting
in the battle at Muktasar—a definitive battle in this period of conflict—and for
inspiring the Guru's hesitant followers to take up arms again.

  The narration returns to the Dalla household, and then goes on to relate the interaction of the Guru with Dayal Das' relatives at Chakk Fateh Singhwala, which
houses a collection of objects related to the Guru, as has been noted (see figure 4.1):[35]

  In the village of Chakk,
  where Ram Singh had made preparations,
  there the Guru arrived
  and brought joy to his disciples.

---

31. Santokh Singh, *Sūraj Granth*, 6079.

32. Santokh Singh, *Sūraj Granth*, 6081–84.

33. The name for the site is given in Santokh Singh, *Sūraj Granth*, Ain 1, Ansu 21, 6079; also in
Attar Singh, ed. and trans., "Travels," 56.

34. See the discussion in Anne Murphy, "Objects, Ethics, and the Gendering of Sikh Memory"
Early Modern Women: An Interdisciplinary Journal 4 (2009): 161–68.

35. See Murphy, "Objects, Ethics, and the Gendering of Sikh Memory."

Below the Peepul tree,
he was cooled in a small hut of branches.
There the Guru stopped,
left his horse and went inside.[36]

These preparations and other forms of service are still remembered in contemporary representations of the story at Chakk Fateh Singhwala, including an extensive object collection that derives from this visit. The *Sūraj Granth* version also includes a description of the meeting of the Guru with a "woman of the house," who gifted the Guru with a shawl.[37] The rivalry between the brothers in the family is resolved by the Guru, as is currently remembered as well. The son of the family (who is not named) is also remembered, for his special relationship with the Guru during this visit.[38]

The *Sūraj Granth* thus describes the interactions of Dalla and other devotees with the Guru in detail. In "Travels," too, details are provided of meetings of the Guru with disciples and gifts exchanged, including those given and received by the Guru's wives.[39] It is noted in *sākhī* 3 that the Guru halted on his way and that "the place at which he stopped is still held in great veneration."[40] This pattern is repeated throughout the text: meetings of the Guru with disciples, substantiation of relationships through gifting, and the notation of reverence accorded to places associated with the Guru. In return, the Guru presented devotees with gifts, often turbans, which in the cultural vocabulary of the day expressed a hierarchical relationship of Guru and devotee, and established and solidified a connection, as well as a differential in power, between them. This substantiates the webs of relationships being described in the text, in keeping with the practices related to hierarchy, gifting, and the cultural semantics of clothing and authority that were discussed in chapter 2.

The objects or gifts described are therefore related to general memorial and gifting traditions: within royal contexts, such as the practice of *khil'at*, the exchange of gold coins and clothing and other valuables between king and subject, and within familial ones, wherein objects related to elders are preserved and honored.[41] Although Attar Singh's translation of the "The Travels" refers directly to the *khil'at*, in the Punjabi version of this text the term used is *sirepao* or "From

---

36. Santokh Singh, *Sūraj Granth*, 6087–88.

37. Santokh Singh, *Sūraj Granth*, 6089.

38. Santokh Singh, *Sūraj Granth*, 6090.

39. For example, Attar Singh, ed. and trans., "Travels," 22–23, 57.

40. Attar Singh, ed. and trans., "Travels," 23.

41. On *khil'at*, see Cohn *Colonialism*, 114ff. On clothes and gifting practices, see C.A. Bayly, "The Origins of Swadeshi"; Gordon, ed., *Robes and Honor*; Gordon, *Robes of Honour*. See chapter 2.

Head to Foot," otherwise known as *siropā*, and generally translated as "robe of honor"—a meaning parallel to the *khil'at*. Indeed, the mention of the set of three gifts for the wives of the Guru in the *Sūraj Granth*, referred to above, references the conventions associated with the practice of *khil'at*.[42] Here, the practice of the exchange of gifts has been explicitly mobilized to substantiate the authority of the Guru, and the "The Travels" makes the status of these objects of giving clear. After a description of the particularly dedicated service of Dalla to the Guru, and his taking of the *amrit* or initiation into the Khalsa, the author tells us:

> This so pleased the Guru, that he presented Dalla with a sword, a shield, and bangles studded with precious stones worth 2,000 rupees, together with a cloak. "These I will not wear," said Dalla, "I will only worship them."[43]

In such a passage we see the cultural vocabulary of authority and sovereignty, articulated in preliminary forms in *Gur Sobhā* and the *rahitnāmā* literature in relation to the articulation of history, fully engaged. History in the context of this text entails the representation of relationships and, further, the representation of the evidence of these relationships, substantiated through gifted clothing and weapons, which contain and pass on the authorizing function of the Guru. Such functions are inherent to the practice of *khil'at*. This sense of sovereignty is key to the Malwa region, the area under consideration, for which settlement and authority to rule are granted through the Guru. This is stated explicitly in the "Travels" in relation to the ancestor founders of Patiala state. In these sections of the text, the author makes clear that the Guru is the source of the authority of these leaders and their claim to sovereignty. The Guru asks Ram and Tiloka Singh to ask for a boon in recognition of their great contribution of provisions and their performance of funeral rites for his sons. Upon hearing that they lack a home, the Guru declares, "Your feet will become well placed. Your rule will remain from seat to seat, between Delhi and Lahore. . . ."[44] A *hukamnāmā* issued to them by Guru Gobind Singh attests to this relationship; the Guru calls their home his.[45]

This kind of narration relates to broader political histories being written in the eighteenth and early nineteenth centuries and the development of political power

42. Cohn, *Colonialism*, 115. See my discussion in chapter 2.

43. Attar Singh, ed. and trans., "Travels," 69. See the reference to control of land through the blessing of the Guru in the next *sākhī*, on p. 70.

44. Attar Singh, ed. and trans., "Travels," 69–70.

45. Ganda Singh, *Hukamnāme*, 23.

in Malwa under the Phulkian states and other small settlers.[46] The foundational myths associated with these rulers functioned on multiple levels: to assert a higher social status, in some cases; to promote *birādarī* or kinship ties through a patriarchal ancestor; and also to document the relationship of families and founders to the Gurus, particularly with reference to the settlement of the region and its conversion to Sikhism.[47] Stories of the Guru are thus related to these political histories and constructions of authority, as are the physical forms of evidence of these histories and their substantiation of sovereignty—whether on a local village level or a state level as seen in the formation of the Phulkian states—through the Guru. Malwa, therefore, as a Sikh place and Malwa as a political space are in question in these sections of these texts—the relation of the history of the Guru in the region, his relationship with the structures of authority that exist in Malwa, and what substantiates that authority, in relation to the Guru. One *sākhī* from the "Travels" sums up the sense of place that is articulated in relation to the Guru: Malwa appears to the Sikhs and the Guru tells how she had been cursed by the gods. Only with the forgiveness of the Guru was the region able to thrive again.[48] Presence within place is central here, in relation to the articulation of the religious sovereignty of the Guru—and, as noted, his authority to grant sovereignty to his followers. Here we see the specificity of person and event in direct relationship to the authority vested in the Guru and what is associated with him, a form of history concerned ultimately with describing and proving this authority through the stories that constitute it and the forms of evidence—gifts that still exist in family hands, as shown—that substantiate it.

By the end of the nineteenth century, a new genre of literature developed: the "gurdwara guide," which provided a listing not only of important historical gurdwaras, but also (in many cases) lists of sacred objects associated with the Gurus. Tara Singh Narotam's *Gurū Tīrth Saṅgraih* provides an early example. These kinds of texts will be discussed at greater length in the next section, but here we may simply notice the ways in which they drew upon early antecedents such as the *Purātan Janam-sākhī*, which records the places visited (and therefore sanctified) by Guru Nanak; we can see this as the vision present in "Travels" and the *Sūraj Granth* as well, with their accounts of people, places, and objects and their relationship with the articulation of the authority of the Guru.[49] Harjot Oberoi

---

46. Dhavan, *When Sparrows Became Hawks*, chapter 5.

47. For a history of the individual families of the Phulkian states, see: Conran and Craik *Chiefs and Families of Note*, 393–98 (for Patiala); 405–10 (for Jind); and 411–14 (for Nabha).

48. Attar Singh, ed. and trans., "Travels," 64–65.

49. Mann, "Sources for the Study," 230 n. 9.

highlights the role of Narotam in articulating aspects of "Sanatan Sikh" ideology, as represented in general by Nirmala scholars like him.[50] We do not need to see the organization of religious practice around sacred sites to be "Sanatan," however: such practices can be seen as a part of a larger historiographical endeavor that sought evidence for the authority of the Guru within place, object, and lineage, utilizing the cultural vocabulary of *khil'at*, which was as concerned with secular authority—the domain of politics—as it was with religious authority, depending on context. The proliferation of formal encyclopedias, such as Bhai Kahn Singh Nabha's *Mahānkosh* and the *Nāvāṅ te Thāvāṅ dā Kosh* ("A treasury of names and places") attests to the ways in which knowledge was reformulated, drawing on earlier antecedents, in modern forms in the early twentieth century.[51]

A Theory of History

Rattan Singh Bhangu's *Prācīn Panth Parkāsh* provides an important example of the ways in which the Sikh writing of the past was formed within colonial power dynamics and in relation to a complex array of historiographical forces: European, Persianate, and Sikh/Punjabi. The text was written in 1841 (although there is some doubt about this date).[52] It has been called "perhaps the most important of all Sikh examples of the *gur-bilās* genre" by Fenech; according to McLeod the text "vigorously affirms the distinctive nature of the Khalsa identity and the claim that this was the identity which Guru Gobind Singh intended his followers to adopt."[53] The work must be understood within a complex array of intertextual relationships. Bhangu wrote in response to an account provided to the British by a non-Sikh, mentioned above; he describes the need to counter the history of Punjab of Bute Shah: "when would a Musalman praise the Sikhs?" Or it may have been "Hindus": in the edited and published version of this text, the line reads "he would not praise the Sikhs," but Fenech reveals that the early twentieth-century scholar/author Bhai Vir Singh (discussed below) generally changed references to "Hindus"

---

50. Oberoi, *Construction*, 124ff.

51. Mahitab Singh, *Nāvāṅ te Thāvāṅ dā Kosh* (Amritsar: Singh Brothers, 1991); Kahn Singh, *Mahānkosh: Encyclopedia of Sikh Literature* (New Delhi: National Book Trust, 2000). (see discussion in chapter 7).

52. Dhavan. "Reading the Texture," 516 n. 4. For discussion of the text, see McLeod, *Who is a Sikh?* 67; McLeod, ed., *Textual Sources*, 12–13; and Pashaura Singh, *Guru Granth Sahib*, 223.

53. Louis Fenech, "Martyrdom and the Execution of Guru Arjan in Early Sikh Sources," *Journal of the American Oriental Society*, 121, 1 (2001): 20–31, see p. 27; McLeod, *Textual Sources*, 67.

to "Sikhs" in his editing of it.[54] The overt Khalsa-orientation of the text and concern for legitimation of Sikh rule, identified by so many readers, thus must not be seen in isolation; they are born in relation to British interests in Punjabi and Sikh history, other historiographical and cultural interests, and the eventual decline of the Sikh state and ascendancy of the British in Punjab. Dhavan therefore argues that the text is "in part a nostalgic account of the Sikh's 'golden age' at a time when the morale of most Khalsa Sikhs was fairly low."[55] By the 1840s and before, both political power and religious social formations were shifting in Punjab, such that "these nineteenth-century texts," Dhavan writes, "were an effort to memorialize and capture those very identities and intellectual practices that were in dramatic flux" at this time.[56] By the middle of the nineteenth century, as this example shows, history had become a discursive battlefield with multiple participants.

As Dhavan notes, however, Bhangu's text was clearly written for a Punjabi-speaking Sikh audience, rather than a British one.[57] The text does retain the interests of earlier narrations of the Gurus, but with a strong emphasis on the post-Guru period, and the ascendancy of the Sikhs in Punjab in the eighteenth and early nineteenth century. In this, it differs significantly from the roughly contemporary *Sūraj Granth*. In addition, the Malwa families addressed in detail within the *Sūraj Granth* are mentioned in a much-abbreviated fashion in Bhangu's text.[58] Much more prominently featured are the stories of these families in the context of the rise of the Phulkian states—the rise of centralized Sikh political power is what

---

54. Fenech, *Martyrdom*, 189–90 n. 59. For the phrasing in the edited volume (that is, with the modification), see Bhangu, *Panth Parkāsh*, 20. On the context for the writing of the text, see Dhavan, "Reading the Texture," 519. For discussion of textual issues with this passage, see Dhavan, "Reading the Texture," 515. I reproduce this original reading by relying upon Fenech and his sources. It should be noted that we cannot identify Bhangu's use of the term "Hindu" with our modern notion of the bounded religious community, so the "problem" of its use is itself somewhat illusory. There is no evidence that it described a single religious identity in this period. The use of "Hindu" prior to the consolidation of the meaning of this term (particularly in Punjab, which was not yet under British control) does not in any way mean that Sikhism was considered religiously part of Hinduism. The term might refer to non-Turks (a term used in Bhangu's text), or have a more general sense of those in Hindustan, without referring to religious identity per se: the use of the term alone does not tell us what we would like to know regarding the status of Sikhs vis-à-vis Hindus, and to assume it does is to interpolate a reading of "Hindu" into material where this reading is not warranted. See my related discussion, Anne Murphy, "The *Gurbilās* Literature and the Idea of 'Religion'" in *The Punjab Reader*, ed. Anshu Malhotra and Farina Mir, 93–115 (New York and New Delhi: Oxford University Press, 2012).

55. Dhavan, *When Sparrows Became Hawks*, 120.

56. Dhavan, "Reading the Texture," 516.

57. Dhavan, "Reading the Texture," 521.

58. Bhangu, *Panth Parkāsh*, 70–72. Dhavan notes that this may reflect the famous rivalry between those from the Majha region with those from Malwa (Dhavan, *When Sparrows Became Hawks*, 119).

matters for this author.[59] At the same time, Bhangu's characterization of Sikh sovereignty or power emphasizes not "successful or opportunistic rebellion against the
Mughals but . . . the fulfillment of the divine mandate of their Gurus." The collective
will of the community of the Khalsa is emphasized.[60] Bhangu's critical stance towards
Alha Singh, the founder of the Patiala state, is in keeping with such an emphasis, as
not fulfilling the heroic ideals of the Khalsa as an ideal.[61] As Purnima Dhavan has
made plain, the primary concern of Bhangu's text is therefore the description of the
Khalsa community in very particular terms. He asks the "the Khalsa Sikh reader to
participate in both witnessing and rememorializing the Sikh past . . . both as a form of
spiritual practice and as a curb on the self-interest of the Khalsa warrior." He focuses
on those moments in the recent Sikh past where Sikh political contestants worked in
concert, rather than for the fulfillment of individual ambitions. His was an interest in
collective political organization.[62] While his approach overall is different from that
found in the *Sūraj Granth*, we can with this also find commonality. Like the portrayals in the *Sūraj Granth*, the *Panth Parkāsh* presents the web of connections that
contribute to ongoing authority in the Sikh community, as well as the establishment
of sovereignty. Thus here we see a reiteration of that close relationship between the
Tenth Guru and the family of Phul, the progenitor of the Phulkian states, and the
granting of land to the lineage.[63] Land therefore—as it is portrayed in these texts—is
not only the location for memory of the Guru, although that too is emphasized. It
is also that which can be granted by the Guru, promised by him. This is mobilized
by Bhangu in his history of an explanation of the right of the Sikhs to rule—it is
extended to the contention that Guru Nanak had in fact granted the right to rule to
the Mughals, who had betrayed the promise implicit in that "divine mandate" and
therefore lost the right to rule.[64]

   As noted, Rattan Singh Bhangu's text was heavily edited by Bhai Vir Singh, an
important figure in the articulation of Sikh and Khalsa identity at the beginning
of the twentieth century (and author of the text examined below). Fenech argues
that "in editing this text, it seems that Vir Singh both deleted anything he felt was
contrary to his vision of Sikhism and added passages which supplemented his Tat
Khalsa–aligned interpretation."[65] Vir Singh was, as Fenech notes and as will be

59. Bhangu, *Panth Parkāsh*, 457ff.

60. Dhavan, "Reading the Texture," 520–22, 520 for quote.

61. Dhavan, *When Sparrows Became Hawks*, 119.

62. Dhavan, "Reading the Texture," 521–22, 521 for quote.

63. Bhangu, *Panth Parkāsh*, 459.

64. Dhavan, "Reading the Texture," 520. Guru Nanak comments critically on the invasion of
the Mughal emperor Babur (Guru Granth Sahib, p. 360).

65. Fenech, *Martyrdom*, 189. "Tat Khalsa" here is used to refer to a Khalsa-centric ideology, or
to those who adhere to one. The term is also sometimes used more specifically to describe the

discussed, fundamentally concerned with the representation of Sikh pasts—utilizing "model" Sikhs from the past as a means to exhort his present-day fellow Sikhs to follow appropriate Khalsa behavior.[66] The representation of the past within Bhangu's text, therefore, was of great importance, particularly, as Dhavan notes, with its "emphasis on the primacy of the community's right to organize its own affairs"—something that resonates in the early twentieth-century efforts of the community to devise a voice for Sikh interests, as explored in Section 2.[67] Vir Singh was also involved in the editing of Santokh Singh's *Sūraj Granth*, and his comments as interspersed throughout the edited text tend to explain puranic or "non-Sikh" elements to his readers, as Fenech has also noted.[68] Vir Singh was not alone in his condemnation of the "inaccuracies, inconsistencies, and hybrid statements" of the literature of Santokh Singh.[69] We must understand this focus on Sikh identity in relation to history within the larger colonial context that shaped it—as the next part of this chapter, and the second section of this book, will explore.

The introduction to the *Sūraj Granth*, written in 1931, the year of the second printing of the text, demonstrates a well-developed and thoroughly articulated philosophy of history, framed within references to Christian and Hegelian ideas regarding the role of history in the development of civilization. In this, we see the fulfillment of a process visible in its incipient form in the nineteenth century. According to the author of one of these introductions (who is unnamed), the basis of Sikh faith is godly wisdom, or *daivī giān*. The Ten Gurus appeared on earth to provide the word and order (*bāṇī te hukam*) of God, and this provides the basis of Sikh faith (*is par sikkhī īmān dī nīṅh hai*). Sikh faith does not in any way depend on historical events[70]—yet, history is important, since it describes the Gurus' actions in the world; it achieves a status below the *bāṇī* (word) and *hukam* (order) of the Guru.[71] This position

---

approach to the Sikh tradition espoused by members of the Singh Sabha movement, as it is in this instance. As this range of usage indicates, there is much ambiguity in the term, however, so it is not one I rely upon analytically.

66. This was part of a larger movement, among Sikhs and others in Punjab, as well as across the country; see the discussion of Bhai Vir Singh below.

67. Dhavan, "Reading the Texture," 527.

68. Fenech, *Martyrdom*, 172 n. 44. The *Sūraj Granth* was also a source for several texts by Vir Singh that compiled information on the Gurus, including the *Gurū Niraṅkārī Cāmatkār*.

69. From a letter from Harnam Singh of Rawalpindi (*Khālsā Advocate* Vol. 18, No. 24 (1920), 2.) Harnam Singh was also concerned with the negative portrayal of Majha Sikhs in *Panth Parkāsh*.

70. Santokh Singh, *Sūraj Granth*, 27, 34.

71. Santokh Singh, *Sūraj Granth*, 34–35.

reflects a set of polemics around history and its relationship with religion informed by much broader sources in North India, and well established in Europe—and, as has been noted, retains a remarkable resilience in the representation of South Asian religions even today.[72] Similarly, in the introduction to his edited version of Sainapati's text, Ganda Singh claims that Sainapati's text is "history," and in fact the first history of the Guru ever written.[73] At the same time, Singh distinguishes between Islamic/Christian senses of historicity and religion, and those "in Hindustan." He argues that a religion based on a single birth, such as Christianity and Islam, is uniquely concerned with the historical, since it is only in one's single life that one can make one's mark—and it is on the basis of this single life that one is judged.[74] It is in memory of this single life that memorials—both written and physical—are created.[75] Singh in this way replicates Western colonial conceptions of the Hindu worldview: that those who believe in multiple lives do not value the events of the world, and that Hinduism is concerned primarily with the world as illusion.[76] In fact, Singh goes on to argue, Hindustanis (and of these, particularly Hindus) have refused the influence of Muslim and Christian historiography, even up to the present. Colonial formulations here resonate.

The representation of the Sikh past has been transformed within colonial and postcolonial contexts and has also taken various textual and material forms prior to the colonial intervention—forms that were not any less constructed out of the political and social concerns of their day, as this and the previous chapter demonstrate. As such, these forms of representation reveal much about the discursive construction of the Sikh community and individual subjects in different historical contexts. The history so constructed narrates a Sikh claim to the sovereignty of the Guru in constituting his community, and the relationships that comprise that community. A history of the community is thus written, manifest in the evidence that was itself born of the relationships that constitute the narrative. Texts like Sainapati's and Santokh Singh's, therefore, acted in a fashion parallel to that identified by William Pinch for the *Bhaktamāl*, an early sixteenth-century hagiography about *bhaktī* saints—to define the parameters of the religious community,

72. Santokh Singh, *Sūraj Granth*, 32ff. On the influence of Hegel in the evolving self-understanding of the Sikh tradition, see Mandair, *Religion and the Specter of the West*.

73. He cites Sainapati's position as a witness to the events he describes as justification for this (Sainapati, *Gur Sobha*, 102).

74. Sainapati, *Gur Sobha*, ix.

75. Sainapati, *Gur Sobha*, x.

76. Thapar, "Time as a Metaphor of History," 5ff.

who comprised it, and how authority was to be articulated in relation to it.[77] The objects that provide evidence of history interact in complex ways with literary history, as the sovereignty of Guru and community is determined and proved through both.

The "sovereignty" thus defined should not be construed to map directly to the foundation of a state; Guru Gobind Singh's ongoing negotiations with the Mughal emperor in the years before his death exemplify the ways in which his claims to authority took place within a complex set of political and social relations, with differing levels of sovereignty articulated within them. This is indicative of larger trends in the period of the waning of centralized Mughal authority. Indeed, as we have seen, Mughal sovereignty itself was determined in relation to a complex set of religious and quasi-religious practices and ideologies. In some ways, the sovereignty of the Guru reflects the complex sovereign relations within Mughal state-building itself, with its system of vassal-suzerain alliances: the Guru as quasi-sovereign within a larger Mughal system. The behavior evidenced in the court of the Guru suggests this, with evidence of recognition of the authority of the Guru from outside and that the Tenth Guru "recognized and accepted the suzerainty of the Timurid line of which Aurangzeb was most certainly a part without embracing the person of the emperor himself."[78] This should not surprise us, since Mughal power was normalized at that time; as Allison Busch has shown, by the early seventeenth century, "Mughal rule had become fully routinized, and was entirely comprehensible within the traditional Sanskritic episteme of Hindu *dharma* and kingship" in the work of the Hindi poet Keshavdas.[79] In *Gur Sobhā*, the notion of sovereignty mobilized operates over the community outside of (or alongside of) the operation of the state. The sovereignty of the Guru in the foundation and perpetuation of the community of his followers was clearly articulated within a range of practices and events: the founding of the Khalsa, the gifting strategies reflected in the objects of memory that are collected by the Guru's followers, and the historical representations of the Guru and his community that were created (and are explored here). Articulating the form and substance of that sovereignty, and the shape of the community of the sovereign, became one major concern of the precolonial Sikh use of the past.

---

77. William Pinch, "History, Devotion and the Search for Nabhadas of Galta." in *Invoking the Past: The Uses of History in South Asia*, ed. Daud Ali (New Delhi: Oxford University Press, 1999), 366–99.

78. Fenech, *Darbar of the Sikh Gurus*, 19 for first point, 212 for latter quotation.

79. Allison Busch, "Literary Responses to the Mughal Imperium: The Historical Poems of Kesavdās," *South Asia Research* 25, 1 (2005): 31–54, 47 for quotation. See also Busch, *Poetry of Kings*, 60.

End of the Century: Writing the Sikh Past Under the Raj

Historical discourse in the colonial context in Punjabi and in Sikh terms is related to a larger discourse on the past found within the colonial public sphere, and a flourishing new print environment, which saw tremendous growth in the number and accessibility of Punjabi-language texts.[80] The late nineteenth century is in particular characterized by the explosion of "tract" literature: cheaply produced literature for a newly emerging readership. Most of these texts were highly polemical in nature, responding to a competitive print environment as well as a competitive ideological one. Newspapers also flourished in the early twentieth century: of approximately 260 newspapers extant in Punjab in 1905, 17 were in Punjabi in the Gurmukhi script, while 198 were in Urdu.[81] These numbers describe the relative status of Punjabi and Urdu: Urdu was the official language of the provincial administration, and Punjabi held no formal administrative status (although it was recognized as important in the daily life of governance).[82] Yet, as Mir has shown, Punjabi flourished in this environment, outside of the direct influence of colonial governance.[83] This relative independence from colonial support (and therefore control) enabled Punjabi literary texts to retain a greater connection to precolonial interests and forms, exhibiting a form of resilience throughout the colonial period.[84] This is particularly true, perhaps, of the *qissā* literature, but it is also true in fact of the reformist tract literature, which for the most part was also similarly written in verse.

Within the tract literature, historical inquiry played a prominent role.[85] It was a time of a literal profusion of literature on history. As Tony Ballantyne has observed: "history writing became a crucial tool for community leaders who crafted epic poems, polemic pamphlets, and commentaries on 'scripture' in the

---

80. On the impact of print technology on Punjabi language and literary production, see *The Social Space of Language*, 32ff.

81. N. G. Barrier, "Vernacular Publishing and Sikh Public Life in the Punjab, 1880–1910," in *Religious Controversy in British India: Dialogues in South Asian Languages*, ed. Kenneth W. Jones (Albany: State University of New York Press, 1992), 201. On newspapers, see also Mir, *Social Space of Language*, 76ff.

82. Mir, *Social Space of Language*, 60.

83. See Mir, *Social Space of Language*, overall, but especially p. 4.

84. Mir, *The Social Space of Language*, 15 and elsewhere.

85. Barrier attributes the growth in this literature to the introduction of the printing press and the western interest in history; N. G. Barrier, *The Punjab in Nineteenth-Century Tracts: An Introduction to the Pamphlet Collections in the British Museum and India Office* (East Lansing, MI: Research Committee on the Punjab and Asian Studies Center, Michigan State University, 1969), 7.

hope that by clearly defining the community's past they would be able to cement their own vision of the community's present and future."[86] Barrier's survey of the India Office collections found that "the earlier tendency to publish scriptural tracts or standard works had given way by the 1890s to emphasis on Sikh history, religion and contemporary problems."[87] Communal publications also grew in prevalence, although as Mir has so vividly shown and even a brief examination of the India Office collections reveals, publication of literature accessible across religious boundaries—such as the *qissā* literature—continued unabated and indeed with increasing success through the early twentieth century.[88] Indeed, as will be shown in brief below but is generally true, authors of religiously-oriented tracts were sometimes also authors of *qissā* and similar texts. Thus, while Mir argues that "*qissā* poets were a heterogeneous group that cohered—conceptually, across time, space, class, caste and religion—around the *qissā* tradition" and that it is important not to overemphasize the polemical literature of reformist movements due to their rich archive of publications, it is also the case that these disparate orientations toward religious identity and difference shared the same literary space. That is, those who adhered to a more capacious sense of Punjabi culture—as expressed in the *qissā*—also did at times embrace a more religiously singular stance.[89] There is not an absolute distinction between the "Punjabi literary formation," as Mir calls this shared literary space among Punjabi speakers of a wide range of social positions, and a more communalized rhetorical sphere.[90]

The Khalsa Tract Society was particularly active in producing texts of these kinds, and was a major force in the publication of tracts related to the Singh Sabha movement of the late nineteenth and early twentieth centuries.[91] The Singh Sabha movement was the site of the articulation of multiple visions of what it meant to be Sikh in the period. Competing ideologies arose among the Amritsar and Lahore organizations, as explored at length by Harjot Oberoi, in what he identifies as a conflict between a Tat Khalsa and a "Sanatan Sikh" perspective on the

86. Ballantyne, *Between Colonialism and Diaspora*, 5.

87. Barrier, *Punjab in Nineteenth-Century Tracts*, 13.

88. Barrier, *Punjab in Nineteent-Century Tracts*, 14. Mir, *Social Space of Language.*

89. Mir, *Social Space of Language*, 89.

90. This coincides with Dhavan's observation that both narrow sectarian and expansive cosmopolitan positions are articulated by the same authors/texts in the eighteenth century (Dhavan, *When Sparrows Became Hawks*, 151); see discussion in chapter 3.

91. On other publications associated with Singh Sabha reform, see Barrier, "Vernacular Publishing," 206ff.

Sikh tradition. The latter, he argues, was open to an "enchanted universe" in which multiplicity and hybridity were the norm; the former was invested in articulating a bounded definition of being Sikh that denied commonality, in particular, with Hinduism. Thus, he argues that an "older, pluralist paradigm of Sikh faith was displaced forever by a highly uniform Sikh identity, to one we know today as modern Sikhism."[92] It would be wrong, however, to overstate this displacement. Ballantyne for example has cogently argued that the history of the migration of Punjabis in the same period, and the production of alternative visions of Sikhness in that context, cannot allow anyone to claim victory for any one way of being Sikh, as multiple identities were also articulated and acted out during this time of reform and consolidation.[93] The publications that gave voice to these definitions of being Sikh—and the effort to enforce such definitions—thus are only a part of a larger, more complicated set of transformations. Overall, there were three main preoccupations in the flowering religious tract literature of the period: managing and defining Sikh behavior, history, and gurdwara reform. Discussion of martyrdom, which came to be an important theme in the twentieth century in the movement for gurdwara reform, was also an important sub-theme.[94] What is important about the tracts of this period is the direct relationship they demonstrate between the "the ethos of reform and revival among Sikhs," in Barrier's words, and the concerns that came to the forefront among Sikhs in the 1920s regarding history, identity, and gurdwara reform.[95] The sentiments expressed in this literature thus mirror the political and religious aspirations that animated the Gurdwara Reform Movement, which will be discussed at length in following chapters.

Authors of the period generally wrote on all three subjects, interweaving these themes in their works. Giani Kartar Singh, head *granthī* at the Golden Temple, thus spoke of historical martyrdom in relation to the persecution of Sikhs in the Gurdwara Reform Movement.[96] He gave a history of the gurdwara as an institution in his introduction to the account of the Nankana Sahib incident—a major opening conflict of the Gurdwara Reform Movement.[97] He also wrote works on the history of the Sikhs in the eighteenth century, such as a three-part series called

---

92. Oberoi, *Construction*, 25.

93. Ballantyne, *Between Colonialism and Diaspora*, 166–67 and chapter 2 in general.

94. Fenech, *Martyrdom*.

95. Barrier, *Punjab in Nineteenth-Century Tracts*, 13.

96. Giani Kartar Singh Kalasvalia, *Khūnī Shahīdāṅ Arthāt Sākkā Srī Nanakāṅā Sāhib Jī* (Amritsar: Darbar Press, 1922), 2. IOL 14162.gg.39.(4).

97. Kalasvalia, *Khūnī Shahīdāṅ*, 2–4.

Jauhari Khālsā, the "Precious Jewel Khalsa." In one part of this, the *Teg Khālsā*, he describes:

> The injustice of the Turk rulers of Punjab, the grief to the Hindu people, the cruelties upon the heads of the Sikhs, the holocaust of the Sikhs, the attacks of Ahmad Shah Abdali on Punjab and India, and the situation of the flights of Zaman Shah, the great war of the Afghani emperor on the Sikhs ... the defeats of the emperors of Afghanistan and Delhi by the Sikhs, the rule of the 12 militias in Punjab, the happiness of the rule of the British, and even more different kinds of anecdotes of battles. . . .[98]

The battle for gurdwara reform and the events at Nankana Sahib are seamlessly included in this narrative. Bhai Kartar Singh's account of the Nankana Sahib incident describes the range of works he created, on a wide range of topics: "*srī dasmesh prakāsh, bābā bandā bahādur, sidak khālsā, teg khālsā, raj khālsā, akālī jot, niranjanī jot, nirankārī jot, bīr saputtr, jīvan sudhār, bābe dī ber, prahilād bhagat, vārān dharm shahīdān, ādik.*"[99] What is particularly interesting about this list is that it contains both general mythological material, such as the material on the devotee Prahlād, and specifically Sikh material, both in theological terms and more historical terms, such as the work on Guru Gobind Singh, Banda Bahadur, and the definition of the Khalsa. One of these describes martyrs for religion: *Hero Martyrs for Dharma* (*Vīr Dharam Shahīd*).

The range of works by a given author reveals how interdependent these themes were. Many authors were concerned with regulating Sikh behavior, alongside their interest in history. Some of these works self-consciously address distinctions between Hindus and Sikhs, such as those by Bhai Nahar Singh of the village of Dhalla in Ferozepur district. He deals with issues around Sikh practice in his *Kalūkāl dā Puāṛā*, "Debate of the Times," particularly with reference to women. In it, a husband exhorts his bride not to take part in certain practices: "Do not do worship at cremation grounds, funeral pyres, or graves; Do not abandon the name of Ram and follow others."[100] The husband then exclaims, *māī de khiāl nūn heṅ merī aichaḍḍīṅ, guge bhairo sītalā nūṅ ḍaṇḍe se kaḍhīṅ*, "Abandon these womanly thoughts, I will put a stick to Guga, Bhairo and Shitala."[101] Guga was commonly

---

98. Giani Kartar Singh Kalasvalia, *Tegh Khālsā* (Lahore: Ladha Singh and Sons, 1918?). IOL 14162.gg.39.

99. Kalasvalia, *Khūni Shahīdāṅ*, front cover.

100. Bhai Nahar Singh, *Kalūkāl dā Puāṛā* (Amritsar: Sri Gurmat Press, 1916), 3. IOL Panj F 391.

101. Bhai Nahar Singh, *Kalūkāl dā Puāṛā*, 3.

worshipped in villages in Punjab as a safeguard against snakebites, and Bhairo (the fearsome form of Shiva) and Shitala (the smallpox goddess) were also commonly supplicated.[102] Women are addressed again in his *Farebī Tiṅṅaṇ arthāt Desh vic Ulaṭ Cālāṅ* or "The deceitful group of spinning women, or Ways that have gone astray in the country," in which the contemporary state of life is bemoaned, including the abandonment of the spinning wheel (*charkhā*).[103] His *Dilī Muhabbatāṅ* or "Loves of the Heart" tells of the tragic events at Nankana Sahib, while his *Prem de Tīr te Dardāṅ dīāṅ Puṛīāṅ* or "The arrows of love and the wounds of pain" exhorts fellow Sikhs to act to protect and maintain their faith—including (as a part of this) for women to listen to men.[104]

Bhai Bhagat Singh also wrote of the Nankana Sahib tragedy, and about what constitutes a good wife through the mytho-historical figure of Bibi Rajni, who is said to have invoked the wrath of her father with her extreme piety, causing him to marry her to a leper, whom she served with devotion.[105] Bhai Bhagat Singh wrote three further books on very different subjects that crystallize the interests of the day: a work on a chaste woman, one on the Nankana Sahib tragedy, and a more theologically oriented work on the meanings and roles of *amrit* in Sikh thought and practice, alongside other key concepts (such as *sahij*, the experience of oneness and equanimity that is found within spiritual practice).[106] In this last work, the author bemoans the factionalism (*pakhyavādī*) that now obscures the true meaning of *amrit*, or nectar, a word that has multiple meanings, but generally stands for the purity and practice of the Khalsa.[107]

---

102. See Anne Murphy, "Texts of the Guga Tradition: Texts and Contexts." M.A. Thesis, University of Washington, 1995, and Anne Murphy, "The Uses of the 'Folk': Towards a Cultural History of the Guga Traditon," paper delivered at "Cultural Studies in the Indian Context," National Seminar at Panjab University, March 2–3, 2012. To be published in forthcoming conference proceedings.

103. Bhai Nahar Singh, *Farebī Tiṅṅaṇ arthāt Kesh vic Ulaṭ Cālāṅ* (Amritsar: Panjab Khalsa Press, n.d.). IOL Panj 1048. Marked in on the document as entering the India Office in 1929. For the spinning wheel reference, see page 2.

104. Bhai Nāhar Singh, *Prem de tīr te Dardāṅ dīāṅ Puṛīāṅ* (Amritsar: Sri Gurmat Press, 1923), 6. IOL Panj F 1049. Bhai Nahar Singh, *Dilī Muhabbatāṅ* (Amritsar: Sri Gurmat Press, n.d.). IOL Panj F 709. Date noted by hand as 1921.

105. Bhai Bhagat Singh, *Shahīdī Nankāṇā Sāhib* (Amritsar: City Press, n.d.). IOL Panj F 412 (incomplete). Bhai Bhagat Singh, *Patibratā Bībī Rajnī Jī* (Amritsar: Bharat Printing Press and Bhai Chatar Singh Jiwan Singh, n.d.). Catalog says 1923.

106. Bhai Bhagat Singh, *Sār Amritdhār* (No publication information). IOL Panj D 521. Other works by the author hail from 1921, on the Nankana tragedy (IOL Panj F 412) and 1923, on chastity (IOL Panj F 808, 923). See references in Ganesh Gaur, compiler, *India Office Library: Panjabi Printed Books 1902–1964* (London: Foreign and Commonwealth Office, 1975).

107. Bhai Bhagat Singh, *Sār Amritdhār*, 1.

Another striking example in the early twentieth century of an author with wide-ranging interests is Bhai Variam Singh.[108] He wrote extensively and prolifically to dictate and amend Sikh behavior, such as through his *Kuṛī Vecāṅ dā Hāl*, or the "Practice of selling daughters," in 1928, which sought to abolish the selling of daughters.[109] He also produced tracts in support of recruitment for the First World War, in both the Gurmukhi and Shahmukhi scripts and *Māro Jarman nūṅ Jarūr Ralke, Cakkī Vāṅg Daliā Banao Dalke*, "Come together, and certainly destroy the Germans! Having become like a mill, crush them to make flour!"[110] He wrote in fact a series of loyalist tracts throughout the late teens of the twentieth century. He also wrote more traditional *qissās*—the narrative story genre so common in the period—and poems. In light of his relatively loyalist commitments, it might seem surprising that not too many years after the works on recruitment, Variam Singh wrote on events at Guru kā Bāg—another important incident in the Gurdwara Reform Movement, which is discussed at length in chapter 6—like many other authors of his time, in a work entitled *Guru ke Bāg dā Shāṅt maī Jaṅg ate Bājāṅ vāle Guru de Akālī Sūrme*, "The peaceful battle for Guru kā Bāg and the brave Akalis of the Falconed Guru."[111] The government utilized force to disperse protesters who had gathered at the gurdwara, and Variam Singh's short account emphasizes over and over again the "peaceful" fight of the Akalis, in the face of the violence of the state.[112]

We will return in a later chapter to the portrayal of the Gurdwara Reform Movement. Our main concern here, in explicating the representation of the past in the discourse of the period, is with one exemplary and particularly important novel from the period—but we must remember its connections to this larger field of works, concerned with the past and with behavior. The author of the novel is Bhai Vir Singh (1872–1957, hereafter BVS), an extraordinary

---

108. Listed as Varyam in IOL catalog, and under the pen name Varyam Singh Kavisar: Gaur, *India Office Library*, 299–301.

109. Bhai Variam Singh, *Kuṛī Vecāṅdā Hāl* (Amritsar: Sri Gurmat Press, n.d.). IOL Panj F 1159. The text entered the India Office in 1930, and was recorded in the catalog as having been produced in 1928. See also the similar: Bhai Variam Singh, *Atha Ikk Nek Calaṇ Bībī dī Jabānoṅ Lobhī Māpiāṅ nūṅ Chaṅgī Sikkhyā* (Hissā Tīsarā) (Amritsar: Sri Gurmat Press, n.d.). IOL Panj F 1223.

110. Bhai Variam Singh, *Bharatī Nāmā* (Amritsar: Sri Gurmat Press, n.d.), 9. IOL Panj F 545 and Panj D 1176. Marked by hand as 1918, accessioned into India Office in 1922.

111. Bhai Variam Singh, *Guru ke Bāg dā Shāṅt maī Jaṅg ate Bājāṅ vāle Guru de Akālī Sūrme* (Amritsar: Gurmat Press, n.d.). IOL Panj F 799. Marked in catalog as 1923.

112. Bhai Variam Singh, *Guru ke Bāg*, 7. The hawk of the Guru was said to have appeared and inspired all, pp. 8ff.

literary and cultural figure who fundamentally shaped both theological and modern Punjabi literary traditions. He is of particular interest not only because of his stature and influence—which are both considerable—but also because of his vision of Sikhism as a religion, and as a historical process. BVS was active in and founder of the Khalsa Tract Society in 1893, which produced many tracts like those described above, and the year before that founder of the *Wazīr-e-Hind* Press and after it, the *Khālsā Samācār* (or, "Khalsa News") newspaper.[113] He is also widely regarded as a founding figure for modern Punjabi literature as a whole. In this way, he is much like Bharatendu Harishchandra of Banaras, a prominent Hindi-language author commonly regarded as a founding father of modern Hindi literature, and a major defining voice in the framing of Hindu interests in the first half of the nineteenth century. While BVS is generally seen as quintessentially modern, particularly in literary terms, like Harishchandra, because of his religious commitments, he is also perceived to be traditionalist.[114] BVS's 1905 poetic work, *Rāṇā Sūrat Singh*, for example, has been described by Sant Singh Sekhon as "largely modern in form" but "oriental" and "premodern" in spirit, with its "stress on otherworldliness."[115] In similar but perhaps more generous terms, Christopher Shackle has noted with reference to that work that the author "is able to draw naturally upon the still living traditions of the past . . . [and] recast these in the then still emerging language of the present."[116] Less generously, Sekhon and Kartar Singh Duggal note that BVS's devotion to Sikh thought and religious philosophy "submerged the thinker in him, and bound him down to what he inherited in the Sikh tradition."[117] Yet elsewhere, they say he "upheld the torch of modernism in Punjabi literature."[118] This conflation of the "modern" and "traditional" in BVS, however, is less of a contradiction than might appear. BVS's Sikhism was

---

113. A useful biography is: G. S. Khosla, *Bhai Vir Singh: An Analytical Study* (New Delhi: Heritage Publishers, 1984). See also J. S. Guleria, *Bhai Vir Singh: A Literary Portrait* (Delhi: National Book Shop, 1985.

114. Vasudha Dalmia, *The Nationalization of Hindu Traditions: Bharatendu Harischandra and Nineteenth-Century Banaras* (New Delhi: Oxford University Press, 1999), 49.

115. Sant Singh Sekhon and Kartar Singh Duggal, *A History of Punjabi Literature* (Delhi: Sahitya Akedemi, 1992), 124.

116. Christopher Shackle "A Sikh Spiritual Classic: Vīr Singh's *Rāṇā Sūrat Singh*" in *Classics of Modern South Asian Literature*, ed. Rupert Snell and I. M. P. Raeside, 183–209 (Wiesbaden: Harrassowitz, 1998), 183.

117. Sekhon and Duggal, *History of Punjabi Literature*, 110.

118. Sekhon and Duggal, *History of Punjabi Literature*, 109. For more discussion of the issue see 111–13.

very much modern, as Arvind Mandair has shown, and his vision of the Sikh past was no less so.[119]

The book under examination here, *Sundarī* (1898), was Bhai Vir Singh's first novel and is also known as the first modern Punjabi novel.[120] It was based on a song popular in northern India.[121] Though longer than most tract literature, the novel is typical in many ways of such work of the period in how it simultaneously sets up an ideal model for women, and criticizes both women and men for un-Sikh behavior. As Anshu Malhotra has vividly shown, the tract literature of the period was highly regulatory in its approach to women, seeking to set up almost-impossible ideals, and then chastising women for not fulfilling them.[122] Gurpreet Bal thus calls *Sundarī* "the culmination, objectification, and justification" of reformist Singh Sabha identity formation.[123] While this is true, it also reflects a more complicated set of influences and expressions. The novel tells the story of a young woman who is abducted by a Mughal official at the time of her *muklāvā*, the time of the commencement of married life. She is saved by her Sikh brother, and then decides to dedicate her life to the Sikh way. Her life and its trials—and her dedication to the Sikh path—constitute the central thematic of the novel. It is fiction, but through it, BVS also tells a history. Or rather histories—there are multiple historical imaginaries at work in the novel: the history of the Khalsa, of the nation, of the people or *parjā*. The work has been criticized for just this characteristic: its simultaneously historical and fictional nature.[124] In this thinking, the novel fails on both counts: it does not make good history, nor good literature. However, we may view the novel as exemplary of a particular moment in the

---

119. On the impact of BVS on the development of Sikh theology as a modern discourse, see Arvind-pal Singh Mandair "The Emergence of Modern 'Sikh Theology': Reassessing the Passage of Ideas from Trumpp to Bhai Vir Singh," *Bulletin of the School of Oriental and African Studies* 68, 2 (2005): 253–75.

120. The edition utilized here is Bhai Vir Singh, *Sundarī* (New Delhi: Bhai Vir Singh Sahit Sadan, 2003). Hereafter cited as BVS. All translations are mine.

121. Khosla, *Bhai Vir Singh*, 30.

122. See Anshu Malhotra, *Gender, Caste, and Religious Identities: Restructuring Class in Colonial Punjab* (New Delhi: Oxford University Press, 2002), chapter 4 (116–63).

123. Gurpreet Bal, "Construction of Gender and Religious Identities in the First Punjabi Novel, *Sundarī*," *Economic and Political Weekly*, August 12, 2006, 3528–3534, for quotation, 3533.

124. Nikky Guninder Kaur Singh, *The Feminine Principle in the Sikh Vision of the Transcendent* (Cambridge: Cambridge University Press, 1993), 203. Harcharan Singh Sobti has blamed the ills of the novel on its being targeted toward female readers; as such, the book fails as an art form but does "preech effectively." Harcharan Singh Sobti, *Studies in Panjabi Fiction* (Delhi: Eastern Book Linkers, 1987), 2.

production of historical imagination in Punjab and in relation to Sikh tradition through an understanding of the very important results of this "failure."

In considering a parallel case just decades before *Sundarī* was published, Sudipta Kaviraj has noted of Bengali historians of the colonial period that "[i]f judged in rationalistic terms, their efforts often fell far short of the European ideal of constructing a *reliable* account of the people's past; in some other ways, in giving an *imaginative* unity to it, it went far beyond."[125] BVS's *Sundarī* makes a similar fractured achievement, forged within the power differentials of the British Raj. *Sundarī*, then, is an imaginary history; and it is in this form that it stands alongside the other works in BVS's oeuvre: works of textual criticism, poetry, and (importantly for our purposes here) historical inquiry. He was not concerned only with the novel, nor only with history. Again, parallels can be made with Bengali writers of the same period and, in colonial terms, of similar position, as highlighted by Kaviraj: those who undertake both academic and imaginative history.[126] Thus Bankimchandra Chattopadhyay's call in 1880 that "we must have a history" is echoed quickly by Bhai Vir Singh's similar statement in 1898.[127] It must also be noted that BVS is less strident in his call for historical awareness in later work, such as *Satwant Kaur*—which is far more concerned with defining Sikh belief and practice—but does continue to locate his central stories in the eighteenth century.[128] This call to history is very particular to the late nineteenth century.

Imaginative history is achieved in *Sundarī* in multiple ways. BVS enters into extensive and imaginative descriptions of how Sikhs lived, setting the scene vividly. This is part history, part novel: an imaginary history. The author at times also speaks directly to the reader: *ithe asīṅ bhīṛī jūh de ik samāgam dā varṇan karde hāṅ*, "Here we will describe the gathering in a forest" (BVS 9), violating stylistic conventions of the novel. Nikky-Guninder Singh Kaur notes that these moments of transgression in the novelistic form and the third-person conventions associated with it have been viewed as examples of the weakness of the novel.[129] This form of

---

125. Sudipta Kaviraj, *The Unhappy Consciousness: Bankimchandra Chattopadhyay and the Formation of Nationalist Discourse in India* (New Delhi: Oxford University Press, 1998), 108.

126. Kaviraj, *Unhappy Consciousness*, 111.

127. Partha Chatterjee, *The Nation and Its Fragments: Colonial and Postcolonial Histories* (Princeton, NJ: Princeton University Press, 1993), 76.

128. Bhai Vir Singh, *Satwant Kaur* (New Delhi: Bhai Vir Singh Sahitya Sadan, 1968 [1918]). On the eighteenth century and its importance in modern Sikh discourse, see: McLeod, *Exploring Sikhism*, chapter 5, 70–90.

129. Nikky Guninder-Kaur Singh, *Feminine Principle*, 203.

speech, however, can also be seen in a different light, reminiscent of Bengali narrators of the period. As Chatterjee notes: "Looking at the pages of some of the most popular novels in Bengali it is often difficult to tell whether one is reading a novel or a play. Having created a modern prose language in the fashion of the approved modular forms, the literati, in its search for artistic truthfulness, apparently found it necessary to escape as often as possible the rigidities of that prose."[130] From this perspective, Partha Chatterjee suggests, such articulations might be seen as important moments in the construction of this text as an imaginary history in the terms set out by Kaviraj, where we become conscious of the writer as the creator of this imaginary history, his intervention in the imaginative creation of the past. The historical basis of his story is of great importance—*itahāsāṅ toṅ patā lagdā hai ki . . .*, "We know from history that. . . ." (BVS 82)—and BVS intervenes as the recipient and deliverer of historical knowledge. His intimacy with the past, and its direct physical effect, is brought into the novel. Indeed, the telling of the story of the past creates a personal, physical response, in dramatic terms:

> *tavārīkh te purāṇe granthāṅ nūṅ paṛhke sarīr kaṁb uṭhdā hai. jo jo kahir us sameṅ khālse ne bahādarī nāl sahāre lekhṇī likh nahīṅ sakdī, akkhāṅ paṛh nahīṅ sakdīāṅ, kaṅn suṇ nahīṅ sakde.*

> Reading histories and old texts, the body begins to shake. Those trials that the Khalsa had to endure with bravery in those days, the pen cannot write, the eyes cannot read, the ears cannot hear. (BVS 55)

The past here is directly, physically, and dramatically experienced.

BVS is clear about the task before him: he tells the reader directly: *he sikh dharam de sajjaṇo! is pavitr sameṅ nūṅ yād karke ik verī tāṅ do pavitr haṅjhū ḍeg diu,* "Oh Good Sikh men of Dharma! Remembering this holy time, one time let two holy tears fall!" (BVS 22). The purpose of this history is to delineate a Satijug, a holy time, the kind of holiness that the Gurus themselves had taught and that Sikhs must now remember, mourn the loss of, and emulate. The violence and suffering of the past shape the present. Indeed, this is why the Sikh community must remember the sufferings of the community, but—BVS argues—haven't sufficiently to date:

> *kaī itihāskārāṅ dī rāi hai ki aṭṭh ku hazār de lag pag khālsā es jaṅg vic shahīd hoiā. koī is saṅkhyā nūṅ das bārāṅ hazār tīk dassde han, par ratan siṅgh jī likhde han ki koi cālī, koī paṅjāh hazār dassdā hai, giṇtī dā ṭhīk patā nahīṅ.*

---

130. Chatterjee, *Nation*, 8.

par ināṅ bahādarāṅ dī yādgār sikkhī ne vī kāim nahīṅ kītī. jagat dīāṅ hor kaumāṅ ne āpṇe vaḍḍiāṅ de rāī jinne upakār bī merū karke manne te yadgārāṅ baṇāiāṅ, par dhaṅn dhaṅn sikkh jinnhāṅ ne parbatāṅ jiḍḍe upakār cete bī nahīṅ rakkhe, sagoṅ āpṇā itihās bī nahīṅ saṁbhāliā. (BVS 73)

A few historians are of the opinion that approximately eight thousand Khalsa members were martyred in this battle. Some might say that this number would go up to ten or twelve thousand, but Rattan Singh writes that some say forty or fifty thousand; the number is not well known. But no memorial to these brave ones has been established by the Sikhs. The other races of the world have made whatever they perceive of their beneficence into Mount Meru, and made memorials of them, but praise to the Sikhs, who have paid no mind to [their own] mountain-like selfless service and have paid no mind to their own history.

This is a cry for history, indeed. Such history writing was effective on multiple levels, as Partha Chatterjee has pointed out: "in this mode of recalling the past, the power to represent oneself is nothing other than political power itself."[131] As was the case for Bankimchandra Chattopadhyay, this reclamation of history is worked out in the pre-British past. Bankimchandra and other historians of Bengal made a clear equivalence between British and Muslim rule, defining the identity of rulers in relation to their right to rule. There are some clear commonalities between this and BVS's understanding of the Sikh past. But while BVS also locates his exploration of political and personal ideals in the pre-British past, in relation to Muslim rulers, the articulation of his history, I believe, is also somewhat different.

This brings us to the specifics of this novel. Historical references come to dominate the novel at points—as seen above, BVS extensively refers to the work of Rattan Singh Bhangu and in the later chapters of the book, there are direct quotations from his work. BVS utilizes *Panth Parkāsh* as an authoritative text, within his own colonial historical imaginary, where the past must provide the Sikhs of the present with a way of being.[132] His use of Bhangu becomes particularly dramatic in the latter half of the novel, such as in the twelfth chapter—in the description of the *choṭa ghallūghāra*, the small holocaust perpetrated by Lakhpat Rai—when historical background dominates so much that the author has to

---

131. Chatterjee, *Nation*, 76. Chatterjee refers to Chattopadhyay's cry for history here.

132. BVS also quotes from the Guru Granth Sahib, or Sikh scripture, but less extensively. See BVS 59.

reintroduce with a somewhat heavy hand the original thread of the story about the young woman, Sundari (BVS 57).[133]

The author becomes clearer about the uses of the past as the novel progresses, within the thirteenth chapter, where further forms of violence and humiliation are described, and Sikhs are subjected to depredation and persecution while fleeing their opponents in the forests and hills. BVS utilizes these moments of violence as a counterpoint to the dignity and honor of the Singhs, the members of the Khalsa who fight for justice throughout. As such, he portrays the utopia of the past and demonstrates what community is, and how good government is constituted, for the present:

> is vele jo vicārāṅ ar dalīlāṅ te dānāī dī bahis hoī us dī upamā nahīṅ ho sakdī. nitt dīāṅ loṛāṅ te dukhāṅ ne jo akal us vele sikkhāṅ nūṅ sikhāī sī te jo jān unhāṅ vic gur ādarsh ne bharī sī, us dā hulsāu unhāṅ nūṅ sakke vīr baṇā ke amalī, akalāṅ sikhāldā sī. (BVS 61)

> There is no possible comparison to the wise discussion, thoughts, and arguments at this time. The joy found in the wisdom gained from the lessons learned in their daily trials and the model of the Guru made all the Sikhs true brothers, and taught them proper conduct and knowledge.

The multiple references to good government constitute one of the most important ways this novel relates to a broader literature. The notion of *parjā* or "the people" and the right to govern is explicitly identified, and is part of a larger South Asian colonial imaginary in which the conditions of possibility for the construction of the nation are found.[134] As is clear in the quotations above, good governance in the past operates to critique the present. This governance, as articulated through a kind of sovereignty in multiple modes in the past, is an essential aspect of the imaginary history in *Sundarī*. Indeed, in its opening pages, the narrative of good governance is quickly addressed; it takes place by page 3. This occurs when the father of the heroine of the story, Saraswati, who is renamed Sundari, goes to the *hākam* or leader of the region who has captured Sundari while out hunting.

---

133. The *choṭā ghallūghārā* took place in 1746, when a Mughal official named Lakhpat Rai exacted fierce revenge for the death of his brother at Sikh hands; the *vaḍḍā ghallūghārā* took place in 1762, with the death of many Sikhs at the hands of the forces of the Afghan Ahmad Shah Abdali, who was vying for power in Punjab.

134. The theme of the *parjā* and how the people are treated at the hands of unjust ruler is a concern of *Satwant Kaur* as well. See BVS, *Satwant Kaur*, 17. A variant spelling of this term in Punjabi is *prajā*; this is the standard spelling in Hindi. I favor the more common Punjabi spelling of the word here.

He pleads: *hākam parjā de māī bāp hunde han*, "The Hakam is the mother and father of of the people" (BVS 3). This line of attack and cajoling continues throughout: Saraswati's husband-in-waiting (since married life has not quite begun yet) begs the Hakam at his feet, *main āp dī parjā hān, parjā dī lāj rāj nūn hundī hai . . . āp merī lāj sharam rakh lao*, "I am your people, it is the duty of the ruler to maintain the honor/shame of the people. Please protect my honor" (BVS 4).

The role of the Khalsa as guarantor of rights, and sometimes as sovereign, is explored at multiple locations in the novel. Sham Singh, the leader of the Khalsa forces Sundari is with, asks members of a village Panchayat for food and asserts that *ais vele pātshāh khālsā hai*, "The Khalsa is the *pādshāh* (emperor) now." This is denied by village representative: *khālse dā kī patā hai? baddal chāiā vāng huṇe hai te huṇe gumm tusīn kall khabare kithe hovoge*, "What do we know of the Khalsa? Like clouds and shadows, now they are here and then who knows where they will be tomorrow?" (BVS 17). Sham Singh continues, asserting that the Khalsa will pay for its food, that *parjā nūn luṭṭṇā yā mārnā khālse dā kamm nahīn. pātshāhī sainā dī akkhī ghaṭṭā pāuṇā faujān nūn harā ke khazāne luṭṭ lai jāṇe sāḍā kamm hai. asīn zulam de vairī hān parjā de dushman nahīn hān*, "It is not the task of the Khalsa to kill or steal. It is our job to throw dirt in the eyes of the imperial soldiers and to loot their treasury houses. We are the opponents of tyranny, not the enemies of the people" (BVS 17). At the center of the portrayal of the Khalsa is the concept of good governance, and this also constitutes the central motif in portrayals of male Sikhs. Overall, the affective experience of being Sikh is defined by women in this novel: the experience and effect of the recitation of the sacred Word is demonstrated through Sundari. Being Sikh, as manifested in males, is envisioned as a certain kind of governance, articulated above, and a set of related behaviors, such as expressed for example in the behavior of Balwant Singh when he defends the women associated with the Nawab from harassment—this makes his sister Sundari very happy (*bharā dī ih gambhīrtā vekh ke sundarī bāg bāg ho gaī* [BVS 31]).

The vision of the novel—and the nation and people it constructs imaginatively— is at times sectarian. Crucially, at times it is not. The text speaks in multiple registers about government and religion, people and community. I would like to consider this novel in particular—unlike BVS's later more "comfortable," less transitional works—as representative of a certain moment in the production of a popular historical imaginary that draws on both preexisting Sikh historical imaginaries and, at times uncomfortably, Western and nationalist visions of the past. Like other texts of the period, there is certainly the portrayal of what might be termed, in Chattopadhyay's terms, "Muslim oppression," a feature that Chatterjee argues has contributed to how "the materials of Hindu-extremist political rhetoric current in postcolonial India were fashioned from the very birth of nationalist historiography."[135] For example, a Muslim leader is incensed that the Sikhs have been fed by local people—this occurs after the episode described above, where the Khalsa is described as being the ruler, or *pādshāh*; such behavior has an explicit relationship with sovereignty. As a result, the Muslim Sardar, as he is called, has the villagers beaten, causing the deaths of several Hindus. This is done *nā koī pucch nā gicch, nā dosh sabūt kītā*, "without asking, without proof of guilt." The husband of one woman is killed in this assault; she is then captured to be forced into remarriage. She is killed after daring to strike her captor (BVS 18). Such portrayals of the tyranny of rulers of that time—identified as Muslim—continue in the text. There are other distinctions clearly delineated. Brahmins are oppressed, forced into *vagārī naukrī* or forced labor (BVS 13). Hindus are consistently portrayed as weak: *hindū tāṅ makkhaṇ, par ih kaṭhor patthar han*, "Hindus are butter but these [Sikhs] are rock." Shopkeepers are defined as being without energy and sad (*nimāṇe, sust, udās* [BVS 11, 13]). A Hindu faints at the treatment of his wife; he is not ready to fight, or even to able to face death (BVS 26). This same person is transformed physically and mentally upon becoming a Sikh (BVS 36); the theme of conversion is one that preoccupies BVS's imagination in his other works as well.[136]

On the other hand, there are sections where BVS is careful in his portrayal of Hindus and Muslims, to distinguish between Muslims as a group of people and Muslims as rulers, and to define Muslims as being *within* the people of the nation. He notes the response of the members of the village to Saraswati's abduction: *kī hindū kī musalmān ugalāṅ ṭuk ṭuk rahi gae, 'hāi haner' 'ih anarth*' "What Hindu, what Muslim, they all bit their fingers and proclaimed, 'What injustice!', 'Such misfortune!' (BVS 5). He also describes those who have a grievance against a particular nawab, as *jis jis mazlūm hindū ne te koī garīb musalmānāṅ ne vī āpne dukh kise turak valoṅ roe*, "Whichever oppressed Hindu and whatever poor Muslim who cried after having been wronged by a Turk." Two women are portrayed as coming before the Singhs for justice: an elderly Hindu woman who calls them *rabb de ghalle hoe pātshāh*, "God-sent *padshah*" and a young Muslim woman with children, whose husband was wrongly killed by the nawab, who exclaims that *tūṅ jarvāṇiāṅ dā sir-bhaṅn jāpdā hai, kujh maiṅ dukhiārī dā bhī uparālā kar*, "You

---

135. Chatterjee, *Nation*, 94. C. Christine Fair emphasizes the ways this novel, like other novels by BVS, sets up boundaries between communities, although she notes that these boundaries are not always static: Fair, "The Novels of Bhai Vir Singh and the Imagination of Sikh Identity, Community, and Nation," in *Sikhism and Women: History, Texts and Experience*, ed. Doris R. Jakobsh, 115–33 (New Delhi: Oxford University Press, 2010), 124–25.

136. See for instance the portrayal of Fatima's conversion to Sikhism in *Satwant Kaur*, and particularly the transformation in her nature through recitation (*Satwant Kaur*, 33).

look like someone to break the heads of the tyrants, please make efforts for one as unhappy as me." (BVS 31). This evenhandedness is taken further in an interlude regarding the concept of right governance, discussed below. (BVS 32–34).

The use of the terminology of Turk and Muslim is ambiguous. Sometimes Turk is a political category, such as when the power of the Turks is defined in the region: *turkā dā zor hai . . .*, "The power of the Turks . . ." (BVS 16); and when a Sikh takes on the guise of a Mughal, it seems that Turk designates a soldier of some kind (BVS 10). At other times it is a religious label. When the conversion of Saraswati is discussed, it is noted that she will become a "Musalman" (BVS 11), but elsewhere that she will become a "Turk" (BVS 12); this is repeated in the description of the possible conversion of a female Khatri, who becomes Dharam Kaur when she joins the Khalsa (BVS 26). The ambiguity of the portrayal of identities persists. Sikhs remain outside of the binary of Hindu versus Muslim and must negotiate a place in relation to both. For example, when questioned by a Brahmin about the magnanimous treatment of the Muslim woman discussed above, whose husband had been wrongly killed by the nawab, Sham Singh defends his actions, and positions Sikh action in relation to the communities of Hindus and Muslims. "Listen O Brahmin," Sham Singh exclaims,

> *ih sāḍā ghar pakkhpātī nahīṅ hai nā sānūṅ kise nāl vair hai, hiṅdū musalmān kī sāḍe satgurāṅ nūṅ kise nāl bī vair nahīṅ sī, sārī srishṭi sānūṅ ik samān hai. asāṅ tāṅ anyāi nāsh karnā hai te pūrā tolṇā hai. is vele jo hākm zulam kar rahe han, asāṅ tāṅ uhnāṅ nūṅ sodhṇā hai, uhnāṅnūṅ sodhṇā zulam nūṅ sodhṅā hai.*

> Our home is not prejudiced, nor do we have any enmity with anyone; our Gurus had no enmity with Hindus or Muslims, either. All of creation is one to us. We have come to destroy injustice and finish with it. At this time we have come to correct those rulers who are oppressive. (BVS 33)

Sham Singh is further questioned by the Brahmin regarding this stance toward the Turks: why do the Sikhs not just make alliances with the Turks, if they have no special enmity for them? Sham Singh elaborates his position:

> *sāḍā turkāṅ nāl ki paṭhāṇāṅ nāl uhnāṅ de masalmān hoṇ piche koī vair nahīṅ te nā hī vair virodh vic paike asīṅ unhāṅ dā rāj guā rahe hāṅ, sāḍā mugalāṅ de rāj nūṅ nāsh karan dā matlab ih hai ki uh pātshāh ho ke parjā nūṅ dukh deṅde han, niāuṅ nahīṅ karde han begunāhāṅ te nirdoshiāṅ nūṅ marvā suṭde han, māmlā laiṅde han par parjā dī rākhī nahīṅ karde. dharm vic dakhal deṅde han, malo mali dharam hīn karde han. eh pāp han,*

rājā dā dharm ih nahiṅ hai, is karke asiṅ uhnāṅ de zulam de rāj dā nāsh kar rahe hāṅ. kise jāt jāṅ mat nāl sānūṅ koī vair nahiṅ. sāḍe satigur dharm phailāvan āe san, so uhnāṅ dā nāsh karde hāṅ jo adharam karde han ar akāl purakh dī parcā [should be *parjā*] *ṛūṅ* [should be *nūṅ*] *dukhāuṅde han. tusīṅ dekho ethe mutāṇe te jarvāṇe ho rahe han, nā hī inhāṅ nūṅ khauf khudā dā hai te nā hī lāhaur dillī dā koī roab rahi giā hai.*

We have no enmity with the Turks and Pathans on account of their being Muslim and do not because of this oppose their rule. The reason we destroy the rule of the Mughals is that, having become rulers, they give grief to the people, they are not just, and they cause innocent, sinless people to be killed. They take tax but they do not protect the people. They enter into matters of religion and by force cause people to lose their religions. This is sin, this is not the *dharm* of rule. Because of this we destroy their rule of cruelty. We have no enmity with any caste or way of thought. Our Gurus came to spread religion, so we destroy those people who cause *adharm* [that which is against *dharm*] and give grief to the people. Look, here, you see that this leader was cruel and violent, he had no fear of God, nor is there any power in Lahore or Delhi [to control him]. (BVS 33–34)

There are several things that are notable about this exchange. It defines good governance and the role of the Sikhs—the governance of the Sikhs is a corrective one, to restore a universally conceived form of justice. In the power vacuum of the early to mid eighteenth century caused by the decline of the formal structures of Mughal rule, and the development of successor powers within Punjab and its environs, there is no power to stay the hand of local power brokers. The Sikhs are guarantors of justice in this chaotic environment, and are not against Muslims or any other religious community in *religious* terms. Cruelty and intolerance: these features of rule inspire Sikh opposition.

It is in the formulation of the *des* or country in relation to this notion of good government that one can see strong parallels between Bhai Vir Singh and the literature of the nation as expressed in Bankimchandra Chattopadhyay. This rhetoric of the *des* in this novel does at times feature tropes of Muslim oppression and Hindu suffering, as demonstrated above—familiar tropes in the portrayal of the nation, as Partha Chatterjee has so vividly shown—but it also transcends such characterizations, and the notion of *des* seems larger: larger than religious identity, and indeed (as will be discussed), larger than the Khalsa itself. Discussion of the *des* takes several forms. It is first mentioned and discussed in the novel when the Khatri is describing the loss of his wife and property: *uh kī pāp hai jis kar ke sāḍe des ute iḍḍā kahir ho rihā hai? kiuṅ sāḍe bhā dī kaṅbakhtī ā rahī hai? . . . rikhī munī kiuṅ nahīṅ bahuṛde? he Shiv! he Vishnu! devate dukhī han, bahuṛo! . . . ih kī kahir vart giā? malechāṅ dā nāsh kiuṅ nahīṅ huṅdā? ih upaddar kiuṅ nahīṅ ṭaldā?* "What is this sin, because of which such calamity falls upon our country? Why is there such misfortune of our brothers? . . . Why do the rishis and sages not return? Oh Shiva! Oh Vishnu! The gods are unhappy, return! . . . What is this calamity? Why is there no destruction of the foreigners (*mlechās*)? Why [are we] not spared this violence?" (BVS 26–27). The exchange with Sundari makes clear that the current situation is the result of bad action, the abandoning of real service of God and the doing of false actions. Even more so, the problem is lack of unity: *bharāupane te bhāu nāl juṛe hoe ki tākat baṇ jānde han. vikolittriāṅ rahiṇā sāḍe desh dī kamzorī dā kāran hai. sāḍe āpo vic pāṭe rahiṇā ik maṅd karam hai, jis dī mazā asīṅ bhugat rahe hāṅ,* "If we join together with the spirit of brotherhood, then we will become strong. The reason for our country's weakness is our remaining separate. Our remaining torn apart amongst ourselves is a bad thing, and it is punishment for this that we now enjoy" (BVS 27).

In this context, the Khalsa may be the emperor or *pādshāh*, but the *des* is complicated in what it signifies and who rightfully rules it; the Khalsa acts as its guarantor but is not synonymous with it. At the same time, the idea of the Khalsa is larger than life, not to be contained within limited political relations.[137] The Khalsa even takes up the role of Hindu deities, replacing their agency with its own. This is clearly portrayed at several points, such as when the Khatri woman expresses her amazement at her being saved "just" in time: *jaisī rākhī dropatī dī lāj,* "Just as the shame of Draupadi was protected" (BVS 30). Thus, unlike examples from Bengali historiography of the period in which "English-educated Bengalis abandoned the criteria of divine intervention, religious value, and the norms of right conduct in judging the rise and fall of kingdoms," within the "amoral pursuit of *raison d'état*," the politics of power in BVS's *Sundarī* are imagined in non-statist terms that assert a moral order determined outside of state power.[138]

Although the past is used as a mirror for the present throughout the book, it is toward its conclusion that the process of reflection becomes direct, and this past is used directly as a form of commentary on the present. The transition is slow. At first the ideal is demonstrated. Then it is made clear what characteristics the Sikhs of Bhai Vir Singh's time did *not* possess:

---

137. Such sentiments continue to hold sway in BVS's historical novel *Satwant Kaur*, where BVS describes the Khalsa as fighting sin and tyranny (197).

138. Chatterjee, *Nation*, 90.

us vele bāṇī dā prem sī, jīvan uce san paṅthak pyār ati dā sī, khudgarjī sikhāṅ vic nahīṅ sī, paṅthak kaṁmāṅ toṅ āpā varde san. us rāt dā gurmatā koī āpo vic dī dhaṛebāzī dī kameṭī nahīṅ sī, nā nij peṭ-pālū dharam-hitaishīāṅ kukaṛā vālī laṛāī sī, nā āpṇī nijj dī dushmanī picche kise bharā dā beṛā garak karan dā mansūbā sī. nā koī fūṅ fāṅ te dikhāve dā jalsā sī.

At that time there was love of the *banī* [the word of the Gurus], life was noble, and there was real love for the *panth* [the path, the community]. There was no selfishness among the Sikhs, and they sacrificed themselves for the work of the *panth*. There was no factionalism among them within that *gurmatā* [decision of the body of Sikhs, in the name of the Guru], there was no cock-fight among the self-interests of individuals, nor any plan to drown the ship of any of the brothers out of enmity for another. Nor was there any rally to show vanities. (BVS 61)

Then there is the use of the past to comment on today:

us vele gurmatā sacce sikkhāṅ dī us dānāī de pūrniāṅ ute turan dā āhar sī, jo gurū gobind siṅgh jī āpṇe piāre puttarāṅ nūṅ sikhā gae san, ar jis nūṅ shok hai ki ajj kal de chufergaṛie sikkh bhulā rahe han. us vele de sir paṅth dī āuṇ vālī dashā dā sārā nirbhar sī. jo us vele de gurmate vic ajj kal de kaī pālisībāz, akal de maṭṭ sikkhāṅ varge siṅgh huṅde tāṅ patā nahīṅ ki sikkhāṅ dā bhavikhatt kī huṅdā? guru mahārāj jī paṅth de vālī sadā aṅg saṅg han, ar sacce siṅghāṅ de har vele sahāī han.

At that time there was zeal to act upon the ideals of the wise ones among the true Sikhs in the *gurmatā*, which Guru Gobind Singh had taught to his beloved sons, and which today's fickle Sikhs have tragically forgotten. The state of the *panth* was entirely dependant upon the *gurmatā* of that time. If there were the same kind of clever, pitchers of intellect Singhs as there are today in the *gurmatā* of that time, then who knows what the future of the Sikhs would have been. The Great Guru is always with the *panth* as its companion, and is the supporter of the true Singhs, at all times. (BVS 61)

The writing of a history is necessary—but never sufficient: *mīr maṅnūṅ de zulam ḍāḍhe kahir de san, sāre likhīe tāṅ ik pustak loṛīe . . .*, "It would require a book to write about all the terrible cruelties of Mir Mannu [an infamous governor of Punjab known for his persecution of Sikhs] . . ." (BVS 86). This interest in the past has soteriological dimensions: the main character of *Sundarī* must face her past before the Guru at her death, to make an accounting of herself as a Sikh and as a spiritual daughter of the Guru (BVS 93).

Sundarī is exemplary of a broader engagement with the past in the modern period. Such representations are meaningful in the presents that they are created to serve. What is striking about this text as a historical document is what it both shares and does not share with roughly contemporary Bengali works, such as by Bankimchandra Chattopadhyay. Whereas for these, "the idea of the singularity of national history has inevitably led to a single source of Indian tradition, namely, ancient Hindu civilization," BVS reflects a more contingent position, where the Sikhs are located among other religious communities within the *parjā* and for whom the past demonstrates political ideas that must be executed in a plural political field, suggesting a vision of history within which "the very relation between parts and the whole ... [are] open for negotiation."[139] As Chatterjee argues, "if there is any unity in these alternative histories, it is not national but confederal."[140] We see traces of this in BVS's imaginary history, reflecting the possibilities within plural Sikh imaginations of territory and its relation to the nation. In the next section, we will see the material concerns that shaped the formation of the Sikh past in the colonial period. The ideological formations we see emerging in Bhai Vir Singh are accompanied by more concrete changes that will fundamentally shape how the Sikh past comes to be imagined. In *Sundarī* we see a crossing-over point. The Khalsa operates in this text in a broad, deterritorialized mode, but we have entered a discursive field where the representation of the past is tied to the imagination of the nation in modern—and colonial— terms. This represents a move toward the marriage of the nation and history that we are familiar with from the broader history of historiography around the world. But in *Sundarī*, that move is incomplete and open.

Conclusions

The examples given in this chapter, like those examined in chapter 3, demonstrate the intimate connection between the writing of history and the narrative construction of the Sikh community. That community took different forms, as did history itself. The writing of history became a highly polemical field of activity among the British as well as among Punjabis of all kinds, in the decades leading up to and after the annexation of Punjab by the East India Company. The writing of Sikh history in particular, by the British as well as

---

139. Chatterjee, *Nation*, 113 (first quotation); 115 (second quotation).

140. Chatterjee, *Nation*, 115.

by Sikhs after the intervention of British rule, had a profound impact on the way the Sikhs were understood within the evolving conditions of the early decades of the British Raj.[141] As Barrier notes, "it is not surprising that at the same time [as producing theological treatises and initiating conversion programs] Sikhs were exhibiting fresh interest in their past and historical literature in general. Much of the theological discourse rested upon evaluation of history and documents," citing the exemplary work of Professor Gurmukh Singh (1849–98) and Bhai Kahn Singh of Nabha (1867–1938).[142] As I have shown here with the example of Bhai Vir Singh and his contemporaries, historical work accompanied multiple literary and intellectual engagements: fictional, poetic, and theological. The multiple histories that were written did not function in a vacuum. As will be shown in the next section, they were mobilized in various ways within colonial governance, making the articulation of history and the appropriation of the past a highly political project. The political as well as religious nature of the past is not new, but the ways in which this past was mobilized within the workings of colonial government represented a new role for the past in the present, and a new role for representations of that past.

Arvind Mandair has shown how the modern understanding of *gurmat* (which is often translated as "Sikh theology" but would be more rightly construed as "the teachings of the Gurus") was produced through a translation process or "language event" within which Western ideological formations were imposed on Sikh teachings. As such, even among Sikhs, the very idea of *gurmat* could only be produced within a discourse already determined within European theological and philosophical terms.[143] Ernest Trumpp's description of Sikhism, dismissed by many as biased, nevertheless effectively "managed to shift the ground of future discourse on Sikh scripture under the purview of the Western intellectual and religious tradition, and specifically into the context of current debates in theology

---

141. This has been detailed by a number of scholars. See for example: Ganda Singh, ed., *Early European Accounts* and Fauja Singh, *Historians*; on the Sikhs and their literature, see N. G. Barrier, *Sikhs and their Literature: A Guide to Tracts, Books, and Periodicals, 1849–1919* (Delhi: Manohar Book Service, 1970). Ballantyne, *Between Colonialism and Diaspora* provides important recent exploration of this terrain, showing the ways in which Sikhism as a religion was constructed within colonial discourse.

142. Barrier, *Sikhs and their Literature*, xxi.

143. Mandair, "Emergence." Arvind-pal Singh Mandair, "The Politics of Non-duality: Reassessing the Work of Transcendence in Modern Sikh Theology," *Journal of the American Academy of Religion* 74, 3 (September 2006): 646–73, see 646. See also Mandair, *Religion and the Specter of the West*, 25–26.

and philosophy."[144] The understanding of *gurmat* within the work of Bhai Vir Singh, for example, featured a preoccupation with describing the nature of God, and therefore the monotheistic status of the Sikh religion. Thus through a "process of intercultural mimesis," a particular "systematic narrative and a theological concept of God" came to dominate in *gurmat* by the 1920s, providing "a discursive regime that provided the conceptual framework within which the future discourse on modern Sikhism would be received."[145] In this way, Sikhness came to be objectified as a set of beliefs about the nature of God.

History too was changed in the late nineteenth and early twentieth centuries, as it came to serve a new set of social and political concerns. As we have seen in this exploration of the narration of the past in key Sikh texts in the mid to late nineteenth century, relationships—and their articulation within history—have been a focus of Sikh cultural and intellectual production. At the center of the Sikh historical imagination was the description of the community around the Guru, and the history of its formation. Objects and sites form a part of this historical imaginary, evidence of the past and of the relationships that constitute that past. In the Sikh case, as can be seen in the work of Rattan Singh Bhangu, Santokh Singh, and Bhai Vir Singh—as well as before, such as in Sainapati—the idea of the Sikh collectivity, the Khalsa, in relation to the representation of the past existed before the historical became tied to the national. That vision, however, took multiple forms.

The Sikh interest in history, therefore, is not a modern and colonial phenomenon. But its form and emphasis has never been static. Increasingly, this interest in history came to focus less on the affective ties of the community to the Guru. This explains the later criticism of Bhai Vir Singh's *Sundarī* as failing to produce the correct distinction between fiction and history: history is different from fiction, and history is not theology. *Sundarī* provides an important transition point. The production of the community, within *Sundarī*, is located within the production of history, here in imaginary terms—befitting the need for history in the colonial context—but not in the narration of relationships that constitute the community, as one finds in Santokh Singh. We do see a similar idealized role for the Khalsa, reminiscent of Bhangu, in Bhai Vir Singh's text, so there are strong affinities. Santokh Singh's approach to the shape of the community differs more significantly, although the ideal for the community is present in it too. In these texts, the formation of the community of Sikhs is as an ideal to be achieved; this

---

144. Mandair, "Politics of Non-duality," 260.

145. Mandair, "Politics of Non-duality," 262 for first quotation; Mandair, *Religion and the Specter of the West*, 176 for the second.

results in Bhangu's relatively critical stance towards those Sikhs who have achieved political power in his time. The Khalsa is not limited to state sovereignty; it represents a greater ideal. Perhaps there are resonances of Santokh Singh's approach even in Bhai Vir Singh; perhaps it is the drive to create an intimate history that had him to write his history as fiction, to bring to life the personal domain in his reconstruction of the Sikh past, the affective ties that constitute the community. With the development of a more *impersonal* history, outside of a history of complex relationships that constitutes the community, we see a transformation in the conceptualization of being Sikh that is parallel to what Mandair highlights.[146] This culminates, in one register, in the historiographical preoccupations of Sikh territorial discourse, as discussed in chapter 1.

The material representations of the Sikh past—objects and sites—come to operate in a new way in the colonial period. This change is not discerned primarily in discursive contexts. History is transformed in relation to the Sikh past with reference to the landscape of Punjab itself, where the territorial evidence of the Sikh past comes to be privileged. It is thus informed by material changes in the relationship of history to the landscape—located in the specific administrative mechanisms of the colonial state—that will be highlighted in the next section. Through these mechanisms, we can see the further development of the imagination of the community in relation to the nation that we see beginning to coalesce in Bhai Vir Singh's *Sundarī*, and a change in the way that objects and sites of memory are integrated into and provide proof of the history of the community.

---

146. Mandair notes that historical accounts are the main *other* response to the regime of translation produced in the colonial encounter, to produce modern Sikhism, alongside the production of Sikh theology (Mandair, *Religion and the Specter of the West*, 194).

SECTION II

Possessing the Past

5

A History of Possession

IN 1783, A Sikh leader named Baghel Singh Dhaliwal led the Karorsinghia *misal*, alongside others, into Delhi and entered the Red Fort. This is commonly remembered as a moment of Sikh supremacy, when Sikhs conquered Delhi: Jassa Singh Ahluwalia, leader of the *misal* of that lineage, is said to have sat briefly upon the Mughal peacock throne. After negotiations, Baghel Singh and his forces agreed to leave Delhi and reinstate then–Mughal Emperor Shah Alam II. The conditions of their retreat included the construction and protection of seven historical gurdwaras in Delhi associated with the Sikh Gurus, including Rakabganj, where the headless body of the Ninth Guru had been cremated, and Sis Ganj, where he was executed. As Rattan Singh Bhangu tells us:

> *srī teg bahādur deh jahiṅ hutī thī dādhī ṭhaur*
> *ḍihro chevoṅ tahiṅ racayo jhaṅḍo gaḍyo kar dhauṛ*
> *kar kaṛāh tahiṅ siṅghan bahu layāikar dīovartāi*
> *turkan ghar sogo bhayo au siṅghan man sukh pāi*
> In that place where the body of Sri Teg Bahadur was burned,
> They made the sixth doorway [gurdwara] and hoisted the flag there.
> Then they made *kaṛāh parshād* and distributed it to many.
> The Turks were grieved in their homes, and the minds of the Singhs
>   were contented.[1]

Baghel Singh is said to have remained in Delhi to oversee the construction of these sites.[2] According to the description now available at the museum at Sis Ganj, "The Sikhs proved that their desire to serve the Gurus was greater than their desire to rule over Delhi." In this narrative, the construction of gurdwaras challenges sovereign state authority and establishes a subsidiary form of sovereignty for the community—sovereignty over representations of the community's past.

---

1. Bhangu, *Panth Parkāsh*, 451.

2. See Bhagat Singh, *History of the Sikh Misals*, 276–81, and Bhangu, *Panth Parkāsh*, 447–56 For more evidence on Sis Ganj, see Mann, "Sources for the Study," 234.

The figure of Baghel Singh represents today the fight for Sikh gurdwaras in the Mughal context, a fight that has been perceived to have been fought repeatedly since then. Indeed, the Sikh prayer of Ardas, recited daily in gurdwaras and in private prayer, references Sikh shrines in Pakistan, which are remembered alongside important shrines in India (according to the translation provided by the SGPC): "O, Almighty, Protector and Helper Ever of the Panth, Restore to us the Right and Privilege of unhindered management and free service of and access to Nankana Sahib [which commemorates the birthplace of Guru Nanak] and other centres of the Sikh Religion, the Gurdwaras, out of which we have been forcibly evicted."[3] Only limited numbers of Sikhs from outside Pakistan are allowed to visit the shrine every year, making very real this sense of separation.[4] Contemporary discourse over the control of Sikh sacred historical sites, as reflected in Ardas, was formed in a movement that has also fundamentally shaped Sikh political life since the early twentieth century: the battle for reform and control over Sikh gurdwaras, known as the Akali or Gurdwara Reform Movement. This struggle was articulated as continuing an ongoing effort to protect and control the sites of the Sikh past—as Baghel Singh is said to have done—with reference to ideas about history and its relationship to the community that had also evolved in the colonial environment. We see such a sentiment beginning to take shape in Bhai Vir Singh's vision of the need for Sikh history ("We have not even cared for our own history!" *āpṇā itihās bī nahīṅ sambhāliā*).[5] It draws on the broader precolonial Sikh historical imaginary explicated in the last two chapters. It is not, therefore, new; it does, however, take a form, expression, and effect particular to the colonial context.

Gurdwaras that commemorate historical locations and events associated with the Gurus, and their past presence, are found across both Indian Punjab and Pakistani Punjab.[6] We have seen that these sites are accompanied by objects that function in a similar way, but which today occupy a less prominent place in the

---

3. This is the text and translation given on the SGPC website. (My translation would be different, but I provide the SGPC translation to demonstrate their perspective.) There are variant versions of the prayer. For English translation of the first line, see http://www.sgpc.net/ardas/ ardas_en3.asp; for the Punjabi, see http://www.sgpc.net/ardas/ardas_pb3.asp.; for the latter line, see http://www.sgpc.net/ardas/ardas_pb4.asp for the Punjabi and http://www.sgpc.net/ ardas/ardas_en4.asp for the English.

4. Indeed, one reliable indicator of the status of Indian-Pakistani relations at any given time is the ability of Sikh pilgrims to visit Sikh shrines across the border.

5. Bhai Vir Singh, *Sundarī*, 73.

6. See for example, Hari Singh, ed., *Sikh Heritage, Gurdwaras, and Memorials in Pakistan* (New Delhi: Asian Publication Services, 1994) and Iqbal Qaiser, *Historical Sikh Shrines in Pakistan* (Lahore: Punjab History Board, 1998).

Sikh memorial landscape. These sites and objects operated within a larger logic of the representation of the past in the imagination of the Sikh *panth*, as expressed in textual traditions and practices in the eighteenth and early nineteenth centuries. The past and the relationship of the community to it took varying forms with reference to the formation of community in the eighteenth and early nineteenth centuries: the sovereignty of the community in non-statist terms, and the sovereignty of the state, were both visible. As we will see here, a historical imaginary was born in the nineteenth and twentieth centuries that shaped how the past was located in historical sites in a new way. The past came to be represented in terms that expressed an intermixture of colonial and precolonial Sikh concerns, an example of the kind of confluence Ballantyne calls "points of recognition" between colonized and colonizer, where "exchanges took place within the highly uneven power relations of developing colonialism."[7]

This section details the transformation in the meaning of historical sites from the end of the precolonial period under the Lahore state into the colonial period and the major Sikh movement of the early twentieth century for gurdwara reform. The transformation of history in the colonial period was tied to a series of discursive transformations in the imagination of being Sikh; these have been examined in the past by a range of scholars.[8] This section will show that this transformation was not mainly discursive; material changes in land ownership and understandings of the representation of the past in relation to it reconfigured the Sikh experience of the landscape and the definition of the contours of the community, toward the production of a territorialized understanding of the representation of the community. Farina Mir has described the persistence in colonial-period *qissā* literature of a precolonial imagination of Punjab within which the region took form as "an imagined ensemble of natal places within a particular topography (rivers, riverbanks, forests and mountains) and religious geography (Sufi shrines and Hindu monasteries)," a different sense of territory not equivalent to the colonial administrative understanding of Punjab as a fixed geographic and governed space, but instead as a place characterized by dynamic forms of belonging and difference.[9] This is parallel to the prehistory of the imagination of place with reference to the articulation of Sikh history described in previous chapters—a landscape animated with

---

7. Ballantyne, *Between Colonialism and Diaspora*, 28–29.

8. Oberoi, *Construction of Religious Boundaries* and Mandair, *Religion and the Specter of the West* are exemplary of a large body of work that has explored how Sikh intellectual and cultural production was reshaped in the late nineteenth and early twentieth century to reconfigure the definition, and in so doing the experience, of being Sikh. See discussion below.

9. Mir, *Social Space of Language*, 134; for quotation, 137.

events associated with and relationships with the Gurus—which can be contrasted with a modern territorialized understanding of the Sikh past. Historical sites became a particularly charged arena for the articulation of Sikh positions within a range of evolving colonial realms of signification, as the "historical gurdwara" came to be fixed as property, in direct relation to polemics over who is a Sikh. "Sikhness" thus came to be constituted as a singular and unchanging category in relation to property, which provided objectivized evidence of the Sikh past, alongside the movement toward the objectification of Sikhness as a set of beliefs (rather than a history of relationships and community) identified in chapter 4. It has been shown that history and the past mattered a great deal in precolonial Sikh discourses. But in the colonial regime of meaning and power, Sikhness was wedded to history in relation to place as possession in relation to a particular politicized notion of identity. This produced a new kind of territoriality.

Objects become increasingly secondary in the property logic of the colonial period and, therefore, come to represent a different logic of the past and its possession. This is due to two major factors: first, the specifics of the rule of property established by the British, and its relationship with religious sites, and second, the connection between history and territory established under the British (drawing but also expanding on precolonial practices). Both of these culminate in the particular way the community is linked historically to territory in Gurdwara Reform Movement of the early twentieth century. Thus, the marking and territorialization of Punjab in Sikh terms became increasingly important in the colonial and postcolonial periods, representing a transformation from the imagination of place and history expressed prior to and in the early stages of the colonial intervention. The relationship of the community to property that followed entailed, in the words of Matthew Jeremy Nelson, "the inauguration of a new causal logic, a new causal mechanism,"[10] with profound effect upon the landscape of the Sikh past.

* * *

The Gurdwara Reform or Akali Movement of the 1920s brought into being the major religious and political organized body of the Sikhs in Punjab—the Shiromani Gurdwara Parbandhak Committee (SGPC)—in direct relation to the idea of a Sikh historical territory articulated through gurdwaras. Thus, while gurdwaras reflect a long precolonial history, their modern management reflects the interaction of the precolonial logic of the gurdwara with colonial and related social and

10. Matthew Jeremy Nelson, "Land, Law, and the Logic of Local Politics in the Punjab, 1849–1999," PhD diss. (Columbia University, 2002), 133.

political forces. The Akali Movement and the issues involved in it do not arise *ex nihilo*; they relate to earlier forms of management of religious sites in South Asia, and in some senses are extensions of preexisting concerns, in a new environment. In this chapter, I shall examine these preexisting concerns in some detail to highlight how the new colonial environment altered the terms of the debate. I discuss the administrative/governmental formation of religious sites in three contexts: (1) precolonial property in general, (2) the role and status of specifically religious property in the precolonial period, and (3) the British intervention and the formations of their property regime with reference to precolonial formations. I include new readings of the court records of the Lahore state under Maharaja Ranjit Singh that provide a sense of the precolonial order of religious sites at the time of annexation. The goal here is to trace the ways in which the support of gurdwaras was articulated within broader sociopolitical and cultural contexts, within numerous working idioms for the support and role of religious institutions, such that the form of the gurdwara today, and its institutionalization, can be seen as a particularly modern form of commemoration and representation of Sikh pasts—with full recognition of earlier forms of the gurdwara that also constitute the modern gurdwara imaginary. Objects, as we will see in the final chapter of this section, are increasingly peripheral to the new form this gurdwara imaginary takes.

The Question of Ownership

The debate over who controls a religious site came to be of central importance in the battle for control over gurdwaras that takes place in the 1920s, the Gurdwara Reform Movement. That Movement is the subject of this and the following chapters. To understand how this movement developed in the context of colonial rule, we turn here first to the notion of property in South Asia and its evolution from the precolonial to the colonial period, to provide a framework for further exploration of how the management of religious sites must be understood. David Ludden has shown how religious institutions in the premodern period functioned within a broader kind of agrarian territoriality that centered on the state.[11] The status and management of such religious sites therefore did not exist in a separate order from more general policies toward land management and entitlements. Revenue-free grants, dedicated to religious institutions and individuals, in Mughal and pre-Mughal terms were related to general assignments of income-producing lands,

11. David Ludden, *The New Cambridge History of India*, IV: 4, *An Agrarian History of South Asia* (Cambridge: Cambridge University Press, 1999), chapter 2.

known as *iqṭāʾ*, and after Emperor Akbar, *jagīr*. In Mughal contexts, *madad-i-maʾāsh* was the term used for revenue-free grants, meaning that the revenue from the land was not remitted to the state and was dedicated to the care of the holder.[12] In a similar way, *iqṭāʾ* represents a way in which landed property was made to support particular interests; it was instituted by the Sultanate rulers of India as a way to support commanders and other officials of the state, who then were responsible for supplying military forces for service to the state. Akbar modified this system slightly in instituting the *jagīr* system, according to which the crown assigned lands to officers for their support, but not permanently; this provision was meant to prevent recipients from gaining local power around their *jagīr*.[13] The control and exchange of land was of course intimately tied to the maintenance of sovereignty within South Asia. Rulers retained the right to negotiate treaties and to make grants and gifts of land to allies, as well as to religious institutions. There was a clearly political nature to land rights in general, as well as to religious grants, as Dirks observes in South India.[14] When lands were granted to individuals and/ or institutions, the rights to occupancy and cultivation of such lands were left intact; the recipient gained access to revenue from the land, rather than "ownership."[15] Thus, as Brian Caton has observed, the *sanad*s or documents issued to protect rights to control of land were political rather than legal documents, the former designating political rights and relationships to land, and the latter an objective relationship to land as property.[16]

---

12. Jigar Mohammed, *Revenue Free Land Grants in Mughal India: Awadh Region in the Seventeenth and Eighteenth Centuries (1658–1765)* (New Delhi: Manohar, 2002), 23; Irfan Habib, *The Agrarian System of Mughal India 1556–1707* (1963; 2nd, rev. ed., New York: Oxford University Press, 1999), 342ff. (unless otherwise mentioned, all references are to the 1999 edition). A later term used was *aʾimma*, the plural of *imām* ("religious leader"), for grantees and then for lands thus designated, in which context the term for the grantee became *aʾimma-dār* (Habib, *Agrarian System*, 342).

13. Gregory C. Kozlowski, *Muslim Endowments and Society in British India* (Cambridge: Cambridge University Press, 1985), 26. Habib, *Agrarian System* provides an extensive overview of the system of land administration under the Mughals. On *jagīr*s in particular, see 298ff.

14. Dirks, *Hollow Crown*, 7.

15. Compare Habib, *Agrarian System* and Banga, *Agrarian System*. Interestingly, Banga's 1978 study of the agrarian system of the Sikhs assumes property ownership, but given its reliance upon British records, this is not surprising.

16. See Brian Caton, "Settling for the State: Pastoralists and Colonial Rule in Southwestern Panjab, 1840–1900," PhD diss. (University of Pennsylvania, 2003), 161ff. for a discussion of the problem in relation to evolving British notions of property. Changes in the leadership of religious institutions also required confirmation of grants. Also see Goswamy and Grewal, *Mughals and the Jogis of Jakhbar*, 31. This was in keeping with Mughal administrative policies:

As Habib noted in 1963, "the search after the 'owner of the soil' in India before the British conquest has exercised the ingenuity of many modern writers,"[17] leading to the central question: was private property the "fatal gift" of the British to Punjabis and other South Asians, or not?[18] Habib and a large number of writers who have followed him have, in general, argued that the status of land changed under the British, although details on how and why have varied.[19] Political control of land as a sovereign related to the political defense of land, rather than to ownership of the land per se.[20] Mughal interests focused on the produce of the land, rather than the land itself, and rights were articulated in relation to that produce. The power of the king lay in his ability to confer rights to land, not his ownership of the land (as the British had assumed):[21] "The king's mastery of the land, far from being opposed to the . . . rights in land held by peasant cultivators, complemented, indeed made possible, those rights, for . . . entitlement to land was usually conferred by a higher agency, preferably a king."[22] The language and

---

each subsequent ruler confirmed the revenue-free grants granted by prior rulers, because these grants were fundamentally political in nature; even when Aurangzeb designated such rights as heritable, he emphasized their status as loans. Thus, the example Goswamy and Grewal present from Pindori, which indicates the sale of *madad-i-ma'āsh* property. Goswamy and Grewal, *Mughal and Sikh Rulers and the Vaishnavas of Pindori*, 35, 185–88. See Andrew J. Major, *Return to Empire: Punjab under the Sikhs and British in the Mid-Nineteenth Century* (New Delhi: Sterling Publishers, 1996), 25ff.

17. Habib, *Agrarian System*, 111 (1963 edition).

18. See Shadi Lal, MA BCL, *The Punjab Alienation of Land Act (XIII of 1900) with Exhaustive Commentary, Notifications, Circulars and Proceedings of the Legislative Council* (Lahore: Addison Press, 1905), 173 for a related discussion in the Legislative Council Debate. See also below.

19. Dirks, *Hollow Crown*; Nicholas B. Dirks, "From Little King to Landlord: Colonial Discourse and Colonial Rule," in *Colonialism and Culture*, ed. Nicholas Dirks, 175–208 (Ann Arbor: University of Michigan Press, 1992); Ranajit Guha, *A Rule of Property for Bengal: An Essay on the Idea of Permanent Settlement* (1981, repr. Durham, NC: Duke University Press, 1996); J. Mark Baker, "Colonial Influences on Property, Community, and Land Use in Kangra, Himachal Pradesh," in *Agrarian Environments: Resources, Representations, and Rule in India*, ed. Arun Agrawal and K. Sivaramakrishnan, 47–67 (Durham, NC: Duke University Press, 2000); Veena Talwar Oldenburg, *Dowry Murder: The Imperial Origins of a Cultural Crime* (Oxford: Oxford University Press, 2002); and others. For an overview of academic approaches to agrarian policies in British India, see Burton Stein, ed., *The Making of Agrarian Policy in British India, 1770–1900* (New Delhi: Oxford University Press, 1992), and particularly his introduction (1–32). See also the 1999 edition of Habib's *Agrarian System*.

20. Dirks, "From Little King to Landlord"; Oldenburg, *Dowry Murder*, 109.

21. See Habib, *Agrarian System*, 169ff. on the rights of *zamīndārs*; also Dirks, "From Little King to Landlord," 124ff. and 178ff.

22. Dirks, "From Little King to Landlord," 178–79.

rights of sovereignty pervaded endowments and the articulation of rights to land.[23] As Habib concludes in the revised edition of his 1963 study of the agrarian system of the Mughals, while the right to *zamīndārī* or holding of a share in land was indeed saleable, and therefore proprietary, and peasants had limited proprietary rights (at least where *zamīndārs* prevailed), it is difficult to say that there was an exclusive right to property in any one person. Instead, "the system contained a network of transferable rights and obligations, with different claimants (the king or his assignee; the *zamīndār*; and, finally, the peasant) to differently defined shares in the produce from the same land."[24]

As it was for Mughal land tenure, so it was in post-Mughal Punjab, where Andrew Major argues that "under Sikh rule landownership was not simply a question of abstract principles or time-honoured rights and responsibilities. It was, rather, a highly political question involving the strength and fiscal imperatives of the state on the one hand and the resilience or adaptability of the cultivating communities on the other."[25] Things changed somewhat dramatically under British rule. This shift has been described by Walter Neale as one of being from political control, with land as territory that is ruled, in the Mughal and post-Mughal view, to land as something that can be owned, in the eyes of the British. "Differences in thought" divided the Indian and English understanding of "the objectives of secular life, about how these objectives fitted together, and differences in the situations in which the Indian and the Englishman reasoned."[26] Thus, as J. M. Douie noted in his Settlement Manual on Punjab in 1915, demonstrating both British recognition of the complexity of the situation and their overstatement of the power of the king:

> Individuals exercising a permanent right . . . subject only to payment of the dues of the State have been recognized by us as "owners" or "proprietors," but it would be a mistake to assume that these words, as used in India, imply all that they do in England. . . . As long as the sovereign was entitled to a portion of the produce of all land and there was no fixed limit to that

23. Kozlowski, *Muslim Endowments*, 48.

24. The reference to *zamīndārī* saleability is from Habib, *Agrarian System*, 194; the later quotation is from 134–35. See also Walter C. Neale, "Land is to Rule" in *Land Control and Social Structure in Indian History* (Madison, Milwaukee, and London: University of Wisconsin Press, 1969), 5.

25. Major, *Return to Empire*, 24.

26. Neale, "Land is to Rule," 6. I am indebted to Caton, "Settling for the State," for the references to the two Neale essays in this chapter.

portion, practically the sovereign was so far owner of the land as to be able to exclude all other persons from enjoying any portion of new produce.[27]

Revenue payment within the post-Mughal Lahore state established by Ranjit Singh gave a person the right to control a piece of land in order to continue its productivity, so that the payment of revenue was fundamentally connected to control; failure to perform through payment would compromise one's right to land.[28] The fact that sales and mortgages could still occur and that *aspects* of ownership in the modern sense were visible only reflects the fact of the political nature of such rights: they were contingent and negotiated, as Major points out. The ensuing change engaged by the British reflected, in the words of Radha Sharma, a "British inability to free themselves of the notion of an absolute and exclusive form of proprietorship when interests in land were traditionally [in the Lahore state] multiple and inclusive."[29]

Endowments and the Logic of Granting in the Precolonial Period

Gurdwaras, like other religious sites, are provided for by the state as a type of property as *dharamarth* or "for the purpose of *dharam*." They are designated thus in relation to the state, and thus become part of a type across religious traditions.

---

27. J. M. Douie, *Punjab Settlement Manual* (1899; 3rd ed. Lahore: Government Printing, 1915), see preface to 1st ed., 1–2. Douie notes, however, that in Punjab several proprietors of the land were strong enough to be seen as holding "a real proprietary right in the soil." (Douie, *Punjab Settlement Manual*, 2).

28. Caton, "Settling for the State," 154ff. Walter C. Neale, "Property in Land as Cultural Imperialism: or, Why Ethnocentric Ideas Won't Work in India and Africa," *Journal of Economic Issues* 19, 4 (1985): 955. See Banga, *Agrarian System*, 171–72; Major, *Return to Empire*, 24–25. Banga, *Agrarian System*, contends that Sikh rulers "encouraged the actual cultivators as against the holders of superior ownership" (171); her sources in this section, however, are primarily British, which leaves room for debate, since the comments so clearly reflect the debates that ensued regarding who were the holders of ownership (the cultivators or hereditary village leaders). Major describes the Lahore state as "proto-modern," in that "its territorial sovereignty, especially along the western and southern boundaries, was frequently but a ritualistic hegemony backed up by periodic displays of naked force," encouraging relative autonomy at the peripheries and effective administrative control only at the centre (Major, *Return to Empire*, 19).

29. Radha Sharma, *Peasantry and the State: Early Nineteenth Century Punjab* (New Delhi: K.K. Publishers and Distributors, 2000), 177; elsewhere she argues that "agricultural land was heritable and alienable through sale, gift or mortgage." Sharma, "The State and Agrarian Society in the Early Nineteenth Century Punjab," in *Precolonial and Colonial Punjab, Society, Economy, Politics, and Culture: Essays for Indu Banga*, ed. Reeta Grewal and Sheena Pall (Delhi: Manohar, 2005), 143–55, see 144.

Overall, the evidence demonstrates that the intervention of the precolonial state in the support of religious institutions cannot be seen as driven by purely religious motivations, such that we can assume Muslim rulers were primarily patrons of Muslim sites, for example, because of devotional or sectarian interests. As such, a category of "religious institution" was granted and its rights conferred *across* religious traditions.[30] Such grants were also seen to be a part of state formation itself. As Irfan Habib notes, in the Mughal period "the state had its own interest in maintaining this class [of religious grantees]. . . . The grantees were . . . [the empire's] natural apologists and propagandists . . . [and] a bastion of conservatism, because they had nothing except their orthodoxy to justify their claims on the state's bounty."[31] Indeed, Jahangir defined these individuals as members of "the army of prayer," and this army contained non-Muslims alongside Muslims (a sensibility that continued under successors to the Mughals).[32] This link between the religious institution and the issue of sovereignty is therefore one of great importance; we will see a continuation of this relationship in the British period in a not identical but similar form.

There is now a large literature countering the historically unsupported and yet recently popular contention that relationships among religious communities in South Asia in the precolonial period were characterized primarily by conflict, and ample evidence to deny the related belief that religious difference prompted the wholesale destruction of religious sites by invading armies and members of other religious communities. The popular representation of this seemingly essential conflict has reached its most infamous expression in the Ram Janmabhumi discourse of the Hindu Right, which vilifies Muslim rulers (and by extension, all Muslims) as destroyers of Hindu temples in general, and a temple commemorating the

30. As observed by Fleming for an earlier period, "the 'sacred' as a category and as it is defined within the context of the Candra land-grants is both ecumenical and trans-religious." Benjamin Fleming, "Making Land Sacred: Land Grant Inscriptions in the Candra Dynasty," unpublished paper presented at the American Academy of Religion Annual Meeting (Chicago, 2008), 7. I thank the author for making his paper available to me.

31. Habib, *Agrarian System*, 355. See also Mohammed, *Revenue Free Land Grants*, 47–48. This is notably similar to the role local religious elites played under colonial rule in Punjab, as discussed at length by David Gilmartin, *Empire and Islam: Punjab and the Making of Pakistan* (Berkeley: University of California Press, 1988).

32. On the army of prayer, see Mohammed, *Revenue Free Land Grants*, 32. For the example of non-Muslim supporters of the Mughals, see B. N. Goswamy and J. S. Grewal, *The Mughals and the Jogis of Jakhbar: Some Madad-i Ma'āsh and Other Documents* (Simla: Indian Institute of Advanced Study, 1967), 36, 164. On the army of prayer for a Sikh leader, see B. N. Goswamy and J. S. Grewal, *The Mughal and Sikh Rulers and the Vaishnavas of Pindori* (Simla: Indian Institute of Advanced Study, 1968), 247–49. See also Banga, *Agrarian System*, chapter 7. Indeed, Benjamin Fleming (Making Land Sacred) notes that this is the reason for the Buddhist Bengali king's patronage of Brahmins in his kingdom.

birthplace of Ram in particular. A wealth of scholarly evidence refutes the historicity of such claims.[33] The evidence which complicates this simple opposition between religious communities vis-à-vis religious sites is directly relevant to the material in question here, for it demonstrates the historical reality of the complicated patronage of religious institutions within all forms of polity in southern Asia and how generic categories of "religious institutions" were created within such patronage systems. This specific case, therefore, adds further weight to the observations of a range of scholars that emphasize the complicated interactions between Muslim and other religious identities in the subcontinent in the precolonial period, in religious as well as secular domains.[34]

Through the form of "religious grant," Muslim rulers sometimes endowed Hindu temples and other religious establishments, such as the Jogi center at Jakhbar in Punjab documented by Goswamy and Grewal.[35] As will be discussed further, patronage of a range of religious institutions by Sikh rulers, such as Ranjit Singh, was also commonplace. As noted by Mukherjee and Habib, Mughal administration was actively engaged in the management of Hindu temples, and the Mughal court adjudicated disputes, determined management and personnel, and so on. In their words, thus, "it becomes obvious that the Mughal administration saw it as a function as well as a right to exercise power of ultimate control over the management of temples; its authority was, in any case, indispensable for the protection of any installed management against pretentious usurpers."[36] Thus, in the

---

33. See Eaton, "Temple Desecration and Indo-Muslim States"; Sarvepalli Gopal, ed. *Anatomy of a Confrontation: The Babri-Masjid-Ramjanmabhumi Issue* (New Delhi: Viking, Penguin Books India, 1991).

34. Phillip B. Wagoner, "Sultan among Hindu Kings: Dress, Titles, and the Islamicization of Hindu Culture at Vijayanagara," *Journal of Asian Studies* 55, 4 (1996): 851–80.

35. Emperor Akbar was particularly known for regulating the *madad-i-ma'āsh* grants to Muslim theologians who challenged his syncretic views, and for opening such grants up to non-Muslim religious leaders; the first known example of this was in 1565. Akbar not only confirmed existing grants but initiated them, such as for the Jogi Udant Nath in Jakhbar. Extensive support for the Jogis is in evidence over two centuries of Mughal rule in the collection of documents examined by Goswamy and Grewal, establishing a continuing commitment to the support of a major non-Muslim institution in Punjab since 1571. This occurs in religious and other terms; a document from Aurangzeb expresses interest in the then-*mahant*'s medicinal preparation. See Goswamy and Grewal, *Mughals and the Jogis of Jakhbar*, 16, for the reference to the Aurangzeb letter. The Punjabi term "*jogi*" may be more familiar to some readers as "*yogi*."

36. Tarapada Mukherjee and Irfan Habib, "The Mughal Administration and the Temples of Vrindavan During the Reigns of Jahangir and Shahjahan," *Proceedings of the Indian History Congress: Forty-Ninth Session, Karnatak University, Dharwad, 1988* (Delhi: Indian History Congress, Department of History, University of Delhi/Anamika Publications, 1989), 291. On Mughal patronage in the Braj region, see Alan Entwistle, *Braj: Centre of Krishna Pilgrimage* (Groningen: Egbert Forsten, 1987), 157–60, 173–75, 180–83.

words of Kapila Vatsyayan, "mutual dialogue and support was more the rule than the exception in the sixteenth century." This can even be said of the generally-less-tolerant Aurangzeb.[37] Similarly, the Peshwas and the Nizams of Hyderabad competed as patrons for the Sufi shrines of Aurangabad in the Deccan in the way the Mughals had competed with the sultans of the Deccan for these sites, as a means of asserting control over the region.[38]

Land grants were said to have been made to the Sikh community as well, in the early period of the tradition, when the Gurus established their centers throughout Punjab. These, however, are generally unattested in the Mughal imperial record. A land grant was supposed to have been made to Guru Amardas through his daughter Bibi Bhani in Amritsar district, but corroboration of this does not exist.[39] A land grant seems to have been made to Ramdas and his sons by Emperor Akbar, although again there is no mention of this in the records.[40] The grant, however, was accepted as factual by the British in their *Gazetteer* and land revenue administration records later in the nineteenth century, in which it was stated that the "land of Darbar Sahib was a revenue-free grant."[41] While revenue records are silent on the granting of the land of Kartarpur, which according to Sikh tradition was granted by Akbar, the elder grandson of Guru Hargobind, Dhir Mal, received a revenue-free grant in 1643 from Emperor Shah Jahan for the city and according to most writers, such as Pashaura Singh, this is seen as a "reinstatement of an earlier revenue-free grant offered to Guru Ram Das and his sons by emperor Akbar."[42] An alleged copy of an imperial

----

37. Kapila Vatsyayan, "Introduction," in *Govindadeva: A Dialogue in Stone*, ed. Margaret H. Case (New Delhi: Indira Gandhi National Centre for the Arts, 1996), 3–8, see 6. See the article in the same volume by Bahura for more on patronage in the sixteenth century. On Aurangzeb and his issuance of firmans in favor of institutions in the Braj region, see Entwistle, *Braj*, 183.

38. Nile Green, *Indian Sufism since the Seventeenth Century: Saints, Books and Empires in the Muslim Deccan* (London: Routledge, 2011), 61.

39. Pashaura Singh, *Life and Work of Guru Arjan: History, Memory, and Biography in the Sikh Tradition* (New Delhi: Oxford University Press, 2006), 18, 107. This is mentioned in the *Sūraj Granth*, p. 1684, quoted in Madanjit Kaur, *The Golden Temple: Past and Present* (Amritsar, Punjab: Department of Guru Nanak Studies, Guru Nanak Dev University Press, 1983), 4–6, but as she also notes, there is no corroboration of this in the imperial records.

40. Pashaura Singh, *Life and Work of Guru Arjan*, 81.

41. Madanjit Kaur, *Golden Temple*, 6, quotation from 7; see Appendix 1 (191–92) for the text of the land settlement records of Amritsar.

42. Pashaura Singh, *Life and Work of Guru Arjan*, 77. Goswamy and Grewal, *Mughals and the Jogis of Jakhbar*, 21 concurs. According to the latter, the Shah Jahan document is transcribed in Ganda Singh, *Makhiz-i-Tawarikh-i-Sikhan* (Amritsar, 1949), but this is not confirmed.

order regarding the grant of land to Guru Arjan by Emperor Jahangir is produced in later Gurmukhi texts.[43]

The category of "religious grant" was one that operated across religious
communities. Hindu temples were central to state formation, such that "a do-
nation to Brahmans, monasteries, monks, or temples represented an investment in agrarian territoriality."[44] There is not, however, one single monolithic
"law of endowments" in Hindu traditions, Arjun Appadurai notes, because
"the activities of Hindu kings in respect to temples were 'administrative' and
not 'legislative,' [as later British colonial control would be,] and because their
resolutions were context specific and not absorbed into a general body of
evolving case law."[45] Overall, given the central place of Punjab in the polities of
Muslim rulers established in the second millennium of the Common Era from
the time of the Ghaznavid empire in the eleventh century onward, more recently introduced Islamic legal definitions and management policies for religious and charitable sites are most significant for understanding the status of
religious sites in the Sikh context. Indeed, other than the term *dharamarth*, the
vocabulary associated with later grants of this type under Sikh rulers in the
eighteenth and nineteenth centuries was drawn mostly from Persianate tradition.
Mughal granting traditions provide the central model. As Goswamy and Grewal
note in their exploration of the grants associated with the Jogis of Jakhbar in
Punjab—a collection that includes both Mughal and post-Mughal documents
regarding revenue grants—"the *madad-i-maʿāsh* [or "aid for subsistence"] was
no longer simply a Muslim institution," and indeed, over time, Sikh documents
regarding land management become more and not less similar to Mughal documents of the same type.[46]

There are multiple imaginaries at work in the Indo-Muslim legal and cultural
world for grants for religious and/or charitable purposes. *Madad-i-maʿāsh* were
similar to other kinds of land grants in pre-Mughal and Mughal administration:
they were controlled by the state, and rights thus conferred were done so at the

---

43. Pashaura Singh, *Life and Work of Guru Arjan*, 75. On the meeting of Guru Arjan with
Emperor Akbar in 1598, see Grewal and Habib, *Sikh History from Persian Sources*, 55.

44. Ludden, *Agrarian History of South Asia*, 80.

45. Arjun Appadurai, *Worship and Conflict under Colonial Rule* (Cambridge: Cambridge
University Press, 1981), 169.

46. Goswamy and Grewal, *Mughals and the Jogis of Jakhbar*, 24. It was also used by the Hindu
chiefs of the Punjab Hills (37). On the practices of Sikh chiefs, see Goswamy and Grewal,
Mughal and Sikh Rulers and the Vaishnavas of Pindori, 30–31; on the resemblance between Sikh
and Mughal documents, 44. On the involvement of Ranjit Singh and other Sikh chiefs in such
grants, see Banga, *Agrarian System*, 150–51, and for an example of one chief's grants overall, see
166.

will of the state. They could be resumed, and the resumption of such grants was an ongoing political matter.[47] Aurangzeb defined such grants as equivalent to a kind of loan, such that full proprietary possession was not implied.[48] Rulers offered confirmations of these grants made by previous rulers in the Mughal period, and thus they were not a completely independent proprietary, inheritable property.[49] Such practices continued in the period after the Mughals, under Sikh and other rulers in Punjab, when such land grants continued to function as an aspect of state formation and rule. Later rulers—such as Maharaja Ranjit Singh—generally offered confirmations of the grants made by previous rulers;

A crucial distinction that comes into play in the later management of religious sites under the British concerns the recipients of such grants: were they individuals, or corporate bodies? This was significant in the Mughal period as well, as evidenced by the transition under Akbar to the recognition of institutions as recipients, over individuals. This ensured the continuance of grants, since institutions in theory persisted far beyond the lifespan of an ordinary person.[50] Donations were made, for example, to Hindu temples in name of the deity, but they also served the temples as institutions.[51] The distinction between individual and corporate bodies of ownership is parallel to the distinction, to some degree,

---

47. For example, Aurangzeb defined the principles by which confirmation and resumption of such grants would be governed in 1661, but these were subverted by later policies: Mohammed, *Revenue Free Land Grants*, 52–53. Non-Muslim *madad-i-ma'āsh* were later ordered, as a whole, for resumption by Aurangzeb (1672–73), but this policy was never fully enforced. See Habib, *Agrarian System*, 356ff. Indeed, some grants to Hindu *madad-i-ma'āsh* holders were confirmed and renewed from 1672 on (Mohammed, *Revenue Free Land Grants*, 38).

48. Habib, *Agrarian System*, 348–49. Aurangzeb did make these grants hereditary in 1690, but retained control over the grants by imperial authorities (rather than by Shari'at) and asserted their status as loans. Habib, *Agrarian System* 1999 ed., 351; see also Mohammed, *Revenue Free Land Grants*, 53. Later, in Awadh, *milkiyat* or proprietary rights were conferred, paralleling the transition that took place under the British with respect to gurdwaras (Mohammed, *Revenue Free Land Grants*, 39).

49. Examples of such confirmations are given in Goswamy and Grewal, *Mughals and the Jogis of Jakhbar*, 27–28, 79–86, 95–99, but according to Banga, confirming *sanad*s were not issued for all Mughal grants; see Banga, *Agrarian System*, 155. Banga argues that such grants were alienable and constituted ownership, but she does qualify this by saying that they were "given *practically* in perpetuity" (Banga, *Agrarian System*, 152–53; emphasis mine). As will be discussed, the evidence she uses for this from the Khalsa Darbar Records (the records of the state of Maharaja Ranjit Singh and heirs) requires some reinterpretation.

50. Tarapada Mukherjee and Irfan Habib, "Akbar and the Temples of Mathura and Its Environs," in *Proceedings of the Indian History Congress (PIHC)* 48 (1987), 234–50.

51. Davis, *Lives*, 249. While in the precolonial period the deity was understood, in Davis' words, not as "a juristic personality but as a divine person," the status of the deity changes in the colonial period. See discussion of temple administration in chapter 6 and Appadurai, *Worship and Conflict*, 20–21, 173–74.

between *madad-i-maʿāsh* grants and those known as *waqf* within Islamic contexts. The latter term (and its plural form, *awaqāf*) is deployed in Islamic legal contexts to signify a kind of property that cannot change hands by inheritance, sale, or seizure; that is, it is reserved from the normal inheritance procedures (governed by Islamic law, or *sharīʿa*) and made into a special entity, with a different set of management and inheritance rules and requirements than hold for other types of personal property.[52] This is the term that comes to dominate in later colonial discourse on the management of Muslim sites. In general terms, the person who designates a *waqf* gives up formal ownership rights to such a property, but in doing so is allowed to appoint a custodian to manage the property; this person is known as a *mutawallī*, literally meaning "one who is trusted." Another term, *mutasaddī*, is also used for managers. The key contentious issue in the Gurdwara Reform Movement concerns who has the right to "own" a site. As will be shown, the accusation of innovation on the part of the British Government of India may not lie in this arena, as is generally assumed.

Immediate Antecedents in Punjab: the Post-Mughal, Pre–East India Company Period

According to Gregory Kozlowski, "when the Mughal empire entered its long decline in the first decades of the eighteenth century, most of those striving to become its heirs shared similar attitudes about the nature of property."[53] The confirmation of prior religious grants by later Sikh chiefs reflects such a dynamic.[54] This does not mean that new rulers did not have particular emphases in their religious granting programs. The rulers of Awadh, for example, maintained the Mughal system of endowments as much as possible, but in particular were great patrons of Shīʿa institutions in the state, in keeping with their religious commitments.[55]

---

52. See Kozlowski, *Muslim Endowments*. For Islamic legal positions on *waqf*, see Murat Cizakca, *A History of Philanthropic Foundations: The Islamic World From the Seventh Century to the Present* (Istanbul: Bogazici University Press, 2000), 27–42; and Kozlowski, *Muslim Endowments*, 13ff. Immovable property, in particular, is associated with endowments, particularly because the patterns of inheritance established for property most easily applies to movable and not immovable property. *Awaqāf* were also determined for cash and movable properties, however, particularly for those dedicated primarily to the maintenance of the family (Kozlowski, *Muslim Endowments*, 13. See Cizakca, *History of Philanthropic Foundations*, 27ff.).

53. Kozlowski, *Muslim Endowments*, 27.

54. Goswamy and Grewal, *Mughals and the Jogis of Jakhbar*, 38. Mughal grants were confirmed by Sikh leaders who preceded the rise of Ranjit Singh's centralized administration, as well as by Ranjit Singh himself; see the examples in Goswamy and Grewal, *Mughal and Sikh Rulers and the Vaishnavas of Pindori*, 227–29, 235–37, 251–54, 271–73.

55. Kozlowski, *Muslim Endowments*, 29–31.

A similar maintenance of preexisting traditions, with special attention to Sikh religious interests, can be seen among Sikhs who gained political control in the eighteenth century, including the Lahore state of Maharaja Ranjit Singh, where religious revenue-free lands were estimated at 7% of the total land revenues at the end of the Lahore-state period.[56] As Banga and Grewal note, it is not surprising that documents related to such *dharamarth* grants are rare in the collection they examined of over 450 orders from Ranjit Singh's court: unlike other kinds of land grants, "grants given by way of charity were never transferred and seldom quashed."[57] Such grants are referred to as "coming down from olden times" or being in accordance with "former practice" or "ways of old" (commonly as *ba qarār-i-qadīm, az qadīm al-ayyām* or *ba dastūr-i-sābeq*).[58] Thus, they were not automatically transferred, but established precedent based on prior grants was recognized. Grants also refer to collections of documents (called *isnād*) and provide summary histories of prior grants.[59]

The *dharamarth* records of the Khalsa Darbar, or the court of the Lahore state under Maharaja Ranjit Singh (ruled 1799–1839), demonstrate the political nature of such grants and their need for confirmation. The grants were clearly gathered together in 1849 at the time of annexation and constituted not a diachronic and comprehensive record of past practices, but a set of claims being made before the new rulers, the East India Company: as political documents, such grants had to be affirmed by the new political order. *Dharamarth* records are largely absent from the yearly records of the court (except for exceptional instances in the beginning of the nineteenth century). A place is identified for the grants in the yearly records, but the place is left blank. The grants as they exist now were instead

---

56. On the maintenance of precedents, see Indu Banga and J.S.Grewal, *Civil and Military Affairs of Maharaja Ranjit Singh: A Study of 450 Orders in Persian* (Amritsar: Guru Nanak Dev University, 1987), 68. On the percentage of revenue-free lands, see Banga, *Agrarian System*, 167.

57. Banga and Grewal, *Civil and Military Affairs*, 68.

58. These terms are used so ubiquitously throughout the Khalsa Darbar Records that individual instances are not useful to cite; for a few examples (all in Khalsa Darbar Records Bundle 5, with volume numbers abbreviated as vol. 1, etc.): see for *az* or *ba qarār-i-qadim*, vol. 6 #269; vol. 8 #181, 227; vol. 11 #9; vol. 12 #5; for *az qadīm al-ayyām*, vol. 3 #19; vol. 8 #177; for *ba dastūr-i-sābeq*, vol. 8 #161; vol. 14 #13; for *az qadīm-i-ma'āf*, vol. 8 #175. See Goswamy and Grewal, *Mughal and Sikh Rulers and the Vaishnavas of Pindori*, 31, for a similar observation on a more limited scale. See also Banga and Grewal, *Civil and Military Affairs*, 69; documents 123, 129, 199, 262, 323, 372. Banga and Grewal note that the reason that *dharamarth* grants figure in the documents they examine is that there were problems associated with them, in terms of recognition and/or interference, so clearly there was some inconsistency or controversy in the maintenance of such grants. As will be shown, the Khalsa Darbar Records too reflect a contentious situation at the end of independent rule in Punjab. For prior discussion of the Khalsa Darbar Records, see Banga, *Agrarian System*, 149.

59. For a good example of how prior grants are listed, see as just one of many examples Khalsa Darbar Records vol. 7 #7.

collected in a single set of volumes at the end of the yearly listings of the court, dated with the Christian year 1849, as well as with the year in the Indian calendar, Samvat 1906, with explicit reference to the British and their accounting of land revenue rights.[60] In these records, histories of past grants are given, clearly as an attempt to make a claim to "right" based on past practice and historical precedent.

For both Sikh and non-Sikh sites, religious grants under Maharaja Ranjit Singh, as well as among earlier and contemporary Sikh chiefs, were modeled along the lines of those of the Mughal court. Individuals—or rather, lineages of individuals—are the recipients, so that a grant might become quasi-hereditary.[61] Indeed, the *dharamarth* records associated with the Khalsa Darbar are organized according to the broad category of recipient, with entire books dedicated to the Sodhis, Bedis, and Bhallas, the prominent family lineages of the Gurus.[62] The descendants of the Gurus' families were given generous grants through the period of Sikh ascendancy in the eighteenth century; later British patronage of these same families (particularly, for example, the Bedi and Bhalla families) was thus in keeping with established customs in this regard.[63] The Sodhis benefited particularly from grants from Sikh rulers, and "held revenue free lands in nearly all parts of the Punjab."[64] It should be noted that a wide range of members of this and other families benefited from patronage. The Khalsa Darbar records reveal this in detail. Overall, Banga notes that the largess enjoyed by the Bedis and Sodhis, or families of the Gurus, certainly reflected the rulers' "piety and catholic outlook," but also their "practical good sense"[65] and, as Major has similarly argued, demonstrates the role of such religious figures as "warrior-priests and militant

---

60. See for example Khalsa Darbar Records vol. 8 #43 and 159, which mentions the *kitāb-i-angrez* and a *maʿāf* entered in it.

61. Veena Sachdeva, *Polity and Economy of the Punjab during the Late Eighteenth Century* (New Delhi: Mahohar, 1993), 122–23. See also Banga and Grewal, *Civil and Military Affairs*, 73; document 383.

62. The material here is discussed in a different context in Anne Murphy, "Configuring Community in Colonial and Pre-colonial Imaginaries: Insights from the Khalsa Darbar Records," in *Modernity, Diversity and the Public Sphere: Negotiating Religious Identities in 18th-20th Century India*, ed. Martin Fuchs and Vasudha Dalmia (Delhi: Oxford University Press, forthcoming).

63. The Bedis benefited immensely, particularly the family of Sahib Singh of Una (on grants to the Bedis, see Khalsa Darbar Records B. 5, vol. 3; and Caton, "Settling for the State," 48, 181, 194ff., and Banga, *Agrarian System*, 157 n. 47, and 157–58). The Bhalla family received a smaller number of grants (on the Bhalla family grants, see Khalsa Darbar Records B. 5, vol. 4 and Banga, *Agrarian System*, 158).

64. Banga, *Agrarian System*, 156. For the Sodhi grants, see Khalsa Darbar Records B. 5, vol. 9.

65. Banga, *Agrarian System*, 167.

champions of the principle of Sikh theocracy."[66] Alongside these and other, Sikh recipients, such as *granthis* or Sikh textual specialists, Hindu religious specialists and Muslim shrines and saints as well were honored with grants and past grants confirmed;[67] thus in the Khalsa Darbar records, entire volumes were dedicated to *sādh*s and Udasi (Bundle 5, Volume 2), Brahmins and *purohit*s (Bundle 5, Volumes 5 and 7), *sayyid*s and *faqīr*s (Bundle 5, Volume 11), and "famous Sardars and dependants" (Bundle 5, Volume 12). Banga argues that "the Muslim grantees received essentially the same treatment from the Sikh rulers as the Hindu or Sikh grantees,"[68] although this cannot be confirmed without a more detailed comparative study of the granting practices of Lahore state in relation to prior state patronage. Support of a range of religious specialists, she argues, reflects the "self-interest of the rulers" to act as patrons of those influential with the general population.[69] As noted earlier, Sikh rulers were also following a South Asia–wide precedent in granting broad protection for religious persons and institutions. Political interests thus informed the support given to religious institutions, alongside devotional and communitarian concerns.

Sachdeva notes that in the eighteenth century, "[r]evenue-free lands were granted to various Gurdwaras,"[70] such as those described by Banga.[71] Exactly how such grants functioned, however, is not delineated in the existing secondary scholarship. This is in fact a crucial question, given the debate that ensues in the twentieth century regarding who should be granted the right to manage Sikh shrines. Only by understanding how they were treated in the precolonial period can we understand what changed in the colonial period. The *dharamarth* records

---

66. Major, *Return to Empire*, 145.

67. See the findings of Indu Banga, "Running the State (The Maharaja's Own Orders)," in *Maharaja Ranjit Singh: The State and Society*, ed. Indu Banga and J.S. Grewal, 102–30 (Amritsar: Guru Nanak Dev University, 2001), see 105. Banga highlights the following documents: 123, 129, 186, 199, 202, 238, 244, 262, 323, 327, 372. On *dharamarth* grants to Udasis and Nirmalas, see Banga, *Agrarian System*, 160, and to *dhādi*s and other religious specialists, 166. See, in general, Banga and Grewal, *Civil and Military Affairs*. Akalis and Nihangs are also identified as recipients (Banga, *Agrarian System*, 160–61). Also see the discussion in Major, *Return to Empire*, 145.

68. Banga, *Agrarian System*, 164. On the honoring of Brahmins, see Banga and Grewal, *Civil and Military Affairs*, document 74; on Hindu establishments and religious specialists, see Banga, *Agrarian System*, 161–64. On a grant to a *faqīr*, see Banga and Grewal, *Civil and Military Affairs*, document 33, pp. 105–6; see also document 154, p. 130; on such grants in general, see Banga, *Agrarian System*, 164–65.

69. Banga, *Agrarian System*, 167. For a similar point, see also Banga and Grewal, *Civil and Military Affairs*, 69.

70. Sachdeva, *Polity and Economy of the Punjab*, 123.

71. Banga, *Agrarian System*, 159 n. 58.

of the Khalsa Darbar reveal the logic of such grants as a set of claims made before the colonial state: it is based in persons and lineages, rather than focused on sites themselves. Most grants there are structured the same way, with indication of the recipient or recipients of a grant, and their heritage: the father and grandfather of a recipient is named, or, in the case of disciples, the lineage of teachers. Most of the Khalsa Darbar grants then detail the history associated with the grant under consideration, also providing a brief history of associated grants and their confirmation, usually with reference to Maharaja Ranjit Singh or his successors, Kharak Singh, Sher Singh, or Dalip Singh. For all but the first volume in the extant collection (discussed below), the organizing principle is based on the designation of individuals or groups of people as recipients, under broad categories associated with their lineage (e.g., descendant of the Guru), caste (Brahmin), or role (*sādh, udāsī, purohit, faqīr*). Two volumes are recorded as "miscellaneous," and these volumes too indicate individual recipients of grants, without much detail on the reasons for the grants or the specific roles associated with grantees.[72] The term Bhai was utilized in particular to denote persons associated with Sikh institutions or practices; it is ubiquitous in the Khalsa Darbar records, and used as a section heading to denote an entire category of recipients.[73] Thus both the Khalsa Darbar records, and those examined by Banga/Grewal and Goswamy/Grewal elsewhere, provide many examples of grants to individuals.[74] There is some ambiguity, in rare cases.[75] One exemplary exception was found by Banga and Grewal,

---

72. Khalsa Darbar Records vol.13 and 14.

73. Banga and Grewal, *Civil and Military Affairs*, 70. See for example document 129, p. 124. On the use of the term as a general category, see Khalsa Darbar Records vol. 10, Part 1. On the term, see Oberoi, "Brotherhood of the Pure," 162ff.

74. The individual orientation of such grants is made even clearer by the necessity of grantees to have non-hereditary grants (which all *madad-i-maʿāsh* grants were before 1690) confirmed after a change in institution leadership. For examples of individual grants, see Goswamy and Grewal, *Mughal and Sikh Rulers and the Vaishnavas of Pindori*, document XXVII, pp. 239–41. Many other examples are given in this volume.

75. In document 23 of the Pindori documents analyzed by Goswamy and Grewal, for example, a memorandum (which confirmed an existing grant) was issued regarding the village of Lahri Gosain, as a *dharamarth*, "in equal parts upon the *mahant*s of Pindori and Baba Sahib Badbhag Singh Jio," who the authors identify as Sodhi Badbhag Singh of Kartarpur or another saint of a Dera in Hoshiarpur District (See Goswamy and Grewal, *Mughal and Sikh Rulers and the Vaishnavas of Pindori*, document XXIII, pp. 223–25). The "*mahant*s" act as a corporate body in the grant; this is continued in other examples from that collection. (Goswamy and Grewal, *Mughal and Sikh Rulers and the Vaishnavas of Pindori*, document XXI, pp. 217–18; document XXVIII, pp. 243–45.) In one grant studied by Banga and Grewal, "one of the preserves held by Sardar Ratan Singh Garjakhia should be given by him to the Gujjars of the city of Lahore," thus delineating a corporate body ("the Gujjars") as recipient. (Banga and Grewal, *Civil and Military Affairs*, document 302, p. 166.) The idea of the community as the recipient is found also in the documents associated with the Jogis of Jakhbar. (Goswamy and Grewal, *Mughals and the Jogis of Jakhbar*, 10–11.)

where the Guru Granth Sahib itself was considered a grantee. However, although Banga and Grewal assert that this is a grant to the Guru Granth Sahib, it is in fact articulated through a human caretaker.[76] Thus while the reason for the grant may be the sacred text, it is to an individual. Even this exceptional case, therefore, reveals the overwhelming preference for individual recipients and the rarity of corporate bodies or non-persons as designated owners.

If it is indeed the case that the sacred scripture could be the recipient of a grant, it seems that the most likely parallel example in the Khalsa Darbar records would be found in relation to the Adi Granth (the 1604 version of the canon, known as the Kartarpur Pothi) and Guru Granth Sahib, the final canonical version of the text. Here the Khalsa Darbar records seem, at first, to give a clear answer. The first volume of the series declares itself to be about the *granth sāhibān*, or the esteemed texts, the Adi Granth and the Baba Granth Sahib. Of the twenty-seven grants listed there, however, the overwhelming majority clearly define an individual or individuals as the recipients. One is given to the Adi Granth, in the name of the Sodhi Sahib at Kartarpur. Another mentions John Lawrence, a member of the Punjab Board of Administration of post-annexation Punjab (and major architect of the paternalist and authoritarian "Punjab School" of administration in the early years of British control).[77] There are two grants which do not clearly define an individual human recipient, seeming to be for the *granth* itself, and one that seems to be for the *granth* and for an individual associated with it as a *granthī*.[78] Most of the recipients are male (and in all cases genealogy is defined in patrilineal terms), but women are mentioned in two grants.[79] Thus, individual designation prevails, with few exceptions.

How, then, was the Darbar Sahib or Harmandir Sahib (known popularly in English as the Golden Temple)—one of the most important of Sikh institutions—treated, and how were grants related to it assigned? This site provides an important case for consideration along these lines. To it was dedicated an entire volume in the Khalsa Darbar records (Bundle 5, Volume 8). The history of the control of the Darbar Sahib is similar to that of other Sikh religious sites: it was controlled by

---

76. The grant reads: "A well in village Chane has been held by Bhai Mal Singh since olden times in *dharamarth* on account of Sri Granth Sahib Jio at Ram Garh" (dated Lahore, 1 Har 1891 / 12 June 1834). (Banga and Grewal, *Civil and Military Affairs*, 70; document 262, p. 157–58).

77. Khalsa Darbar Records vol. 1, #3 for first example, #9 for second.

78. Khalsa Darbar Records vol. 1, #5 and 35 for the *granth* alone, and #21 for the *granth* and an individual.

79. In one, the *ahliye* of a male are noted as recipients, and this term is used throughout the Records for female descendants; in another, women with a role in relation to the *granth* are indicated. Khalsa Darbar Records B. 5, vol. 1, #23 for first, #53 for second instance.

various parties over the course of the seventeenth and eighteenth centuries. Prithi Chand and his son Harji controlled the site in the second half of the seventeenth century, after the time of Guru Hargobind, and it remained under the control of this apostate group, the "Minas" as they are traditionally called, until the time of Guru Gobind Singh.[80] The proprietary rights of Chak Guru, the name of the present city of Amritsar, were later given to Baba Ajit Singh (the adopted son of Mata Sundari, the widow of Guru Gobind Singh) by the Mughal emperor Bahadur Shah I, to be managed by Bhai Mani Singh, a major figure in the period. This reflects ongoing tensions within the community between the followers of the wives of the Guru and Banda Bahadur.[81] This grant is said to have been later resumed by the state, although evidence for this is also lacking.[82]

The Golden Temple was said to have received a number of revenue-free grants from Ranjit Singh. Several scholars have noted that grants were also made to important personnel; indeed, Banga argues that the Darbar Sahib received so many grants from so many different rulers and chiefs that separate *mutasaddīs* (managers) were appointed to manage the revenues.[83] The Khalsa Darbar records, however, in current form, overwhelmingly indicate that individuals were given grants, rather than the Darbar Sahib itself. Of the total 115 grants in the corpus (and an additional narrative about a *granthī* who had lost his rights), all but four—made out to the Akal Bunga, on the site of the Darbar Sahib, rather than to the Darbar Sahib itself—are made out to individuals.[84] *Granthī*s received a total of twenty-eight grants, with the additional narrative regarding the claims of one *granthī* who fared badly under British rule—and a total of thirteen grants were made for *mutasaddīs* and *pūjārīs*. Additional grants were made to others associated with the administration and ritual functioning of the institution: *rabābīs* and *rāgīs*, who performed there (eleven grants); *ardāsīe*, responsible for the recitation of *Ardās* (six grants); *amle* or staff/workers (including *dhupīe* or

80. Madanjit Kaur, *Golden Temple*, 26.

81. See Madanjit Kaur, *Golden Temple*, 32 n. 70. See Ganda Singh, "The Punjab News in the Akhbar-i-Darbar-i-Mualla," *Punjab Past and Present* 2 (October 1970): 225. A later *jagīr* was issued in 1749, but the direct recipient of this is unclear. Madanjit Kaur, *Golden Temple*, 43. It also should be noted that the destruction of the Golden Temple in this period, like the assignment of rights to it, also was determined within a larger set of political relations. See Eaton, "Temple Desecration," which provides the larger political model for such destructions.

82. Madanjit Kaur, *Golden Temple*, 39.

83. Banga, *Agrarian System*, 159; see also Pashaura Singh, *Life and Work of Guru Arjan*, 120, Madanjit Kaur, *Golden Temple*, 52. On grants to personnel, see Madanjit Kaur, *Golden Temple*, 55 and Banga, *Agrarian System* 159, footnote 57.

84. Khalsa Darbar Records B. 5, V. 8, records 141, 143, 145, 159.

incense lighters, a candle lighter, and the holder of keys: seven grants); and people associated with *bungā* or dwelling places and other institutions associated with the Darbar Sahib: the Akal Bunga or Akal Takhat (thirty-three grants); Dera Baba Atal Sahib and Gurdwara Bheek Singh (two grants each); Jandh Bunga (eight grants); and Bunga Sarkarwala (one grant).[85] It must be remembered however that, as mentioned above, these records are not necessarily accurate representations of all types of grants related to *dharamarth*, and may reflect the intrusion of personal interests brought before a new state body in Punjab (the East India Company administration). But it is notable that the language of personal rights prevails within these records.

Who, then, ultimately was proprietor of the Darbar Sahib, and who was responsible for its administration? One can see intimations of the rhetoric of community in the efforts the wives of the Guru are said to have made to intervene in the management of the Darbar Sahib during the early eighteenth century, but evidence of this is reserved for later, such as in the writings of Kesar Singh Chibber and Rattan Singh Bhangu.[86] In Chibber's account, Mata Sahib Devi advised the Sikhs of Delhi not to celebrate Sikh holidays due to the sensitive political situation. After taking a *gurmatā*, leaders of the community left Delhi and established control over the Darbar Sahib.[87] According to Madanjit Kaur, Ranjit Singh appointed a committee to manage this sacred site,[88] and she argues that "the fact that his authority to look after the general management of the Harmandir was questioned by none, indicates that it was based on a general acceptance."[89] Ian Kerr argues, instead, that Ranjit Singh did away with committee management and appointed a temple manager.[90] Based on the evidence of the Khalsa Darbar

85. The Bunge at Darbar Sahib are described in Chibber, *Bansāvalīnāmā*, 213.

86. Madanjit Kaur, *Golden Temple*, 34. The evidence Kaur presents for control of the site is based on the reading of a history of Amritsar, the date of which is unclear (Madanjit Kaur, *Golden Temple*, 103–4).

87. Chibber, *Bansāvalīnāmā*, chapter 13, 214–15.

88. Madanjit Kaur, *Golden Temple*, 52, 104.

89. Madandjit Kaur, *Golden Temple*, 58.

90. Ian Kerr, "The British and the Administration of the Golden Temple in 1859," *Panjab Past and Present* 10, 2 (serial no. 20, October 1976): 306–21, see 310. When the British began indirect rule in March 1849, Sirdar Lehna Singh Majithia was in charge of Darbar Sahib (in addition to holding other important posts). (Kerr cites *The Punjab Chiefs*, Vol. 1, 270.) His father Desa Singh had held this post before him, and had been appointed by Ranjit Singh, who had "abolished the system of collective management of the Temple by representatives of influential sirdars that had existed during the period of the Sikh misals and taken upon himself the task of appointing a Temple manager" (Kerr, "British and the Administration of the Golden Temple," 308, citing "Memorandum on the Sikh Temple, Amritsar," NAI, Home Public A Proceedings, Confidential February 1881, nos. 65–71).

records, it seems that through the period of Ranjit Singh and his successors, the logic of the individual as recipient prevails. Rattan Singh Bhangu's description of the granting of a *jagīr* to Kapur Singh "for the *panth*" reflects this practice as well.[91] This pattern only changes with the intervention of British rule in the subcontinent, when we see a new logic proposed for the designation of authority over religious sites. With these changes, a new direct relationship is established between the community as a bounded, corporate body and the territory of its past, through the gurdwara. This new relationship draws on the understanding of the landscape of the Sikh past that was explored in previous chapters but with a new understanding of property and its relationship to the community.

British Rule and the Politics of Land Administration: Continuity and Transformation

The officer submitting the first regular land settlement in 1860, R. E. Egerton, observed that tenants in Lahore District did not generally pay rent to village *zamīndārs* and that many of the "proprietors decline[d] to assert their claims."[92] Indeed, Egerton felt these *zamīndārs* "misunderstood" their own rights to the land and thus considered them a liability:[93]

> The people had not themselves received such preliminary training as would enable them to appreciate an elaborate system; and though possessing adequate notions of ancestral rights, and extremely tenacious of them in practice, they yet did not care to cause their interests to be accurately recorded. They consequently rendered no aid whatever; indeed, by loose and erroneous statements, they constantly misled the settlement officials, and thus in reality offered passive obstructions.[94]

Later British administrators believed the Sikh land-administration system had caused land to be "completely insecure and therefore utterly worthless" (and that

---

91. Dhavan, *When Sparrows Became Hawks*, 63.

92. Quoted in Nelson, "Land, Law, and the Logic of Local Politics," 90.

93. For more on the representation of precolonial policy within British sources, see Nelson, "Land, Law, and the Logic of Local Politics," 123 and 151, where some rather biased accounts of the prior system are described.

94. Selections from the Records of the Government of India, 1849–1937. IOR v/23/1. No. 8: *General Report on the Administration of the Punjab Territories, Comprising the Punjab Proper and the Cis and Trans-Sutlej States, for the Years 1851–52 and 1852–53* (Calcutta: Calcutta Gazette Press, 1854), 106.

the government of Ranjit Singh had been a "rude and simple one").[95] This view was not universal, however; Douie argued that "[t]he Sikhs were anxious to increase the revenue by extending cultivation and at the same time to diminish the influence of the ancient landowning tribes and ruling families. With these objects they effected in some parts of the country a great, and on the whole benef- icent, revolution in landed property by founding in the extensive waste lands of the older estates numerous settlements of industrious cultivators of lower castes."[96] It was estimated at the time of annexation that 29% of the total revenue of Ranjit Singh's kingdom in the late 1830s was given out as *jagīr*; Henry Law- rence estimated the same percentage was reserved as revenue-free in 1847.[97] The remaining lands were reserved for direct payment to the state, or *khālisā*.[98]

Reluctance to assert claims to land disappeared when the notion of the value of land was transformed within the British system. Land became an objective thing to be owned, made more valuable by the increasing commercialization of agriculture and the limitation of alternative means of income for South Asians in the new East India Company–dominated economy.[99] Early British land adminis- trators expressed a sense of a precolonial organization of land rights that did not rely upon the designation of exclusionary "owners" of the land. But, as Banga notes, "the practical interest of the British rulers demanded a simple and rational classification of land tenures in the Panjab," in the face of the "infinite variety" of isolated tenures arising from "the various social circumstances of the people and the past history of the administration of the different parts of the country"; according to one revenue official, Robert Cust, who wrote the first land settlement

---

95. For the first quotation, see Nelson, "Land, Law, and the Logic of Local Politics," 50. For the quotation on Ranjit Singh, see *Selections from the Records of the Government of India, 1849–1937. IOR v/23/1. No. 2: Report on the Administration of the Punjab for the Years 1849–50 and 1850–51* (Calcutta: Calcutta Gazette Office, 1853), 8.

96. Douie, *Punjabi Settlement Manual*, 21. Radha Sharma argues that the policies of the Lahore state had actively supported agricultural development (Radha Sharma, "State and Agrarian Society," 152–53).

97. Cited in Kerr, "The Punjab Province and the Lahore District, 1849–1872: A Case Study." (PhD diss., University of Minnesota, 1975), 259. For extensive discussion of *jagīrs* with exam- ples, see Banga and Grewal, *Civil and Military Affairs*, 64ff.

98. See Banga and Grewal, *Civil and Military Affairs*, 66ff.

99. Importantly, the economic and agrarian transitions in the colonial period that Habib highlights are not based solely in the redefinition of property rights, but also the pressure on land that resulted from the limitation of options outside of the agricultural arena for peasants. None of these transitions, therefore, acts in isolation in generating social change (Habib, *Agrarian System*, 134). On the limitations on Indians within the colonial economy, see Sudipta Sen, *Empire of Free Trade: The East India Company and Making of the Colonial Marketplace* (Philadelphia: University of Pennsylvania Press, 1998).

manual for Punjab in 1866, it was "clear that native Governments give a very imperfect recognition of proprietary right."[100]

We must remember the larger context for this discussion. Land management came to constitute a critical feature of East India Company administration in South Asia after the assumption of the right to *diwānī* or taxation, by the East India Company in Bengal in the middle of the eighteenth century. Several policies regarding landownership and regularization were enacted in the decades between this series of events and the imposition of direct East India Company rule in Punjab in 1849, after the annexation of the Lahore state a decade after the death of its founder, Ranjit Singh. The basic process by which British agricultural interests intervened and subverted prior agricultural rights and privileges was common across diverse areas, even when the actual mechanisms put in place by British policies varied greatly throughout East India Company and later British Crown territories. As Cornwallis aptly put it: "[i]t is immaterial to government what individual possesses the land, provided he cultivates it, protects the *ryot* [cultivator] and pays public revenue"[101] There was not one universal perspective on the issue; utilitarians like Jeremy Bentham and James Mill, for example, felt that the *zamīndār*s were not the "right" people for the job.[102] Regardless of the system, however, it must be noted that the fundamental premise of the British system was consistent in Punjab as elsewhere: "every function of the colonial state, from the establishment of district boundaries to the collection of excise taxes to the operation of elementary schools, depended upon the establishment of an unambiguous title in land."[103] Cust called the collection of land revenue a chess game, one of great importance to the government.[104]

While the overall approach to resolving the question of land ownership was parallel in different locations, the specific logic of property in Punjab is quite distinctive among the models of property relations implemented in British-controlled South Asia. In the province, the British instituted the "village system" of periodic land revenue settlements, as developed in the Northwestern Provinces earlier in the nineteenth century, in contrast to the system in place in the provinces

---

100. First quotation: Banga, *Agrarian System*, 168; Banga quotes from *The General Report upon the Administration of the Punjab Proper (1849–50 & 1850–51)*, 104. Second quotation: Robert Cust, *Manual for the Guidance of Revenue Officers in the Punjab* (Lahore: Koh-i-Noor Press, 1866).

101. Quoted in R. Guha, *Rule of Property for Bengal*, 8, 5–17.

102. See Eric Stokes, *The English Utilitarians and India* (Oxford: Clarendon Press, 1959), 5–6.

103. Caton, "Settling for the State," 174.

104. Cust, *Manual for the Guidance of Revenue Officers*, 134. Discussion of lineage of manuals/guides for land settlement in Punjab is given in Douie, *Punjab Settlement Manual*, 1.

of Madras and Bombay (where settlements were made directly with individual cultivators, or *ryots*), on the one hand, and, on the other, in Bengal and environs, and parts of Madras (where permanent settlement was made with landlords, or *zamīndārs*).[105] The idealized village body lay at the center of the Punjabi system.[106] There were complications with the settlements all over British India.[107] As a colonial official wrote in 1870s in response to the situation in Bengal: "The greatest wrong we did to the Mussalman aristocracy was in defining their rights. Up to that period their title had not been permanent, but neither had it been fixed . . . we gave them their tenures in perpetuity, but in doing so, we rendered them inelastic."[108] Aspects of the preexisting system were thus continued, but were embedded within a new overall order.[109] It has been argued that prior to the British East India Company's reorganization of property in South Asia "capitalist class relations had made their appearance."[110] The debate that has ensued, however, need not detain us, because even if this were the case, it is still true that "full-blown agrarian capitalism" was a product of the later nineteenth century, in general, across South Asia, after colonial reformulation of property relations took hold.[111]

In Punjab, property rights were conceived of as nonindividual—as Cust noted, "property has existed in this Province from time immemorial; tracts have been occupied by tribes and families, and are called by their names"[112]—in a way that was distinct from the articulation of property interests in other parts of the subcontinent, an innovation that provided an important context for the imagination of control of the community over land. Possession in this context was seen as

---

105. Richard Saumarez Smith, *Rule by Records: Land Registration and Village Custom in Early British Panjab* (New Delhi: Oxford University Press, 1996), 43; for further discussion, see Dirks, *Hollow Crown*, 22ff., Nelson, "Land, Law, and the Logic of Local Politics," 17. For a discussion of the different forms of land settlement, see Burton Stein, "Introduction," in *The Making of Agrarian Policy in British India: 1770–1900* (New Delhi: Oxford University Press, 1992), 14.

106. Nelson, "Land, Law, and the Logic of Local Politics," 52.

107. In Kangra, for example, not only were British formulations of land use and ownership inappropriate and foreign, so too were systems imported from the plains. (Baker, "Colonial Influences," 48). For an overview of the British land revenue policy from the perspective of the Government of India, mainly as a response to critics such as R.C. Dutt, formerly Acting Commissioner of Burdwan, see *Land Revenue Policy of the Indian Government* (Calcutta: Office of the Superintendent, Government Printing, 1902).

108. W.W. Hunter, *The Indian Musalmans* (repr., Lahore: Premier Book House, 1974), 139; quoted in Kozlowski, *Muslim Endowments*, 37.

109. Dirks, "From Little King to Landlord," 176.

110. Stein, "Introduction," 22.

111. Stein, "Introduction," 23.

112. Cust, *Manual for the Guidance of Revenue Officers*, 21.

something that "has trodden down ancestral right," and the rightful owner of land was difficult to determine, according to Cust, "among a people with a feline attachment to the soil and yet with little or no written records, an entire incapacity to grasp an abstract general principle, or see justice in any other result but individual triumph." The task of determining a general principle lay with the Revenue Collector.[113] Further, in the Punjab the operation of customary law, "like the logic of the colonial land revenue administration, subordinated individual rights to collective responsibilities."[114]

A view of the changes enacted within the British system is visible within R. S. Smith's exploration of the inconsistencies in the operation of the first or "regular" settlement of Ludhiana District in 1853 in Punjab. Smith's work shows an "alternative view of land holding at the start of British rule" and how agrarian relations were classified and transformed within the British colonial context.[115] The settlement of revenue enacted by the British did not only determine revenue, but also "defined rights to land; and the records, in which the rights of everyone with an identifiable interest in the land were registered, defined a new idiom for the cultivator just as they defined a new level of involvement of the State in the cultivator's interests."[116] The mandate declared for the Board of Administration for the Punjab in 1849, Smith notes, demanded that the village remain the administrative unit and that "Native institutions" should be upheld "in all their integrity."[117] Yet, the use of indigenous terms in this process does not define continuities, but instead was meant to "bind colonial institutions more effectively to local traditions," as a means of shoring up colonial authority and control. Ideologically, this was also in keeping with a British paternalist attraction to the reinstatement of idealized pastoral relations in Punjab that mirrored such an idealized (and disappearing, to the extent it ever existed) landscape in Britain.[118] In so doing, formerly flexible meanings were made rigid.[119]

---

113. Cust, *Manual for the Guidance of Revenue Officers*, 23.

114. Nelson, "Land, Law, and the Logic of Local Politics," 17.

115. Smith, *Rule by Records*, 16; see also for details on the sequence and scope of settlements.

116. Smith, *Rule by Records*, vii.

117. Quoted in Smith, *Rule by Records*, 45. See also David Gilmartin, "Migration and Modernity: The State, the Punjabi Village, and the Settling of the Canal Colonies," in *People on the Move: Punjabi Colonial, and Post-Colonial Migration*, ed. Ian Talbot and Shinder Thandi, 3–20 (Oxford: Oxford University Press, 2004).

118. Nelson, "Land, Law, and the Logic of Local Politics," 55; see also the overall argument in David Cannadine, *Ornamentalism: How the British Saw Their Empire* (London: Allen Lane, 2001).

119. Smith, *Rule by Records*, 17.

The system that came to prevail in Punjab reflected the different ideologies followed by two central protagonists of the debate: Edward Augustus (E. A.) Prinsep, a subordinate revenue officer and later Settlement Commissioner, and Richard Temple, who worked in revenue and settlement in Punjab prior to undertaking illustrious positions outside the province.[120] What came to distinguish the owners identified in Punjab from those in other locations in India, such as Bengal and Madras, was not their status as cultivators per se, but their supposed link in ancestral and "tribal" terms to the village founder. The right to property was thus determined through a historical relationship to a founder.[121] According to Matthew Nelson, Prinsep "threw prevailing ideas about the relative importance of individual and collective landed property rights into complete disarray" throughout British-held India with his shift in focus away from individual toward collective rights, first defined at the village level and then in relation to "tribes," "discarding, as it were, more than one hundred years of accumulated administrative experience along the way."[122] The early preliminary settlement enacted by Temple—which is reflected in the Tenancy Act of 1868—followed patterns established by the Punjab School of governance to protect the village body and as such recognized the possession of cultivators, as measured in terms of ploughs. At the time, Nelson argues, Temple found that "members of the village proprietary body . . . were only too willing to include as many cultivators as possible. After all, proprietorship had been a burden more than a benefit under the Sikhs, so there was little reason to resist when Temple proposed a wider distribution of the government demand."[123] Things had changed by the time Prinsep began his settlement work, partially as a result of the increasing commercial value of land. Proprietors, according to Prinsep, began to identify their rights in terms of ancestral shares, causing the exclusion of occupying tenants. Prinsep supported these claims, ending the system Temple had instituted and reflecting an aristocratic turn in post-1857 British India.[124] The Punjab Laws Act of 1872 enacted his findings. These were later shored up by the Punjab Alienation of

---

120. For an overview of the history of the settlements, see Douie, *Punjab Settlement Manual*, 24ff. On the conflict between the "Aristocratic Reaction" and the "Punjab Tradition," terms that Hambly notes were in use in the 1860s, as represented by Prinsep and Temple, see G. R. G. Hambly, "Richard Temple and the Punjab Tenancy Act of 1868," *English Historical Review* 79, 310 (January 1964): 47–66.

121. Nelson, "Land, Law, and the Logic of Local Politics," 70.

122. Nelson, "Land, Law, and the Logic of Local Politics," 41.

123. Nelson, "Land, Law, and the Logic of Local Politics," 97.

124. Hambly, "Richard Temple," 59.

Land Act of 1900,[125] which "subordinated individual rights to collective obligations once and for all," relying fundamentally on "late-nineteenth-century assumptions about the nature of the village proprietary body and tribal custom."[126]

Shareholding as determined within the colonial Punjab revenue settlement was fundamentally related to birth status within an ancestral community and thus tied to the idea of private property with reference primarily to village, caste, and *history*. When faced with sets of shares, the British chose to grant ownership status to those claiming ancestral control and priority over village territory and to exclude others—who might have come to the village later and were not related by blood to the founders—who were transformed into "tenants": "under British rule it was the genealogy of proprietors that was taken to represent shareholding, not the pattern of allotments on the ground."[127] Temple's system was largely set aside for Prinsep's, which embraced the historical formation of claims in direct relation to caste. Thus, as Caton argues, "the British property regime transformed the ways Panjabi notables sought to maintain their status."[128] At the same time, many claims to *jagīrs* that *were* filed with the British administration after annexation were rejected, particularly those of the court elites in the Lahore state, whose claim to land rested in their political status. Land grants were rigorously interrogated by the British after annexation; delaying such evaluation, Dalhousie feared, would only allow grants to appear inevitable and legitimate.[129] Quick resolution of claims would "disabuse" the "native mind" of their "inherent rights . . . [in] their tenures in virtue of long possession."[130] John Lawrence, unlike Henry Lawrence, argued against maintaining grants to courtly elites, and thus many grants were resumed and only "those who had remained aloof from the 1848 rebellion [that rejected British influence in Punjab] were confirmed in their *jagīrs*."[131] As noted by A. Kensington regarding families in the Ambala district, "the more serious offenders were visited with signal punishment. Their possessions were

---

125. For an extensive further discussion of the distinctions between the positions of Temple and Prinsep, see Nelson, "Land, Law, and the Logic of Local Politics," chapters 1 and 2.

126. Nelson, "Land, Law, and the Logic of Local Politics," 126.

127. Smith, *Rule by Records*, 32; for quotation, 383.

128. Caton, "Settling for the State," 33.

129. H. E. Elliot, Secretary to the Government of India with the Governor General to the Board of Administration for the Affairs of the Punjab, dated March 31, 1849, Home Miscellaneous Series, Vol. 760, pp. 1–21, Quoted in Kerr, "Punjab Province," 263.

130. Elliot, quotations in Kerr, "Punjab Province," 263–64. Most *jagīrs* were cancelled by the British; Caton, "Settling for the State," 177. See also Major, *Return to Empire*.

131. Major, *Return to Empire*, 145.

confiscated to government, and in some cases they were themselves removed as prisoners from the Province."[132] The amount of *jagīr* lands was thus greatly reduced under the British, with a mere 20% in 1860, and then to 11.8% in 1870.[133]

British attitudes toward elites, and resulting policies, changed after the Rebellion of 1857, which nearly cost Britain its Indian empire. One can see the benefits of loyalty—and the risks of disloyalty—in the histories of some of the most prominent families in the province.[134] Baba Khem Singh Bedi, within the family lineage of Guru Nanak, provides a good example of the benefits.[135] With the opening of the canal colonies—new areas of land brought under irrigation and therefore cultivation—in Western Punjab in the opening decades of the twentieth century, his became a major landholding family: fully 10% of the Sohag Para Colony, or almost 8,000 acres of land, were allotted to him. As Imran Ali has argued, "by providing families like the Bedis with land, the British not only dissuaded them from any thoughts of opposition, but also cemented both their loyalty and their authority by enhancing their economic power."[136] The Una branch of the family, on the other hand, had suffered much for their participation in the resistance to the British presence in 1849. Service allowed that family, too, to reinstate itself. Thus in the post-1857 period, "the preservation of the old aristocracy in the Punjab—the chieftain/military families of the western districts and the dominant peasant proprietors and rural notables of central and eastern Punjab—was indeed central to the imperial enterprise in the province."[137]

The production of an elite that supported the Government of India involved the establishment of a *landed* gentry, rather than a court-based, political one. Property therefore was crucial. Given the role of the Sikhs in Lahore state, Rishi Singh has argued that Sikhs were clearly preferred over members of other religious communities in the court of the Lahore state; disregard for court elites by the colonial state therefore disproportionally impacted the Sikh population of the

---

132. Cited in Conran and Craik, *Chiefs and Families*, 58.

133. The status of religious sites in particular, however, was to be protected: Kerr, "Punjab Province," 264.

134. For example, see Conran and Craik, *Chiefs and Families*, 26, 42, 71, etc. See also Kerr on loyalty, "Punjab Province," 294.

135. A short publication in his honor was written by Bhai Avtar Singh Vahiria, *Shok Pattr* (Lahore: Sri Gurmat Press, n.d.) IOL Panj B 1380. Received by the India Office in 1909.

136. Imran Ali, *Punjab under Imperialism, 1885–1947* (Princeton, NJ: Princeton University Press, 1988), 17.

137. Tai Yong Tan, *The Garrison State: The Military, Government and Society in Colonial Punjab, 1849–1947* (New Delhi: Sage, 2005), 240.

province.[138] Although Nelson argues that religion did not operate centrally in these developments—and that the emphasis on ancestry over religion distinguished Punjab from much of British India[139]—this was not in fact entirely the case, as he himself notes at another point. As religion was also believed to be tied to agricultural tribe identity, there was in fact a communal cast to these processes, and certain castes and religious communities were seen to be more "quintessentially" related to property. This was particularly notable in the rural indebtedness crisis that resulted in the 1900 Punjab Land Alienation Act, which prevented the transfer of land from agriculturalists to non-agriculturalists. According to the Act:

> A person who desires to make a permanent alienation of his land shall be at liberty to make such alienation where (a) the alienor is not a member of an agricultural tribe; or (b) the alienor is a member of an agricultural tribe and the alienee holds lands as an agriculturist in the village where the land alienated is situated; or (c) the alienor is a member of an agricultural tribe and the alienee is a member of the same tribe or of a tribe in the same group.[140]

The effort was to find a way by which, in the words of Harnam Singh Ahluwalia in a Minute of Dissent arguing that the bill did not do enough, "the agriculturalists may be saved from their own improvidence and utter ruin."[141] The indebtedness crisis of the late nineteenth century—and the selling of land that it caused—had complex causes, related both to the increase in property value that resulted from the commercialization of agriculture under the British and the increase in litigation that resulted with the introduction of British legal structures in Punjab; the "improvidence" of cultivators is not the most convincing of these causes.[142] Regardless, alienations increased significantly in the years after annexation, having been relatively rare before it.[143]

---

138. Rishi Singh, "State Formation and the Establishment of Non-Muslim Hegemony in the Post Mughal Nineteenth Century Punjab" (PhD diss., School of Oriental and African Studies, 2009).

139. Nelson, "Land, Law, and the Logic of Local Politics," 148.

140. Lal, *Punjab Alienation of Land Act*, 13.

141. Lal, *Punjab Alienation of Land Act*, 189. For a discussion of Harnam Singh's dissent, see N. G. Barrier, *The Punjab Alienation of Land Bill of 1900* (Durham, NC: Duke University Program in Comparative Studies on Southern Asia, 1966), 65–66.

142. For an extensive discussion of contributing causes, see Barrier, *Punjab Alienation of Land Bill*, chapter 1. See also the discussion in Oldenburg, *Dowry Murder*.

143. Lal, *Punjab Alienation of Land Act*, 173.

The indebtedness crisis that faced cultivators in the late nineteenth century threatened the foundational power of the colonial regime since the state of Punjab had become the central recruiting location for the army, and these "sturdy landholders" furnished "the flower of the Native Army of India"; it was clear that "the expropriation of the hereditary agriculturalist in many parts of the Province through the machinery of unrestricted sale and mortgage has been regarded for years past as a serious political danger."[144] Since the moneylenders who came to possess land were identified as Hindu, and cultivators/landowners as overwhelmingly Muslim or Sikh, the definition of these roles was religiously charged.[145] It may be the case that "what mattered in the district courts of colonial Punjab [adjudicating land cases] was not religion or caste *per se*, but the relationship between hereditary status and landownership."[146] However, since these were mutually produced categories, religious identity cannot be extricated easily from the equation. Barrier notes that although religion was not explicitly named as a reason for naming Muslims as agriculturalists within the implementation of the 1900 Land Alienation Act, such a policy had advocates, and there are clear cases of its influence: "For example, Brahmins were often agriculturalists, and yet the revenue authorities continually hesitated at including them because of their religion."[147] Hindu Jats could also be barred from transferring land to Muslim Jats, even if they lived in the same village.[148] This legislation particularly impacted the Jat-dominated Sikh community, determined within the colonial logic to be an agricultural community. Historical relations to land, therefore, came to be articulated through both caste and religion. The 1900 Act was not novel in this effect, since the entire conception of property rights in Punjab relied upon "the feeling in favour of the prior rights of the village community and on the recognition of the principle of tribal organization which are well known powerful factors in the social economy of the agricultural classes of Punjab."[149]

Three points are salient here, all of which come to impact the status of the gurdwara in the twentieth century. First: in the evolving property order, the proof of a history of ownership in the past becomes central to ownership in the present. History is an essential part of the discourse on ownership. Second, a

---

144. Lal, *Punjab Alienation of Land Act*, 174 first quote, 163 second quote.

145. Nelson, "Land, Law, and the Logic of Local Politics," 115, 122–23. 163.

146. Nelson, "Land, Law, and the Logic of Local Politics," 183, and see also 190.

147. Barrier, *Punjab Alienation of Land Bill*, 113.

148. Barrier, *Punjab Alienation of Land Bill*, 74.

149. See Legislative Council discussion of the Bill, in Lal, *Punjab Alienation of Land Act*, 170–71.

notion of the community was articulated in relation to the administration of property rights in general, over individual rights. This will prove to have a powerful impact in the debate over who should control gurdwaras, in the early twentieth century. Individual possession comes to be countered by community right to ownership, utilizing a broader discourse regarding the "history" of a site and its historical relationship to a community. Third, the assertion of singular proprietary rights made ownership in general more absolute than had existed in previous periods, at the same time that these hereditary rights came to be communally inflected. There were various *kinds* of ownership at work in Punjab, prior to the colonial period; there was neither absolute difference between the colonial order and what preceded it, nor complete continuity. At the same time, there *was* a change in the assertion of singular proprietary rights, making ownership less politically- and context-sensitive, than it had been in previous periods, such as can be seen in the reissuance of *sanad*s under new rulers. These three features of the understanding of property in combination constituted the fundamental conditions of possibility for the Gurdwara Reform Movement, with its challenge of individual property (as defined by the British colonial state) and the creation of the notion of a group—the Sikh *panth*—as the rightful owner, based on historical precedent. This process operated alongside others in colonial India to define the community with rights produced in the past. It was articulated specifically in relation to the religious institution as property, as will be discussed, but this more general discourse on property had an impact as well. The "Third Sikh War," as Richard Fox called the Gurdwara Reform Movement, must be understood in these terms, in addition to the broader economic and cultural constructivist concerns Fox highlights.[150]

Conclusion

Central to the understanding of the gurdwara that emerges in the early twentieth century is the notion of territoriality. This idea is not one that was invented with colonialism. David Ludden's discussion of agrarian territoriality is useful here. We can understand the transformation of the Sikh historical imaginary as one fundamentally related to a new sense of territoriality that emerges in the colonial period, drawing upon and significantly modifying preexisting precolonial/early modern formations of territoriality in an agrarian context. In the medieval and early modern periods, Ludden has argued, state formation was characterized by "flexible agrarian alliances among farmers, warriors, merchants, ritualists, kings,

---

150. Richard Fox, *Lions of the Punjab: Culture in the Making* (Berkeley: University of California Press, 1985).

and literati," that participated in sacred territorialization projects.[151] Landholding thus took place alongside a wide range of economic and social practices in the premodern and early modern periods, in relation to the granting of honors and emblems, to articulate forms of sovereignty. In the precolonial period, the gifts the king made, as land and as object, acted fundamentally, in Dirks' words, as "signs of sovereignty."[152] Gifts, whether they be emblems and honors or land rights, represented the sovereignty of the king and the state, and provided the means for participation with it. At some level, they were as much a "contributing factor" to this sovereignty, as a sign of it, as Dirks notes.[153] This territorialty, however, took a different shape in the colonial modern.

Cohn has described how such symbolic forms of sovereignty continued into the colonial period, to generate a colonial symbolic logic of sovereignty in relation to the gift. Certain elements were transformed, at the same time. We have seen in the data presented above that most commonly individuals were named within religious grants; occasionally other recipients were named, such as the Guru Granth Sahib (but through a human caretaker), or the Jogis at Jakhbar. This is an important point, given that the body to be designated as the rightful owner/controller of religious property becomes a highly contentious issue early on in the formation of the East India Company state, and even more so under direct Crown rule. This issue becomes a highly political matter that touches on one of the most profound ways the colonial state impacted South Asian cultural forms: the reification of religious and other community boundaries, in agonistic relation to each other. It also contributes foundationally to the movement for Sikh control of gurdwaras, based on a community's right to its historical property. The fight for Sikh control of gurdwaras expressed in the Gurdwara Reform Movement thus represented the culmination of a transition in the making of the historicality of place in the Sikh imaginary, in relation to a new kind of colonial territoriality and a new sense of the logic of ownership by and for the community.

The Darbar Sahib provides a compelling example of this transition in property and the logic of ownership that impacts the status of the gurdwara in relation to community. When the Darbar Sahib came under the control of the British administration of Punjab, it was managed through a committee. An allowance was granted for the Golden Temple and a *jagīr* granted to its head *granthī* in

---

151. Ludden, *Agrarian History of South Asia*, 65.

152. Dirks, "From Little King to Landlord," 180.

153. Dirks, *Hollow Crown*, 134.

1847.[154] Ian Kerr notes that "the British willingness to provide this financial support came from their belief that if [*sic*; it] politically benefited the Raj by (1) providing the British with a way to influence and pressure the influential functionaries of the Temple, and by (2) gaining the gratitude of the Sikh community (which at least could be translated into passive acceptance of British rule) because of the generous treatment of Sikhism's premier shrine. Conversely, the continued alienation of land revenue to the Temple also reflected British unwillingness to create discontent by ending the long-established practice in the Punjab of providing state support for religious institutions."[155] As will be discussed in the next chapter, British support for religious institutions was widespread and controversial across the subcontinent.

The appointed managing committee framed a set of rules and regulations for the Golden Temple's administration, entitled the *Dastur-ul' Amal*, in which ownership was defined as follows: "the sole proprietor of this sacred institution for ever is Guru Ramdass: no person else has any title to proprietorship. The claim to the noviciate or chelaship belongs to the whole 'Khalsa' body. The Pujaris and others receive their wages from the offerings according to their appointed dues for service performed."[156] As we have seen, this does not follow the previously established model for the designation of proprietorship at a site. In the precolonial period, under Ranjit Singh and his successors, individual service-providers received grants; so too did institutions within the Darbar Sahib (e.g. the Akal Bunga). With the early British period document, which identifies the Guru as the continuing proprietor of the site, and the Khalsa as his *chelā* or disciple, we see a transition into the management by the community that resonates through Sikh political and religious mobilization through the nineteenth and twentieth centuries, drawing on precolonial antecedents but changing them significantly. We will see in the next chapter that this document is not unusual; it reflects a general orientation to the management of religious sites that developed in British administration. The document draws on an already existing collective imaginary—the Khalsa—but articulates it with reference to the control of sites in a way that we have not seen in precolonial examples. This is why in the *hukamnāme* or orders of the Guru collected and edited by Ganda Singh, the

---

154. Cited in Kerr, "Administration of the Golden Temple." See *Lahore Political Diaries 1847–1848, Vol. III Political Diaries of the Agent to the Governor-general North-West Frontier and Resident at Lahore from 1st January 1847 to 4th March 1848* (Allahabad 1909), 355, 363.

155. Kerr, "Administration of the Golden Temple," 310.

156. See reference in Madanjit Kaur, *Golden Temple*, 62 and Appendix IV (199–203). See Kerr, "Administration of the Golden Temple," 316–19. He includes the Administration Paper for the Sikh Temple, dated September 15, 1859, as an appendix (317–19).

term Khalsa is used to address the community—it was clearly an important way of articulating the emerging consciousness of the community, as we saw in *Gur Sobhā* onwards—but orders are not issued in an institutional sense, on behalf of the Khalsa corporate body, until after 1850, when the Golden Temple's administration had already been framed with reference to the community of the Khalsa as owner.[157] The territory of the community began to take shape in a new way at this time.

The logic of property in Punjab provides an important context for the Gurdwara Reform Movement, which will be discussed at length in the next two chapters, because of its definition of property in relation to a designation of "the community," a logic that takes center stage—although in a different register—in the Movement. In the Punjabi land system, proof of a history of ownership in the past becomes central to ownership in the present, and a historical relationship with a founder determined rights in the modern debate over property. This becomes relevant to discourses over religious institutions and their ownership, and the debate that will ensue in which possession in the past by individuals is countered by community right to ownership in ancestral terms. We can see this in the designation of the Darbar Sahib as the property of the Khalsa body, the way the community is defined as a cohesive whole, as owner. This kind of religious articulation with reference to the land contributes to the ways that the landscape of Punjab was territorialized as Sikh.

Sites and objects have constituted an important type of evidence of the past, toward the construction of memory and the writing of history around these types of evidence: they do so in the present and, as argued earlier, did so in the past. The value and meaning of the evidence of the past—sites and objects— were articulated differently (but not replaced) however, within and after the intervention of colonial forms of knowledge. We have explored this transition here specifically with respect to the understanding of a religious site as property, in relation to the broader idea of property that coalesces in the colonial period. The next chapter will delve deeper into the status of the religious site in administrative terms under colonial rule, shaping not only the way the gurdwara is conceptualized in the modernizing order of Punjab, but also how the community is conceived in relation to the site. David Ludden has argued that "many social movements that moderns might call 'religious' might be better understood as formations of agrarian territorialism."[158] The movement for gurdwara management, and the formation of the SGPC, can be seen in such a light,

---

157. Ganda Singh, *Hukamnāme*, 233–36.

158. Ludden, *Agrarian History of South Asia*, 85.

reflecting medieval/early modern forms of agrarian territorialism, altered and inflected within the territorial logic of the East India Company and later Crown rule of property, to create a new Sikh territorialism with shifting relations to state sovereignty and animated by a communitarian imagination of the past that was inherited from earlier times.

6

Colonial Governance and Gurdwara Reform

gur sikkhāṅ valloṅ ih khoj saṅbhāl te sevā kise lobh vāste nahīṅ
sī es vāste jitthe 2 jo bhale purash mile uthoṅ uthoṅ dī dhārmak
maṅdarāṅ te saṅgatāṅ nūṅ shubh upadesh karan dī sevā unhāṅ
de hī sapurad karke nekī dā somāṅ jārī kar ditā!

This search, care, and service [of the gurdwaras] on the part
of the Gursikhs [those dedicated to the Guru] is not born
of any kind of greed, but for the cause of the virtue initiated
wherever two good people come together and make it their
duty to serve and teach communities at religious places.

—BHAI MOHAN SINGH VAID[1]

It should not be understood that the Sikhs do not want to
reform the Sikh religious and charitable public trusts, other
than historical, which are mismanaged. It is hoped that
when the main problem of the historical Gurdwaras is
solved, there will be no difficulty in improving the conditions of other religious institutions by securing their management according to the conditions of their foundation.
The present struggle, however, is confined to historical
Gurdwaras alone.

—LETTER TO M. K. GANDHI FROM THE SGPC, APRIL
20, 1924[2]

---

1. Bhai Mohan Singh Vaid, *Bhayānak Sākkā*. (Amritsar: Wazir Hind Press, n.d.), 3. IOL
14162.n.8 (1). Vaid was municipal commissioner of Tarn Taran. On Vaid, see N. G. Barrier,
"Vernacular Publishing and Sikh Public Life in the Punjab, 1880–1910." In *Religious Contro-*
versy in British India: Dialogues in South Asian Languages, ed. Kenneth W. Jones. (Albany:
State University of New York Press, 1992), 219–21.

2. Ganda Singh, ed., *Some Confidential Papers of the Akali Movement* (Amritsar: Shiromani
Gurdwara Parbandhak Committee, Sikh Itihas Research Board, 1965), 63.

PLACES AND OBJECTS related to the Gurus were important in the precolonial historical imaginary. They provided evidence of a history of relationships in the past—parallel to that narrated within textual historiography—that constructed the community around the Guru, the Sikhs, in the ongoing present. The landscape of the Sikh past was commemorated by the establishment of gurdwaras, particularly with the achievement of political power by Sikh leaders in eighteenth-century, post-Mughal Punjab, reflecting the shared historical imaginary within which both objects and sites were revered. Support for religious sites provided a means for the production of a landscape of the Sikh past, but this landscape was only one way of reading the religious landscape in multi-religious Punjab, alongside more secular readings. That diverse religious landscape is fully represented, for example, in the court records of the Lahore state, under Maharaja Ranjit Singh and his successors. As we saw in chapter 5, the precolonial record saw the control of such sites by individuals who represented lineages, families, or sites themselves, reflecting the precolonial understanding of ownership as political and negotiated, articulated through persons, and entailing a range of different rights to land and the produce of land. As has been shown in the previous chapter, colonial period administration of property focused on property as an enduring, proprietary right, rather than a political process. Thus while land was highly valued in both the precolonial and the colonial imagination, its status in the British Raj was fundamentally changed. As property came to be linked to an individual as heritable, enduring, and alienable, the relationship of individuals in control of religious grants to the land changed. This change in the nature of property rights meant that the designation of individuals in control of religious sites was no longer viable. This situation, in the Sikh case, led to the quest for control of gurdwaras, known as the Gurdwara Reform or Akali Movement. Through this movement, the Sikh past came to be linked to territory in a new way, in relation to an idea of the Sikh community that drew on long existing formulations of the Khalsa *panth* but utilized them in administrative terms in new ways.

These phenomena of course had broader implications. The Gurdwara Reform or Akali Movement proved to be the first significant and widespread mobilization of Sikhs in opposition to British power in the subcontinent, as other forms of resistance also coalesced in the early 1920s. The Ghadar or "Revolution" Movement, then later the 1919 unrest (and the infamous Jallianwala Bagh incident) and the Non-Cooperation and Khilafat Movements, expressed a growing sentiment against colonial rule, as South Asians and particularly Punjabis returned from fighting in significant numbers for the British in World War I. In 1922, V. W. Smith, superintendent of police in the Criminal Investigation Department of

Punjab, declared the Akali Movement a "cause of much greater concern and anxiety than civil disobedience campaign instituted by Mr. Gandhi." He gives reasons for this:

> A spirit of fanaticism which cannot be exorcised has permeated the ranks of the Akalis. Gandhi's propaganda makes its appeal mainly to the urban classes, which lack both the stamina and physical courage to oppose successfully even small bodies of police; the Akali campaign is essentially a rural movement, and its followers are men of fine physique with a national history of which the martial characteristics have been purposely kept alive both by Government and the Sikhs themselves. Finally, the national volunteer is unarmed, whereas the Akali has acquired the right to arm himself with an obsolete, but none the less formidable, offensive weapon.[3]

This statement is rife with the stereotypes that shaped the British perception of the Sikhs vis-à-vis others, such as the lack of "stamina and physical courage" of the urban classes, compared to the "spirit of fanaticism" and "fine physique" of the Sikhs. The statement also notes "the martial characteristics have been purposely kept alive both by Government and the Sikhs themselves," revealing the self-understanding of colonial administrators as patrons of Sikhism.[4] It also shows a central, related concern of the government: the need to maintain the premiere recruiting territory of the Indian Army in Punjab.[5]

Sikh and Punjabi loyalty loomed large in the concerns voiced in government communications and Legislative Council debates at the provincial level, where gurdwara reform was debated at length. The debates in the provincial council reflect an important component of a changing governance structure in British India: such councils provided a key mode of "modified" colonial governance after the passage of the Indian Councils Act of 1861, which brought the

---

3. *Home Department, Political*, File No. 459 of 1922, Serial Nos. 1–10: 27. National Archives of India, New Delhi.

4. This is something that is all too often accepted as simply true in both popular and academic historiography; the classic example is Fox, *Lions of the Punjab*.

5. Discussed by Tai Yong Tan, "Assuaging the Sikhs: Government Responses to the Akali Movement, 1920–25," *Modern Asian Studies* 29, 3 (1995): 655–703; see 655–56. The importance of Punjab as a recruitment ground is stated clearly by British administrators, sometimes even impacting the level of revenue assessment demanded by the state; see, for example, *Dept of Revenue and Agricultural Proceedings* No. 30. Nov 1912, IOR P/8918: 17.

promise, if not the reality, of representative structures.[6] This debate over gurdwara reform—which took place in a newly elected Council—demonstrates the shape of colonial governance generally, but also specifically the way the representation of the Sikh community was configured within it. As the notations for each member of the committee below demonstrate, the Council imagined its members as not individuals, or representatives of geographically defined entities, but as representative of community types: urban or rural, Sikh or Muslim. The debate shows, with vivid detail, how the case was made for the production of a Sikh governing body for gurdwaras, and in this sense, how colonial governance interacted with Sikh and other interests in the Legislative Council context to produce a particular imagination of the Sikh community, in administrative terms and in relation to the representation of the past through the Sikh gurdwara.

The all-India context creates a crucial frame for the Gurdwara Reform Movement, one that is often neglected in scholarly treatment of it.[7] We will in this chapter examine all-India concerns regarding the management of religious sites, particularly with reference to Hindu temples and Muslim institutions, before turning to the movement for gurdwara reform, with particular attention to the ways in which the case was made for Sikh community governance of Sikh shrines. Arjun Appadurai showed in his early work how the evolving conditions of the colonial state's role in managing South Indian Hindu temples provided a local instance of broader discourse over the management of religious sites, whereby caste and sect acted as determining factors in the definition of an institution's community.[8] In the gurdwara context, historical precedent and the ensuing right of the community were invoked, in relation to the codification of the definition of who is a Sikh—a preoccupation of the colonial state in general. Our examination of the specific case of the gurdwara and the fight for control over the Sikh historical site that ensued in the early 1920s leads, in the next chapter, to consideration of how and why religious-site-as-property has in this context been decoupled from the historical object, which once shared a place in the imagination of the

---

6. In the Government of India Act of 1919 (the Montagu-Chelmsford Reforms), under which elections were held in 1920, a two-level centralized and provincial system was established, such that ministries were split between those "reserved" for government appointments and those for which ministers could be elected. By 1935, provincial representation became more complete, but reserved ministries continued.

7. Most accounts explore the movement in relation to the development of Sikh identity, without attention to the all-India context, such as Mohinder Singh, *The Akali Movement* (1978; repr., New Delhi: National Institute of Punjab Studies, 1997).

8. Appadurai, *Worship and Conflict*, 188–89.

past, and how the forces described in the last chapter and this one contributed to the articulation of a territorialized Sikh identity in the materialization of the Sikh past in the colonial period.

Ownership, Management, and Religious Sites in the British Raj

While the establishment of British rule brought great changes to the assignment of land in Punjab, and many grants were resumed, it was argued in the early 1850s that "the priestly classes have . . . every reason to bless their new masters. The Seikh [*sic*] holy places have been respected . . . [and] liberality has indeed been extended to all religious characters, even to mendicant friars and village ascetics."[9] The impact of the British administration on endowments for religious institutions however was more complex than such a statement might indicate and had a wide range of sometimes unintended consequences, born of both Sikh and British interests. Indeed, as Appadurai has argued regarding the British administration of Hindu temples in the Tamil region, British management of temple conflict forced the British both to adhere to local needs and to shape local articulation of rights and claims, reflecting therefore a dialectic between colonial and South Asian forms of knowledge in the formation of the realms of action in relation to the religious site.[10] The same can be said of the dynamics of gurdwara reform.

Thus "traditional" forms of the management of religious sites took new shape within the circumstances produced by East India Company and British Crown administration, and interference by the state grew in intensity through the second half of the nineteenth century—at the very time that efforts were ostensibly made to lessen the colonial state's role in the management of such sites. The Religious Endowments Act of 1863 (Act XX of that year) was passed to allow the Board of Revenue to withdraw from active oversight of religious sites, and specifically to undo the precedents set by Regulation XIX of the Bengal Code in 1810 and Regulation VII of the Madras Code in 1817, which had allowed for "support of mosques, Hindoo temples, colleges, and for other pious and beneficial purposes".[11] The 1863 Act created the context for the management of religious endowments until its modification in 1936 and, therefore, was the legislation that governed the management of religious institutions throughout India—Hindu,

9. Kerr, "Punjab Province," 292, and for quotation, Selections from the Records of the Government of India, 1849–1937. IOR v/23/1. No.8, 212–214.

10. Appadurai, *Worship and Conflict*, 17.

11. For quotation, see: Regulation XIX, Bengal Code 1810. Regulations, 1804–1814. IOR v/8/18; 412; see also Act No. XX of 1863, India Acts, IOR v/8/39, section 1.

Muslim, or Sikh. As such, it is integrally related to the Gurdwara Reform Act of 1925—which determined who had the right to manage gurdwaras, and who was their legal owner—as well as legislation of the same period concerning other religious establishments.[12] Due to concern that the government would be abandoning the care of religious and charitable organizations, the final Act of 1863 repealed the two regulations in question but with "special provisions."[13] According to the Act, there were two types of endowments: first, those which would be managed by their present trustees, and thus would require no major modification of current arrangements; second, those that would require such "special provisions to be made for their management."[14] A committee of at least three persons would make such provisions. This committee would be appointed by the local government (or, if government so determined, by election) and include persons "professing the religion for the purposes of which the Mosque, Temple, or other religious establishment, was founded, or is now maintained." The Act determined that "as soon as possible after the passing of this Act" the government would "transfer to such Trustee, Manager or Superintendent, all the landed or other property which, at the time of the passing of this Act, shall be under the superintendence or in the possession of the Board of Revenue, or any local Agent, and belonging to such Mosque, Temple, or other religious establishment."[15]

The status of the owner of the institution becomes a central one in this legislation, and is defined in radically different ways for different religious communities in British India; it is the acceptance of these different modes of description that in many ways reinscribes differences and conflicts among communities and differentiates the solution to the problem for Sikhs from others. The manner of management and control of religious sites therefore had profound implications for the relationship between the state and religious communities. The Religious Societies Act I of 1880 attempted to "simplify the manner in which certain bodies of persons (other than Hindus, Mahomedans and Buddhists), associated for the purpose of maintaining religious worship may hold property acquired for such

12. The Hindu Religious Endowments Board in Madras Presidency, examined by Appadurai, provides one example (Appadurai, *Worship and Conflict*, 52). See discussion below.

13. Act No. XX of 1863, Bills, Objects and Reasons. IOR L/P&J/5/3, "Statement of Objects and Reasons," February 5, 1862, p. 1.

14. Act No. XX of 1863, Bills, Objects and Reasons. IOR L/P&J/5/3, "A Paper related to the Bill to enable the Government to divest itself of the management of Religious Endowments," May 9, 1862, p. 1.

15. Act No. XX of 1863, Bills, Objects and Reasons. IOR L/P&J/5/3, see sections VIII of final Act (first quote) and IV (second quote).

purpose."[16] In colonial courts, worshipers gained the right to management in the absence of a manager, or when defined as possessing a legitimate interest. This was an all-India phenomenon. Thus, Appadurai names two "radical generative consequences" of British Indian treatment of religious endowments with respect to the Sri Partasarati Swami Temple: first, that the community that had the "exclusive right" to control the temple was defined, and second, that "various subgroups and individuals within this Tenkalai community were encouraged to emphasize the heterogeneity of their interests and to formulate their *special* rights in a mutually antagonistic way, thus making authority in the temple even more fragile than it previously had been."[17]

In a parallel example from the late nineteenth century regarding Muslim endowments, decisions were handed down by the High Courts of India and the Privy Council that declared invalid any *waqf* that benefited the families of founders.[18] Instead, Quranic injunction had to be followed: "if the *Quran* demanded a partition of estates, Muslims must not evade the rigours of their own legal system."[19] Through this process, the British assumed a position of arbitration over which aspects of Muslim belief and practice constituted *legitimate* religious action (for example, by subordinating Hadith to the Quran). Kozlowski notes that the British assumed that Muslims were, as a rule, orthodox and uniform, and that their legal system was not responsive to historical circumstances.[20] The distinctions explicitly accepted within Muslim discursive settings, between ethnic and linguistic groups or different class groups, were not acknowledged, and Muslim unity was emphasized. Kozlowski notes that in this sense, British policy "contributed to the work of the religious and political reformers who have had so much influence on the shape of Muslim history in the twentieth century."[21] This is in keeping with what we see elsewhere, the agreement between increasingly politicized religious identities and colonial

---

16. Abinaschandra Ghosh, *The law of endowments (Hindu & Mahomedan): With introduction, history of the origin and development of the charitable and religious institutions in India, and the laws governing them: including the procedure, and all the imperial and local acts, model forms of deeds, pleadings and rules* (Calcutta: Eastern Law House, 1938), 53.

17. Appadurai, *Worship and Conflict*, 176. On "interest," see the text of "Charitable and Religious Trusts Act, 1920," Act. No. XIV of 1920, in IOR v/8/70, p. 87.

18. Kozlowski, *Muslim Endowments*, 5, 38. 5, 38. See *Abul Fatah Mahomed Ishak v. Rasamaya Dhur Chowdhuri* 22 I.A. 76: 22 Cal. 619 (P.C.), cited in Ghosh, *Law of Endowments*, 524. This was referred to the Privy Council in 1894, which declared family forms of this *waqf* invalid because not pious.

19. Kozlowski, *Muslim Endowments*, 5.

20. Kozlowski, *Muslim Endowments*, 97.

21. Kozlowski, *Muslim Endowments*, 7.

policies: British legal and Islamist political discourse were in fact aligned and mutu-ally productive. The intervention of the British courts into the arena of Muslim en-dowments caused political controversy that led to the Mussalman Wakf Validating Act of 1913, meant to ensure that a Muslim(s) retain the right to establish a *waqf* (or religious endowment) on their "own terms," but *as defined by the state*. The Mus-salman Wakf Act of 1923 followed, requiring registration of such institutions, in keeping with the provisions spelled out in the Charitable and Religious Trusts Act of 1920, which sought to define trusts (and, as Ritu Birla notes, ensuing ideas of public and private) and bring them under the control of the state.[22] Gurdwara reform legislation took shape in this context, solidifying definitions of the Sikh com-munity in the language of the Gurdwara Reform Act, as will be seen in chapter 7.

The Punjabi Context: Economic and Social Change, 1880–1920

The movement for gurdwara reform at the beginning of the twentieth century must be located within the tensions over the definition of religious communities that fueled the all-India legislation named above. It must simultaneously be located within the particular material and other circumstances of Punjab and the Sikh community. Punjab has been considered unique in colonial India for several reasons. It was annexed by the East India Company late—less than ten years before the 1857 rebel-lion against the East India Company—and was administered through a system of "paternalistic despotism" that came to be known as the Punjab School of Administra-tion.[23] One aspect of that administration was the investment in agricultural develop-ment in what came to be called the "canal colonies"—settlements in western Punjab dependant upon new canals built by the colonial administration—which provided not only for agricultural expansion in the region, but also the retrenchment of the political forces that supported British rule. In Punjab, unlike in some parts of India, the British thus vigorously promoted agricultural development, particularly in the beginning of the twentieth century. As Imran Ali has emphasized, however, one cannot see the Punjab economy as being developed *overall* under the British: its underdevelopment took place through a process of "economic expansion rather than stagnation or decline," as colonization policies were developed to shore up imperial interests at the expense of the development of resources and technologies.[24] As the

---

22. Ritu Birla, *Stages of Capital: Law, Culture, and Market Governance in Late Colonial India* (Durham: Duke University Press, 2009), ch. 2 and 3. See also: Charitable and Religious Trusts Act, 1920. Act. No. XIV of 1920, IOR v/8/70.

23. Tan, *Garrison State*, 17.

24. Ali, *Punjab under Imperialism*, 6; see also 237ff.

market infiltrated the pre-canal colony peasant-based agricultural centers in Punjab
after annexation, peasants in the central region of the province became what Richard
Fox calls "petty commodity producers," and an increasingly international market
came to have more importance in agricultural life than had previously been the case.
The Jats, at the center of the Punjabi agricultural landscape, and in the traditionally
well-developed agricultural areas in the province, played a special role in this new
economy. A good number of them were Sikh.

Military service was also a major agent of change in the region, and one
that ensured that the British would protect the interests of Punjabis. Before
the 1857 Rebellion—called quite rightly by some the first war of Indian independence, but known as "the Mutiny" in colonial sources—the Bengal army
was dominated by higher-caste recruits from eastern India. With insurrection
spreading among East India Company troops, Punjabis played a crucial role in
the protracted battle that ensued to reestablish British control in the subcontinent: between May and December of that year approximately 34,000 Punjabis joined the British forces, including some who had been demobilized by
the same government previously.[25] As Tan notes, "although British rhetoric at
that time spoke of the Punjabis' 'splendid and noble response to the call of
duty,' there were no illusions that the Punjabis had responded to the British
call out of a sense of loyalty."[26] The precarious position of Punjabi, and particularly Sikh, elites in post-annexation Punjab ensured that they would welcome any opportunity to reinstate themselves. The benefits of both service
and supporting recruitment were real: the participation of Punjabis in the
conflict in defense of British interests helped secure them a significant place in
the military machinery of empire. With the advent of the "Great Game" in
the 1880s, when British concerns over Russian designs on the subcontinent
became paramount, the theory of the martial races took precedence in recruitment and Punjabis came to dominate overall.[27] It was at this time that the
personal preferences of particular leaders in the army consolidated into a
"full-blown recruiting doctrine which the military and the state in colonial
India faithfully adhered to for the next fifty years." By 1900, more than 50% of
men in the Indian Army—newly consolidated as a single army out of the three
presidency armies in 1895—were from Punjab; at the eve of World War I, 66%

---

25. Tan, *Garrison State*, 46.

26. Tan, *Garrison State*, 47. Quotation is from Captain H. R. James, Offg. Sec to Chief Commissioner, Punjab to Sec, Government of India, Foreign Department, May 17, 1857, in *Mutiny
Records (Correspondence)* Vol. 7 (i), 36, as quoted in Tan.

27. See the discussion in Tan, *Garrison State*, 57ff.

of the cavalry, 87% of the artillery, and 45% of the infantry of the Indian Army were Punjabi.[28]

At first no particular preponderance of one group among Punjabis was maintained; later, the model advocated by the "Punjab Committee" (including administrator John Lawrence) established provincial regiments with companies dominated by different groups, to prevent these from joining forces. This meant, typically, that a Punjabi regiment would have a company of Sikhs, two of Pathans, and one of Hindu Jats. Within the Punjab contingent, divisions based on religious, class, and caste difference were thus maintained "to reproduce . . . the historical cleavages that existed within their society."[29] Such a policy was also pursued in the settlement of the canal colonies, where "a cardinal principle of colonisation remained that men of different castes should not be mixed in the same village . . . [so that] in an area where production for the market was well advanced, the emphasis on caste signified a strengthening of traditional forms of social organisation."[30] Thus, as Tan argues, "while the army in India, with its European-style organizational structure, uniforms, weapons systems and tactical doctrines, was in many ways a modern Anglo-Indian institution, its effect on society, especially where recruitment was concerned, was to reinforce and perpetuate the old order of rural Punjab."[31] Military service and the development of agriculture under British rule were thus connected forces of change, in terms of how they were implemented; they were even further connected, since so many grants to land in newly opened areas were made to benefit those serving in the military, or those who raised horses or provided other services. This represented in some ways an expansion of the precolonial logic of the *jagīr* system, in support of imperial interests, but with the added reinforcement of purportedly traditional forms of social organization.[32]

The impact of World War I cannot be underemphasized. Of the approximately seven hundred thousand combatants recruited in India between 1914 and 1918 to serve in World War I, approximately 60% came from Punjab. During the war, "Punjab was converted into a virtual 'home front,' with the state firmly oriented toward supporting the war effort." When recruitment opened up to wider sections of Punjabi society as the pressures on recruitment increased dramatically

28. Tan, *Garrison State*, 68, 18, 64 for quote.

29. Tan, *Garrison State*, 52–53, 76 for quote.

30. Ali, *Punjab under Imperialism*, 64.

31. Tan, *Garrison State*, 76–77.

32. Ali, *Punjab under Imperialism*, 122–23.

toward the end of World War I, more Punjabis took advantage of these benefits, with the strong support of local elites in the recruitment effort.[33] The main groups chosen in the early twentieth century—Jat Sikhs from the central Punjab or Majha region (and to a lesser extent Hoshiarpur and Ludhiana), aristocratic Muslims from western Punjab, and Hindu and Muslim Jats from eastern Punjab and the hills—entered the army for different reasons.[34] For Sikhs from Majha, whose land was productive and well-irrigated, the prosperity associated with the land brought its own problems: heavy pressure on soil and the fragmentation of agricultural land due to population pressure. Military service was a way to escape debt and to maintain and even add to a family's landholdings.[35] Migration abroad was also an option for some, particularly for those who served in the army. As long as these options were open to the "petty commodity producer," and as long as the government fought to protect him, conditions remained somewhat stable in central Punjab.[36]

As Richard Fox and others have shown, in the period 1880–1920 the delicate economic balance established under the Raj was disrupted. Small producers in central Punjab found themselves at a distinct disadvantage in comparison to those cultivators in the canal colonies who were not saddled by debt and whose economy had benefited from the development-oriented intervention of the British. Central Punjab could not compete with canal colony production. A series of factors related to this, Fox argues, brought about the crisis that thrust the petty commodity producer into conflict with the state in the 1920s: (1) unequal market competition and unequal exchange with the canal colonies; (2) the removal of external options for revenue production, such as a decrease in army recruits and in migration, in light of increasingly restrictive immigration policies in destinations like the United States and Canada, which had adopted racist laws meant to discourage Asian migration; (3) waterlogging in central Punjab; and (4) a decrease in the number of canal colony grants available.[37]

The Land Alienation Act of 1900 was an early attempt by the government to protect peasant proprietors in Punjab by limiting the alienation of land to nonagricultural tribes/groups, and therefore preventing moneylenders from having the

---

33. Tan, *Garrison State*, 99ff, 98–99 for quote. On the opening up of recruiting for new groups, see 116ff.

34. Tan, *Garrison State*, 74–75.

35. Tan, *Garrison State*, 86–88.

36. Fox, *Lions of the Punjab*, 48–49.

37. See Fox, *Lions of the Punjab*, particularly chapter 4.

ability to collect on debts through the acquisition of land. This was clearly done for the sake of the stability and loyalty of the army: "the argument that further alienation could inevitably hurt the interests of the military classes, whose loyalty the state could not afford to compromise, was incontrovertible."[38] To some degree, Fox argues, this freed small producers from the hegemony of merchant capital, but debt to rich farmers took its place. In addition, the Act exacerbated differences between rural and urban members of society, and among castes. These factors, coupled with soaring land prices after the First World War, gave rise to violent rural protest, as the Singhs fought to "free themselves and their land from the British tether."[39]

A Context for Protest

The Gurdwara Reform Movement was not the only source of unrest in the period. The Khilafat Movement, linked at times to the larger Non-Cooperation Movement led by M. K. Gandhi, was meant to defend the caliphate in the face of attacks on Turkey and its eventual defeat in World War I. With the abolition of the caliphate by Ataturk, the movement was disbanded.[40] The Khilafat Movement took hold in Punjab just as the Akali Movement was radicalizing, threatening the disloyalty of the central pieces of the British military puzzle: Punjabi Muslims and Sikhs.[41] The Muslim League, Congress, and numerous other groups united behind this issue temporarily; in concert, these constituted a major challenge to the colonial government. The other, larger movement that coincided with the movement for gurdwara reform was the Non-Cooperation Movement, which pledged to fight the British colonial regime through non-cooperation or peaceful resistance. Ruchi Ram Sahni (1863–1948), Punjabi intellectual, witness to the Gurdwara Reform Movement, and member of the Punjabi Legislative Council who participated in the passing of legislation to address gurdwara reform, described the gurdwara movement as "the best and most inspiring instance of Mahatma Gandhi's teachings of non-violence in thought, word and deed," and declared that "Mahatma Gandhi himself could not have expected more faithful followers to carry out his non-violent non-cooperative struggle in

---

38. Tan, *Garrison State*, 92.

39. Fox, *Lions of the Punjab*, 11. See chapter 5 on the Act and its impact.

40. See Gail Minault, *The Khilafat Movement: Religious Symbolism and Political Mobilization in India* (New York: Columbia University Press, 1982).

41. Tan, *Garrison State*, 148. There are discursive links between the two movements as well, as will be discussed.

the face of the gravest provocation."[42] Indeed, as described in SGPC papers, "our mode of suffering is perfectly non-violent,"[43] and in the words of Mohan Singh Vaid, municipal commissioner of Tarn Taran and prominent reformist leader:

> *asīṅ kise te*
> *zulam karnā nahīṅ zulam sahiṇā hai!*
> *burā kahiṇā nahīṅ burā sahiṇā hai!*
> *dukh deṇā nahīṅ dukh jarnā hai!*
> *marnā nahīṅ āp marnā hai!*
> *kahiṇā nahīṅ karke dasṇā hai!*
> *par asūlāṅ dā ghāt nahīṅ hoṇ deṇā!*
> *kaumī āṅ nūṅ vataṅ nahīṅ laggaṇ deṇā.*[44]

We, unto anyone else:
>   We will not be cruel, but will endure cruelty!
>   We will not speak badly, but will endure the bad!
>   We will not give trouble, but will bear it!
>   We will not kill others, but will die!
>   We will not speak, but having done will tell!
But we will not allow murder of our principles!
We will not allow the oppression of the members of our community!

Based on the philosophy of *satyāgraha* or "truth force," non-cooperation was initiated by M. K. Gandhi in the first decade of the twentieth century in South Africa, and became his central mode of non-violent resistance to colonial rule in India upon his return there. In 1919–20, non-cooperation was adopted by Congress in its all-India demonstrations against the Rowlatt Acts, made infamous by the Jallianwala Bagh incident, in which a large crowd of mostly Sikh peaceful demonstrators were fired upon by the forces of the state. Self-governing institutions were announced with the Montagu-Chelmsford Reforms of 1919, but these were slow to be enacted. The electorate comprised a tenth of the male population, and was specifically designed, in the Punjab, to favor the "rural-military elites," as Tan calls them, who were the backbone of the British Indian Punjabi political framework and explicitly promoted by government authorities to support the military-political establishment in Punjab.

---

42. Ruchi Ram Sahni, *The Akali Movement: Struggle for Reform in Sikh Shrines* (Amritsar: Sikh Ithas Research Board, [1940s?] 1960–69[?]), i (first quotation), iv (second quotation).

43. Ganda Singh, *Some Confidential Papers*, 64.

44. Bhai Mohan Singh Vaid, *Bhayānak Sākkā*, 7.

Another important context for the activism around gurdwara reform was the Ghadar Movement.[45] Earlier, the promise of the return of Maharaja Dalip Singh (the son of Maharaja Ranjit Singh who had signed over his kingdom to the East India Company at annexation) in the 1880s had been seen as a possible opportunity to return to glories of the past. This had come to naught, however, and the Maharaja never returned to Punjab. The Ghadar Movement was initiated in 1913 within the Sikh diaspora, primarily in North America—particularly in California, Oregon, Washington, and British Columbia—and reflects the development of a national consciousness amongst South Asians (mostly Punjabis and Sikhs) within a North American environment that was hostile to their presence. Inequalities and injustice in colonial India were seen to mirror the discrimination Punjabis faced in Canada and the United States; supporters of *ghadar* or revolution perceived the connections between the two situations in a shared imperial and global economic system. As Maia Ramnath thus notes, "the impact of racial discrimination and its crucial intersection with class cannot be underestimated as a catalyst for the radicalization of South Asians in North America. Yet only when this frame was overlaid on the geopolitical reality of India's colonized status would American discontent transmute into Indian mutiny."[46] The hostility migrants faced in North America is demonstrated most vividly in the 1914 Komagata Maru incident in Vancouver BC, where a boatload of almost four hundred South Asian (overwhelmingly Punjabi and Sikh) migrants were refused entry into Canada as a result of the passage of immigration regulations meant specifically to stop the flow of South Asian (and other Asian) migration.[47] This incident invigorated the Ghadar Movement in 1914–15. Contacts were made between Ghadar activists and former and current members of the Indian Army in the countryside, and Ghadar revolutionary cells were said to exist within the army. Indeed, many members of the Ghadar Party had significant ties to the Indian Army, with as many as 50% being ex-soldiers.[48] Three thousand Ghadarites returned to Punjab from North America in this period, and nearly a thousand were imprisoned by the colonial state. Ghadar never gained wide acceptance and failed to initiate the general uprising it sought. Sikh elites indeed played a crucial role in limiting its influence, and the

---

45. Harish K. Puri *Ghadar Movement: Ideology, Organization, and Strategy* (Amritsar: Guru Nanak Dev University, 1983).

46. Maia Ramnath *Haj to Utopia: How the Ghadar Movement Charted Global Radicalism and Attempted to Overthrow the British Empire* (Berkeley: University of California Press, 2011), 33.

47. Hugh Johnston *The Voyage of the Komagata Maru: The Sikh Challenge to Canada's Colour Bar* (New Delhi: Oxford University Press, 1979).

48. Tan, *Garrison State*, 113, 112 n. 45.

Chief Khalsa Diwan and Singh Sabhas issued manifestos against Ghadar activities.[49] The movement did, however, set the stage for later increased nationalist activity.

Despite such forces, Punjab overall remained the bulwark of the imperial presence at the beginning of the twentieth century. Extensive rewards, in the form of swords of honor, annual financial settlements, and land grants were given to the loyal, and particularly to those who garnered support for the war effort.[50] Many of the province's old aristocracy in particular benefited, receiving income and land for their cooperation with the state in supporting the war and combating dissent.[51] This collaboration of elites and the civil-military nexus in Punjab was formidable, particularly among Sikhs involved in the armed forces, and in turn the colonial administration relied heavily on the Punjab's rural landed elites to maintain loyalty in the army. The resultant quiescence did not, however, continue into the 1920s. Demilitarized soldiers after World War I were both a threat and a promise to the government. Some could be counted on to remain loyal, but others could not. District Soldiers' Boards and other mechanisms were formed to manage dissent among former soldiers. But these means proved less successful in the central districts of Punjab, due to a relatively smaller group of elites available to maintain them. As Tan notes, "the onus of maintaining the 'loyalty' of the army . . . lay not so much on British regimental officers as on local governments and district officers, for it was in the recruiting districts and the homes of soldiers that the 'loyalty' of the army was often won or lost."[52] Management proved extremely difficult to achieve for the government with the advent of the movement for gurdwara reform.

Imagining the Gurdwara in the New Colonial Economy

A new gurdwara-episteme was created in the dynamic interaction of colonial interests and administration and the preexisting Sikh commitment to the commemoration of the Sikh past, and this episteme was articulated and acted upon within the Gurdwara Reform Movement. Fox describes this "Third Sikh War" as a massive rural protest movement against colonial rule that he argues was driven by the instability wrought by economic change in the province. It would be wrong to see it as

---

49. Tan, *Garrison State*, 126.

50. See table of rewards in Tan, *Garrison State*, 123.

51. Tan, *Garrison State*, 128; see 132 for examples of Bhai Arjan Singh Bagrian and Bhai Khem Singh Bedi of Rawalpindi.

52. Tan, *Garrison State*, 163, 167, 240, see 184 for quote.

primarily economic. Fundamentally, the movement was about who had the right to control gurdwaras and the lands associated with them. Importantly, in general terms, it was also "the most sustained and widespread case of military dissent in British Punjab."[53] It was strongly rural in character and was dominated by Jats. At first, conflict was between, in Fox's words, "different sorts of Sikhs,"[54] as the Singh reformers sought to wrest control of the gurdwaras from *mahant*s and *sarbrah*s (appointed managers). Later, it grew into direct conflict with the state. The definition of who was a Sikh was already by this time open to serious and contentious debate; the definition (and the act of setting one) had become highly politicized since the second quarter of the nineteenth century, with the founding of the Sri Guru Singh Sabha of Amritsar in 1873, followed by Lahore Sabha in 1879. Hundreds more Singh Sabhas were founded in the last two decades of the nineteenth century, reflecting what J. S. Grewal has called a "new consciousness of common identity" and a time of the production of "tradition" in a new modern form, with reference to the past.[55]

The rhetoric of the movement centrally addressed the question of who was the right *kind* of person to manage a Sikh shrine, and who was truly a Sikh, all with reference to the specter of the past as the source of tradition. For example, a 1922 pamphlet criticizes those who engage in yogic practices:

sādh nahīṅ hove dehī āpnī nūṅ gaḍ khaṛe sādh nahīṅ huṅde jāṇ dhūṇīāṅ ca jalatāṅ

They are not good, who pierce their bodies. They are not good who burn in the fire of ascetics. . . .

sādh nahīṅ hove sir rakh le jaṛvālā sādh nahīṅ hove jo sarīr ko munāe jī

They are not good, who wear dreadlocks on their head. They are not good who trim [the hair on] their bodies.

sādh nahīṅ hove jo suāh ko lagāve jādā sādh nahīṅ hove bhekh bahute banae jī

They are not good, who apply ashes. They are not good who engage in the wearing of the dress of a religious order.[56]

---

53. Tan, *Garrison State*, 188.

54. Fox, *Lions of the Punjab*, 84.

55. Grewal, *Sikhs of the Punjab*, 145; Ballantyne, *Between Colonialism and Diaspora*, 35.

56. Bachan Singh, *Srī Nankāṇā Sāhib dā Sākā tathā Dard Bhare Dukhaṛe Bahut Vadhīā Jisnūṅ Kavi Bacan Siṅgh Siddhamāṅ Nivāsī ne Baiṅtāṅ, Kabitāṅ Surāṅ, te Chaṅdāṅ vic Racke Chapvāyā* (Amritsar: Sri Gurmat Press, Sardar Budh Singh, 1922), 4. IOL Panj F497.

As has been discussed, debate over the control of religious sites was not new in colonial India, and was given a new sense of urgency within the Khilafat Movement. The British initially perceived the gurdwara movement as religious—and thus were eager to pursue a policy of "conciliatory inactivity," in Tan's words, but the political overtones of the movement, which increased over time, were increasingly troubling to the government.[57] The confused differentiation between the religious and political aspects of reform is made clear in the Punjab Legislative Council Debates of the period, where it was much discussed, as well as in other papers and correspondence of the SGPC, where the religious and "non-political" nature of the movement was emphasized.[58] To be legitimate, Gurdwara Reform had to be deemed religious; to succeed, however, it had to be political.

Sikh shrines or gurdwaras were centers of communication in rural areas and earned incomes, which made them important to both reformers and nationalists. Managing a Sikh shrine became a particularly lucrative endeavor with the political ascendancy of the Sikhs in Punjab in the eighteenth century, and therefore a desirable position. British policies had also long afforded a great deal of influence to religious leaders, such as to Muslim *pīr*s and to descendants of the Sikh Gurus, so these positions were inherently political as well as religious. But why did gurdwaras matter so much? Along parallel lines in South India, Appadurai asks, "why should temples generate intense conflict between local men of power, their publicists, and their lawyers at just the period when *new* arenas for the accumulation and disposal of resources . . . are multiplying?" His answer is that temples were unique in how they manifested three features: cultural continuity, structural virtuosity, and political utility.[59] Thus, temples provided "culturally valued markers of the recipient's status as the leader of his group, as a partial replica of the sovereignty of the deity, and as a co-sharer in a larger system of gift and honor in which other notables were involved," and in this way they "represented a last resort for working out political entitlement in an old and well-understood cultural framework."[60] We can observe a similar situation for the gurdwara (as well as other religious sites), which through the *dharamarth* grant in the precolonial period provided a way for local elites to articulate their power and political status, and thus were a link in the colonial

---

57. Tan, *Garrison State*, 200, 220.

58. Fox, *Lions of the Punjab*, 85. Punjab Legislative Council, *Punjab Legislative Council Debates* (Lahore, Punjab: Printed by the Superintendent, Government Printers, 1922), 41; Punjab Legislative Council, *Punjab Legislative Council Debates* (Lahore, Punjab: Printed by the Superintendent, Government Printers, 1924), 606ff. Ganda Singh, *Some Confidential Papers*, 57ff.

59. Appadurai, *Worship and Conflict*, 222.

60. Appadurai, *Worship and Conflict*, 223.

period to preexisting formations of sovereignty. The gurdwara was also already established, as has been shown in prior chapters, as a powerful form of representation of the past, a long-standing Sikh interest. Here, in the legislative context of the Raj, the sovereignty of the community and the representation of its past came to be articulated in an evolving political framework that privileged communitarian political formations.[61] The status of the gurdwara was worked out in this context.

The property status of the gurdwaras was the central issue of contention for those agitating for control of the sites in question; the situation was summarized by Mian Fazl-i-Husain Khan (in whose portfolio as Minister of Education the management of religious institutions fell)[62] in the Punjab Legislative Council Debates of 1921 as follows:

> It is alleged that these *mahants* and *pujari* have on account of circumstances over which they, the beneficiaries, have had no control assumed in some cases the role of proprietors, that instead of being appointed as servants of the institutions, they have arrogated to themselves the right to succeed on account of being bodily or spiritual heirs of the last *mahants*. . . .[63]

The role of the *mahant* came to be hereditary, within lineages, under Ranjit Singh and even earlier: this can be seen in the way such lineages were defined in the land grants of the Khalsa Darbar examined in the last chapter. The grants *themselves*, however, as was also shown, were political in nature in the pre-British period, and not absolute. After 1849, under British administration, importantly, the managers were granted legal ownership of the shrines and attached lands; given the increasing value of land in the province, these grants were valuable indeed. This change in the nature of control and ownership had a profound impact on the relationship of the shrines to the public. Since the lands attached to the shrines were so valuable, it was not necessary even to gather alms from the congregation, further alienating the manager from the public in attendance at the gurdwara.[64]

61. See Jones's foundational work on the census: Kenneth Jones, "Religious Identity and the Indian Census," in *The Census in British India: New Perspectives*, ed. N. G. Barrier, 73–101 (New Delhi: Manohar, 1981).

62. Tan, *Garrison State*, 206–7.

63. Punjab Legislative Council, *Punjab Legislative Council Debates* (Lahore, Punjab: Printed by the Superintendent, Government Printers, 1921), 532.

64. Tan, "Assuaging the Sikhs," 663.

Often managers were Udasis. The term *"udāsī,"* it should be noted, is multivalent in Punjabi. It refers to the period of Guru Nanak's travels, when he was an itinerant preacher and renunciant. It is also a general term that refers in general to religious specialists who do not marry.[65] It is also a term used specifically to describe the followers of Sri Chand, the son of Guru Nanak who became a renunciant. Udasis have historically maintained a rather ambiguous relationship with the mainstream Sikh tradition, at times working closely with the community, and at times clearly distinct from it. The Udasis were constituted as a legally recognized, organized body in 1899.[66] As noted earlier, they were also designated as a category within the Khalsa Darbar records prior to colonial rule. The control of Sikh sites by Udasis, it was argued throughout the Legislative Council Debates, was deemed unacceptable: "they (the Udasis) were bound to be dispossessed of them (their properties), because the days are gone when any religious place or institution can be allowed to remain under the control of an individual uncontrolled by the community to which that religious institution may belong."[67] Such discourses resonate with larger debates about the control of Muslim places of worship, within the Khilafat Movement, as well as the debates on an all-India level over the management of religious sites.[68] According to the positions presented in the Punjab Legislative Council Debates, there were insufficient provisions for the resolution of conflicts on related issues according to the law as written, making the position of those in control unassailable.[69] The right of property was a fundamental one in the British system, requiring new legislation to deal with the reassignment of ownership from those assigned. The gurdwara management cases were, according to the governor of Punjab, not ones "which our civil courts, with their regard for established possession and settled usage, could attempt to rectify" because they challenged the right to property that stood at the center of British sovereignty.[70] There was also political necessity involved: as Ian Kerr has shown, control of the Golden Temple (which was managed by a government appointee—another source of friction between the government and Sikh

---

65. Many of these would now be termed "Hindu."

66. *Punjab Legislative Council Debates* 1921, 551.

67. *Punjab Legislative Council Debates* (Lahore, Punjab: Printed by the Superintendent, Government Printers, 1925), 1214.

68. Minault, *Khilafat*, 35–36.

69. See *Punjab Legislative Council Debates* 1921, 532ff., for the main legal arguments for revision of the existing laws.

70. *Punjab Legislative Council Debates* 1925, 1302; see also 1216ff.

reformers) was highly political.[71] The British were drawn into local religious affairs and management in their relationships with local Muslim shrines as well, as David Gilmartin has shown, and the complexity of the arrangement between state and religious institutions was not unique to Punjab.[72]

Also central to this debate was the issue of good management: it was not only that the wrong people were in charge of Sikh shrines, but that they also were engaging in incorrect practices in these sacred places. Thus, according to an account of an early conflict at Nankana Sahib, it was said that:

> In the middle of the place of holiness (*pavitratā dī thāṅ*) they started to do this, in the place of Kirtan (*kīrtan jagā*) they had dancing and prostitutes.
> They uttered falsehood and tricks, and girding their loins they went against religion (*adharam*), abandoning religion.
> They needed to do good, but then they practiced vice, those who abandoned contentment of the soul and pursued malice.
> They abandoned good company (*satsaṅg*) and started to keep bad company (*kusaṅgatāṅ karan lage*); abandoning service of the community (*kaumī sevā*), they did lowly things.
> *kabitt:*
> Abandoning poverty, they engaged in bullying, and in places of the good (*satīāṅ de thāṅ*), by force, they made their *own* good.
> Filled with pride (*ahaṅkār*), they abandoned duty, and instead of exhibiting patience, they pursued bad deeds (*badcalnī calāṅmde*).[73]

This language of "proper management" was one generally known in the larger debate over religious sites in British India, regarding *who* has the right to control religious sites, and *how* responsible bodies can be identified.

Yet, lest we see activities related to the control of gurdwaras in strictly Sikh terms, we must remember that even early activity around the management of Sikh shrines took on a nationalist cast. This can be seen in the Rakabganj incident in Delhi, prior to the World War. In this case, the wall of the gurdwara in Delhi that honors the site where the Ninth Guru, Tegh Bahadur, was cremated, was damaged by colonial authorities in the construction of a road. Agitation for the repair of the

---

71. Ian Kerr, "British Relationships with the Golden Temple, 1849–90," *Indian Economic and Social History Review* 21, 2 (1984): 139–51.

72. David Gilmartin, *Empire and Islam: Punjab and the Making of Pakistan* (Berkeley: University of California Press, 1988), 48ff.

73. Bachan Singh. *Srī Nankāṇā Sāhib dā Sākā*, 3.

wall was interrupted by World War I, but an organization called the Central Sikh League was founded in 1919 partially to address the issue.[74] It also sought to gain control of the Khalsa College and gurdwaras, and, importantly, to seek independence. In the same year, the Jallianwala Bagh incident incited Sikhs and other Punjabis against the government. In the second session of the League in 1920, it resolved to support the Non-Cooperation Movement initiated by Congress. The Government of India was troubled by the potential impact of this cohesion of forces and was conciliatory at first.[75] In 1920, therefore, in response to criticism of the management of the Golden Temple and the request for independent governance, the Government of India formed a thirty-six-person council to manage the site; reformists in turn formed their own committee instead, including those serving on the government council.[76] With this, the SGPC, or Shiromani Gurdwara Parbandhak Committee—which would come to have tremendous political power in Punjab after Independence as well as before—was born. It was formed with 175 members, and as a unit was designed to manage the Golden Temple and all the important shrines in Punjab. As was noted in the quotation at the beginning of this chapter, it was the *historical* gurdwaras—rather than every place where the Guru Granth Sahib lies in state, as a congregational site—over which that management was sought. As this organization attempted to position itself as the only legitimate authority over gurdwaras—in contrast to the government's appointees and the "owners" of gurdwaras (as defined by colonial law)—groups organized across Punjab to orchestrate the forcible takeover of certain shrines.[77]

It was the development of such independent and extra-legal means to take control of gurdwaras that made the issue of gurdwara reform so controversial. *Jathās*, volunteer groups led by individuals called *jathedārs*, were formed to spearhead the movement to bring Sikh shrines under Sikh control and force *mahants* out of gurdwaras across Punjab. The SGPC formed the Shiromani Akali Dal (later a separate political party) in December 1920 as the central body that would

---

74. Grewal, *Sikhs of the Punjab*, 157ff. The Central Sikh League mobilized hundreds to repair the Rakabganj wall; the government responded quickly, and fixed it.

75. Tan, *Garrison State*, 201–3. Tan argues that this conciliatory attitude only emboldened the movement.

76. Criticisms of the government's management of the Golden Temple were outlined, for example, in an editorial in the *Khālsā Samācar*, Vol. 21, No. 48 (September 30, 1920), 3; see also *Khālsā Advocate*, Vol. 21, No. 6 (February 10, 1920), 3–4. For further information on these publications, see N. G. Barrier, *Sikhs and Their Literature: A Guide to Tracts, Books, and Periodicals, 1849–1919* (New Delhi: Manohar Book Service, 1970), xxix, 79, and 81–82.

77. In the same year, 1920, the Khalsa College was made independent under a Sikh president, after having been managed by district commissioner of Amritsar since 1908 because of the government's financial control. This concession proved to be one of several meant to appease the movement.

coordinate activities among the *jathās* that had been formed.[78] This body made a formal decision to pursue control of Nankana Sahib, the birthplace of Guru Nanak, which was under the control of a *mahant*.[79] Indeed, accounts of the Nankana Sahib incident tend to emphasize this as the point at which the resolve was formed within the community to take on the *mahants*.[80] A particularly bloody episode at Nankana Sahib followed, radicalizing the movement. There a heavily armed *mahant* had defended his position and, in doing so, killed a number of Akalis, as the members of the *jathās* were called. This aroused not only a great outcry against the *mahant*, who was quickly dismissed by the British, but also against British authorities, who were seen as complicit.[81] An account of the Nankana Sahib incident from February 1922 called upon the Khalsa to come together and consider events there, where "sin" was occurring;[82] the Khalsa was called upon to stop the incorrect practices of those in control of all gurdwaras:

> *nānaksar jithe bāl karī līlhā gurūā suṇī biān jo meriāṅ nūṅ*

> Listen to my description of that place Nanaksar where the Guru did his play of youth . . .

> [mentions several other gurdwaras associated with Guru Nanak] . . .

> *tere dhāmāṅ de vic kī hoṅvdā hai vekho huṇ pujārī luṭeriāṅ nūṅ*

> What is happening in your holy places, look! Now the Pujaris are looting them.[83]

It was in this context that the rhetoric of martyrdom was mobilized to great effect, as Fenech has demonstrated.[84] An example of this sentiment is as follows:

> Oh Khalsa! In the world, no race/nation can live without martyrdom
> (*khālsā jī! sansār vicc koī kaum bhī shahādat de bināṅ jiuṅdī nahīṅ rahi*

---

78. Tan, "Assuaging the Sikhs," 665–66.

79. Text of this decision is provided in: Bhai Mohan Singh Vaid, *Bhayānak Sākkā*, 9.

80. Bhai Bhagat Singh, *Shahīdī Nankāṇā Sāhib*. (Amritsar: City Press, n.d.), 3. IOL Panj F 412 (incomplete). Listed as 1921 in IOL catalog. Such a description is very common, as is the description of the gathering of Singhs and their going to Nankana Sahib.

81. Tan, *Garrison State*, 205.

82. Bacan Singh, *Srī Nankāṇā Sāhib dā Sākā*, 2.

83. Bacan Singh, *Srī Nankāṇā Sāhib dā Sākā*, 2.

84. Fenech, *Martyrdom*.

sakkdī). Only that race can advance (*unnatī*) which can endure the greatest trouble . . . and still remain resolved. Sikh history is filled with sacrifices, more than most, and even at enduring great pains the Sikh people have never lost their nerve. In the way that especially upon Sikhs great tyranny was delivered, in that way they remained brave in destroying tyranny.[85]

The literature of the period is rife with reference to the martyrdom of those who took part in the Gurdwara Reform Movement, invoking—at the same time— historical instances of martyrdom. Indeed, in the example above, the author continues to name historical instances of torture, noting that *huṇ enhāṅ shahīdāṅ ne is sameṅ vicc vī karke sāmṇe vikhā dittā hai*, "Now in this time as well these martyrs have shown this before [us]."[86] We see this again in another example:

shaktī apṇī khālse vicc pāvo pran eh shahīdī dā karan lagge

We obtain our power in the Khalsa because of the sacrifice/martyrdom of life.

tārū siṅgh jehe sānūṅ sidak bakhsho maṇī siṅgh vāṅgū nahīṅ ḍaran lagge

Ask for faith like Taru Singh, that like (Bhai) Mani Singh there be no fear.[87]

A *granthī* from the Golden Temple, Bhai Kartar Singh Giani, described the Nankana Sahib events in detail, again relating them to forgotten events of the past:

In this way, the Singhs sacrificed themselves (*sīs kurbān kīte)*, and I will describe their faith . . .

Time passed, and these matters people completely forgot.

Mani Singh, Mataab Singh, Taru Singh, their historical happenings were taken from [their] hearts.

Time passed, and relieved pain; and sleep lifted these matters from [their] hearts (*diloṅ uṭhā baiṭhe*).[88]

---

85. Bhai Mohan Singh Vaid, *Bhayānak Sākkā*, 47.

86. Bhai Mohan Singh Vaid, *Bhayānak Sākkā*, 47.

87. Bacan Singh, *Srī Nankāṇā Sāhib dā Sākā*, 8.

88. Giani Kartar Singh Kalasvalia (Head Granthi, Darbar Sahib, Amritsar), *Khūni Shahīdāṅ arthāt Sākkā Srī ṇNankāṇā Sāhib Ji* (Darbar Press, Amritsar, n.d.), 1–2. IOL 14162.gg.39.(4) (No date given on the publication itself; catalog indicates date of publication as 1922.) The British Library's Asian and African Studies Collection, for example, features numerous examples.

Remembering Nankana Sahib, within the context of this larger movement, was itself an important act. Indeed, a *gurmatā* or decision was passed toward the conclusion of the series of events to ensure this: that at the place where rites had been held for the martyrs of these events, a memorial would be constructed as a "Khalsa Shahid Ganj," and that all Sikhs would annually gather together on the 24th of April to honor their sacrifice.[89] The history of the community, as it was occurring, would be commemorated.

The designation of "Sikh" versus "Hindu" was a key feature of debate over a bill introduced to the Legislative Council in 1921 as a means to address the conflict, since "identity" as one of the two was fundamental to the issue as construed in the Council: a Hindu could not care for the gurdwara in question without sacrificing aspects of the "Sikhness" of the site. The exact construal of this provided one reason the Akalis rejected this bill: the Akalis demanded that the definition of Sikh be limited to Khalsa Sikhs, while *Sahajdhārī* (defined as those who do not adhere to all aspects of the Khalsa *rahit*) Sikhs and Hindus protested the criticism of some *mahant*s, and wanted to maintain aspects of the status quo. As Rai Bahadur Lala Hari Chand argued in the April 16 meeting of the 1921 Punjab Legislative Assembly, "The Sahjd-haris, the Nirmalas, and the Udasis are bitterly opposed to the Bill. . . ."[90] A Sikh member of the Council countered that the bill was being opposed by "Hindus who posing as Sahjdhari Sikhs want to obstruct the passing of the Bill."[91] Reflecting larger debates regarding the relationship of Sikhs to Hindus, Rai Bahadur Lala Sewak Ram countered Bakhtawar Singh by arguing that the Hindus in question do not mean to obstruct the bill, but that "the only idea in their minds is that the Hindus are a nation which includes the Sikhs as well. The Sikhs are practically Hindus."[92] When defending the rights of Sahajdhari Sikhs, therefore, Hindus "believe that this is our affair as well, embodying as we do the Hindu sects and the various sects that are classed as Sikhs."[93] The larger questions of identity within the colonial frame were thus central to the question of gurdwara reform, and to the designation of the community of right, in relation to the religious site, as can be seen in other parallel situations in colonial India.

---

89. Bhai Mohan Singh Vaid, *Bhayānak Sākkā*, 50.

90. *Punjab Legislative Council Debates* 1921, 581. The spelling of *Sahajdhārī* is as in the original.

91. *Punjab Legislative Council Debates* 1921, 582.

92. *Punjab Legislative Council Debates* 1921, 582; see also *Punjab Legislative Council Debates* 1925, 1276ff.

93. *Punjab Legislative Council Debates* 1921, 582.

Several incidents that heightened tensions quickly followed in 1921 and 1922, particularly over the treasury of the Golden Temple.[94] On November 7, 1921, the government took away the keys to the treasury of the Golden Temple—in what became known as the "Keys Affair"—from the manager, Sardar Sundar Singh Ramgarhia, asserting its control. In 1922, the agitation over the keys was merged with the Non-Cooperation Movement, which was gaining ground across India, and in January of that year, the Central Sikh League determined that independence or Swaraj was its goal, and pledged commitment to non-cooperation.[95] This alliance with the larger freedom movement would be rearticulated later as well.[96] Sikh soldiers began to exhibit signs that the conflict was impacting their loyalty, and as a result the government backed down and handed over the keys to the Golden Temple treasury to the SGPC.[97] M. K. Gandhi's telegram to Sardar Kharak Singh, president of the SGPC at the time, reads: "first decisive battle for India's freedom won, congratulations."[98] With the simultaneous waning of the Khilafat Movement and later non-cooperation, a relative calm did return to the province until the incident at Guru ka Bagh occurred in the summer of 1922. As Mian Fazl-i-Husain Khan put it in the meeting of the Punjab Legislative Council on November 7, 1922, that incident "made these matters [regarding gurdwara legislation] more complicated than they were before."[99]

In the rhetoric associated with the Guru ka Bagh incident as well we see the recurrence of the discourse of bad management and bad character. The *mahant* in this case was described as follows in a pamphlet of the time:

Oh brothers, Sundar Das is the name of the *mahant* who is a very
    depraved enemy of the *panth*.
He was a worker for a sweet maker (*halvāī dā sī naukar*) in Amritsar, oh
    brothers, and he was filled with licentiousness (*durācār*). . . .
Slothful and indolent, evil, riotous, and a friend of thieves, oh brothers!

94. For more detail, see Tan, "Assuaging the Sikhs," and Tan, *Garrison State*, 209ff.

95. Tan, "Assuaging the Sikhs," 681. See also Tan, *Garrison State*, 215.

96. Ganda Singh, *Akali Movement*, 53ff.

97. Tan, "Assuaging the Sikhs," 681–83; Tan, *Garrison State*, 214–17; on the impact on the army, see 215–17.

98. Ganda Singh, *Akali Movement*, xi, 11.

99. *Punjab Legislative Council Debates* 1922, 3.

Abandoning his work he sat in the Guru's garden, using it up and doing
   nothing of use, oh brothers. . . .
No meditation, no recitation (*na tap na jap*), says Kartar Singh, relaxing,
   always engaged in sin, oh brothers![100]

It should be noted that the behavior of the *mahant* is here emphasized—not his
identity. But beyond this, the key issue was, as always, one of ownership: at Guru
ka Bagh, the *mahant* had relinquished control of the gurdwara, but not associated lands. He then took issue with firewood being cut from this land for the
langar or communal meal at the gurdwara. After the arrest of several Sikhs, Akali
*jathā*s gathered to assert their right to take firewood for the *langar* and were dispersed by the government with force: as one eyewitness put it, *magar vāh re
bahādur sikh ki voh phir āge baṛhne kā kasad kartā thā aur phir usī tarhe mār
khātā thā*, "But those brave Sikhs, indeed, they kept moving forward, enduring
all, and in this way they took their beating."[101] Large numbers came from all over
central Punjab to engage in non-violent resistance to government force.[102] As one
pamphlet described it:

For six months the Committee [SGPC] gave the order (*hukam*) and
   hundreds of *jathā*s responded.
When there was an order from the Akal Takhat, then all the *jathā*s went
   to Guru ka Bagh.
On the road when they stopped they were surrounded by the soldiers of
   the cruel sinner.
He gave the order to attack the *jathā*s with clubs, and they suffered
   [lit. "caused their bodies to swell," *badan sujāṅvde ne*].
The soldier beat them with *lāṭhī* [sticks], and beating the people, they fell
   [lit "were spread out below," *heṭhāṅ vachānde*).[103]

---

100. Giani Kartar Singh Kalasvalia (Head Granthi, Darbar Sahib, Amritsar), *Sidak Nazāre
arthāt Bīr Khālsā* (Amritsar: Bhai Gurdiaal Singh Deepindra Singh, n.d.), 5. IOL 14162.gg.
39.(7)

101. Ganda Singh, *Akali Movement*, 306. Observations by Maulana Kifayatullah, September 10,
1922. A *jatha* of Sikhs from the United States were prepared to participate in the Morcha as well,
but were unable to do so in time; they did contribute to the cause. See Giani Anokh Singh,
Shahīdī Valvale (Amritsar: Khalsa Pradesi Malwa Press and Sardar Kartar Singh Printer, 1929?).
IOL Panj B 1128.

102. Tan, "Assuaging the Sikhs," 688–90.

103. Bhai Dharam Singh, *Sākā Guru Bāg* (Amritsar: Sri Gurmat Press, 1923), 5. IOL Panj F 1053.

The Guru ka Bagh protests only stopped when a Hindu leased the land under dispute next to the gurdwara and allowed Akalis use of it.[104] The conflict then dissipated, although some members of the Akali Movement saw government involvement in this resolution as disingenuous.[105] The Government of India went on the offensive, propaganda-wise, against the SGPC and the SGPC agreed to negotiate, but talks stalled over the release of prisoners: authorities would not agree to release them unless the SGPC rejected the strategy of seizing shrines by extra-legal means. The SGPC would not do so, and negotiations came to nothing.[106] The government, in the meantime, became less amenable to negotiation. The non-cooperation agitation had been discontinued by Gandhi because of the violence perpetrated in its name at Chauri Chaura in February 1922. This, and the dissipation of the Khilafat agitation, made the government more willing to risk the continuing displeasure of members of the Sikh community involved in the gurdwara action.

There were later incidents related to the quest for gurdwara reform, such as the forced abdication of the Maharaja of Nabha, a cause taken up by the SGPC.[107] Interpreting this as an attack on the Akali Movement, of which the Maharaja of Nabha had been a strong supporter, Akali *jathā*s sprang into action and began agitating for the Maharaja's reinstatement.[108] The incident culminated in the "Jaito struggle": an Akhand Path at the gurdwara at Jaito in support of the Maharaja was convened and the government attempted to thwart it; *jathā*s rose up in defense of the right to religious observance. The Government of India initiated the formation of local *sudhār* or Reform associations, led by a provincial association designed to subvert the SGPC, which were moderate and pro-government. These anti-Akali associations "attacked the SGPC's tactics while urging the fulfillment of Sikh religious aspirations."[109] By 1924, they successfully challenged the

---

104. In the midst of the ongoing conflict over Guru ka Bagh, a new gurdwara management bill was introduced in the Legislative Council in August of 1922. The bill was passed, but could not be implemented because the SGPC and Sikh Members of the Legislative Council refused to nominate the members of the Board of Commissioners. Council members made it clear this would happen, *Punjab Legislative Council Debates* 1922, 38. For a discussion of the opposition, see *Punjab Legislative Council Debates* 1922, 12 and Tan *Garrison State*, 222ff. For non-Sikh opinion on the bill, which generally also opposed it, see *Punjab Legislative Council Debates* 1922, 14–15.

105. According to Mian Fazl-i-Husain on November 7, 1922 (*Punjab Legislative Council Debates* 1922, 3).

106. Tan, "Assuaging the Sikhs," 691–93.

107. See Ganda Singh, *Akali Movement*, 18–24.

108. Tan, "Assuaging the Sikhs," 693–94.

109. Tan, *Garrison State*, 234.

power of the SGPC; at the same time, authorities took a hard line against the organization. Argument continued over the status of the prisoners.[110]

The turmoil associated with the struggle for control of gurdwaras was only ameliorated with the passage of the Gurdwara Reform Act in 1925. The relevant debates of the legislative assembly centered on the notion of good government or proper management. Sardar Bakhtawar Singh, a rural member of the Council from Hoshiarpur and Kangra, thus asked: "How could they [the Sikhs] have tolerated autocracy in the *gurdwaras*? The mahants desire that they should not be required to give an account of the money that was given to them for the poor and for religion, and that they should be allowed to lead dissipated lives in the shrines without ever being called upon for an explanation. When there is no autocratic rule in the shrines belonging to other communities the Sikhs too cannot tolerate that the Mahants should behave despotically."[111]

By far the greatest emphasis was placed upon reform, the ideal of good government, and the role of the *mahants* in mismanaging gurdwaras. The cause for the movement was described early on in the Council by Mian Fazl-i-Husain as follows, speaking for "those who seek to alter the existing conditions" within the Sikh community:

They [the Sikhs] allege that their *gurdwaras* and shrines are in a deplorable condition. They contend that the *mahants* and *pujaris* in charge of most of their *gurdwaras* and shrines are men of bad character, men who misappropriate the funds of these institutions, men who instead of being saintly and thus likely to exert a salutary influence on the worshippers of the shrines, are evil minded; wicked, vicious, and in fact so low and depraved as to contaminate the simple faithful worshippers of these shrines.[112]

The central conceit of the gurdwara reform agitation was thus that the gurdwaras of the Sikhs were being mismanaged, and that a new system of oversight was required to remedy this situation. This rationale held through the entire movement, as articulated in March of 1924 in this statement from Ruchi Ram Sahni: the Akalis only sought to rescue "their Gurdwaras and their places of worship from the hands of corrupt and debauched *mahants* and priests." The cause of the Akali disturbances, in Sahni's view, was to be found not in any fault on the part of the Akalis, but in the

---

110. *Punjab Legislative Council Debates* 1924, 610.

111. *Punjab Legislative Council Debates* 1922, 13.

112. *Punjab Legislative Council Debates* 1921, 532.

law itself: "What Government should have done and which, I submit, Government did not do, is that they did not pay any attention to this defect in the law."[113]

The *resolution* of these difficulties, however, visible from early on in the Legislative Council Debates, lay in evaluation not only of the relative quality of the *mahants* in question, but also in two other factors: first, identity, and second, of the historical nature of sites and their relationships with present-day practitioners. Husain's speech before the Punjab Legislative Council in 1921 clearly expressed the conflation of elements of history, identity, and "reform" that made up the full underlying rationale for the movement—and defined "history" in relation to place and evidence. After addressing the claims of the Sikhs, as identified above, Husain noted that three issues are "simple and clear": first, that no corrupt person has a right to manage any religious institution; second, that all the income to a religious site should be "spent in promoting the objects of that shrine"; and third, a shrine must remain in the hands of the sect it "belongs" to: "Where a shrine is obviously a shrine belonging to a particular sect it should remain in charge of that sect. I understand there is no desire on the part of Sikh reformers to take possession of sectarian shrines, that is to say, the shrines which are, for instance, essentially Udasi shrines, having been founded by Udasis for the benefit of their sect."[114] The gurdwara legislation passed in 1925 also hinged on the intimate connection established between the definition of a Sikh and the definition of a gurdwara. A religious site must be governed by its community as historically constituted. To identify that community, the "identity" of a Sikh was defined. History and identity were wedded, in the definition of the gurdwara.

Identity and History

We see a conflation of several elements in the language of debate under review here: good government and reform in relation to a shrine's property and administration; the shrine's history; and its "identity"—whether it was determined to be Sikh or non-Sikh. Religious identity of a site is here constructed within this legislative discourse as an effect of history, for which evidence in historical terms can be provided. The points at issue between the reformist Sikhs and the *mahants*, as identified by Husain, represent this array of interests:

(1) Is a particular *mahant* of bad character, vicious habits and unsuited to the high dignity of his exalted office as the spiritual head of a shrine or not?
(2) Are the funds of a particular shrine being misappropriated, misused,

---

113. *Punjab Legislative Council Debates* 1924, for both quotes, see 611.

114. *Punjab Legislative Council Debates* 1921, 533.

diverted to objects personal to the *mahant* or not? (3) Are the particular estates the property of the shrine or the private property of the *mahant*? (4) Whether a particular shrine or *gurdwara* has been endowed by the Sikh community, of a guru, and dedicated not to a particular sect but to the community as a whole. (5) The best scheme of administration. (6) The most suitable way of holding religious observances and ceremonies.

Husain noted that it will not be possible to resolve disputes in these matters until "we know the history of every institution which comes into dispute." That which must be countered is history, as well: Bakhtawar Singh went on to argue that "the Mahants are wrong when they say that they have held possession of the *gurdwaras* for a long time." This history was fundamentally related to a determination of who is a Sikh, as we shall see in the court cases that followed in the wake of the Act. The definition of a Sikh that was constituted within the legislation was addressed throughout the debate, as different parties endeavored to provide an authoritative definition. For example, a group of *mahants* from Hardwar argued that the "term Sikh is too vague and liable to misinterpretation. Sikh at present connotes Hindus who are followers of Guru Nanak forming a vast majority as well as those who call themselves Tatkhalsas and Non-Hindus." Soon after in the same session, Sardar Mehtab Singh argued that matters were much clearer than put forward by earlier speakers, because: "We do not intend to take possession of any *thākurdwārā* or temple. We do not lay claim to the private property of any person simply because the Granth Sahib is kept there. We claim only those historical places, which are regarded sacred by all the Sikhs, and which are the common property of the whole of the Sikh community."[115]

According to the formulation, Sikh sites are defined as such through the delineation of their history. At the same time, this required definition of the Sikh community, to allow for designation of the historical community of a site *as Sikh.* Similar thoughts were articulated in other contexts of the time, outside of the Legislative Council debates; an article entitled "History and the Sikhs" noted that history is the life of the nation, its "breath and glory."[116] Gaining back their history, therefore, was a means for gaining much more for the Sikhs. We saw this sentiment clearly expressed by Bhai Vir Singh, in his novel *Sundarī,* and in the general preoccupation of writers of the time with the three major themes of Sikh

---

115. *Punjab Legislative Council Debates* 1921, 533–34 (first two quotations); 1922, 13; 1921, 543 and 545 (final two).

116. "*Itihās Kaumiat dī Jān Hai, Itihās Kaumāṅ de Prāṇ Hai, Itihās Kaumāṅ dī Shān Hai*" *Khālsā Samācar,* Vol. 22, No. 29 (1921), 3.

behavior, Sikh history, and gurdwara reform. These themes provided a backdrop to the quest for gurdwara reform. As has been mentioned, the martyrdom of Sikhs in the movement was seen to continue a preexisting lineage of Sikh martyrs, and direct analogies were made between contemporary and historical forms of martyrdom. A pamphlet from the period makes an analogy between the situation in the twentieth century, with the *mahant* control of gurdwaras, and that of the eighteenth, when *masands* had a role in the community until the office was abolished by Guru Gobind Singh with the formation of the Khalsa:

> Wherever there were *jagīrs*, there the Masands took up residency.
> They left a little bit for the Gurus, but the rest they took for themselves (*āpṇe kabze*).
> Blind worldly illusion has done a lot, knowingly sin and bad acts commenced.
> The wealth that came for the sake of *dharam* came to be used for bad deeds.[117]

Thus, the movement was seen as a continuation, a repetition of a past, a dynamic we have seen before as a feature of modern Sikh discourse.[118] The history that was invoked in the argument for a community's relation to a site was also marked by historical assumptions within colonial administration. Thus the issues that animated the Gurdwara Reform Movement were not unique to the Sikh community—religious institutions and their management were contested all over India, in response to an inconsistent and sometimes contradictory state orientation toward them. The quest for gurdwara reform, however, featured its own particular valences, with respect to the representation of the community in historical terms in relation to such sites. This reflects an orientation to the Sikh shrine that encompassed preexisting, precolonial historical imaginaries— as described in earlier chapters—and those that were born of colonial conceptions of property and history, and the ability of the state to define a bounded community of interest with respect to a religious site. The community of a religious site had to be determined: this was the basic premise of the legislation that sought to decouple the state from religious sites. The designation of that community, however, took place in different terms in different locations. Caste and sect were determining factors for Hindu temples; Islamic law, read as singular for all Muslims, was crucial for Muslim sites. History and the clear

---

117. Kalasvalia, *Khūnī Shahīdāṅ*, 4.

118. See discussion in chapter 2.

definition of who is a Sikh in historical relation to a site provided those terms for the Sikhs.

Richard Fox provides an important materialist explanation for the Gurdwara Reform Movement, through a portrait of an agrarian economy under duress due to the effects of colonialism, and the anticolonial sentiment it aroused. Fox finds this cultural materialist answer to be insufficient, however, for it does not explain the religious elements that were so central to the movement, as "religious" and "class" identities were not coterminous. He argues for an understanding of Sikh cultural agency that recognizes its non-materialist aspects, while locating its formation mostly within the colonial state. Both the materialist argument, and the argument that ascribes all agency to the colonial state, are insufficient. More fruitfully, however, Fox argues that when the Akali activists were protesting and agitating for control over Sikh shrines, they were "in the act of defining what was a Sikh shrine; that is, as they carried out their collective action to capture shrines, they were creating the boundaries of their religious tradition."[119] This comment usefully highlights the ways in which protesters were, in many ways, creating a new idea of the Sikh shrine through their endeavors. I do not mean that such shrines were actually *created* in the movement: the Darbar Sahib existed long before the Gurdwara Reform Movement, as did many, many other sites whose significance was based in the representation of the past as a formative ground for the community. We have seen the precolonial logic for the importance of the representation of the community's past in the form of sites as well as objects in prior chapters. As a result of the Movement, however, these sites changed in their *meaning, functioning,* and *relationship* with other elements of Sikh life, and particularly with the state. In this sense, participants in the Gurdwara Reform Movement were "creating" these sites, not *ex nihilo*, but out of a prior set of meanings and functions, as they came to be imagined in particular legislative and juridical ways in relation to the colonial state and evolving notions of Sikh identity that were framed within the administrative discourse in it.

Nicholas Dirks has noted that "under the British in India, law became the most effective and the most valued domain for the dispensation of the new truths of colonial rule."[120] We have seen that the Gurdwara Reform Movement fits within a larger colonial discourse over control of religious sites; it was not, therefore, a unique phenomenon. As Appadurai has argued in relation to the management of the Sri Partasarati Svami Temple in Madras, the actions of the English courts between 1878 and 1925 fundamentally shaped the idea of the

---

119. Fox, *Lions of the Punjab*, 114.

120. Dirks, "From Little King to Landlord," 177.

temple's community and created new agonistic modes of governance for the temple's management.[121] The gurdwara phenomenon is illustrative of a parallel process, and reflects a similar tension between the designation of fixity and the notion of diversity. As such, Appadurai continues, "[t]he court's efforts to classify, define, and demarcate the concrete meaning of the concept of the 'Tenkalai community of Triplicane' generated more tensions than it resolved."[122] This very same process can be seen in Punjab, with added dimensions and striking repercussions. While the community "elaborated, refined and codified" in the case Appadurai examines was for one temple, in relation to one local community—with vague reference to an overall Hindu community—the management of gurdwaras in the Punjab was seen to be the preserve of *all* those who could be defined as Sikh, within the state—requiring that all Sikhs be thus defined. This has particular consequences, in tying the definition of Sikhness to the state at the provincial level (the management structure did not hold outside of Punjab); in defining the entire community as "sovereign" over shrines; and, most important in the grounding of the definition of the community and the gurdwaras that it would be sovereign over in the realm of history, in the direct relationship established between the history of the Sikh people (and defining them as such) and Sikh places. Thus while the all-India context for gurdwara reform shows that similar conflicts existed all through British India, governed by a core set of laws, the process of defining communities and rights had particular results in the Punjab, for the Sikhs. In the next chapter, we will look closely at the Act and subsequent court cases to ascertain the functioning of the Act in the definition of history and Sikhness, and the development of a sense of the sovereignty of the community over place.

Concluding Remarks

A crucial distinction that comes into play in the later management of religious sites under the British (and in the Gurdwara Reform Movement) relates to *whom* such grants were made: individuals or corporate bodies.[123] The central question within the movement for control of gurdwaras by the Akalis in the 1920s was: did the managers of such sites—the *mahants*—have the rights to these sites, or should those rights belong to the Sikh community, as a corporate

121. Appadurai, *Worship and Conflict*, 176.

122. Appadurai, *Worship and Conflict*, 178.

123. The distinction between these two types is parallel to the distinction, to some degree, between *madad-i-ma'ash* grants and those known as *waqf*. See chapter 5 for a discussion.

body? The Sikh Gurdwara Act of 1925 decided in favor of the community, and then sought to legislate the contours of that community, as we will see in the next chapter, through the representation of that community's past. As has been shown in the prior chapter, research on the *dharamarth* grants of the pre-British period demonstrates a range of types of recipients of grants. Individual grants are the norm. Some ambiguity in grants is present, and instructive: there are nascent notions of corporate or communitarian ownership expressed. One example is the Darbar Sahib/Golden Temple. The first clear articulation of community management comes in the colonial period, when the "claim to the noviciate or chelaship" was said to belong "to the whole 'Khalsa' body."[124] In this colonial document, the community is identified as the manager/owner of the site, after the Guru, based on ideas of the Khalsa body that certainly did exist, but had not been so voiced in direct relation to ownership. In this way, the British Indian understanding of the religious endowment and its management shaped evolving understandings of who must control the gurdwara, and how that body/person be defined. The community and its relationship to property were thus legislated.

I have tried to highlight here the nascent notion of territoriality found within the evolving idea of the gurdwara in the twentieth century, and its relationship with "community." A Sikh historical imaginary was thus joined to an emerging territoriality, drawing upon but significantly modifying preexisting precolonial/early modern formations of the same.[125] The movement for gurdwara management, and the formation of the managing organization for gurdwaras, the Shiromani Gurdwara Parbandhak Committee, must be seen as reflecting early modern forms of "agrarian territorialism,"[126] formed and re-formed within the property logic of the East India Company and later Crown rule, to create a new Sikh territorialism with shifting relations to sovereignty and competing notions of the representation of the past in relation to the ideas of community and ownership. If, as Sikh reformers associated with the Gurdwara Reform Movement in the early twentieth century claimed, the ownership of gurdwaras had been constituted by the colonial state in a way that was contrary to "tradition," it became imperative for these reformers to establish the contents of this tradition. Simultaneously, the very notion of a managing body of the community was produced within the

---

124. See reference in Madanjit Kaur, *Golden Temple*, 62 and Appendix IV (199–203). See also Kerr, "Administration of the Golden Temple."

125. See the discussion in chapter 5 of the applicability of Ludden's idea of agrarian territoriality.

126. Ludden, *Agrarian History*, 85.

extensive and multiple forms of legislation dedicated to religious site management. Colonial property formations had in some senses (but not all) subverted earlier forms of ownership associated with gurdwaras; at the same time, notions of community that had not previously existed were introduced into the rule of property. The terms of the debate—as fundamentally historical, and communitarian—were framed within British understandings of property and right, as historically constituted entities, such that even claims made to retrieve earlier forms of property relations and corollary relationships between community and property were framed within the terms and concepts of the Raj. This is not a phenomenon that is isolated to the Sikh community; Appadurai has described its forms in South India as well, such that "the broad intention of the judges of the court was to define the boundaries of the Tenkalai community of Triplicane, concerned as an electorate, and to create a machinery, on the contemporary Western model, that would enable this constituency to elect trustees who would manage the temple on their behalf. This task was not, as it turned out, a simple one."[127]

Partha Chatterjee has argued that the SGPC represents an example of the kind of "representative public institutions and practices"[128] that can accompany minority mobilization whereby a minority group articulates a position in relation to a dominant majority that would be granted validity within "strategic politics of toleration," after having satisfied "the condition of representativeness."[129] The nature of this representativity, in the case of the SGPC, in Chatterjee's argument, is its democratic nature, as it was one of the first "legally constituted public bod[ies] in colonial India for which the principle of universal suffrage was recognized."[130] The SGPC, therefore, might offer a unique vision of a self-governing religious minority body, and the space thus marked out might challenge other state-centered definitions of space, territory, and authority. Harjot Oberoi, on the other hand, has argued that groups claiming to represent religious and other minorities "regularly collude in suppressing rights, disrupting lives, stigmatizing bodies, and inflicting pain," as happened within the Akali Movement in the 1920s, when the Babbar Akalis sought an alternative vision of the Sikh community, including economic justice. In this, "a hegemonic discourse of sameness was

---

127. Appadurai, *Worship and Conflict*, 178.

128. Partha Chatterjee, "Religious Minorities and the Secular State: Reflections on an Indian Impasse," *Public Culture* 8, 1 (1995): 11–39, see 37.

129. Chatterjee, "Religious Minorities," 36, 38.

130. Chatterjee, "Religious Minorities," 38.

thoroughly challenged by a counter-canon that dared to include the terrain of internal differences: social, economic, and political."[131]

It is not surprising that the SGPC and organizations/mobilizations like it do not fit easily with simple genealogies of villainy and virtue.[132] Multiple narratives exist within the logic that shapes the gurdwara landscape: a regional articulation of cultural and religious difference, a celebration of an alternative, non-state-centered history of community, and at the same time, a claim to representativity that is dependant upon control. We have here provided the context—in examining precolonial and colonial formations of ownership in relation to religious sites—for this idea of the community in relation to the gurdwara, as a product of colonial and precolonial forms of governance and community formation. Thus, in the way that the SGPC is not simply parochial, nor ideally cosmopolitan, the formations of the modern gurdwara and its managing body reflect complex representations of the Sikh community and its past.[133] As we continue, we will see how the specifics of the idea of the community in the Gurdwara Act work with colonial notions of property to create a territorialized vision of the Sikh past. Objects persist alongside this vision, substantiating an alternative view.

---

131. He thus argues that "the complexities of the past and present instances . . . do not provide sufficient corroboration for Chatterjee's contention," Harjot Oberoi, "What Has a Whale Got to Do With It? A Tale of Pogroms and Biblical Allegories," in *Sikh Religion, Culture, and Ethnicity*, ed. Christopher Shackle, Gurharpal Singh, and Arvind-pal Singh Mandair (Richmond, UK: Curzon Press, 2001), 186–206.

132. In this sense, the story of the modern historical gurdwara and its governing body, the SGPC, speaks to description by Sumathi Ramaswamy of the national-level Sanskrit Commission's work in the 1950s as both subversive and tragic: subversive in that it "dared to pursue an alternative imagination which did not replicate the historical experience of the West . . . [but tragic in that] in the end, its advocates made their case by deploying the logic of (western) nationalism and modernity." (Sumathi Ramaswamy, "Sanskrit for the Nation," *Modern Asian Studies* 33, 2 [1999]: 339–81, see 380.)

133. That is to say, the gurdwara as a *modern* construct is as much a product of the formations of colonial modernity as it is of continuing precolonial meanings of property, right, and community.

7

Territory and the Definition of Being Sikh

IN ORDER TO define the governance of gurdwaras in relation to a community, the shape of that community, and therefore the definition of its individual members, had to be fixed. The Sikh Gurdwara Act of 1925 thus became a pivotal place for the definition of Sikhs as individuals, and as members of a community. It did not represent the first effort to define who is a Sikh in the contrext of British rule. East India Company attempts to define the Sikhs in political as well as religious terms began with the first political interests in the Punjab state, when British political agents sought to understand Sikhism in the context of comprehending the political formations of Ranjit Singh's Lahore state.[1] With the development of British interests in maintaining Punjabi dominance in the army after the Rebellion of 1857, the British became in many senses patrons of Sikhness, in that they encouraged particular definitions of being Sikh and even enforced these definitions among the Sikh members of the British Indian armed forces. Such actions were intended to support British imperial interests. Their impact however should not be overstated, however.[2] Sikh subjectivity was articulated over the course of the sixteenth and seventeenth centuries and was not an invention of the British. Instead, as Arvind Mandair has rightly stated, "what changes in the colonial period is the way in which identity was conceived."[3] Later organization among Sikhs took place in a broader context within which religious identity was instituted as a fundamental governing principle of British India, through the designation of representative institutions designed to mobilize religious community formations as a basic organizing principle.[4]

---

1. Ballantyne, *Between Colonialism and Diaspora*, chapter 2.
2. Such as is evident in Fox, *Lions of the Punjab*.
3. Mandair, *Religion and the Specter of the West*, 236.
4. See Jones, "Religious Identity."

Through the Gurdwara Reform Act, however, something notable came into being in the way that colonial governance interacted with always-evolving definitions of being Sikh. The definition of being Sikh was connected in the Act to the designation of the historical gurdwara, and therefore to the designation of a landscape of the Sikh past articulated through this institution and its control, as well as to the definition of the Sikh community and Sikh individuals who comprise it. It is through this that we see the linking of a particular kind of territoriality with the articulation of what it means to be Sikh and with the inscription of being Sikh onto the representation of the past. In this formula, identity, land, and history were linked in political and administrative terms. This built upon but also transformed existing ideas of the past and its representation in material and geographical forms that we have seen were engaged in diverse ways since the beginning of the eighteenth century, and caused a change in the way the past could be imagined in material terms. Objects, which accompanied sites as a part of a historical imaginary that constructed the community of Sikhs as a web of relationships, occupied a less prominent place in a memorial landscape mapped onto territory.

Who is a Sikh, and What is a Gurdwara?

The final Gurdwara Reform Act defined what constitutes a "Sikh" as follows:

> "Sikh" means a person who professes the Sikh religion. If any question arises as to whether any person is or is not a Sikh, he shall be deemed respectively to be or not to be a Sikh according as he makes or refuses to make in such manner as the Local Government may prescribe the following declaration:
>> "I solemnly affirm that I am a Sikh, that
>> "I believe in the Guru Granth Sahib, that
>> "I believe in the Ten Gurus, and that
>> "I have no other religion."[5]

The Act also defined who would not be nominated to be a member of the Board of Commissioners: a person would not be eligible if he (and that is the pronoun of use):

(i) is less than twenty-one years old;
(ii) is not a Sikh,

---

5. Government of Punjab, Legislative Department, *Sikh Gurdwaras Act, 1925 (Punjab Act No. VIII of 1925).* (Lahore: Superintendent, Government Printing, Punjab, 1927), part I, chapter I, point 9, p. 4. Hereafter will be cited as "*Sikh Gurdwaras Act, 1925*".

(iii) is of unsound mind,

(iv) is an undischarged insolvent,

 (v) is a *patit* [literally, "fallen"],

(vi) is minister of a Notified Sikh Gurdwara other than the head minister of the Darbar Sahib, Amritsar, or of any of the four Sikh Takhts specified in clause (ii) of sub-section 91 of section 43.

(vii) is a paid servant of any Notified Sikh Gurdwara or of the Board, other than a member of the executive committee of the Board.[6]

The definition of a Sikh was therefore central to the Act and its operation. This could be done in both positive and negative terms. Thus the definition of a Sikh—as well as of good governance—was defined in the provisions for dismissal of a hereditary office-holder. Such an office-holder could be dismissed if he:

(a) makes persistent default in the submission of budgets, accounts, reports, or returns which it is his duty to submit, or

(b) willfully disobeys lawful orders issued by the committee, or

(c) is guilty of any malfeasance, misfeasance, breach of trust or neglect of duty in respect of a trust, or

(d) has misappropriated or improperly dealt with the properties of the gurdwara, or

(e) is of unsound mind or physically unfit to discharge the functions of his office, or is guilty of misconduct of such a character as to render him morally unfit for his office, or

(f) fails persistently to perform his duties in connection with the management or performance of public worship or the management or performance of any rituals and ceremonies in accordance with the teachings of Sri Guru Granth Sahib, or

(g) has ceased to be a Sikh.[7]

We can thus see that proper management was at issue in this designation of eligibility to serve in the gurdwaras. But so was identity, which could precipitate dismissal alongside any form of actual mismanagement. A list of behavioral

---

6. *Sikh Gurdwaras Act, 1925*, part III, chapter VI, point 46, p. 34.

7. *Sikh Gurdwaras Act*, 1925, chapter XI, point 134, pp. 66–67.

requirements was thus insufficient; the designation of an identity, in point (g), was required for a hereditary office-holder to be eligible for office. Further restrictions on identity were and have been debated, such as regarding the necessity of being an *amritdhārī* or initiated Sikh versus being a *keshdhārī* or bearer of the long hair prescribed for members of the Khalsa.[8] The use of Punjabi was also debated as a possible requirement, but not included in the bill due to the controversy brought about by the suggestion.[9] Such references to identity had great significance, since the designation of religious identity was directly related to governmental representation, through the system of reserved electorates. Such a designation was therefore charged politically and carried real social and economic power.

Chapter II of the Act defines the manner by which a petition can be made to have a gurdwara designated as a "Sikh Gurdwara"—the Act uses this terminology, noting a difference between a gurdwara as a generic category, and a specifically Sikh Gurdwara (whereas today a "gurdwara" generally is a Sikh Gurdwara, in the Act this needed specification).[10] The factors used in the determination of whether or not a congregational site or gurdwara is a "Sikh Gurdwara" are as follows:

If the tribunal finds that the gurdwara—

(i) was established by, or in memory of any of the Ten Sikh Gurus, or in commemoration of any incident in the life of any of the Ten Sikh Gurus, and is used for public worship by Sikhs, or

(ii) owing to some tradition connected with one of the Ten Sikh Gurus, is used for public worship predominantly by Sikhs, or

(iii) was established for use by the Sikhs for the purpose of public worship and is used for such worship by Sikhs, or

(iv) was established in memory of a Sikh martyr, saint or historical person and is used for public worship by Sikhs, or

(v) owing to some incident connected with the Sikh religion is used for public worship predominantly by Sikhs.[11]

---

8. *Punjab Legislative Council Debates* 1925, 1254ff.

9. *Punjab Legislative Council Debates* 1925, 1245ff.

10. *Sikh Gurdwaras Act, 1925*, chapter II, point 6, p. 7.

11. *Sikh Gurdwaras Act, 1925*, chapter III, point 16.2, p. 16.

What is striking in this designation of a Sikh Gurdwara is the way it differs from the substance of the related debate in the Legislative Council. There, reference to proper management was made throughout; this is particularly the case in the final debates over the bill in 1925, when Master Tara Singh discussed the bill and its importance for the community.[12] In the bill (now Act) itself, what matters is history as the central criteria to determine whether or not a gurdwara is Sikh. Also striking is the way in which worship or use by Sikhs becomes important; designation of a site *as Sikh* requires that the courts define *who is a Sikh*, and therefore who is in the congregation. Attention to who *attends* a gurdwara makes the identity of members of the congregation key to its designation as Sikh. This marriage of identity and sacred site, of "Sikhness" defined through the mapping of Punjab as the location of Sikhness in historical terms, happens within the colonial mode of governance in a manner unprecedented in articulations of the religious and historical landscape of the Sikhs that we saw earlier, when the governance of gurdwaras was not tied to inheritable private property and ownership, and there was no legislated definition of a site based on those in attendance (who, then, must be clearly identified).

Exactly which gurdwaras might be considered as Sikh Gurdwaras is indicated in the "Schedules" section of the Act, after chapter XII.[13] This list did raise a certain amount of debate as the Act was being considered in the Council, and it was in this context the idea of "history" was discussed. An earlier version of the Act contained the schedule, and this was omitted from the 1922 version, after "memorial after memorial began to drop in."[14] The case of a gurdwara in Gurdaspur, for example, provided the opportunity for members of the Council to consider the features that constituted a gurdwara as "historical" or not:

> The leading vernacular daily of Lahore, the *Bande Matram* has made its columns available for the Gurdwara Parbandhak Committee to show its case that is it really a *gurdwara* and also for the Mahants to show that really it is . . . not a *gurdwara*. And Sir, reading it as a lawyer I see that there is a good deal to be said on both sides. . . . So clause 24 which enables this Commission to institute exhaustive inquiry into the foundation of the *gurdwaras*, the objects with which they were founded, the aims that the

---

12. *Punjab Legislative Council Debates* 1925, 1102 ff.

13. *Sikh Gurdwaras Act, 1925*, 76ff.

14. *Punjab Legislative Council Debates* 1922, 10.

founders had in instituting them are all matters of supreme importance;
and I have no doubt this Commission will collect matters of great historical
interest and may be in a position, in course of time, to bring out a gazetteer
of *gurdwaras* which will be a monument of industry and research and will
throw a great light on these difficult matters.[15]

At the same time, in the final speech of Master Tara Singh—a major political
figure in the late colonial period and the first two decades after independence—
to the Punjab Legislative Council, he deemphasized "history" as a constituting
element in defining a gurdwara. Instead, his arguments hinged on property rights
and the role of the gurdwara in the Sikh community:

> Everyone to whichsoever religion he may belong will agree with me
> that the temples are the life and soul of a nation. To the Sikh commu-
> nity especially these Gurdwaras are their life and soul. Their very life is
> dependant upon the purity, upon the emancipation, upon the freedom
> of these Gurdwaras from all corrupt practices. . . . Historians or those
> who study the Sikh history will find that the Sikh religion which is
> pre-eminently a congregational religion and not individualistic was
> founded with temples and the main source of its dissemination was the
> temple.[16]

As Master Tara Singh continued, he argued that control of a gurdwara was never
meant to be hereditary, and was instead meant to rest in the hands of the community itself, in the form of local *sangat*s or communities of believers. Problems were
introduced when *mahant*s came to be "absolute masters,"[17] and consider gurdwara properties as their own. While emphasizing that no "non-Sikh temple" was
the concern of the Sikh community, Singh emphasized that "Sikh Gurdwaras or
shrines are the heritage of the Panth and . . . [should] be controlled and managed
by the Panth."[18] The definition of a gurdwara that Tara Singh goes on to provide
does not, in fact, mention historicality as a factor: there are those gurdwaras
about which "no substantial doubt exists," but no specification is given about the
factors that contribute to that lack of doubt, the proof of Sikhness. "Heritage" is

---

15. *Punjab Legislative Council Debates* 1922, 10, 34.

16. *Punjab Legislative Council Debates* 1925, 1103.

17. *Punjab Legislative Council Debates* 1925, 1104.

18. *Punjab Legislative Council Debates* 1925, 1105.

mentioned in general terms. As described above, however, the Gurdwara Reform
Act itself provides the specification lacking in Master Tara Singh's speech: historicality, and the "Sikhness" of those attending the site.

The "historical" in this context is thus a modern legislative construct of
governance: the SGPC was brought into being within the Gurdwara Reform
Movement and with the passage of the Gurdwara Reform Act of 1925 became
an officially recognized administrative body. And it is under the SGPC that
"historical" gurdwaras are managed and the landscape of Punjab is marked as
Sikh and as historical, and through the passage of the Gurdwara Reform Act
of 1925 that the Takhats or administrative seats associated with the governance of the community (*panth*) were brought into being. It was through the
definition of such locations as Sikh, as historical, and as property that the
colonial imagination intervened in the geography of Sikhness in Punjab, and
through which a change was brought about in the conception and history of
History—and its forms of evidence—within Sikh tradition. History, place as
property, and Sikh "identity" were thus joined in defining the territory of the
community.

Enacting the Act

Sardar Narain Singh declared in 1925, "to the Sikhs the gurdwaras are their very
lives. Without these gurdwaras, the Sikhs are as good as dead bodies."[19] The battle
to retain these vital institutions continued long after the passage of the Gurdwara
Reform Bill, through the numerous court cases that resulted from the Act. The
legal discourse over this property thus presented a means by which the colonial
administration intervened in the configuration of definitions of Sikhness in relation to historical sites, even after the end of the Raj.[20]

A few examples express sufficiently the tenor of the evidence presented in
these kinds of cases. Issues of identity were resolved in these court cases, and
definitions drawn, usually utilizing works of history and culture by British
scholar-administrators as evidence. The Orientalist historical literature engaged
as evidence bespeaks the ways in which the discourse engaged was colonial at its
core. The works of Max Macauliffe (author of a sympathetic account of the
Sikhs called *The Sikh Religion*, in 1909) and Ernest Trumpp (responsible for a

19. *Punjab Legislative Council Debates* 1925, 1217.

20. This larger context is discussed by Dirks, "From Little King to Landlord," 181.

controversial translation of the Guru Granth Sahib in the 1870s) are referred to often in court cases relating to gurdwara management, such as in the case of *Mahant Basant Das (defendant) v. Hem Singh etc. (plaintiffs).*[21] In reversing the original judgment of the case, which had found in favor of the plaintiffs in declaring the site in question to be Sikh, Ali J. Zafar used the work of Trumpp to argue that "all the Gurus, with the exception of the last, remained within the pale of Hinduism."[22] This argument was upheld by the British judge involved, J. Harrison, and he took the assertion of separateness on the part of the Sikh plaintiffs to signify that they had no interest in what was a Hindu institution. Their own assertion of separateness undid their claim, and his evaluation of the claim was based upon the work of Trumpp and Macauliffe.[23] Such work was thus used as authoritative evidence that determined rights, property and identities within the legal system, giving it coercive force.[24]

In this way also, the past was constructed within colonial contexts in a new way: in relation to British notions of property and in relation to the power attached to history within British courts—as written and interpreted by British authors. A fundamental question occupied the courts: the identity of Udasis in relation to Sikhs, and the rights to property that ensued from the definition of that identity. One example was the case of *Ram Prashad v. Shiromani Gurdwara Parbandak Committee.*[25] This case hinged, in appeal, on who exactly founded the site and whether there was a clear connection to the Guru

---

21. High Court of Judicature at Lahore (India); Privy Council, Judicial Committee (Great Britain), *Indian Law Reports: containing cases determined by the High Court at Lahore and by the Judicial Committee of the Privy Council on appeal from that court. Lahore series,* Volume VII (Lahore: Printed by the Suptertendent, Government Printers, Punjab, and published at the Govt. Book Depot, 1926), 275ff. Hereafter this and other volumes will be called *Indian Law Reports.* For a discussion of Trumpp and Macauliffe, see Mandair, *Religion and the Specter of the West* and "Emergence of Sikh Theology."

22. *Indian Law Reports,* Vol. VII, 282.

23. This is particularly troubling, given the negative light Trumpp's work was seen in by most Sikhs at the time; Trumpp's nearly legendary disrespect for basic Sikh practices (e.g., not smoking) undermined any standing his work might have had in the community.

24. This kind of role, as Dirks notes in the Coda to his *Castes of Mind,* demonstrates how forms of colonial knowledge occupied a constitutive and not epiphenomenal importance in the colonial project. (Nicholas Dirks *Castes of Mind: Colonialism and the Making of Modern India* [Princeton, NJ: Princeton University Press, 2001].)

25. *Indian Law Reports,* Vol. XII, 504. This same case drew heavily, like the one cited earlier, on the work of Orientalists, in this case Cunningham's *History of the Sikhs* (1849), the work of Dr. Trumpp, and Rose's *Glossary of Punjab Tribes and Castes* (1911).

himself: "it should be observed that if the respondents were found not to have proved the connection between Bhai Prithi and the tenth Guru, their case would practically break down."[26] The relationships that form the ground for the establishment of "history" within Sikh contexts are here deemed legally constitutive of a right to property. The evidence of history valued in Sikh contexts, expressing a relationship between Guru and devotee, is subject to the "rules of evidence" of the British court, transforming them from markers of relationship, and therefore of community, into legal proof.[27] History—of sites and of Sikhs—was a determining factor: "Having had the advantage of a most careful canvass by the Courts below of the history of the Sikh religion from the time of the first Guru onwards, and of the history of the Udasis from the time of his son Siri Chand, whom the Courts below have held to be the founder of the Udasi sect, their Lordships think it impossible to affirm the proposition that this Udasi shrine was established for use by Sikhs for the purpose of public worship. . . ."[28]

The articulation of possession and identity around sites is mirrored by similar activities around objects, but the results have been quite different, due to the more prominent role of land in defining Sikh history and sovereignty. The case of the Golewala Dera provides an interesting example of how religious identity was debated in relation to the history of the site and the history of the Guru's interaction with it—and of how an object operated at the periphery of this debate. According to family members, several of the objects discussed in this book have been sought by the SGPC, such as the Chola Sahib of the Bedi family of Dera Baba Nanak.[29] They claim that the SGPC has attempted to bring these objects under their control as they did with gurdwaras and lands associated with the Gurus; so far, they have not succeeded. Although independent corroborating evidence of legal cases along such lines is lacking, the SGPC has periodically issued statements indicating its desire to gain control of such objects. The introductory chapter opened with one such statement. In another example, the Sodhi family has been petitioned numerous times as well to give the 1604 version of the scripture to Sikh

26. *Indian Law Reports*, Vol. XII, 514–15.

27. *Indian Law Reports*, Vol. XII, 520.

28. *Indian Law Reports*, Vol. XII, 168.

29. Described in conversation with holders of objects; no legal documents are available to corroborate this. This phenomenon has been noted by others as well; see Mann, *Making of Sikh Scripture*.

authorities. In 2004, the year of the 400th anniversary of the compilation of the Adi Granth or Kartarpur Pothi, strenuous requests were made by SGPC officials and particularly by the Guru Gobind Singh Foundation. The Sodhi family, however, did not comply.[30]

The arguments over historicality and identity are parallel in relation to objects as well, although they are not generally resolved in the same way. For example, the Golewala Dera possesses a *kaṭār*, or waistbelt blade, that once belonged to Guru Gobind Singh (see figure 7.1). The *kaṭār* is said to have been given to Baba Heta Singh by Guru Gobind Singh, to the family at Bahibal Kalan, near Kot Kapura.[31] Guru Gobind Singh had passed close to Bahibal village and camped near a pool of water that is now revered as Guru Sar. It was given to the Dera twenty years later. The Dera has a ritual ceremony (their *maryādā*, or tradition, they call it) enacted in relation to the object. It is only shown to the public on days when preparations are made for *karāh parshād*, the sweet generally given out at gurdwaras to devotees. Ardas is recited, and then the *kaṭār* is brought out for public viewing from its air-conditioned resting place (*sukhāsan*), next to the Guru Granth Sahib. When I viewed the ceremony in the spring of 2002, Kashmir Singh, the current patriarch of the community, led the ceremony, which ends with cries of praise typical of Sikh congregational events—*Bole so nihāl* and *Waheguru Ji kā Khālsā*. The Dera is led by a central *sant*. *Samādh*s or death memorials to each of the past *sant*s are located on the site: Swarup, who founded the Dera, and then Kesar Singh.

There was lengthy litigation over control of the site—that is, whether or not it should be declared Sikh and come under the control of the SGPC, or not—continuing from the 1930s to the 1970s. Although members of the Dera emphasize the role of the dagger in the court battle, this was not actually the case. As early as 1936, a case between Hem Singh and Basant Singh brought the Dera into question. According to the decision in the case, referring to section 2 (iii) of the Sikh Gurdwaras Act, the main "stress under the clause has to be taken by the first part thereof."[32] At that time, a witness testified to the fact that "the institution in

---

30. Chander Suta Dogra, "The Captive Word of a Faith," *Outlook India*, September 6, 2004, http://www.outlookindia.com/article.aspx?225024 (accessed April 20, 2012); "Sodhi Family Asked to Hand over Kartarpuri Bir to SGPC," *The Tribune*, Chandigarh, http://www.tribune india.com/2004/specials/ggs.htm (accessed August 27, 2004).

31. See Gurmukh Singh, *Historical Sikh Shrines*, 239–40.

32. This and all court documents that are referred to here were accessed as unpublished copies found in the archive at Golewala Dera. I thank Kashmir Singh for allowing me to look at these documents.

FIGURE 7.1 Display of the historical weapon kept at Golewala. Photograph by Anne Murphy. May 2002.

dispute is a dera and smadhs [*sic*] are the object of worship at the institution. Kesar Singh mahant . . . wore a langoti and was not a Sikh." The case of *Ram Piari v. Sardar Singh* in 1938 (PLR 82) determined that if not used for public worship, a site could not be declared a gurdwara, and this provided the necessary precedent. In 1964, the Dera won a court case brought by the SGPC, which tried to win control of the Dera and possession of the *katār* as well. The SGPC had sought to have the Dera declared an *itihāsik* gurdwara. The Dera won, arguing that the *katār* had been given to the family elsewhere, so that the Dera was not involved in the gift at all. A decision on April 8, 1964, under section 34 of the Sikh Gurdwaras Act, declared that this place was "not established in memory of any of the ten Sikh Gurus or in commemoration of any incident in the life of any of the ten Sikh Gurus or in memory of Sikh martyrs, saints, or historical persons and was never used for public worship by the Sikhs." Further, it was argued that the site was not used by the Sikhs and was a Dera established by Baba Sarup Singh, "a Nirmala Sadhu of pious and religious bent of mind and revered [*sic*] in the ilaqa"; that the Adi Granth was used at the site, but the Nirmala *samādh*s were worshipped by devotees, and thus the institution was not a gurdwara. Other scriptures (the Adhyatma Ramayana and Bhagavad Gita) were also present. The site was thus declared in the decision to be a private charitable institution, "to provide food and shelter to the wayfarer and the sadhus of the Nirmala fraternity." (Here the court refers to an earlier decision, *Puran Singh v. Mela Singh*, 1934, Lahore 277.) Later, in 1967, Nirmala Sadhus were declared not to be Sikh (*Mahant Harnam Singh v. Gurdial Singh* 1967 PLR 805). On April 8, 1970, an appeal was filed that mentioned the *katār* specifically, but since there was no mention of the dagger in the original case, the appeal was dismissed.[33] The same is true of court documents regarding the control of the lands associated with the Bhais of Bagrian, which sought to distinguish what possessions of the family were private property and what would be deemed a Sikh Gurdwara (and, therefore, would come under the control of the SGPC). The historical objects related to the Gurus were left out of the demarcation of the property of the family and the property of the community.[34]

The issue of *samādh*s, such as those in evidence at Golewala, was also a primary one in the formulation of the Gurdwara Reform Act of 1925. It was promised that such *samādh*s would be looked after when sites were declared Sikh

---

33. Court documents examined did not address the ownership of the dagger itself in relation to control of the site.

34. Thanks are due to Bhai Sikander Singh for sharing the Bagrian court documents with me.

gurdwaras.[35] Yet, as has been shown, the presence of such *samādh*s can be taken, in association with other factors, as proof of a site not being Sikh. In the end, it is the *history* of a site that is crucial in determining its level of Sikhness, and therefore who can possess it. Objects are secondary to this formulation, and generally are accepted as personal private property. Property thus is made central, but certain kinds of historical "property" matter—specifically, land—and others (such as objects), less so. With the colonial intervention, therefore, a category that was once singular and inclusive—modes of representation of the landscape of the Gurus' past, as site or object—was made dual.

Defining Religious Identity in Relation to Place

Appadurai has noted how debate over the management of Hindu temples in Madras led to the definition of the community associated with the temple and the construction of more rigid boundaries. At the same time, there is evidence that there are ways in which this kind of process of definition—which characterizes the Sikh Gurdwara community as well—did not take place in the case of the Hindu community to the same degree. This can be seen with reference to the The Hindu Religious and Charitable Trusts Act, 1924. In his Statement of Objects and Reasons for the Bill, H. S. Gour noted that the bill proposed to provide for the management of the Hindu Trust properties throughout India was based on the "Mussalman Wakf Act":

> The reasons which have led the Legislature to pass the Mussalman Wakf Act apply *a fortiori* to Hindu religious and charitable trusts, and, as the Central Legislature has protected the trusts of one community, it is necessary that it should also protect the trusts of the other community.[36]

The designation of proper management of Hindu temples was seen as a priority also because of recent events with respect to gurdwara reform. Comments by Sardar Sewaram Singh (District and Sessions Judge) noted this: "No time should, in my opinion, be lost in passing this measure, and in introducing it in all provinces, if it be intended to avoid the happenings that have characterised the Sikh Gurdwaras and shrines the last few years, in their effect on the Hindu endowments. A legislation of this nature is not a minute too soon in the present instance."[37]

---

35. *Punjab Legislative Council Debates* 1925, 1227ff.

36. Punjab State Home Proceedings, IOR P/11436. No. 21 (October 1924).

37. Punjab State Home Proceedings, IOR P/11436. Enclosure No. 4 to Pro. No. 23, p. 2.

A. J. O'Brien, Commissioner, Ambala Division, noted that: "religious bodies of all sects should form themselves into registered associations and should decide as to the organization, to govern the working of the matters in which the sect is concerned locally or otherwise."[38]

As O'Brien also notes, the desire for a clear system of management was offset by the realization that "so many religious beliefs in India are fluid and it may not be easy to crystallize believers into registered associations," no matter how necessary such associations might be.[39] Generally, most of the opinions registered about the bill advocated a narrow, provincial-level solution, and many identified ambiguity about who is "Hindu" as a major problem for the bill. It was also noted that any all-India measure along these lines needed to consider the Hindu community in particular terms: "The word 'Hindu' should not be defined positively but negatively, sections of the populations, such as Muslims, Christians, Buddhists, Jains, Parsis and Sikhs, etc., being excluded, and power let to the Local Government to add or exclude from the category of Hindus any persons, families, tribes and communities, whatsoever."[40] This definition (and the idea of Hindu subjectivity it reflects) was all-encompassing, rather than exclusive. The notion of a singular "Hindu" style and organization for management was thus called into question by many in British India, relating to a broader polemic engaged then, as now, about whether or not "Hinduism" is a religious category like "Islam." Although it has been commonly accepted that the formalization of "Hinduism" as a category was a product of colonialism, it has been less commonly acknowledged that so, too, was the notion of Hinduism as an *unbounded* religion. It is not surprise, therefore, as Will Sweetman has noted, that it is "precisely the claim that Hinduism is not a religion which reveals lingering Christian and theological influence even in the works of those who explicitly disclaim such influence."[41] The interpretation of Hinduism as "different" was also a part of British understanding of how Hinduism functioned alongside other religions.

---

38. Punjab State Home Proceedings, IOR P/11436. No. 25, p. 6.

39. Punjab State Home Proceedings, IOR P/11436. No. 25, p. 6.

40. Punjab State Home Proceedings, IOR P/11436. No. 41 (October), pp. 1–2. A Letter (no. 2708-S Home General). From A. Latifi, Esq, OBE ICS (Secretary to Government, Punjab, Transferred Departments) to the Secretary to the Government of India, Legislative Department. Dated Simla, August 16, 1924 on the Subject of the Hindu Religious and Charitable Trusts Bill.

41. Will Sweetman, "'Hinduism' and the History of 'Religion': Protestant Presuppositions in the Critique of the Concept of Hinduism," *Method & Theory in the Study of Religion*, 15, 4 (2003): 329–53, see 330.

Whereas the "solution" for Hindu religious sites was therefore seen to be found in an amorphous definition of the religion as a whole, there are clear parallels between the ways "religions" were configured within the Gurdwara Reform Movement and the movement for improved management of Muslim trusts, such as reflected in the debate leading up to the passage of the Waqf Act of 1923. The sentiments submitted in support of the Waqf Act are strikingly similar to those presented for gurdwara reform:

> For several years past, there has been a growing feeling amongst the Muhammadan community, throughout the country, that the numerous endowments which have been made or are being made daily by pious and public-spirited Muhammadans are being wasted or systematically misappropriated by those whose hands the trusts may have come in the course of time. Instances of such misuse of trust property are unfortunately so very common that a *Waqf* endowment has now come to be regarded by the public as only a clever device to tie up property in order to defeat creditors and generally to evade the law under the cloak of a plausible dedication to the Almighty.

The personal defects of the managers were also, in this case, in question:

> In some cases the *Mutwailis* [sic] are persons who are utterly unfit to carry on the administration of the *Waqf* and who, by their moral delinquencies, bring discredit not merely on the endowment but on the community itself. It is believed that the feeling is unanimous that some steps should be taken in order that incompetent and unscrupulous *Mutwallis* may be checked in their career of waste and mismanagement, and that the endowments themselves may be appropriated to the purposes for which they had been originally dedicated.... There are numerous *Waqf* properties all over the country unknown to the public which the *Mutwallis* are treating as their own private property and dealing with in any way they think fit or necessary.[42]

Comments by Sardar Ali Hussain Khan, Kazilbash, bar-at-law, senior sub-judge to the deputy commissioner, Montgomery, on January 14, 1922, could literally be taken right out of the Gurdwara Reform Movement literature:

42. Both quotations from: Punjab State Home Proceedings, IOR P/11436. Musalman [sic] Waqf Act, 1923, and the Rules Under It. November 1924, Nos. 1–48. Statement of Objects and Reasons, November 24, 1924. Proceeding No. 1, Enclosure 2.

Every educated Muhammadan feels the necessity of controlling the expenses and preventing the abuse of the income derived from the *waqfs* of the public nature. The machinery now provided is very cumbrous and insufficient. It involves litigation extending over several years. The public is not aware of all the facts and the law and their rights under the *waqf* and even if they were they would not like to incur such heavy expenses. This has led the *mutwallis* to feel themselves all powerful. A community which seeks the shelter of the Government in order to ameliorate the condition of its institutions deserves that a helping hand should be extended towards it. Such a help will be a source of the gratitude of the community. Of course the Government being pledged not to interfere with the religion cannot directly control the management but it can help the community in getting the necessary control of its institutions and money which ought to be spent for its benefit.[43]

The Gurdwara Reform Movement thus took place within a much larger field of debate and controversy regarding the religious site and the designation of the community associated with it. It did so in relation to larger assumptions about the definition of religious community and identity, and the relationship of the past to claims of rights to institutions and property in the present. In the Sikh case, a particular form of historical consciousness, in relation to territory and identity, was in this way forged, dependant upon the *narrowing* of the definition of a Sikh that is strikingly different from the vague and expansive understanding of "Hindu" that animated discourse over Hindu sites.

Mapping the Punjab Landscape

The fundamental argument of the Gurdwara Reform Movement was that under the British ownership and control of Sikh shrines had been in error granted to their caretakers. Sardar Narain Singh stated the situation quite plainly in 1925: "The grants of land were of course intended for the support of the institution; and under Sikh rule if a Sadh misbehaved he was at once turned out. But at the regular settlement the incumbent was in every case returned as owner of the land, which was at the same time exempted from revenue for the period of the settlement...."[44] Place came to be conceived as property, and tied to *individuals*. Under the 1925 Act, history and identity (who is a Sikh, who uses a site, and how are they proved as Sikh) came to

---

43. Punjab State Home Proceedings, IOR P/11436. Comments on Act XLII of 1923, No. 6, Enclosure 1.

44. *Punjab Legislative Council Debates* 1925, 1218.

constitute the argument for reevaluating individual ownership of Sikh shrines, and as such scripted a new way of understanding the landscape of Punjab as historically Sikh and under the control of the community as a bounded unit (and in this way very distinct from Hinduism, which was viewed as unbounded and inclusive). Under the new system, ownership was reconstituted in relation to *communities*— discrete and defined, and attested to by historical provenance.[45]

Particular features of gurdwara management and control were reconstituted in the new colonial regime of meaning. *Kār sevā* or volunteer service was a primary means of exerting control and claiming authority over sacred sites, and provided a vocabulary for participation in not only the protection of established sites within the Gurdwara Reform Movement, but also the addition of new sites—as in the case of Gurdwara Bhattha Sahib, discussed in chapter 2, which was "discovered" as a historical site during the movement. The Golden Temple has been a primary location of volunteer service, particularly in the de-silting of the tank around the temple; such an effort took place in 1923, as the Gurdwara Reform Movement gathered pace.[46] Other important shrines were served by the community, or rather a small subsection of the community, and this is true of the refurbishment and establishment of sacred Sikh sites till today.[47] Such projects were described in detail in the Sikh newspapers of the period, which highlighted important *kār sevā* projects and often publicized requests for service by community members, sometimes but not always in the form of financial support.[48] For the 1923 Golden Temple *kār sevā*, for example, the Sikhs of Peshawar sent thousands of mats.[49]

The rhetoric of loss and return, search and recovery, was central to the movement for gurdwara reform. It was seen as a quest to recapture what had been lost, when gurdwaras went out of the hands of the community during the political turmoil of the eighteenth century.[50] Indeed, the search for and discovery of gurdwaras in the early twentieth century is portrayed as part of a continuing process:

---

45. See, for example, a discussion of how religious sites relate to other individual communities, such as in *Punjab Legislative Council Debates* 1925, 1222 and 1263, and passim; on interests in a property as an individual or as an institution, see *Punjab Legislative Council Debates* 1925, 1229.

46. Described in detail in the *Khālsā Samācar* Vol. 24, No. 30 (May 24, 1923), and following.

47. See Murphy, "Mobilizing *Seva*."

48. One example is the Kar Seva of Gurdwara Santokh Sar, *Khālsā Samācar* Vol. 21, No. 29 (May 20, 1920): 2. Another is that of Kartarpur at Dera Baba Nanak, *Khālsā Samācar* Vol. 21, No. 22 (April 1, 1920): 1. An appeal for money is exemplified by a short plea in *Khālsā Samācar* Vol. 22, No. 4 (December 16, 1920): 4; these are common in the period.

49. *Khālsā Samācar* Vol. 24, No. 30 (May 24, 1923): 4.

50. The history of gurdwaras provided in Kartar Singh's account of Guru Ka Bag provides this larger context. Kalasvalia, *Sidak Nazāre*, 2ff.

jadoṅ sikkhāṅ de din palte tadoṅ kujh saṅbhalan sār hī gurdvāryāṅ dī sevā
dā dhiān āyā te āpṇā tan, man, dhan, sarbaṅs takk lagā ke bhī gurdvāryāṅ
dī khoj saṅbhāl te sevā misalāṅ de vele ate shere paṅjāb mahārājā raṇjīt siṅgh
jī ādi valloṅ araṁbh ho gaī [51]

When the days of the Sikhs turned, then there came to be attention to the
service of the Gurdwaras, for the sake of their care. Dedicating bodies,
mind, wealth, and entire family, the search and care for Gurdwaras began
at the time of the militias (*misals*) and the Lion of the Punjab, Maharaja
Ranjit Singh, and others.

Lists of historical sites began to be compiled at the end of the nineteenth century
and the beginning of the twentieth, as a prelude to the Gurdwara Reform Movement that culminated in the Gurdwara Reform Act of 1925. These texts, which I
call "gurdwara guides," began to appear in print in the end of the nineteenth century, by which time the printing press was well established in Punjab and a wide
array of pamphlets, in general, became available. [52] An early form was Tara Singh
Narotam's *Gurū Tīrth Saṅgraih* (1884), a compilation of the holy places of the
Gurus. Later examples of the genre include the *Nāvāṅ te Thāvāṅ dā Kosh*, an ency-
clopedic guide to names and places related to Sikhism, and of course the famous
Mahānkosh by Kahn Singh of Nabha, which is said to be an encyclopedia of Sikh
literature but is more of an all-around reference work on Sikh history.

A comparison of the presentation of information in various gurdwara guides is revealing. Some were organized by district or location, and others, by Guru; in all cases,
they provided information designed to aid the pilgrim in visiting the sacred shrines.
For example, the guide entitled *Cheviṅ Dharam Pothī* is from (it is guessed, given the
references to the Chief Khalsa Diwan and the accession date) the early 1920s. [53] The
text conforms to the traditional convention of listing sites by Guru, but there
are no headings given to indicate as such. It is written in the same form as a
janam-sākhī, telling where and when Guru Nanak (in the initial sections)

---

51. Bhai Mohan Singh Vaid, *Bhayānak Sākkā*, 3.

52. See discussion in chapter 4. Barrier notes that at this time tracts were generally of two types:
appeals (*bentī*) or polemical; see Barrier, *Sikhs and their Literature*, Appendix C for a list of exemplary texts. See also Barrier, *Punjab in Nineteenth-Century Tracts* and N. G. Barrier and Paul Wallace, *The Punjab Press: 1880–1905* (East Lansing, MI: Research Committee on the Punjab and
Asian Studies Center, Michigan State University, 1970); also Grewal, *Sikhs of the Punjab*, 149ff.

53. *Cheviṅ Dharam Pothī* (Amritsar: Wazir Hind Press and the Khalsa Pracarak Vidyalaya
(Chief Khalsa Diwan), 1922?). IOL 14162.n.7.

went, complete with dialogue. Commentary on the status of current gurdwaras is provided in footnotes. Direct references to earlier texts are included,
without full bibliographic reference (e.g., on page 6, a Bhai Gurdas quote is
included). The overall narrative style implies a direct relationship between this
type of text and the earlier form of *janam-sākhī*.[54] Tara Singh Narotam's 1884
text and others like it provided information on the district and town in which
a site was located and information on the best way to get there. However,
Narotam's text also was organized according to Guru, followed by entries for
devotees of the Gurus. Bhai Bhagatu, important in the genealogy of the Chakk
Fateh Singhwala family, is given an entry in the guide, as are others who served
the Gurus.[55] The guides functioned explicitly as pilgrimage guides, helping visitors organize their experience of Punjab, while also highlighting Sikh history
and the people who comprise it—Gurus and devotees—and the evidence of
that history.

It has been argued that colonial forms of governance initiated a change in
how property was configured in Punjab, in general and with reference to religious communities. Another means by which the colonial state intervened in
the imagination of the landscape was through the more generalized process of
mapping and regularization. As Smith notes in his study of Punjabi land settlements, "everywhere the business of mapping and measuring, of registering
holdings as discrete, separately negotiable parcels of land, and of fitting agrarian
relations into a new mould must be considered fundamentally disruptive of an
older order."[56] The paired notions of mapping and property as exemplified by
the gurdwara guide phenomenon show how Sikhs adopted and appropriated
these ways of seeing the landscape. We can see these guides as a Sikh mapping
of Punjab that acts as a corollary to British colonial mapping. Ian Barrow has
argued that map-making constitutes a narrativization of the colonial, inscribing history as a justification for colonialism within the map of the colonized.
History as articulated in the map was a means to legitimate rule: "[A]uthority
could only be fully established if the Company was also recognized as the
legitimate possessor of that territory. Outlining a history of possession could

---

54. Denis Matringe has called attention to the parallels of Vir Singh's work and the *janam-
sākhī*s; given the resonances between this text and the *janam-sākhī*s, this feature of modern Sikh
religious discourse must be expanded and generalized (Matringe, "Re-enactment of Guru
Nanak's Charisma," 213).

55. See chapter 4. Narotam, *Shrī Gurū Tīrth Saṅgraih*, 277.

56. R. S. Smith, *Rule by Records*, 379.

prove invaluable to that endeavor and maps, once again, could help document and show how and when possession was established."[57] Barrow thus argues that while in the eighteenth century history depended upon map-making, in the second half of the nineteenth century map-making was "pressed into the service of history. . . . Thus history's preoccupation with a certain kind of past became cartography's 'mission,' tied to the production of nostalgia for 'originary' moments."[58] Barrow extends his understanding of map-making in this sense outside of the production of actual maps, per se, into the production of various modes of mapping the ground and the imposition of historical narratives upon it, such as narrative descriptions of the history of a place (e.g., the Black Hole of Calcutta). In a parallel and directly related way, history, place, and Sikhness were co-inscribed within the legislation associated with the Sikh Gurdwara Act, and necessitated by the means of representation granted by the British, based as it was on the designation of individual and bounded religious communities in its representation of the past. The mapping of Punjab *as Sikh*, represented in the gurdwara guides and legislated through the Gurdwara Reform Act, was a result.

The transformation of property under the British had multiple consequences within the political economy of Punjab, as well as in other spheres—such as gender relations, as the work of Matthew Nelson and Veena Talwar Oldenburg has shown. For Oldenburg, the historical underpinnings of the late twentieth-century phenomenon of dowry murder lie in the simultaneous codification of customary law and the introduction of private property under the British.[59] The interests of women, who engaged in a wide range of forms of agricultural labor, were in this way excluded and "the precolonial logic for female infanticide was to be unwittingly strengthened by imperial revenue and land-ownership policies, even as the British outlawed the practice in 1870."[60] Here, attention to the actual effects of colonial policies, rather than attention to "motivations," reveals the way in which colonial interventions created sometimes radical disjunctures in "traditional" society. Similarly, the change in land and property rights in Punjab constituted a transformation in the way in which religious sites were conceived.

---

57. Ian J. Barrow, *Mapping History, Drawing Territory: British Mapping in India, c. 1756–1905* (Delhi: Oxford University Press, 2003), 16.

58. Barrow, *Mapping History*, 151.

59. Oldenburg, *Dowry Murder*, 12–13.

60. Oldenburg, *Dowry Murder*, 17.

Objects and Sites: Locations of the Historical,
and of the Sovereign

Finally we return to the *itihāsik* or historical objects that initiated this investigation into the transformation of Sikh historical places. It has been argued that in
the precolonial period objects and sites operated within a single category, revered
for their historical relationship to the Guru and as representations of the history
and relationships that comprised the community around the Guru. Gurdwara
guides too reflect this imagination of the Sikh past. Many of them also featured
lists of *itihāsik objects* related to the Gurus alongside lists of historical *sites*. Those
from the late nineteenth century, like Narotam's text, listed such objects alongside or even within entries for historical sites. After featuring a list of sites by
Guru, and a list of important devotees of the Gurus, Narotam's text features a list
of Gurus' "clothes and weapons."[61] The list makes mention, for example, of the
cholā or apron of Guru Nanak, held by members of the Bedi family now at Dera
Baba Nanak, and the early version of the Sikh scripture said to contain the compositions of Guru Nanak, the Harsahai Pothi, held by members of the Sodhi
family.[62] Longer mention is made, in particular, of objects held by the royal
family of Patiala.[63] The public, experiential nature of both site and object is
striking in these texts. One Gurdwara Guide, for example, the *Gurdhām Dīdār*,
is critical of the Dalla family for not showing the objects owned by the family
often enough:

> *ih vastūāṅ . . . srī dasmes jī dīāṅ han, jo gurū jī ne āpṇe ithoṅ de sikkh sar. ḍal
> siṅgh jī nūṅ bakhshīāṅ san, vaisākhī de mele utte ināṅ gur vastūāṅ de dar-
> shan karāuṅde han, agge picche ghaṭṭ karāuṅde han, jo ih vatīrā chaṅga
> nahīṅ, srī dasmes pitā jī de aṅg dīāṅ vastūāṅ nūṅ darshan karke nihāl hoṇ
> vāle tarasde sajjanāṅ nūṅ har sameṅ darshan karāuṇe cāhīde han*[64]

These things . . . are those of the tenth Guru, which he gave to his disciple
Dalla Singh. They make these objects available for viewing for the festival

61. Thank you to the Library of Punjab University in Patiala for providing a photocopy; a copy
is also available in the British Library's IOL collection, 14162.n7 (2). Pages referred to in what
follows refer to the 1971 edition from the Patiala library.

62. This text is no longer extant; see discussion in Mann, *Making of Sikh Scripture*, and brief
overview of its significance in chapter 2.

63. Narotam, *Shrī Gurū Tīrth Saṅgraih*, 291–92.

64. *Gurdhām Dīdār Arthāt Gurdhām Darpan (Mukaṅmal Tinn Hisse)* (Amritsar: Lal Devi
Das Janaki Das and Bhai Sham Singh Sohan Singh, n.d.), 380. IOL Panj B 1186.

of Vaisakhi. They are infrequently shown at other times and this behavior is not good. The things related to the Guru should be on view for enthusiastic viewers at all times, to bring them joy.

The text defines what is a historical site, what is an object related to the Guru, how each should be treated—and who has a right to take part in viewing them.

In the eighteenth and nineteenth centuries, sites and objects were seen to hold an important power, a power related to their historical association with the Gurus. The collection of objects was a way to express a series of relationships to the Guru. It was also a means by which sovereignty was articulated, in different modes, by Sikh rulers in the nineteenth century: Maharaja Ranjit Singh collected objects—not just those gifted by other rulers, but objects related to the Gurus themselves.[65] His famous *toshākhānā*, or treasure house, contained weapons of the Gurus and important Sikh heroes, as well as works of art and jewels. The *kalgī* or plume of the Tenth Guru was given to the Maharaja by a Bedi descendant of Guru Nanak in 1824.[66] He made a special room in his Lahore fort for the original volume of the Adi Granth prepared by Guru Arjan Dev. As J. S. Grewal has noted, Ranjit Singh patronized the families of the Gurus, as did other Sikh chiefs, and "the improvement in their material means as much as their descent gave them a peculiar prestige in the Sikh social order."[67] Indeed, as we have seen, these individuals were commonly granted rights to land and other honors. Such honor was apparently not exclusively for the Gurus' descendants and objects; the Maharaja is said to have also paid reverence to objects related to Prophet Muhammad.[68]

The constellation of historical connections to the Guru—family, object, and site—thus were afforded high status under Sikh patronage. The same was true for important Sikh religious sites, which were patronized under Ranjit Singh's Raj—the golden exterior to the Harmandir or Darbar Sahib, or as it came to be

---

65. See my discussion in Murphy "The Guru's Weapons." Archer mentions that Ranjit Singh went on a collecting spree in the 1820s and '30s, see Archer Papers, IOL Mss. Eur F 236, 214. For some details on "relic" objects given to Ranjit Singh from a number of diverse sources, see: Mohinder Singh, "Jewels and Relics from Maharaja Ranjit Singh's Toshakhana," *The Tribune*, August 4, 2001. http://www.tribuneindia.com/2001/20010408/spectrum/main8.htm

66. Mohinder Singh and Rishi Singh, *Maharaja Ranjit Singh*, 79. On the *kalgī* and other objects from the *toshākhānā*, see Murphy, "1849 Lahore."

67. Grewal, *Sikhs of the Punjab*, 96; see also Banga, *Agrarian System*, 156–57.

68. Mohinder Singh and Rishi Singh, *Maharaja Ranjit Singh*, 79; Mohinder Singh, "Jewels and Relics."

known, the Golden Temple, was affixed through the Maharaja's beneficence—as well as many other types of religious establishments to which the Sikh ruler granted revenue-free lands.[69] This was the duty of a sovereign ruler. The cultural economy of *khil'at* also continued under Ranjit Singh and was a constituting feature of contact both among the Sikh *misal*s, and between the Lahore state and the British at the beginning of the nineteenth century. As Stronge shows, the magnificence of the Punjabi court's collection and beneficence dazzled an array of European visitors.[70] Throughout the period of the ascendancy of post-Mughal sovereignty in the Punjab, the forging of alliances among various Sikh rulers was constituted by the establishment of historical relationships among them (such as through the production of historical accounts of their reign), and material exchanges, such as *khil'at*.[71] It must be noted that the value ascribed to sites associated with the Gurus did not always require political possession of the territory of the gurdwaras, as was the case with the gurdwaras of Delhi at the time of Baghel Singh. The marking of Sikh space did not necessitate Sikh sovereign control of Delhi and the denial of sovereignty to the Mughal emperor—but could be mobilized, such as by Ranjit Singh, to declare sovereignty and authority. The possession of objects related to the Guru worked in concert with other representations to symbolize sovereignty, before the intervention of British rule, but also through it, as I have argued elsewhere.[72] The historical achieved a particular importance under the British, as a means to articulate positions of power, hereditary rights, and "identity." It achieved its clearest manifestation and long-term impact within the Gurdwara Reform Movement of 1920–25, where history was inscribed on the land of Punjab, and on being Sikh within colonial legislative and juridical contexts.

The importance of objects alongside sites in the precolonial historical imaginary is in striking contrast to the discourse over gurdwaras that has predominated since the Gurdwara Reform Movement, and as reflected in the guides; in later compilations on historical gurdwaras, objects are generally ignored. Such texts therefore participated in the broader ideology of the Gurdwara Reform Movement and were part of a larger regulatory process over

---

69. Grewal, *Sikhs of the Punjab*, 96.

70. Susan Stronge, "The Sikh Treasury: The Sikh Kingdom and the British Raj," in *Sikh Art and Literature*, ed. Kerry Brown (New York: Routledge, 1999), 72–88. See also Mohinder Singh, "Jewels and Relics."

71. See Dhavan, *When Sparrows Became Hawks*.

72. Murphy, "Guru's Weapons."

objects and sites, and the definition of the community's relationship and rights with regard to them. Objects grew increasingly irrelevant in this discourse. Sovereignty—symbolic and real—was located in property in the Raj, which coincides (as has been noted above) with the British preoccupation with land revenue settlement and the articulation of ownership—by communities—through history. Objects did occupy a place in this narrative, but they did so secondarily, and with decreasing importance over time. Gurdwara guides from the 1920s and later tend, therefore, to confine themselves to a landscape of historical gurdwaras. The preference for listing sites and *not* objects has continued into the present, where objects are seen as peripheral to the cultural economy of historicality as expressed in the historical gurdwara. The *difference* between object and site was most notably expressed within the court cases that resulted from the Gurdwara Reform Act of 1925, through which the ownership of sites was articulated and rights were enforced. Objects did not generally figure substantially in such cases.

Conclusion

There is an intimate connection between the object and site visible in precolonial as well as in some colonial-era sources. In these, the two things form a kind of single category—the *itihāsik* or historical object and the *itihāsik* site, even though there is no one single term in Punjabi to contain them both, or even for historical objects as a category as such (such as the English term commonly used for them, "relic"). The process I have described here shows how objects and sites were determined to be historical. Sacred sites then came to occupy a primary position as "historical" and as property in the British Raj, and came to be tied to a clearly defined notion of being Sikh that was a direct result of the legislative and juridical order put in place by the British. The Legislative Council Debates referred to above provide glimpses into this process.

The difference in the way that historical sites and objects were and are treated is revealing. Sacred *sites* were addressed by the Gurdwara Reform Movement and had to be managed through the relevant Act, because the right to private property was a fundamental one in the colonial context and any reevaluation of the right to land as property required special provisions. Objects were peripheral to the central debate, which hinged on ownership of land; they maintained their status as "private property" and in general were not granted to the SGPC when it sought possession.[73] Families could retain such objects. Gurdwaras, as

---

73. Anecdotally described to me by a number of collectors of historical objects, such as Manjit Singh of Dera Baba Nanak and Jasbir Singh of Chakk Fateh Singhwala. See above.

property, however, came to belong to the community, the contours of which were defined. Thus sites came to be the location of the articulation community and territory, in relation to the definition of being Sikh. This was necessary, since to fulfill the requirements of the Gurdwara Reform Act, Sikhness and history had to be proven and directly related to land. As a result, is there any reason to question why history, Sikhness, and land as territory should occupy a prominent place in the postcolonial mind of Sikh Punjabis, as observed by Oberoi, Das, and others?[74]

The Sikh example demonstrates a larger phenomenon. The early twentieth century witnessed the transformation of the evidence of history into the evidence of "nation" within the Indian response to colonial historiography.[75] However, the prior interest in history in the Sikh tradition, and the ways in which this interest was partially subverted, and partially continued under colonial rule, in a territorialized mode, make it stand apart. With the colonial state's strict regulation of history and identity in relation to the definition of property rights, Sikhness, history, and place came to be implicated and linked in relation to the historical gurdwara in a way that did not occur for other religious communities in the same way. The historical object, in this context, was placed within the category of personal property. The articulation of sovereignty through it was less central in the new economy. Thus, the object and its historicality escaped some of the pressures put upon the site as the embodiment of the historical. This, in the end, explains the relative silence on these objects in Sikh sources until more recently, since their historicality did not resonate with property in the same troubled way, and was not wrapped up in the process of proving a history of being Sikh, as happened in relation to territorialized *place*. It is only recently that attention has been paid to these objects, through a project at the National Institute for Punjab Studies that sought to document the historical objects available, in 2000, and increased attention to the families who own objects, such as the Bhai Rupa family, which has recently experienced more frequent invitations to display objects both in India and abroad.[76]

This realization of the difference between site and object allows us to consider anew the kinds of representations offered at the opening of the book and the different imaginations of the landscape of the Sikh past that they offer. In

---

74. See citations, chapter 1.

75. See Chatterjee, *Nation*; Sumit Sarkar, *Beyond Nationalist Frames: Postmodernism, Hindu Fundamentalism, History* (Bloomington: Indiana University Press, 2002).

76. See the works by Mohinder Singh. The Bhai Rupa family was discussed in brief in chapter 1.

the next chapter, I will consider briefly how objects participate in a transnational order of representation that utilizes them toward multiple ends, depending on the audience and context for the representation, and in a way that distinguishes them from a more territorial representation of the Sikh. This allows for multiple readings of Sikh objects, and multiple occasions for their postcolonial "lives"—to use Richard Davis's term—with precolonial references, to come into being.

Conclusion

COMMUNITY, TERRITORY, AND THE
AFTERLIFE OF THE OBJECT

> So it is with memory: it is a complex and deceptive experience.
> It appears to be preeminently a matter of the past, yet it is as
> much an affair of the present. It appears to be preeminently a
> matter of time, yet it is as much an affair of space.
>
> —J.Z. SMITH[1]

A Community of History

The Sikh community is constituted in relation to the personal authority and vision of the Gurus, which is embodied in the sacred text that occupies the central principle and experience of the community today, the Guru Granth Sahib. As has been explored in this book, it is also importantly shaped through the historical imaginary that occupies a central place in Sikh intellectual production in the eighteenth century and following, and is substantiated, experienced, and made present in the object and site. This historical project produces the community around the remembered figure of the Guru and relationships with him. The Guru is the object of memories, instantiated through material and discursive means, and the Guru's continuing community is what comes into being through *history*, the narration of the past and a series of relationships attested to and substantiated through textual and material forms of representation. This concern for the past of the Guru in historical terms has been a central imaginary through which the community has been constituted and Sikh subjectivity expressed, as we have seen in the texts examined from the eighteenth and early nineteenth centuries. It continues in the present, but not always in the same register. This imagination of the community came to be linked to territory in a new way in the twentieth century,

---

1. Smith, *To Take Place*, 25.

within a broader colonial episteme centered on property, but was tied to an earlier imagination of the Sikh historical landscape.

The marking of Sikh territory, based on the evidence of the past, was required within the category of "property" in relation to religious community under the Raj, which inscribed identity and history onto land in a new way, and in the designation of a community in relation to a religious institution. We saw in the precolonial record that land was generally granted to individuals who stood for lineages or communities, or sometimes for institutions/sites, but that grants in this context were treated as political documents that required negotiation and confirmation to remain authoritative. The transition to a more stable and less malleable (and therefore less nuanced) form of property in the colonial period, and the efforts made to define responsible parties for religious institutions in that context, initiated a new relationship between the historical landscape and communities, now defined through a new legislative and juridical framework. We see, therefore, a transition in this period, even as elements of the prior system were maintained. As Ian Barrow has argued, "territoriality does not just occur and territory itself is not just empty space. For land to be turned into territory it needs to be inhabited, appropriated, or recognized in some form."[2] If sovereignty moved from being a form of control over people to control over territory in seventeenth-century Europe, we can see a similar but incomplete process taking place in relation to the mapping of Sikh space vis-à-vis the community.[3] Whereas objects and sites participated in the articulation of a community in the textual formations of the eighteenth and nineteenth centuries, and the practices of reverence recorded there, it was the determination of the value and status of property, and the designation of communities wedded to place through the demarcation of identity, in the Raj that transformed the historically inflected landscape of the community into one of *territory*. Community and territory came to be coterminous. This has contributed to the fraught position of the historical within Sikh territorial discourse in the postcolonial period, and the political presence of history in the recent Sikh past.

The articulation of the community has thus occupied a central, but shifting, focus of the account of the past as history in Sikh contexts. This can be seen in the literary representations examined in the first section, which narrate the Sikh past in various modes in relation to the articulation of the Sikhs as a community and, in some cases, in relation to sovereignty. It can also be seen in the changing nature of the historical in relation to shifting colonial definitions of ownership and

---

2. Barrow, *Mapping History*, 13.

3. Barrow, *Mapping History*.

property, and the identities based on those definitions. The Sikh historical project overall does not position the Sikh community in singular sovereign statist terms, but rather makes the community sovereign in multiple and contingent ways, mapped to the land and to objects as sites of history in an array of ways. The territorialization of this history was produced in the particular administrative and legislative approaches to the management of religious sites within the colonial state. In considering the ways modern understandings of Sikh theology have shaped Sikh political discourse, Arvind Mandair has asked us to consider "[t]o what extent is the notion of an exclusive Sikh territory, and ultimately the partitioning among nations/peoples/religions, a logical consequence of a theoaesthetic principle based on the static immutable One in relation to which time is configured as space or area?"[4] If we add to this principle the process by which the Sikh community became a community for whom the past was foremost expressed in relation to land,[5] and through which the community itself would be constituted in relation to the representation of that past, we can understand in a new way the territorialization of the Sikh commmunity, and the Sikh past.

Central among my interests here has been the question of representation: how Sikh forms of visuality and materiality both connect with and are distinct from representations and, particularly, notions of embodiment, that are associated with other religious traditions. I also suggest a transformation in Sikh representational forms within the transition from the precolonial to the colonial, allowing a more complex genealogy of representation than that afforded by exclusive attention to either precolonial forms of representation or colonial forms.[6] This process must be emphasized, because just as it would be wrong to assume absolute rupture between the precolonial and colonial, it would be as grave an error to posit a simple line of continuity. Every site, every collection—in private and in public gurdwaras—has been constituted and reconstituted in particular ways under precolonial, colonial, and subsequent postcolonial regimes of property and history, in relation to different ways of forming the community, such as through gifting and the honoring of gifted objects, or an understanding of the larger Sikh/Khalsa community in relation to the consolidation of Sikh sovereign power in Punjab in the late eighteenth century. These transformations can enrich our understanding of history itself, as a genre and form of representation, and refocus attention on the ways in which history is authorized and mobilized—and

---

4. Mandair, *Religion and the Specter of the West*, 237.

5. Mandair, *Religion and the Specter of the West*, 190.

6. See Cohn, *Colonialism*, and discussion of the debate on the relative influence of colonialism in Murphy, "Guru's Weapons."

what it *authorizes*. In the same way that, as Dirks has argued, along lines described by Hayden White and others, the "movement from annals to chronicles to historical narratives is the progression from different forms of kingship to the naturalized reality of the nation-state,"[7] the progression of history within Sikh sources may also be constituted by alternative forms of sovereignty that in modernity have found contingent and problematic relationships with the nation-state—not subsumed within it, and yet not entirely separate. The past as history is articulated in the texts addressed here in relation to multiple notions of sovereignty and authority. The overall history of "history" within Sikh tradition can also be seen to reflect more generally the contingent relationship between the authorizing function of the state and the production of history. A fruitful way to think about such a reorientation is to move from the state to a more diffused understanding of *sovereignty*, and consider ways in which alternative formulations of political and social organization and power may have constituted diverse forms of history, within Sikh and other contexts. Thus, alongside statist articulations of sovereignty, exploration of texts and traditions that claim alternative non-state forms of sovereignty—such as the historical imaginary of Sainapati's text and the forms of representation described in Santokh Singh's *Sūraj Granth*—enables a way of complicating our understanding of the formations of the Sikh past. Deol has argued for a unique articulation of sovereignty in relation to the Khalsa within *rahitnāmā* literature, but sovereignty in this context must be seen in relation to broader changes in political and social relations brought on by the weakening of centralized Mughal rule in the eighteenth century. This phenomenon was not limited to Punjab. Indeed, forms of sovereignty were present within many different religious institutional formations in the foundational period of the Sikh tradition, as Shandip Saha has shown for the Vallabha community.[8] There were multiple engagements with the language of the sovereign at work, and not all were tied to state formation. Communities and different kinds of formal organizations, too, occupied alternative forms of sovereign status.

Our contemporary understanding of the discursive role of history within Sikh political discourse in the past fifty years has generally not taken into consideration the multivalent and long-standing meanings of history in Sikh tradition—and the ways they have changed.[9] One result of this has been the assumption that

---

7. Nicholas B. Dirks, "History as a Sign of the Modern," *Public Culture* 2, 2 (1990): 25; see also Hayden White, *Content of the Form: Narrative Discourse and Historical Representation* (Baltimore, MD: John Hopkins University Press, 1987).

8. Shandip Saha, "The Movement of *Bhakti* along a North-West Axis."

9. See Murphy, "History in the Sikh Past."

to combat separatist politics (or at least the violence associated with them, if not the related but separate goal of self-determination) one must deny claims to sovereignty and even to the existence of "history." Yet, it may be that an appreciation of the history of the imagination of history, alongside an appreciation of the multivalent notions of sovereignty in Sikh tradition, will open the door not to the *necessity* of a nation-state, but instead to a more fluid and textured understanding of sovereignty and the making of the community in the past and present. The use of history in the production of forms of sovereignty requires attention rather than vilification; it is related to the historical processes described here and to the formation of a modern Sikh public. In this, it is reminiscent of Michael Warner's sense of the formation of a public: through participation in it, the public achieves a form of sovereignty.[10] The articulation of sovereignty need not necessitate or translate into the nation-state. Regardless, as David Scott suggests, it is not in the past where this conflict must be fought and resolved, but instead in a present for which "history" is allowed multiplicity and alternative engagements with the modern.[11] Failure to pay attention to such dynamics only limits our understanding of the present itself. As was suggested in chapter 2, in many ways the representation of the Sikh past is as much about the present as are the practice and experience of the sacred scripture, producing a multivalent temporal aspect to experience of Sikh tradition.

I noted at the beginning of this work that I intended to call attention to the fact that "history" has a history in Sikh discursive contexts prior to the colonial intervention. Thus, the kind of civilizational divide proposed by some theorists of South Asian religions and culture is unwarranted. More important, I have argued that history has occupied a central location in the articulation of the Sikh community around the relationships between the Guru and devotees, which were substantiated through gifting traditions and memorial technologies established in relation to the Guru and the past presence of the Guru. While "history" has a history in South Asia and has served divergent purposes, in the Sikh case, the narration of the past provides a means for relating the teachings of the Guru, significant events of his life on earth, and the key relationships with devotees that constituted his authority over the community around him. Historical events (and locations) are a means for the articulation of the Guru's "light" (*prakāsh, sobhā*, as in the text *Gur Sobhā*), as are his teachings—and objects and places instantiate and provide evidence of the Guru's intervention in the world

---

10. Michael Warner, *Publics and Counterpublics* (Brooklyn, NY: Zone Books, 2002).

11. Scott, *Refashioning Futures*, chapter 4.

and his relationships with his devotees. Attention to this fact may allow us to approach an analysis that allows history to be associated with alternative notions of sovereignty, and to coexist with religion. It also allows us to consider how history takes material as well as textual forms, and enrich our understanding of how material religiosity interacts with textual forms of representation.

The texts and objects examined here prompt us to consider not only why it has mattered to tell the story of the Guru, and why in a "historical" mode—a mode that verified the actual presence of the Guru and the relationships built around him, in relation to the creation of the object of history, the community—but also the various forms the representations themselves take. The "material" aspects of Sikh history should not be simply equated with Hindu *murtī* practices, as is often assumed by some, but represent a Sikh set of memorial practices that are mobilized in the articulation of the history of the community in relation to the memory of the Guru. These practices are located within broader discourses of history and were shaped by the changing imagination of the past and the relationship of the community to the past that emerges through the tremendous changes occuring in the eighteenth and nineteenth centuries. Attention to materiality opens up new ways of thinking through Sikh intellectual and cultural production in text as well as other forms—the "deep shape" of belief described by scholar of Christianity and material religion David Morgan, which accounts for the full range of material and embodied practices—and should not be simply equated with other practices to which it may bear superficial resemblance.[12]

The Museum Imaginary

A particular territorialized imagination of the Sikh past was produced in the colonial period, drawing upon existing attachments to sites (alongside objects) that contributed to the living memory of the Gurus and their teachings for the Sikh community. This territorialized historical imagination was among the multiple effects of the particularities of the administration of land, generally, and religious sites, specifically, under British rule. Historical sites and objects formed a kind of single category in the precolonial period, where both constituted a technology of memory for the community formed around the Gurus. They were treated differently within the context of colonial rule, because of the centrality of land as property within the colonial regime of value and the use of the past in that context.

---

12. David Morgan, *Religion and Material Culture: The Matter of Belief* (London: Routledge, 2010), 5.

The increasingly territorialized landscape of the Sikh past created was thus a museumized space, produced for consumption of the land as the Sikh past. This should not surprise us, this connection between the museum and territory. The museum, according to Benedict Anderson's now well-known formulation, acted along with the census and the map to shape "the way in which the colonial state imagined its dominion—the nature of the human beings it ruled, the geography of its domain, and the legitimacy of its ancestry," serving the very political purpose of justifying British rule.[13] This was accomplished in different ways within the metropole and colony, whereby the imperial museum in the metropole constructed a comprehensive vision of the imperial object, and the colonial museum produced, as Guha-Thakurta among others has noted, a local, utilitarian vision of the colony that would focus on "local knowledge that was specific to the needs and context of the Indian empire."[14] The gurdwara guides examined demonstrate this tour-museum sensibility in a Sikh mode, with which the landscape of the past is articulated in the historical gurdwara. A museological mode has thus been created around the site and object, with reference to a preexisting culture of collecting and value, such that both objects and sites constitute a form of museological representation today, articulated in relation to a dynamic modern community-narrative. This can be seen in the case of the Dalla family collection, associated with the Takhat Sri Damdama Sahib in the southwest of Indian Punjab, discussed in chapter 2. There, signs direct the visitor from the historical gurdwara to the home of Bhai Dalla Singh, and a museological mode of engagement is created within a private family home. This explicit museological form of representation is modern—the Dalla family began to display the objects in this way in the 1960s at the initiative of one of the patriarchs of the family, drawing upon existing practices regarding the collection and display of, and reverence for, objects. As has been discussed, *itihāsik* gurdwaras, associated with the Ten Sikh Gurus and other heroes and martyrs, are managed by the SGPC—thus, they are also "collected" as a kind of museum representation. Managed by the SGPC and listed officially as "historical," they act as a geographical museum of the travels of and events associated with the Gurus. The gurdwara guides of the late nineteenth and early twentieth centuries narrate this geography. To it we can add the new Khalsa Heritage Complex, the

13. Benedict Anderson, *Imagined Communities: Reflections on the Origin and Spread of Nationalism* (London, New York: Verso, [1983] 1991), 164.

14. Tapati Guha-Thakurta, *Monuments, Objects, Histories: Institutions of Art in Colonial and Postcolonial India* (New Delhi: Permanent Black, 2004), 43. See also, as cited by Guha-Thakurta, Thomas Richards, *The Imperial Archive: Knowledge and the Fantasy of Empire* (London: Verso, 1993).

first part of which has opened in Punjab, in which the organizing theme is, as we would expect, history.

Arjun Appadurai and Carol Breckenridge have noted that museums in India look in two directions simultaneously: "they are a part of a transnational order of cultural forms that has emerged in the last two centuries and now unites much of the world, especially its urban areas . . . [and] belong to the alternative forms of modern life and thought that are emerging in nations and societies throughout the world."[15] If, as the two scholars and many others have argued, museums represent a fundamentally "modern" mode of being, then the museology I suggest here represents a "Sikh modernity" writ to diverse visions of community, territory, and the constitution of both national and transnational subjects.[16] I do not argue here for this as an "alternative modernity"; to do so would grant a normative status to a Western and European modernity. Instead, a Sikh modernity, as embodied in the museum, participates in modernity as wholly and fully as any other cultural location of modernity. It is, like all articulations of the modern, both local and cosmopolitan, sharing in both parallel "aspirations, material standards, and social institutions" and local forms as other forms of modernity.[17] And it is not unconnected to prior cultural forms. The status of the "*itihāsik*" is therefore a modern construct, but historical representation has a long history in the Sikh tradition. The collection of objects and reverence for sites associated with the actions and events of the Ten Gurus of the Sikh tradition is attested to in eighteenth- and early nineteenth-century literature, as we have seen, and relates to general royal

15. Arjun Appadurai and Carol A. Breckenridge, "Museums Are Good To Think: Heritage on View in India," in *Museums and Communities: The Politics of Public Culture*, ed. Ivan Karp, Christine Mullen Kreamer, and Steven D. Lavine (Washington, DC: Smithsonian Institution Press, 1992), 404.

16. Chakrabarty, *Provincializing Europe* and *Habitations of Modernity: Essays in the Wake of Subaltern Studies* (Chicago: University of Chicago Press, 2002); Gyan Prakash, *Another Reason: Science and the Imagination of Modern India* (Princeton, NJ: Princeton University Press, 1999); Arjun Appadurai and Carol Breckenridge, "Public Modernity in India," in *Consuming Modernity: Public Culture in a South Asian World*, ed. Carol Breckenridge (Minneapolis: University of Minnesota Press, 1995); Appadurai and Breckenridge, "Museums"; Arjun Appadurai, *Modernity at Large: Cultural Dimensions of Globalization* (Minneapolis: University of Minnesota Press, 1996); Timothy Mitchell, *Colonising Egypt* (1988; repr., Berkeley: University of California Press, 1991). See also Bruce M. Knauft, ed., *Critically Modern: Alternatives, Alterities, Anthropologies* (Bloomington: Indiana University Press, 2002).

17. Knauft, "Critically Modern: An Introduction" in Knauft, ed., *Critically Modern*, 2. Here modernity has multiple features: notions of progress and development (Knauft, *Critically Modern*, 18); a set of relations among homogenizing global economic and cultural forces and local circumstances; individualism; and a set of governmental and institutional structures and their audiences. It is also characterized by the particular orientation toward history described in earlier chapters, and a set of representational practices that shape Sikh museological engagement.

and religious gifting traditions (for instance, the practice of *khil'at*) and the use of objects as a means to make concrete authoritative relationships with Sikh Gurus. The material presented in prior chapters attests to both the existence of these historical objects and sites (or at least many of them) in the eighteenth and certainly early nineteenth centuries, before British rule in Punjab and the advent of modern museological forms of representation found both in the private home and within the historical gurdwara itself today. Family collections thus participate in their own form of narration—describing local power relations and the authority of the Guru in local contexts—drawing on precolonial royal and religious gifting and collecting traditions. These have been transformed into explicitly museological endeavors in the modern postcolonial state and the diaspora.

A specifically Sikh museum form includes the Gurdwara Museum, in which historical paintings narrate the Sikh past and models of gurdwaras (particularly in the diaspora communities) connect the landscape of the past in Punjab with the present elsewhere. The form is common in India, most famously found in the Central Sikh Museum in the Darbar Sahib complex in Amritsar. The first officially recognized Sikh Museum in England is located in Leicester and was founded in association with a gurdwara (see figure 8.1); this has been followed by the National Sikh Heritage Centre and Holocaust Museum, in association with Sri Guru Singh Sabha Gurdwara, Derby.[18] Exhibitions highlighting the Sikh past and its material culture have also become quite common in mainstream museum settings, having been recently held at the Wing Luke Asian Museum in Seattle, San Francisco's Asian Art Museum, the Smithsonian Institution in Washington DC, and other venues. Historical sites related to Sikh history outside of South Asia have also received attention, such as can be seen with the Sikh Heritage Museum founded in association with the centenary of the Gur Sikh Temple in Abbotsford, British Columbia (Canada), according to Douglas Todd of the Vancouver Sun the first official national heritage site in Canada without English or French heritage.[19] The ubiquitous

---

18. See "National Sikh Heritage Centre and Holocaust Museum," http://www.nationalsikh museum.com/ (accessed May 28, 2012). The content of these museums, however, is diverse, and should not necessarily be considered particularly religious, regardless of their formal association with a gurdwara.

19. On the Abbotsford centenary and the Gur Sikh Temple, see Douglas Todd "B.C. Sikhs have had a long, hard road for 100 years," *Vancouver Sun*, January 11, 2011 http://blogs. vancouversun.com/2011/01/11/b-c-sikhs-have-had-a-long-hard-road-for-100-years/ (accessed May 28, 2012). For more on relevant exhibitions, see Anne Murphy, "Museums and the Making of Sikh History," unpublished paper delivered in panel "Whose Museum? The Collection and Consumption of History, Nation and Community" for the Annual Meeting of the Association for Asian Studies, San Diego, CA, March 2004; Anne Murphy, "The Politics of Possibility and the Commemoration of Trauma," unpublished paper delivered at "After 1984?" conference, Berkeley, CA, September 12–13, 2009.

FIGURE 8.1 The Leicester Sikh Museum. Photograph by Anne Murphy. July 2002.

idiom of the "museum," therefore, should not be taken as homogeneous, but instead is produced locally and, here, *religiously*—albeit in relation to transnational and state-centered interests and competing notions of nation and community. Through these exhibitions at public museums and religious sites, Sikh pasts are represented and made public to both Sikh and non-Sikh, in relation to transnational constructions of diasporic pasts, the religious community, the nation (defined in multiple ways), and various forms of negotiation with state interests (Indian and otherwise). Whereas the political control of Punjab has been contested over time, and the marking of the Punjab landscape *as Sikh* can be seen in direct relation to this contest over control, the marking of object and site as historical is not limited to it. Histories and historicalities as I have explored them here are multiple and reflect diverse genealogies and power relations.

Thus if, as Nicholas Dirks has convincingly shown, "colonial conquest was about the production of an archive of (and for) rule,"[20] the mind to collect and categorize (and occasionally to display) has its own form (and displays its own sets of power relations) outside of Western contexts as well. These different modes interact dynamically in the culture of the Sikh object. John Cort has described this for Jain libraries, and it is exemplified in the Sikh case by Ranjit Singh's famous *toshākhānā*, or treasure house.[21] The genealogy of a Sikh museological imagination is a complex one, therefore, drawing on "indigenous" collecting practices and representations of the past, and adopting and appropriating representational forms associated with the Western museum as needed. Thus we can, with Vasudha Dalmia, appreciate how "tradition" was created in the colonial encounter, in a way that does not undermine the idea of connectedness with the past.[22] I would thus only qualify Appadurai and Breckenridge's statement to the effect that museums look in three, not two directions. The "third" is the existing traditions of collecting and concomitant value, tied as well to legitimation and authority—the "protohistory of cognate indigenous expressions [of modernity] that goes back much further," alluded to but not defined by Appadurai and Breckenridge.[23] Museums, indeed, coexist with other forms of cultural consumption in India and elsewhere, as Appadurai and Breckenridge argue, but

---

20. Dirks, *Castes of Mind*, 107.

21. John Cort, "The Jain Knowledge Warehouses: Traditional Libraries in India," *Journal of the American Oriental Society* 115 (1995): 77–87.

22. Vasudha Dalmia, *Nationalization of Hindu Traditions*, introduction.

23. Appadurai and Breckenridge, "Public Modernity," 14.

do so in complex relation to the modernity defined by the Western museum. There are thus various instances of Sikh museological interest—some existing prior to the colonial intrusion, some clearly born of it, and some born of a uniquely transnational experience and the construction of "community" in relation to that experience.

The objects described in this book have a vibrant transnational religious life that exists alongside other museological efforts to represent the Sikh past, particularly around material culture and historical objects. The Ganga Sagar provides a compelling example of an object that links the Punjab to a larger world through the narrativization of the Sikh past and participation in a global religious imaginary. The object is an urn, which is said to be miraculous: sand is said to fall through the holes in the pitcher, yet it retains water. The object is held by a family based in England and Pakistan, but has traveled widely abroad—including to Fresno, California, in the mid-1990s—and back to Punjab.[24] It was brought back to Punjab in 2004 for the centenary of the death of two of the sons of Guru Hargobind, by Rai Azizullah Khan who is the direct descendant of Nawab of Raikot Kalah III, to whom Guru Gobind Singh had gifted the object, and who was then a member of Pakistan's National Assembly.[25] This is a particularly productive cultural form in the Sikh diaspora: Surrey, British Columbia, as well, has witnessed several major "exhibitions" of religious, historical objects, distinct from the kinds of courtly objects displayed at the Asian Art Museum of San Francisco for example. These exhibitions take place within an explicitly religious setting—the gurdwara—with objects with historical importance directly tied to the Gurus, acting, as was discussed in chapter 2, as "relics." Here, the diaspora does not go to the museumized space of Punjab, or home; the historical comes from home, abroad, in relic form. Objects and,

24. Charles McCarthy, "Sikhs Gather for a Miracle: Sacred Relic Attracts Thousands," *The Fresno Bee*, February 12, 1996, A1. See also: Viji Sundaram, "Thousands Flock to Fresno to View Guru's Miracle Pitcher," *India-West*, March 1, 1996.

25. Neeraj Bagga, "Devotees Throng Gurdwara to Catch a Glimpse of Ganga Sagar," *The Tribune*, December 23, 2004, http://www.tribuneindia.com/2004/20041223/aplus.htm#3 (accessed April 23, 2005); Surinder Bhardwaj "30 Lakh Visit Shahidi Jor Mela Maryada in, Gambling Stalls Out," *The Tribune*, Sunday January 2, 2005, http://www.tribuneindia.com/2005/20050102/punjab1.htm (accessed April 23, 2005); "Ganga Sagar Brought from Britain," *The Tribune*, December 18, 2004 http://www.tribuneindia.com/2004/20041218/main4.htm (accessed April 23, 2005); Jupinderjit Singh, "Raikot Residents Wait for 'Ganga Sagar,'" *The Tribune*, Monday, December 20, 2004 http://www.tribuneindia.com/2004/20041220/punjab1.htm (accessed April 23, 2005).

more generally, museums, therefore participate in the articulation of social and power relations on national and international registers today, contributing to a complex transnational relationship with three nodal points: the Sikh community in global terms, the Sikh past as a living presence, and the location of much of Sikh history, Punjab, as well as sites related to Sikh history outside this region. Connections between Punjab and its diaspora communities are maintained in a variety of ways—through travel in our increasingly mobile world, the production of "Sikh Studies" as a discipline in the West,[26] political and social organizations, and, primarily in religious contexts, a vibrant exchange of *sant*s (religious leaders or holy men), *granthī*s (textual specialists), *kathā vācak*s (specialist interpreters of the sacred text), and *rāgī* or *rāgī jathā* (musicians who perform *bāṇī*, or the Word of the Guru).[27] *Sevā*—important in the history of objects and other related representations—also constitutes a major mode of engagement between "home" and "diaspora" among Sikhs, in general, as well.[28] Transnational interests intervene in the production and management of Sikh gurdwaras in Punjab along such lines, as with the efforts of the Guru Nanak Nishkam Sevak Jatha, based in Birmingham, to assist in the preservation of major historical gurdwaras in India: the refurbishment of the gold exterior of the Darbar Sahib, Amritsar (1995–99); the renovation and expansion of Takhat Keshgarh Sahib, Anandpur (1997–99); and the internal restoration of Takhat Sri Hazoor Sahib, Nanded, Maharashtra (2000–2). The marking of Punjab as a Sikh space and the articulation of the past through the historical object both contribute to a transnational and diasporic narrativization of Sikhness, so activities in the diaspora are directly linked to those in Punjab. The Punjab Heritage News/UK Punjab Heritage Association—led by Amandeep Madra and others in the United Kingdom—provides another example of the active role of members of the Sikh Diaspora in maintaining Sikh heritage and historical sites around the world. This group, as well as others, such as conservationist Gurmeet Kaur Rai, position themselves at times to slow the drive to remember— through the commemoration of the Sikh past with large-scale buildings that replace small, modest, but historical buildings—to allow for a drive for history:

---

26. See Axel, *Nation's Tortured Body*.

27. Darshan Singh Tatla, "Nurturing the Faithful: The Role of the Sant among Britain's Sikhs" *Religion* 22 (1992): 349–74.

28. See Murphy, "Mobilizing *Seva*." Members of the Sikh diaspora were, for example, active in the 2004 desilting of the Golden Temple pool. See: "All Set for Kar Seva at Golden Temple." *Times of India*, April 7, 2004. http://timesofindia.indiatimes.com/articleshow/578806.cms (April 8, 2004).

the preservation of historical buildings rather than their destruction in pursuit of something more "memorable."[29]

Museological representation, on some level, takes place *alongside* territorialization of the Sikh past, as does the life of the relic object. Multiple notions of the community and its sovereignty are articulated here as well, in transnational contexts. We can see in these examples the continuation of multiple "historicalities" or historical imaginaries that escape the categories imposed by a colonial form of knowledge. A complex process of translation has taken—and is taking—place, albeit deeply constituted by colonial and postcolonial power relations. The history of museums may thus be "inseparable from their functioning as signs of Western power," as Gyan Prakash argues. Sikh museological engagement however also reflects a hybrid practice that makes for an "unraveling of the narrative which posits that Western knowledge, fully formed at the center, was tropicalized as it was diffused at the periphery."[30] Sikh museologies (and they are plural, as suggested by the diversity expressed in the Smithsonian Institution exhibition, the Leicester Sikh Museum, and in Abbotsford, BC) defy that narrative and allow us to consider the disjunctures of the colonial intervention alongside the unfinished transformations that coexisted with it.[31]

Timothy Mitchell has argued that a fundamental feature of the European colonial modern has been the construction of things as "objects" in relation to the corresponding construction of the individual and modern "subject."[32] Mitchell's exploration of particular modes of observation and exhibition based on the ordering of power associated with modern European colonialism is useful for understanding the multiplicity of materialities, and interactions with them, that exist in the Sikh representational world, colonial and postcolonial. The multiplicity we see today is made possible only by the relative peripheralization of the object as history within the colonial episteme, as compared with the central role of the sacred site as the territory of sovereignty

29. See: "Architectural Heritage in Jeopardy," http://www.sikhchic.com/architecture/architectural_heritage_in_jeopardy (accessed May 28, 2012); Nonika Singh "Restoring Ranjit Singh's Architectural Legacy" http://www.sikhchic.com/architecture/restoring_ranjit_singhs_architectural_legacy (accessed May 28, 2012) and in general, news.ukpha.org (accessed May 28, 2012).

30. Prakash, *Another Reason*, 46.

31. This material gestures, therefore, toward the "interdependent" modernities that constitute first and third world modernities (see Appadurai and Breckenridge, "Public Modernity"), and the inconsistencies and contradictions inherent to the colonial project (see Dirks, *Castes of Mind*).

32. Mitchell, *Colonising Egypt*.

and possession in this world-as-exhibition and world-as-possession. Objects provide a wider field of meanings, not as clearly tied to territory, and thus provide an opportunity for the articulation of multiple notions of the sovereign community, alluding to the fundamentally de-territorialized imagination of the Sikh community highlighted by Giorgio Shani, who has argued that it "may also be possible to speak of a 'new' counter-hegemonic *diasporic* Sikh identity: an identity made possible by the nationalist project but opposed to its territorializing, reifying imperatives," a project which "implies a *rejection* of the assimilationist project of the nation-state" in keeping with "the contemporary phase of globalization [which] has effectively deterritorialized *sovereignty*."[33]

The possession and representation of the past is thus still tied to the articulation of a sovereign space for the Sikh community, but it is one that need not be mapped as directly to territory in Punjab, but rather to an evolving and de-territorialized notion of the past and the community's relationship to that past. Objects might singularly address the new diasporic mode Shani describes, which has "gone beyond Khalistan in considering the establishment of an independent, sovereign Sikh state unnecessary for the continued survival of a distinct Sikh identity in a globalizing world."[34] This is the ground for its creativity. However, if Mitchell is correct, and the articulation of the world-as-exhibition—the world construed as a perpetual representation for the observing sovereign modern subject, predicated upon an ontological distinction between the "simulated" and "the real," between the exhibition and the world, the "real" and its plan or order— is a fundamentally colonial order, then the Sikh observing subject as a precolonial phenomenon must not be simply equated with that of the colonial and postcolonial subject. But within Mitchell's exploration of the rupture that constitutes the colonial construction of the observing subject is also the possibility of modes of action that mobilize such forms of representation: as Mitchell himself notes, "colonial subjects and their modes of resistance are formed *within* the organizational terrain of the colonial state, rather than some wholly exterior social space."[35] The precolonial valuation of the observed and substantiated past thus works in relation to the colonial apparatus and through it, producing the Sikh simultaneously observing and observed subject. The continuity with the

---

33. Shani, *Sikh Nationalism*, 150 (first two quotations); 156 (last quotation).

34. Shani, *Sikh Nationalism*, 16.

35. Mitchell, *Colonizing Egypt*, xi.

past is one that is contingent and constructed within colonial and postcolonial frame(s) of meaning. Local community, nation, and transnational community are constructed within multiple museologies, with antecedents colonial and precolonial.

We have already arrived at that moment. In today's museum imaginary, Sikhs act as collectors, museum patrons, and museum creators and proprietors, actors creating what Saloni Mathur has called the "new nexus of entanglements between history, religion and heritage," producing what she has described, with reference the Khalsa Heritage Centre in Punjab, as the kind of "myriad emergent formations and cultural representations that we are likely to encounter in the future."[36] The object within the frame of the museum and collection remains a major focus for the articulation of Sikh community control and authority, as possession and control over the interpretation of the past is sought. Certainly, colonial frames of knowledge still abide, and there is contestation over the vision that should guide Sikh museology. But such contestation can be seen be seen as a sign of vitality, rather than fracture alone. Thus, we see a process whereby historical objects and sites become the means through which various modes of engagement with the modern—as Sikh, postcolonial, nationalist, and transnational—have been, and are, articulated, as well as influenced by issues of ownership and control, and audience. This parallels the way objects and sites reflect multiple engagements with the colonial. As Benedict Anderson has noted, "museums, and the museumizing imagination, are both profoundly political."[37] This is so with Sikh museological endeavors, alongside others. The Punjab landscape as Sikh is obviously more closely tied to questions of sovereignty than historical objects are. Objects participate in a less territorially driven, transnational concern for history and the representation of "Sikhness" in relation to that history. But this does not make Punjab irrelevant, in global terms. This "life of the object" as historical representation does not constitute the whole of transnational and postcolonial historical representation; other forms of material and visual historical representation include the historical painting, photograph, text, and gurdwara model—all contained within museological contexts of differing types, and many of which pay careful attention to a more territorial vision of the past.

36. Saloni Mathur, *India by Design: Colonial History and Cultural Display* (Berkeley: University of California, 2007).

37. Benedict Anderson, *Imagined Communities* (1983; repr. London: Verso, 1991), 178. Tony Bennett, *The Birth of the Museum: History, Theory, Politics* (London: Routledge, 1995).

Postcolonial Afterlife of the Object

The postcolonial life of the territorialized understanding of the Sikh past has been given careful scholarly attention; this is not so for the object and its multivalent expression of the past: tied to historical sites in some senses, and yet operating in a different mode. Today, the object embodies multiple forms of knowledge and meaning, partially a result of its disengagement from central arenas of power within colonial administration, as detailed earlier, and in connection with a range of expressions of postcolonial politics.[38] A particularly modern and hybrid form of representation is constituted in the Sikh formation of the museum space—both in the territory of Punjab and in the more conventional institutional sense—and particularly in relation to the *itihāsik* object. The past sought and expressed today reflects the diverse interests of a transnational community and the differing status of objects and sites in the postcolonial context. Issues of control and legitimacy shape the collection and presentation of the object and site with reference to national (of various types) and transnational cultural and power relations.[39] In this way, a multiplicity of historical representations has continued into the postcolonial period, drawing on both precolonial and colonial antecedents but with particular postcolonial valences that both derive from and exceed these prior dynamics. This sketch is incomplete, because it would exceed the parameters of this book to fully define the contours of the range of expressions today. My hope has been to suggest some trajectories such representations have taken, and how they connect to the history articulated here.

We have seen how a set of practices with precolonial references has been reconstituted through the colonial into a postcolonial transnational representational practice to define alternative notions of cultural and religious sovereignty that bear the mark of, but also work through and beyond, colonial interventions. This can bring us back to the past as well. As I have suggested in earlier chapters, we must take the notion of the sovereign articulated in multiple ways in historical Sikh sources seriously, without scripting it directly onto the forms of sovereignty and representation associated with the modern nation-state. At the same time, the postcolonial life of objects and sites provides a metaphor for the formation of modern transnational subjectivities, within a broad transnational system of exchange and memory-making that stands at the center of the production of selfhood for many, both Sikh and non-Sikh, in our transnationally linked as well as dispersed world. They are related to the memory-in-representation found in the museum, but exceed it in the *experience* of the past that

---

38. In some ways, then, the object is parallel to the vibrant life of Punjabi literature in the colonial period *outside of* the direct control and interest of the colonial state. See Mir, *Social Space of Language.*

39. Murphy, "Guru's Weapons."

the object promises, in the present. I opened this chapter with a quote from J. Z. Smith. I end here with his observations regarding the radical change in Christian interest in the earthly life of Jesus, in modernity, which can help us to understand Sikh representation in the past and present, wherein the world-as-exhibition (in Timothy Mitchell's terms) can be seen as community-as-exhibition, the community being represented as the subject of history. Smith notes that interest in the earthly life of Jesus began in the fourth century, and brought with it an emphasis on narrative and temporal relations, transforming Christianity. The transformation of Jerusalem into a set of sacred sites with an all-encompassing, centralized, and coherent liturgy represented "worship as pilgrimage. It reflects the movement of a secure Christianity from an essentially private mode of worship to an overwhelmingly public and civic one of parade and procession."[40] This could be maintained even away from Jerusalem, through the close relationship of liturgical calendar and scripture. More than one millennium later, some Christians rejected this imagination, transferring attention to place to an "inner space" such that "all that remains of Jerusalem is an image, the narrative, and a temporal sequence."[41]

Perhaps the use of the museum as a central representational form reflects a parallel move in Sikh thought and practice, adopting the museum-as-exhibition in a transnationalized and dispersed mode, where relationships that determine the community are externalized and made mobile, on display in public. The community of memory of the Guru is sovereign, in yet another mode, and experience of the community through object and museum representation here provides access for the community to the interstitial space between memory and history. The form of this modernity must be accounted for alongside, not after, Eurocentric models, with reference to complex notions of value and authority in relation to collecting and display, within both Western and South Asian contexts. As has been argued for the idea of history, the only "universal" possible in the idea of the modern is achieved in its fracture.[42] In this, we see the possibility of a postcolonial form of representation not determined by the colonial, but born of the practices that preexisted and continued outside the regulated space of the colonial, as well as those formed within it.[43] The museological imagination at work here offers a map of an alternative Sikh sovereignty, the contours of which—like objects, unbounded by territory, and traveling in time—are unfixed.

---

40. Smith, *To Take Place*, 92. This was discussed briefly in chapter 3.

41. Smith, *To Take Place*, 117.

42. See Knauft, *Critically Modern*, 18ff.

43. Such a space is suggested by Farina Mir's exploration of the Punjabi literary formation under colonial rule in Mir, *Social Space of Language*.

Bibliography

Act No. XX of 1863. Bills, Objects, and Reasons. IOR L/P&J/5/3. India Office Records, British Library, United Kingdom.

Act No. XX of 1863, India Acts. IOR v/8/39. India Office Records, British Library, United Kingdom.

Agrawal, Arun and K. Sivaramakrishnan, eds. *Agrarian Environments: Resources, Representations, and Rule in India*. Durham, NC: Duke University Press, 2000.

Akbar, Arifa. "Sikh Protests Stop Sotheby's Auction of 'Religious Relic.'" http://www.independent.co.uk/news/uk/this-britain/sikh-protests-stop-sothebys-auction-of-religious-relic-806323.html. Accessed June 16, 2008.

Alam, Muzaffar. *The Crisis of Empire in Mughal North India: Awadh and the Punjab, 1707–1748*. New Delhi: Oxford University Press, 1986.

———. "The Culture and Politics of Persian in Precolonial Hindustan." In *Literary Cultures in History: Reconstructions from South Asia*, ed. Sheldon Pollock. New Delhi: Oxford University Press, 2003.

Ali, Daud, ed. *Invoking the Past: The Uses of History in South Asia*. New Delhi: Oxford University Press, 1999.

Ali, Imran. *Punjab under Imperialism, 1885–1947*. Princeton, NJ: Princeton University Press, 1988.

"All Set for Kar Seva at Golden Temple." *Times of India*, April 7, 2004. http://timesofindia.indiatimes.com/articleshow/578806.cms. Accessed April 8, 2004.

Allen-Agostini, Lisa. "In the Sikh Spirit at the Smithsonian." *Washington Post*, Monday, August 13, 2001, C08.

Alpers, Svetlana. "The Museum as a Way of Seeing." In *Exhibiting Cultures: The Poetics and Politics of Museum Display*, edited by Ivan Karp and Steven D. Lavine, 25–32. Washington, DC: Smithsonian Institution Press, 1991.

Anderson, Benedict. *Imagined Communities: Reflections on the Origin and Spread of Nationalism*. London, New York: Verso, [1983] 1991.

Appadurai, Arjun. *Worship and Conflict under Colonial Rule*. Cambridge: Cambridge University Press, 1981.

———. "Introduction: Commodities and the Politics of Value." In *The Social Life of Things: Commodities in Cultural Perspective*, 3–63. Cambridge: Cambridge University Press, 1986.

———. "Sovereignty Without Territoriality: Notes for a Postnational Geography." In *The Geography of Identity*, edited by Patricia Yeager, 40–58. Ann Arbor: University of Michigan, 1996.

———. *Modernity at Large: Cultural Dimensions of Globalization*. Minneapolis: University of Minnesota Press, 1996.

Appadurai, Arjun, ed. *The Social Life of Things: Commodities in Cultural Perspective*. Cambridge: Cambridge University Press, 1986.

Appadurai, Arjun and Carol A. Breckenridge. "Museums Are Good To Think: Heritage on View in India." In *Museums and Communities: The Politics of Public Culture*, edited by Ivan Karp, Christine Mullen Kreamer, and Steven D. Lavine, 34–55. Washington, DC: Smithsonian Institution Press, 1992.

———. "Public Modernity in India." In *Consuming Modernity: Public Culture in a South Asian World*, edited by Carol Breckenridge, 1–20. Minneapolis: University of Minnesota Press, 1995.

Archer Papers, IOL Mss. Eur F236. India Office Library, British Library, United Kingdom.

"Architectural Heritage in Jeopardy" http://www.sikhchic.com/architecture/architectural_heritage_in_jeopardy. Accessed May 28, 2012.

Asad, Talal. "Reading a Modern Classic: W. C. Smith's *The Meaning and End of Religion*." *History of Religions* 40, 3 (2001): 204–22.

———. *Genealogies of Religion: Discipline and Reasons of Power in Christianity and Islam*. Baltimore, MD: Johns Hopkins University Press, 1993.

———. *Formations of the Secular: Christianity, Islam, Modernity*. Stanford, CA: Stanford University Press, 2003.

'Ashok', Shamsher Singh. *Guru Khalse de Rahitname*. Amritsar: Sikh History Research Board, 1979.

Assmann, Jan and Albert J. Baumgarten. *Representation in Religion: Studies in Honor of Moshe Barasch*. Leiden: Brill, 2001.

Axel, Brian Keith. *The Nation's Tortured Body: Violence, Representation, and the Formation of a Sikh "Diaspora."* Durham, NC: Duke University Press, 2001.

———. "Diasporic Sublime: Sikh Martyrs, Internet Mediations, and the Question of the Unimaginable." *Sikh Formations: Religion, Culture, Theory* 1, 1 (2005): 127–54.

Bagga, Neeraj. "Devotees throng gurdwara to catch a glimpse of Ganga Sagar" *The Tribune*, December 23, 2004. http://www.tribuneindia.com/2004/20041223/aplus.htm#3. Accessed April 23, 2005.

Baker, J. Mark. "Colonial Influences on Property, Community, and Land Use in Kangra, Himachal Pradesh." In *Agrarian Environments: Resources, Representations, and Rule in India*, edited by Arun Agrawal and K. Sivaramakrishnan, 47–67. Durham, NC: Duke University Press, 2000.

Bal, Gurpreet. "Construction of Gender and Religious Identities in the First Punjabi Novel *Sundari*." *Economic and Political Weekly* (August 12, 2006): 3528–34.

Ballantyne, Tony. *Between Colonialism and Diaspora: Sikh Cultural Formations in an Imperial World*. Durham, NC: Duke University Press, 2006.

Banga, Indu. *Agrarian System of the Sikhs: Late Eighteenth and Early Nineteenth Century*. New Delhi: Manohar, 1978.

Banga, Indu. "Running the State (The Maharaja's Own Orders)." In *Maharaja Ranjit Singh: The State and Society*, ed. Indu Banga and J.S. Grewal, 102–30. Amritsar: Guru Nanak Dev University, 2001.

Banga, Indu and J. S. Grewal. *Civil and Military Affairs of Maharaja Ranjit Singh: A Study of 450 Orders in Persian*. Amritsar: Guru Nanak Dev University, 1987.

Banga, Indu and J. S. Grewal, eds. *Maharaja Ranjit Singh: The State and Society*. Amritsar: Guru Nanak Dev University, 2001.

Barrier, N. G. *The Punjab Alienation of Land Bill of 1900*. Durham, NC: Duke University Program in Comparative Studies on Southern Asia, 1966.

———. *Punjab in Nineteenth-Century Tracts: An Introduction to the Pamphlet Collections in the British Museum and India Office*. East Lansing: Research Committee on the Punjab and Asian Studies Center, Michigan State University, 1969.

———. *Sikhs and Their Literature: A Guide to Tracts, Books, and Periodicals, 1849–1919*. New Delhi: Manohar Book Service, 1970.

———. *Banned: Controversial Literature and Political Control in British India: 1907–1947*. Columbia: University of Missouri Press, 1974.

———. "Vernacular Publishing and Sikh Public Life in the Punjab, 1880–1910." In *Religious Controversy in British India: Dialogues in South Asian Languages*, edited by Kenneth W. Jones. Albany: State University of New York Press, 1992.

Barrier, N. G. and Verne Dusenbery, eds. *Sikh Diaspora: Migration and Experience Beyond Punjab*. New Delhi: Chanakya, 1989.

Barrier, N. G. and Paul Wallace. *The Punjab Press: 1880–1905*. East Lansing, MI: Research Committee on the Punjab and Asian Studies Center, Michigan State University, 1970.

Barrow, Ian J. *Mapping History, Drawing Territory: British Mapping in India, c. 1756–1905*. New Delhi: Oxford University Press, 2003.

Bayly, C. A. "The Origins of Swadeshi (Home Industry): Cloth and Indian Society, 1700–1930." In *The Social Life of Things: Commodities in Cultural Perspective*, edited by Arjun Appadurai, 285–321. Cambridge: Cambridge University Press, 1986.

———. *Origins of Nationality in South Asia: Patriotism and Ethical Government in the Making of Modern India*. New Delhi: Oxford University Press, 1998.

Bennett, Tony. *The Birth of the Museum: History, Theory, Politics*. London: Routledge, 1995.

———. "The Exhibitionary Complex." In *Representing the Nation: A Reader. Histories, Heritage and Museums*, edited by David Boswell and Jessica Evans, 332–61. New York: Routledge, 1999.

Bhāī Bāle vālī Janam-sākhī. (Punjabi). Amritsar: Bhai Jawahar Singh Kripal Singh and Company, n.d.

Bhamra, Anupreet Sandhu. "Vaisakhi Parade to Feature Float with Holy Articles." *Vancouver Sun*, Saturday, April 14, 2007, B7.

Bhangu, Rattan Singh. *Prācīn Panth Parkāsh*. Edited by Vir Singh, 1841. Reprint, New Delhi: Bhai Vir Singh Sahit Sadan, 1993.

Bhardwaj, Surinder. "30 Lakh Visit Shahidi Jor Mela Maryada in, Gambling Stalls Out." *The Tribune*, Sunday January 2, 2005. http://www.tribuneindia.com/2005/20050102/punjab1.htm. Accessed April 23, 2005.

Birla, Ritu. *Stages of Capital: Law, Culture, and Market Governance in Late Colonial India*. Durham: Duke University Press, 2009.

Boswell, David and Jessica Evans, eds. *Representing the Nation: A Reader. Histories, Heritage and Museums*. New York: Routledge, 1999.

Breckenridge, Carol. "The Aesthetics and Politics of Colonial Collecting: India at World Fairs." *Comparative Studies in History and Society* 31 (1989): 195–216.

———, ed. *Consuming Modernity: Public Culture in a South Asian World*. Minneapolis: University of Minnesota Press, 1995.

Brown, Bill. "Thing Theory." *Critical Theory* 28 (Autumn 2001): 1–22.

———. 2006. "Reification, Reanimation, and the American Uncanny." *Critical Inquiry* 32 (Winter): 175–207.

Brown, Kerry, ed. *Sikh Art and Literature*. London: Routledge, 1999.

Brown, Robert. "Expected Miracles: The Unsurprisingly Miraculous Nature of Buddhist Images." In *Images, Miracles, and Authority in Asian Religious Traditions*, edited by Richard Davis, 23–35. Boulder, CO: Westview Press, 1998.

———. "The Miraculous Buddha Image: Portrait, God, or Object?" In *Images, Miracles, and Authority in Asian Religious Traditions*, edited by Richard Davis, 37–54. Boulder, CO: Westview Press, 1998.

Busch, Allison. "The Anxiety of Innovation: The Practice of Literary Science in the Hindi/*Riti* Tradition." *Comparative Studies of South Asia, Africa, and the Middle East* 24, 2 (2004): 45–59.

———. "Literary Responses to the Mughal Imperium: The Historical Poems of Kesavdās." *South Asia Research* 25, 1 (2005): 31–54.

———. "Hidden in Plain View: Brajbhasha Poets at the Mughal Court." *Modern Asian Studies* 44, 2 (2010): 267–309.

———. *Poetry of Kings: The Classical Hindi Literature of Mughal India*. New York: Oxford University Press, 2011.

Callewaert, Winand M. and Peter G. Friedlander. *The Life and Works of Raidas*. New Delhi: Manohar, 1992.

Callewaert, Winand M. and Rupert Snell, eds. *According to Tradition: Hagiographical Writing in India*. Wiesbaden: Harrassowitz Verlag, 1994.

Cannadine, David. *Ornamentalism: How the British Saw Their Empire*. London: Allen Lane, 2001.

Carr, Annemarie Weyl. "Threads of Authority: The Virgin Mary's Veil in the Middle Ages." In *Robes and Honor: The Medieval World of Investiture*, edited by Stewart Gordon, 59–93. New York: Palgrave, 2001.

Castelli, Elizabeth. *Martyrdom and Memory: Early Christian Culture-Making.* New York: Columbia University Press, 2004.

Caton, Brian. "Settling for the State: Pastoralists and Colonial Rule in Southwestern Panjab, 1840–1900." PhD dissertation, University of Pennsylvania, 2003.

Chakrabarty, Dipesh. *Provincializing Europe: Postcolonial Thought and Historical Difference.* Princeton, NJ: Princeton University Press, 2000.

———. *Habitations of Modernity: Essays in the Wake of Subaltern Studies.* Chicago: University of Chicago Press, 2002.

———. "The Past As Practices: Visualizing, Preserving, and Destroying History." Public talk at The New School for Social Research, December 9, 2004.

Charitable and Religious Trusts Act, 1920. Act. No. XIV of 1920, IOR v/8/70. India Office Records, British Library, United Kingdom.

Chatterjee, Partha. *The Nation and Its Fragments: Colonial and Postcolonial Histories.* Princeton, NJ: Princeton University Press, 1993.

———. "Religious Minorities and the Secular State: Reflections on an Indian Impasse." *Public Culture* 8, 1 (1995): 11–39.

———. "Introduction: History and the Present." In *History and the Present*, edited by Partha Chatterjee and Anjan Ghosh, 1–23. New Delhi: Permanent Black, 2002.

———. "A Singular Modernity?" Conference at Columbia University, March 2006.

Cheviṅ Dharam Pothī. Amritsar: Wazir Hind Press and the Khalsa Pracarak Vidyalaya (Chief Khalsa Diwan), 1922?. IOL 14162.n.7.

Chibber, Kesar Singh. *Baṅsāvalīnāmā Dasāṅ Pātshāhīāṅ kā.* Edited by Piara Singh Padam. Amritsar: Singh Brothers, 1997.

Cizakca, Murat. *A History of Philanthropic Foundations: The Islamic World from the Seventh Century to the Present.* Istanbul: Boğazİcİ University Press, 2000.

"Clarify Stand on Ganga Sagar, SGPC Told." *The Tribune*, December 19, 2004. http://www.tribuneindia.com/2004/20041219/punjab1.htm. Accessed April 23, 2005.

Cohn, Bernard. *Colonialism and Its Forms of Knowledge: The British in India.* Princeton, NJ: Princeton University Press, 1996.

Colas, Gerard. "The Competing Hermeneutics of Image Worship in Hinduism (Fifth to Eleventh Century AD)." In *Images in Asian Religions: Texts and Contexts*, edited by Phyllis Granoff and Koichi Shinohara. Vancouver: UBC Press, 2004.

Connerton, Paul. *How Societies Remember.* Cambridge: Cambridge University Press, 1989.

Conran, W. L. and H. D. Craik. *Chiefs and Families of Note in the Punjab: A Revised edition of "The Punjab Chiefs" by Sir Lepel Griffin and of "Chiefs and Families of Note in the Punjab" by Colonel Charles F. Massy.* Vol. 1. Lahore: Civil and Military Gazette Press, 1909.

Cort, John. "The Jain Knowledge Warehouses: Traditional Libraries in India." *Journal of the American Oriental Society* 115 (1995): 77–87.

Cotter, Holland. "Wonders of Sikh Spirituality Come Alive." *New York Times*, September 18, 2006. http://www.nytimes.com/2006/09/18/arts/design/18sikh.html?ex=1316232000&en=2acdf712f34e9724&ei=5088&partner=rssnyt&emc=rss. Accessed April 5, 2007.

Cunningham, Joseph D. *A History of the Sikhs, From the Origin of the Nation to the Battles of the Sutlej*. London: J. Murray, 1849.

Cust, Robert. *Manual for the Guidance of Revenue Officers in the Punjab*. Lahore: Koh-i-Noor Press, 1866.

Dalmia, Vasudha. *The Nationalization of Hindu Traditions: Bharatendu Harischandra and Nineteenth-Century Banaras*. New Delhi: Oxford University Press, 1999.

———— and H. von Stietencron, eds. *Representing Hinduism: The Construction of Religious Traditions and National Identity*. Thousand Oaks, CA: Sage Publications, 1995.

Dalmia, Vasudha, Angelika Malinar, and Martin Christof, eds. *Charisma and Canon: Essays on the Religious History of the Indian Subcontinent*. New Delhi: Oxford University Press, 2001.

Das, Veena. *Critical Events: An Anthropological Perspective on Contemporary India*. New Delhi: Oxford University Press, 1995.

Davis, Richard. *Lives of Indian Images*. Princeton, NJ: Princeton University Press, 1997.

————. "Indian Image-Worship and Its Discontents." In *Representation in Religion: Studies in Honor of Moshe Barasch*, edited by Jan Assmann and Albert J. Baumgarten, 107–32. Leiden: Brill, 2001.

————, ed. *Images, Miracles, and Authority in Asian Religious Traditions*. Boulder, CO: Westview Press, 1998.

de Certeau, Michel. *The Writing of History*. Translated by Tom Conley. New York: Columbia University Press, 1988.

Dehejia, Vidya. "Aniconism and the Multivalence of Emblems." *Ars Orientalis* 21 (1991): 45–66.

Deol, Jeevan. "Eighteenth-Century Khalsa Identity: Discourse, Praxis, and Narrative." In *Sikh Religion, Culture, and Ethnicity*, edited by Christopher Shackle, Gurharpal Singh, and Arvind-pal Singh Mandair, 25–46. Surrey, UK: Curzon Press, 2001.

————. "Non-Canonical Compositions Attributed to the Seventh and Ninth Sikh Gurus." *Journal of the American Oriental Society* 121, 2 (2001): 193–203.

Dept. of Revenue and Agricultural Proceedings. IOR P/8918. India Office Records, British Library, United Kingdom.

Dhavan, Purnima. "The Warrior's Way: The Making of the Eighteenth-Century *Khalsa* Panth." PhD dissertation, University of Virginia, 2003.

————. "Rehabilitating the Sikh 'Marauder': Changing Colonial Perspectives of Sikhs, 1765–1840." Unpublished paper delivered at the Association for Asian Studies meeting, New York, March 2003.

————. "History, Prophecy, and Power: The Role of Gurbilas Literature in Shaping Khalsa Identity." Unpublished paper delivered at the University of Wisconsin Annual Conference on South Asia, Madison, October 2005.

————. "Redemptive Pasts and Imperiled Futures: The Writing of a Sikh History." *Sikh Formations* 3, 2 (October 2007): 111–24.

————. "Reading the Texture of History and Memory in Early-Nineteenth-Century Punjab." *Comparative Studies of South Asia, Africa, and the Middle East* 29, 3 (2009): 515–27.

———. "Redemptive Pasts and Imperiled Futures: The Writing of a Sikh History." In *Time, History and the Religious Imaginary in South Asia*, edited by Anne Murphy, 40–54. New York: Routledge, 2011.

———. *When Sparrows Became Hawks: The Making of the Sikh Warrior Tradition, 1699–1799*. New York: Oxford University Press, 2011.

Dhillon, Balwant Singh. "Dharamsala: An Early Sikh Religious Centre." In *On Gurdwara Legislation*, edited by Kharak Singh, 36–48. Chandigarh: Institute of Sikh Studies, 1996.

Dhillon, Gurpreet Kaur. *Shrī Gurū Gobind Singh jī dī Bakshish Gur-vastāṅ dā Itihās* (Punjabi). New Delhi: Manpreet Prakashan, 1999.

Dirks, Nicholas B. *The Hollow Crown: Ethnohistory of an Indian Kingdom*. Cambridge: Cambridge University Press, 1987.

———. "History as a Sign of the Modern." *Public Culture* 2, 2 (1990): 25–32.

———, ed. *Colonialism and Culture*. Ann Arbor: University of Michigan Press, 1992.

———. "From Little King to Landlord: Colonial Discourse and Colonial Rule." In *Colonialism and Culture*, 175–208. Ann Arbor: University of Michigan Press, 1992.

———. *Castes of Mind: Colonialism and the Making of Modern India*. Princeton, NJ: Princeton University Press, 2001.

Dogra, Chander Suta. "The Captive Word of a Faith." *Outlook India*, September 6, 2004. http://www.outlookindia.com/article.aspx?225024. Accessed April 20, 2012.

Douie, J. M. *Punjab Settlement Manual* 1899; 3rd ed. Lahore: Government Printing, 1915.

Duncan, Carol. "From the Princely Gallery to the Public Art Museum: The Louvre Museum and the National Gallery, London." In *Representing the Nation: A Reader. Histories, Heritage and Museums*, edited by David Boswell and Jessica Evans. New York: Routledge, 1999.

Dusenbery, Verne. "The Poetics and Politics of Recognition: Diasporan Sikhs in Pluralist Polities." *American Ethnologist* 24, 4 (November 1997): 738–62.

———. *Sikhs at Large: Religion, Culture, and Politics in Global Perspective*. Oxford: Oxford University Press, 2008.

Eaton, Richard M. "The Political and Religious Authority of the Shrine of Baba Farid." In *Moral Conduct and Authority: The Place of* Adab *in South Asian Islam*, edited by Barbara Metcalfe, 262–84. Berkeley: University of California Press, 1984.

———. "Temple Desecration and Indo-Muslim States." In *Essays on Islam and Indian History*, 94–132. New Delhi: Oxford University Press, 2000.

Eck, Diana. *India: A Sacred Geography*. New York: Harmony Books, 2012.

Eliade, Mircea, ed. *The Encyclopedia of Religion*. New York: Macmillan Publishing Company, 1987.

Eley, Geoff and Ronald Grigor Suny, eds. *Becoming National: A Reader*. Oxford: Oxford University Press, 1996.

Entwistle, Alan. *Braj: Centre of Krishna Pilgrimage.* Groningen: Egbert Forsten, 1987.

Fair, C. Christine. "The Novels of Bhai Vir Singh and the Imagination of Sikh Identity, Community, and Nation." In *Sikhism and Women: History, Texts and Experience,* edited by Doris R. Jakobsh, 115–33. New Delhi: Oxford University Press, 2010.

Fasolt, Constantin. *The Limits of History.* Chicago: University of Chicago Press, 2004.

Fenech, Louis. "Martyrdom and the Execution of Guru Arjan in Early Sikh Sources," *Journal of the American Oriental Society,* 121, 1 (2001): 20–31.

———. *Martyrdom in the Sikh Tradition: Playing the "Game of Love."* New Delhi: Oxford University Press, 2000.

———. *The Darbar of the Sikh Gurus: The Court of God in the World of Men.* New Delhi: Oxford University Press, 2008.

Fleming, Benjamin. "Making Land Sacred: Land Grant Inscriptions in the Candra Dynasty." Unpublished paper presented at the American Academy of Religion Annual Meeting, Chicago, 2008.

Flood, Finbarr B. *Objects of Translation: Material Culture and Medieval "Hindu-Muslim" Encounter.* Princeton: Princeton University Press, 2009.

Foucault, Michel. *Discipline and Punish: The Birth of the Prison* 2nd ed. Translated by Alan Sheridan. Westminster MD: Vintage Books, 1995 [1977].

Fox, Richard. *Lions of the Punjab: Culture in the Making.* Berkeley: University of California Press, 1985.

"Ganga Sagar brought from Britain" *The Tribune,* December 18, 2004. http://www.tribuneindia.com/2004/20041218/main4.htm. Accessed April 23, 2005.

Gaur, Ganesh, compiler. *India Office Library: Panjabi Printed Books 1902–1964.* London: Foreign and Commonwealth Office, 1975.

Geary, Patrick J. *Furta Sacra: Thefts of Relics in the Central Middle Ages.* Princeton, NJ: Princeton University Press, 1978.

———. *Living with the Dead in the Middle Ages.* Ithaca, NY: Cornell University Press, 1994.

———. *Phantoms of Remembrance: Memory and Oblivion at the End of the First Millennium.* Princeton NJ: Princeton University Press, 1994.

Gell, Simeran Man Singh. "The Origins of the Sikh 'Look': From Guru Gobind to Dalip Singh." *History & Anthropology* 10, 1 (1996): 37–83.

Germano, David and Kevin Trainor, eds. *Embodying the Dharma: Buddhist Relic Veneration in Asia.* Albany: State University of New York Press, 2004.

Ghosh, Abinaschandra. *The law of endowments (Hindu & Mahomedan): With introduction, history of the origin and development of the charitable and religious institutions in India, and the laws governing them: including the procedure, and all the imperial and local acts, model forms of deeds, pleadings and rules.* Calcutta: Eastern Law House, 1938.

Gilmartin, David. *Empire and Islam: Punjab and the Making of Pakistan.* Berkeley: University of California Press, 1988.

———. "Migration and Modernity: The State, the Punjabi Village, and the Settling of the Canal Colonies." In *People on the Move: Punjabi Colonial and Post-Colonial Migration,* edited by Ian Talbot and Shinder Thandi, 3–20. Oxford: Oxford University Press, 2004.

Golewala Dera Archive, assorted legal documents.

Gopal, Sarvepalli, ed. *Anatomy of a Confrontation: The Babri-Masjid-Ramjanmabhumi Issue.* New Delhi: Viking, Penguin Books India, 1991.

Gordon, Stewart, ed. *Robes and Honor: The Medieval World of Investiture.* New York: Palgrave, 2001.

———. *Robes of Honour:* Khil'at *in Pre-Colonial and Colonial India.* New Delhi: Oxford University Press, 2003.

Gordon, Stewart. "Introduction: Ibn Battuta and a Region of Robing." In *Robes of Honour: Khil'at in Pre-Colonial and Colonial India,* edited by Stewart Gordon, 1–30. New Delhi: Oxford University Press, 2003.

———. "Conclusions." In *Robes of Honour: Khil'at in Pre-Colonial and Colonial India,* edited by Stewart Gordon, 140–46. New Delhi: Oxford University Press, 2003.

Goswamy, B. N. "About the Making of a Throne." *The Tribune,* July 9, 2000. http://www.tribuneindia.com/2000/20000709/spectrum/art.htm. Accessed August 16, 2004.

Goswamy, B. N. and J. S. Grewal, *The Mughals and the Jogis of Jakhbar: Some Madad-i Ma'ash and Other Documents.* Simla: Indian Institute of Advanced Study, 1967.

———. *Mughal and Sikh Rulers and the Vaishnavas of Pindori: A Historical Interpretation of 52 Persian Documents.* Simla: Indian Institute of Advanced Study, 1969.

Government of Punjab, Legislative Department. *Sikh Gurdwaras Act, 1925 (Punjab Act No. VIII of 1925).* Lahore: Superintendent, Government Printing, Punjab, 1927.

Grabar, Oleg. "From the Icon to Aniconism: Islam and the Image." *Museum International* 55, 2 (2003): 46–53.

Granoff, Phyllis. "Images and Their Ritual Use in Medieval India: Hesitations and Contradictions." In *Images in Asian Religions: Texts and Contexts,* edited by Phyllis Granoff and Koichi Shinohara. Vancouver: UBC Press, 2004.

——— and Koichi Shinohara, eds. *Images in Asian Religions: Texts and Contexts.* Vancouver: UBC Press, 2004.

Grewal, J. S. *From Guru Nanak to Maharaja Ranjit Singh.* Amritsar: Department of History, Guru Nanak Dev University, 1982.

———. *The Sikhs of the Punjab.* Cambridge: Cambridge University Press, 1990.

———. *Historical Perspectives on Sikh Identity.* Patiala: Punjabi University, 1997.

———. "Praising the Khalsa: Sainapat's Gursobha." In *The Khalsa: Sikh and Non-Sikh Perspectives,* edited by J. S. Grewal, 35–45. New Delhi: Manohar, 2004.

———. "Brahmanizing the Tradition: Chhibber's Bansāvalīnāma." In *The Khalsa: Sikh and Non-Sikh Perspectives,* edited by J. S. Grewal, 59–101. New Delhi: Manohar, 2004.

———— and S. S. Bal. *Guru Gobind Singh: A Biographical Study*. Chandigarh: Panjab Publication Bureau, 1987 [1967].

Grewal, J. S. and I. Banga, eds. and trans. *Early Nineteenth-Century Panjab: From Ganesh Das's Char Bagh-i-Panjab*. Amritsar: Department of History, Guru Nanak University, 1975.

Grewal, J. S. and Irfan Habib. *Sikh History from Persian Sources: Translations of Major Texts*. New Delhi: Tulika, 2001.

Griffin, Lepel H. *The Panjab Chiefs: Historical and Biographical Notices of the Principal Families in the Territories Under the Panjab Government*. Lahore: T. C. McCarthy-Chronicle Press, 1865.

————. *The Rajas of the Punjab, Being The History of the Principal States in the Punjab and Their Political Relations with the British Government*. 1873. Reprint, Patiala, Punjab: Languages Department, Punjab, 1970.

Guha, Ranajit. *A Rule of Property for Bengal: An Essay on the Idea of Permanent Settlement*. 1981. Reprint, Durham, NC: Duke University Press, 1996.

————. *History at the Limit of World-History*. New York: Columbia University Press, 2002.

Guha, Ranajit and Gayatri Chakravorty Spivak, eds. *Selected Subaltern Studies*. New York: Oxford University Press, 1988.

Guha-Thakurta, Tapati. *Monuments, Objects, Histories: Institutions of Art in Colonial and Postcolonial India*. New Delhi: Permanent Black, 2004.

Guleria, J. S. *Bhai Vir Singh: A Literary Portrait*. Delhi: National Book Shop, 1985.

Gurdhām Dīdār arthāt Gurdhām Darpan (Mukaṅmal Tinn Hisse). Amritsar: Lal Devi Das Janaki Das and Bhai Sham Singh Sohan Singh, no date. IOL Panj B 1186.

Gurdwārā Srī Bhaṭṭhā Sāhib (Punjabi). Amritsar: SGPC, no date.

Guru Gobind Singh Marg: The Great Pilgrimage (Mahan Yatra). Publication information unavailable.

Habib, Irfan. *The Agrarian System of Mughal India, 1556–1707*. Bombay: Asia Publishing House, 1963; 2nd rev. ed., New York: Oxford University Press, 1999.

Halbwachs, Maurice. *On Collective Memory*. Edited, translated, and with an introduction by Lewis A. Coser. Chicago: University of Chicago Press, 1992.

Hambly, G. R. G. "Richard Temple and the Punjab Tenancy Act of 1868." *English Historical Review* 79, 310 (January 1964): 47–66.

Hans, Surjit. *A Reconstruction of Sikh History from Sikh Literature*. Jalandhar: ABS Publications, 1988.

Hardy, Peter. *Historians of Medieval India: Studies in Indo-Muslim Historical Writing*. New Delhi: Munshiram Manoharlal Publishers, 1997.

Hawley, John Stratton. *Krishna, The Butter Thief*. Princeton, NJ: Princeton University Press, 1983.

————. *Surdas: Poet, Singer, Saint*. Seattle: University of Washington Press, 1984.

———. *Songs of the Saints of India*. Text and notes by John Stratton Hawley; translations by J. S. Hawley and Mark Juergensmeyer. New York: Oxford University Press, 1988.

———. "Naming Hinduism." *Wilson Quarterly* 15, 3 (1991): 20–34.

———. "The Nirgun/Sagun Distinction in Early Manuscript Anthologies of Hindu Devotion." In *Bhakti Religion in North India: Community Identity and Political Action*, edited by David N. Lorenzen, 160–80. Albany: State University of New York Press, 1995.

High Court of Judicature at Lahore (India); Privy Council, Judicial Committee (Great Britain). *Indian Law Reports: containing cases determined by the High Court at Lahore and by the Judicial Committee of the Privy Council on appeal from that court.* Lahore series. Volume VII. Lahore: Printed by the Superintendent, Government Printers, Punjab, and published at the Govt. Book Depot, 1926.

———. *Indian Law Reports: containing cases determined by the High Court at Lahore and by the Judicial Committee of the Privy Council on appeal from that court.* Lahore series. Volume XII. Lahore: Printed by the Superintendent, Government Printers, Punjab, and published at the Govt. Book Depot, 1931.

Hirsch, Eric and Charles Stewart. "Ethnographies of Historicity: An Introduction." *History & Anthropology* 16, 3 (2005): 261–74.

Home Department, Political. File No. 459 of 1922, Serial Nos. 1–10: 27. National Archives of India, New Delhi.

Hunter, W. W. *The Indian Musalmans*. Lahore: Premier Book House. Reprint, 1974.

Huntington, Susan. "Early Buddhist Art and the Theory of Aniconism." *Art Journal* 49, 4 (1990): 401–8.

———. "Aniconism and the Multivalence of Emblems: Another Look." *Ars Orientalis* 22 (1991): 111–56.

Hutton, Patrick H. *History as an Art of Memory*. Hanover, NH: University Press of New England, 1993.

Huyssen, Andreas. *Twilight Memories: Marking Time in a Culture of Amnesia*. New York: Routledge, 1993.

———. *Present Pasts: Urban Palimpsests and the Politics of Memory*. Stanford, CA: Stanford University Press, 2003.

Inden, Ronald, Jonathan Walters, and Daud Ali, eds. *Querying the Medieval: Texts and the History of Practices in South Asia*. Oxford: Oxford University Press, 2000.

"Indian Sikhs Furious after Relics Sent to Canada to Raise Funds." *Agence France-Presse*, October 8, 2003. *ClariNet*. http://quickstart.clari.net/qs_se/webnews/wed/cf/Qindia-canada-sikh.Rk_h_DO8.html. Accessed August 16, 2004.

"*Itihās Kaumiat dī Jān Hai, Itihās Kaumāṅ de Prān Hai.*" *Khālsā Samācar* 22, 29 (1921): 3.

Jalal, Ayesha. *Self and Sovereignty: Individual and Community in South Asia since 1850*. London: Routledge, 2000.

Jeffrey, Robin. "Grappling with the Past: Sikh Politicians and the Past." *Pacific Affairs* 60 (1987): 59–72.

Johnston, Hugh. *The Voyage of the Komagata Maru: The Sikh Challenge to Canada's Colour Bar*. New Delhi: Oxford University Press, 1979.

Jones, Jonathan. "Fugitive Pieces: It Was One of Victorian London's Great Attractions, Showing the Wonders of the Raj." *The Guardian*, September 25, 2003, 12.

Jones, Kenneth. *Arya Dharm: Hindu Consciousness in Nineteenth-Century Punjab*. Berkeley: University of California Press, 1976.

———. "Religious Identity and the Indian Census." In *The Census in British India: New Perspectives*, edited by N. G. Barrier, 73–101. New Delhi: Manohar, 1981.

Juergensmeyer, Mark. "The Logic of Religious Violence." *Journal of Strategic Studies* 10 (1987): 172–93.

Kalasvalia, Giani Kartar Singh (Head Granthi, Darbar Sahib, Amritsar). *Sidak Nazāre Arthāt Bīr Khālsā*. Amritsar: Bhai Gurdiaal Singh Deepindra Singh, n.d. IOL 14162.gg.39.(7).

———. *Khūni Shahīdāṅ arthāt Sākkā Srī Nankāṇā Sāhib Jī*. Amritsar: Darbar Press, 1922. IOL 14162.gg.39.(4).

———. *Tegh Khālsā*. Lahore: Ladha Singh and Sons, 1918[?]. IOL 14162.gg.39.

Karp, Ivan and Steven D Lavine, eds. *Exhibiting Cultures: The Poetics and Politics of Museum Display*. Washington, DC: Smithsonian Institution Press, 1991.

Karp, Ivan, Christine Mullen Kreamer, and Steven D. Lavine, eds. *Museums and Communities: The Politics of Public Culture*. Washington, DC: Smithsonian Institution Press, 1992.

Kaur, Madanjit. *The Golden Temple: Past and Present*. Amritsar, Punjab: Department of Guru Nanak Studies, Guru Nanak Dev University Press, 1983.

Kaur, Parvinder and Virbhan Singh. *Kar Sewa of Historical Gurdwaras*. New Delhi: Sapra Publications, 1998.

Kaviraj, Sudipta. *The Unhappy Consciousness: Bankimchandra Chattopadhyay and the Formation of Nationalist Discourse in India*. New Delhi: Oxford University Press, 1998.

King, Richard. *Orientalism and Religion: Post-Colonial Theory, India and the Mystic East*. New York: Routledge, 1999.

Kerr, Ian. "The Punjab Province and the Lahore District, 1849–1872: A Case Study." PhD dissertation, University of Minnesota, 1975.

———. "The British and the Administration of the Golden Temple in 1859." *Panjab Past and Present* 10, 2 (serial no. 20, October 1976): 306–21.

———. "British Relationships with the Golden Temple, 1849–90." *Indian Economic and Social History Review* 21, 2 (1984): 139–51.

Khālsā Advocate, selected editions. Lahore: Tribune Press, 1920.

Khālsā Samācar, selected editions. Amritsar: Wazir Hind Press, 1920–23.

Khan, Zafarul-Islam. "Katiyar Claim Sets Kashmir Valley Aflame." 2005. http://www.milligazette.com/dailyupdate/200203/20020314a.htm. Accessed May 29, 2005.

Khokhar, Giani Pritam Singh. *Brahamgiānī Bhaī Rūp Chaṅd Jī* (Punjabi). Bathinda: Bhai Rup Chand Research and Service Society, 2002.

Khosla, G. S. *Bhai Vir Singh: An Analytical Study*. New Delhi: Heritage Publishers, 1984.

Knauft, Bruce M., ed. *Critically Modern: Alternatives, Alterities, Anthropologies*. Bloomington: Indiana University Press, 2002.

———. "Critically Modern: An Introduction." In *Critically Modern: Alternatives, Alterities, Anthropologies*, edited by Bruce M. Knauft. Bloomington: Indiana University Press, 2002.

Kolff, Dirk. *Naukar, Rajput, and Sepoy: The Ethnohistory of the Military Labour Market in Hindustan, 1450–1850*. Cambridge: Cambridge University Press, 1990.

Kopytoff, Igor. "The Cultural Biography of Things: Commoditization as Process." In *The Social Life of Things*, edited by Arjun Appadurai, 64–91. Cambridge: Cambridge University Press, 1986.

Koselleck, Reinhart. *Futures Past: On the Semantics of Historical Time*. Cambridge, MA: MIT Press, 1985.

Kozlowski, Gregory C. *Muslim Endowments and Society in British India*. Cambridge: Cambridge University Press, 1985.

"Lahore Museum to Set up Sikh Gallery." *The Hindu*, May 17, 2004, online edition: http://www.thehindu.com/2004/05/17/stories/2004051702162000.htm. Accessed June 1, 2004.

Lahore Political Diaries 1847–1848, Vol. III Political Diaries of the Agent to the Governor-general North-West Frontier and Resident at Lahore from 1st January 1847 to 4th March 1848. Allahabad, 1909.

Lal, Shadi, MA BCL. *The Punjab Alienation of Land Act (XIII of 1900) with Exhaustive Commentary, Notifications, Circulars and Proceedings of the Legislative Council*. Lahore: Addison Press, 1905.

Lal, Vinay. "Sikh Kirpans in California Schools: The Social Construction of Symbols, the Cultural Politics of Identity, and the Limits of Multiculturalism." *Amerasia Journal* 22, 1 (1996): 57–90.

Land Revenue Policy of the Indian Government. Calcutta: Office of the Superintendent, Government Printing, 1902.

Launois (Sat Kaur), Anne-Colombe. "The Khalsa Heritage Complex: A Museum for a Community?" In *New Insights into Sikh Art*, edited by Kavita Singh, 134–45. Mumbai: Marg Publications, 2003.

LeGoff, Jacques. *History and Memory*. Translated by Steven Rendall and Elizabeth Claman. 1977. Reprint, New York: Columbia University Press, 1988.

Leonard, Karen Isaksen. *Making Ethnic Choices: California's Punjabi Mexican Americans*. Philadelphia: Temple University Press, 1992.

Login, E. Dalhousie. *Lady Login's Recollections (Court Life and Camp Life—1820–1904)*. Patiala: Punjabi University Language Department, 1970.

Lorenzen, David. "Warrior Ascetics in Indian History." *Journal of the American Oriental Society* (1978): 61–75.

———. "The Kabir Panth: Heretics to Hindus." In *Religious Change and Cultural Domination*, edited by David Lorenzen, 151–71. Mexico: El Collegio de Mexico, 1981.

———. "The Kabir Panth and Social Protest." In *The Sants: Studies in a Devotional Tradition of India*, edited by Karine Schomer and W. H. McLeod, 281–303. Berkeley: Berkeley Religious Studies Series and Motilal Banarsidass, 1987.

———. "Traditions of Non-caste Hinduism." *Contributions to Indian Sociology* 21, 2 (July–December 1987): 263–83.

———. *Praises to a Formless God: Nirguni Texts from North India*. New Delhi: Sri Satguru Publications, 1996.

———. "Who Invented Hinduism." *Comparative Studies in Society and History* 41 (1999): 630–59.

Lucas, A. T. "The Social Role of Relics and Reliquaries in Ancient Ireland." *Journal for the Royal Society of Antiquities of Ireland* 116 (1986): 5–37.

Ludden, David, ed. *Making India Hindu: Religion, Community, and the Politics of Democracy in India*. New Delhi: Oxford University Press, 1996.

———. *The New Cambridge History of India*. IV: 4, *An Agrarian History of South Asia*. Cambridge: Cambridge University Press, 1999.

———. *Reading Subaltern Studies: Critical History, Contested Meaning and the Globalization of South Asia*. London: Anthem Press, 2002.

Lutgendorf, Philip. *The Life of a Text: Performing the Ramcaritmanas of Tulsidas*. Berkeley: University of California Press, 1991.

———. "The Quest for the Legendary Tulsidas." In *According to Tradition: Hagiographical Writing in India*, edited by Winand M. Callewaert and Rupert Snell, 65–85. Wiesbaden: Harrassowitz Verlag, 1994.

Major, Andrew J. *Return to Empire: Punjab under the Sikhs and British in the Mid-Nineteenth Century*. New Delhi: Sterling Publishers, 1996.

Malhotra, Anshu. *Gender, Caste, and Religious Identities: Restructuring Class in Colonial Punjab*. New Delhi: Oxford University Press, 2002.

Mandair, Arvind-pal Singh. "Thinking Differently about Religion and History: Issues for Sikh Studies." In *Sikh Religion, Culture, and Ethnicity*, edited by Christopher Shackle, Gurharpal Singh, and Arvind-pal Singh Mandair, 47–71. Richmond, UK: Curzon Press, 2001.

———. "The Emergence of Modern 'Sikh Theology': Reassessing the Passage of Ideas from Trumpp to Bhai Vir Singh." *Bulletin of the School of Oriental and African Studies* 68, 2 (2005): 253–75.

———. "The Politics of Non-duality: Reassessing the Work of Transcendence in Modern Sikh Theology." *Journal of the American Academy of Religion* 74, 3 (September 2006): 646–73.

———. *Religion and the Specter of the West: Sikhism, India, Postcoloniality, and the Politics of Translation*. New York: Columbia University Press, 2009.

Mann, Gurinder Singh. *The Goindval Pothis: The Earliest Extant Source of the Sikh Canon*. Cambridge, MA: Department of Sanskrit and Indian Studies, Harvard University and Harvard University Press, 1996.

———. *The Making of Sikh Scripture*. Oxford: Oxford University Press, 2001.

———. "Sources for the Study of Guru Gobind Singh's Life and Times." *Journal of Punjab Studies* 15, 1–2 (2008): 229–84.

Marshall, Peter. "Introduction." In *The Eighteenth Century in Indian History: Evolution or Revolution?* edited by Peter Marshall, 1–49. New Delhi: Oxford University Press, 2003.

Mathur, Saloni. *India By Design: Colonial History and Cultural Display*. Berkeley: University of California Press, 2007.

Matringe, Denis. "The Re-enactment of Guru Nanak's Charisma in an Early-Twentieth-Century Panjabi Narrative." In *Charisma and Canon: Essays on the Religious History of the Indian Subcontinent*, edited by Vasudha Dalmia, Angelika Malinar and Martin Christof, 205–22. New Delhi: Oxford University Press, 1996.

Mauss, Marcel. *The Gift: Forms and Functions of Exchange in Archaic Societies*. New York: W. W. Norton, 1967.

McCarthy, Charles. "Sikhs Gather for a Miracle: Sacred Relic Attracts Thousands." *The Fresno Bee*, February 12, 1996, A1.

McLeod, W. H. *Guru Nanak and the Sikh Tradition*. Oxford: Oxford University Press, 1968.

———. *The Evolution of the Sikh Community: Five Essays*. New Delhi: Oxford University Press, 1976.

———. *Early Sikh Tradition: A Study of the Janam-sakhis*. Oxford: Oxford University Press, 1980.

———, ed. *Textual Sources for the Study of Sikhism*. Chicago: University of Chicago Press, 1984.

———. *Who is a Sikh? The Problem of Sikh Identity*. Oxford: Clarendon Press, 1989.

———. *Popular Sikh Art*. Oxford: Oxford University Press, 1991.

———. "The Hagiography of the Sikhs." In *According to Tradition: Hagiographical Writing in India*, edited by Winand M. Callewaert and Rupert Snell, 15–41. Wiesbaden: Harrassowitz Verlag, 1994.

———. *Exploring Sikhism: Aspects of Sikh Identity, Culture, and Thought*. New Delhi: Oxford University Press, 2000.

———. "The Problem of the Panjabi Rahit-namas." In *Exploring Sikhism: Aspects of Sikh Identity, Culture and Thought*, 103–25. New Delhi: Oxford University Press, 2000.

———. *Sikhs of the Khalsa: A History of the Khalsa Rahit*. New Delhi: Oxford University Press, 2003.

Metcalfe, Barbara, ed. *Moral Conduct and Authority: The Place of* Adab *in South Asian Islam*. Berkeley: University of California Press, 1984.

Metcalfe, Thomas. *Land, Landlords, and the British Raj: Northern India in the Nineteenth Century*. Berkeley: University of California Press, 1979.

Minault, Gail. *The Khilafat Movement: Religious Symbolism and Political Mobilization in India*. New York: Columbia University Press, 1982.

———. "The Emperor's Old Clothes: Robing and Sovereignty in Late Mughal and Early British India." In *Robes of Honour: Khil'at in Pre-Colonial and Colonial India*, edited by Stewart Gordon. New Delhi: Oxford University Press, 2003.

Mir, Farina. "Genre and Devotion in Punjabi Popular Narratives: Rethinking Cultural and Religious Syncretism." *Comparative Studies in Society and History* 48, 3 (2006): 727–58.

———. *The Social Space of Language: Vernacular Culture in British Colonial Punjab*. Berkeley: University of California Press, 2010.

Mitchell, Timothy. *Colonising Egypt*. 1988. Reprint, Berkeley: University of California Press, 1991.

Mohammed, Jigar. *Revenue Free Land Grants in Mughal India: Awadh Region in the Seventeenth and Eighteenth Centuries (1658–1765)*. New Delhi: Manohar, 2002.

Morgan, David. *Religion and Material Culture: The Matter of Belief*. London: Routledge, 2010.

Moses, A. Dirk. "Hayden White, Traumatic Nationalism, and the Public Role of History." *History and Theory* 44, 3 (2005): 311–32.

———. "The Public Relevance of Historical Studies: A Rejoinder to Hayden White." *History and Theory* 44, 3 (2005): 339–47.

"MP Faces Trial in Relic Row." BBC website, March 15, 2002. http://news.bbc.co.uk/1/hi/world/south_asia/1874462.stm. Accessed May 29, 2005.

Mukherjee, Tarapada and Irfan Habib. "Akbar and the Temples of Mathura and Its Environs." *Proceedings of the Indian History Congress (PIHC)* 48 (1987): 234–50.

———. "The Mughal Administration and the Temples of Vrindavan during the Reigns of Jahangir and Shahjahan." *Proceedings of the Indian History Congress: Forty-Ninth Session, Karnatak University, Dharwad, 1988*. New Delhi: Indian History Congress, Department of History, University of Delhi/Anamika Publications, 1989.

Murphy, Anne. "Texts of the Guga Tradition: Texts and Contexts." M.A. thesis, University of Washington, 1995.

———. "Museums and the Making of Sikh History." Unpublished paper delivered in panel "Whose Museum? The Collection and Consumption of History, Nation and Community." Annual Meeting of the Association for Asian Studies, San Diego, CA, March 2004.

———. "Mobilizing *Seva* ('Service'): Modes of Sikh Diasporic Action." In *South Asians in Diaspora: Religions and Histories*, edited by Knut Jacobsen and Pratap Kumar, 337–72. Leiden: Brill, 2004.

———. "Materializing Sikh Pasts." *Sikh Formations: Religion, Culture, Theory* 1, 2 (December 2005): 175–200.

———. "History in the Sikh Past." *History and Theory* 46, 2 (October 2007): 345–65.

———. "The Guru's Weapons." *Journal of the American Academy of Religion* 77, 2 (June 2009): 1–30.

———. "The Politics of Possibility and the Commemoration of Trauma." Unpublished paper delivered at "After 1984?" conference, Berkeley, CA, September 12–13, 2009.

———. Review of Louis Fenech's *The Darbar of the Sikh Gurus*. In *Indian Historical Review* 36, 1 (2009): 154–58.

———. "Objects, Ethics, and the Gendering of Sikh Memory." *Early Modern Women: An Interdisciplinary Journal* 4 (2009): 161–68.

———. "March 1849 Lahore, Punjab, India." *Victorian Review* 36, 1 (Spring 2010): 21–26.

———. "Introductory Essay." In *Time, History and the Religious Imaginary in South Asia*, edited by Anne Murphy, 1–11. New York: Routledge, 2011.

———. "The *Gurbilas* Literature and the Idea of 'Religion.'" In *The Punjab Reader*, edited by Anshu Malhotra and Farina Mir, 93–115. New York: Oxford University Press, 2012.

———. "The Gurdwara Landscape and the Territory of Sikh Pasts." In *Negotiating Identity amongst the Religious Minorities of Asia*, edited by Avrum Ehrlich. Leiden: Brill, forthcoming.

———. "The Uses of the 'Folk': Towards a Cultural History of the Guga Tradition." Paper delivered at "Cultural Studies in the Indian Context," National Seminar at Panjab University, March 2–3, 2012. To be published in forthcoming conference proceedings.

———. "Configuring Community in Colonial and Pre-colonial Imaginaries: Insights from the Khalsa Darbar Records." In *Modernity, Diversity and the Public Sphere: Negotiating Religious Identities in 18th-20th Century India*, edited by Martin Fuchs and Vasudha Dalmia. Delhi: Oxford University Press, forthcoming.

Murphy, Anne, ed. *Time, History and the Religious Imaginary in South Asia*. New York: Routledge, 2011.

Nandy, Ashis. "History's Forgotten Doubles." *History and Theory* 34, 2 (1995): 44–66.

Narayana Rao, Velcheru, David Shulman, and Sanjay Subrahmanyam. *Textures of Time: Writing History in South India, 1600–1800*. New Delhi: Permanent Black, 2001.

Narotam, Tara Singh. *Shrī Gurū Tīrth Saṅgraih* (Punjabi). Kankhal: Sri Nirmal Pancaeti Akhara, 1971 [1883]. IOL 14162.n.7 (2).

Neale, Walter C. "Land is to Rule." In *Land Control and Social Structure in Indian History*, 3–15. Madison: University of Wisconsin Press, 1969.

———. "Property in Land as Cultural Imperialism: or, Why Ethnocentric Ideas Won't Work in India and Africa." *Journal of Economic Issues* 19, 4 (1985): 951–58.

Nelson, Matthew Jeremy. "Land, Law, and the Logic of Local Politics in the Punjab, 1849–1999." PhD dissertation, Columbia University, 2002.

Nora, Pierre, ed. *Realms of Memory: Rethinking the French Past*. Translated by Arthur Goldhammer. New York: Columbia University Press, 1996.

———. "Between Memory and History." In *Realms of Memory: Rethinking the French Past*, 1–20. New York: Columbia University Press, 1996.

Novetzke, Christian Lee. "Divining an Author: The Idea of Authorship in an Indian Religious Tradition." *History of Religions* 43 (2003): 213–42.

———. *History, Bhakti, and Public Memory: Namdev in Religious and Secular Traditions*. Ranikhet: Permanent Black, 2009; first published, New York: Columbia University Press, 2008.

Oberoi, Harjot "From Punjab to 'Khalistan': Territoriality and Metacommentary." *Pacific Affairs* 60, 1 (1987): 26–41.

———. "Brotherhood of the Pure: The Poetics and Politics of Cultural Transgression." *Modern Asian Studies* 26, 1 (1992): 157–97

———. "Sikh Fundamentalism: Translating History into Theory." In *Fundamentalisms and the State: Remaking Polities, Economies, and Militance*, edited by Martin E. Marty and Scott Appleby, 256–85. Chicago: University of Chicago Press, 1993.

———. *The Construction of Religious Boundaries: Culture, Identity, and Diversity in the Sikh Tradition*. New Delhi: Oxford University Press, 1994.

———. "What Has a Whale Got to Do With It? A Tale of Pogroms and Biblical Allegories." In *Sikh Religion, Culture, and Ethnicity*, edited by Christopher Shackle, Gurharpal Singh, and Arvind-pal Singh Mandair, 186–206. Richmond, UK: Curzon Press, 2001.

Oldenburg, Veena Talwar. *Dowry Murder: The Imperial Origins of a Cultural Crime*. Oxford: Oxford University Press, 2002.

Olick, Jeffrey and Joyce Robbins. "Social Memory Studies: From 'Collective Memory' to the Historical Sociology of Mnemonic Practices." *Annual Review of Sociology* 24 (1998): 105–40.

Padam, Piara Singh, ed. *Prācīn Pañjābī Gadd*. Patiala: Kalam Mandir, 1978.

Pandey, Gyanendra. *The Construction of Communalism in Colonial North India*. New Delhi: Oxford University Press, 1990.

Parry, Jonathan. "The Gift, The Indian Gift, and the 'Indian Gift.'" *Man* 21, 3 (1986): 453–73.

———. *Death in Banaras*. Cambridge: Cambridge University Press, 1994

Pauwels, Heidi R. M. "Romancing Radha: Nagaridas' Royal Appropriations of Bhakti Themes." *South Asia Research* 25, 1 (2005): 55–78.

Peabody, Norbert. "In Whose Turban Does the Lord Reside? The Objectification of Charisma and the Fetishism of Objects in the Hindu Kingdom of Kota." *Comparative Study in Society and History* 33, 4 (1991): 726–54.

———. *Hindu Kingship and Polity in Precolonial India*. Cambridge: Cambridge University Press, 2003.

Pennington, Brian. *Was Hinduism Invented? Britons, Indians, and the Colonial Construction of Religion*. New York: Oxford University Press, 2005.

Peterson, Indira V. *Poems to Siva: The Hymns of the Tamil Saints*. Princeton, NJ: Princeton University Press, 1989.

Pinch, William. *Peasants and Monks in British India*. Berkeley: University of California Press, 1996.

———. "Subaltern Sadhus? Political Ascetics in Indian Myth, Memory, and History." Draft paper, available on-line at: http://www.virginia.edu/soasia/symsem/kisan/papers/sadhus.html. Accessed April 21, 2012.

———. "History, Devotion and the Search for Nabhadas of Galta." In *Invoking the Past: The Uses of History in South Asia*, edited by Daud Ali, 366–99. New Delhi: Oxford University Press, 1999.

———. "*Bhakti* and the British Empire." *Past and Present* 179 (2003): 159–96.

———. *Warrior Ascetics and Indian Empires*. Cambridge: Cambridge University Press, 2006.

Pollock, Sheldon. "Mimamsa and the Problem of History in Traditional India." *Journal of the American Oriental Society* 109 (1989): 603–10.

Prakash, Gyan. "Writing Post-Orientalist Histories of the Third World: Perspectives from Indian Historiography." *Comparative Studies in Society and History* 32 (1990): 383–408.

———. "Postcolonial Criticism and Indian Historiography." *Social Text* 31/32 (1992): 8–19.

———. "Subaltern Studies as Postcolonial Criticism." *American Historical Review* 99 (1994): 1475–90.

———. "Who's Afraid of Postcoloniality?" *Social Text* 49 (1996): 187–203.

———. *Another Reason: Science and the Imagination of Modern India*. Princeton, NJ: Princeton University Press, 1999.

"Protests over BJP MP's Remarks on Hazratbal." *The Tribune*. March 14, 2002. http://www.tribuneindia.com/2002/20020314/j&k.htm#1. Accessed May 29, 2005.

Punjab Legislative Council. *Punjab Legislative Council Debates*. Lahore, Punjab: Printed by the Superintendent, Government Printers, 1921.

———. *Punjab Legislative Council Debates*. Lahore, Punjab: Printed by the Superintendent, Government Printers, 1922.

———. *Punjab Legislative Council Debates*. Lahore, Punjab: Printed by the Superintendent, Government Printers, 1924.

———. *Punjab Legislative Council Debates*. Lahore, Punjab: Printed by the Superintendent, Government Printers, 1925.

Punjab State Home Proceedings. IOR P/11436. India Office Records, British Library, United Kingdom.

Puri, Harish K. *Ghadar Movement: Ideology, Organizatin, and Strategy*. Amritsar: Guru Nanak Dev University, 1983.

Qaiser, Iqbal. *Historical Sikh Shrines in Pakistan*. Lahore: Punjab History Board, 1998.

Qureshi, M. Naeem. "A Museum for British Lahore." *History Today* 47, 9 (1997): 71–74.

Ramaswamy, Sumathi. "Sanskrit for the Nation." *Modern Asian Studies* 33, 2 (1999): 339–81.

Ramnath, Maia. *Haj to Utopia: How the Ghadar Movement Charted Global Radicalism and Attempted to Overthrow the British Empire*. Berkeley: University of California Press, 2011.

Regulation XIX, Bengal Code 1810. Regulations, 1804–1814. IOR v/8/18. India Office Records, British Library, United Kingdom.

Richards, Thomas. *The Imperial Archive: Knowledge and the Fantasy of Empire*. London: Verso, 1993.

Ricoeur, Paul. *Memory, History, Forgetting*. Translated by Kathleen Blamey and David Pellauer. Chicago: The University of Chicago Press, 2004.

Ridley, Nic. 2002. "A Special City." *Leicester Mercury*, Friday, August 2, 2002, 1, 3–5.

Rinehart, Robin. "Strategies for Interpreting the Dasam Granth." In *Sikhism and History*, edited by Pashaura Singh and N. Gerald Barrier, 135–50. New Delhi: Oxford University Press, 2004.

———. *Debating the Dasam Granth*. New York: Oxford University Press and the American Academy of Religion, 2011.

Roth, Michael. "Foucault's 'History of the Present.'" *History and Theory* 20, 1 (Feb 1981): 32–46.

Roy, Amit. "Sotheby's Pulls Sikh Armour Auction." April 8, 2008. http://www.telegraphindia.com/1080408/jsp/nation/story_9107735.jsp. Accessed June 16, 2008.

Sāhib Srī Gurū Teg Bahādar Jī ate Sāhib Srī Gurū Gobind Siṅgh Jī de Mālwā Desh Raṭan dī Sākhī Pothī. 2nd ed. Amritsar: Khalsa Samachar, 1968.

Sachdeva, Veena. *Polity and Economy of the Punjab during the Late Eighteenth Century*. New Delhi: Mahohar, 1993.

"Sacred Trust: Followers of the Sikh Faith flock to Fresno to View Centuries-old Relics on Loan from India." *The Fresno Bee*, February 21, 2000, A1.

Saha, Shandip. "The Movement of *Bhakti* along a North-West Axis: Tracing the History of the Pustimārg between the Sixteenth and Nineteenth Centuries." *International Journal of Hindu Studies* 11, 3 (December 2007): 299–318.

Sahni, Ruchi Ram. *The Akali Movement: Struggle for Reform in Sikh Shrines*. Amritsar: Sikh Ithas Research Board [1940s?] 1960–69[?].

Sainapati. *Kavi Sainapati Racit Sri Gur Sobha* (Punjabi). Edited by Ganda Singh, 1967. Reprint, Patiala: Publications Bureau, Punjabi University, 1988.

Sākhī Srī Cholā Sāhib Jī (Punjabi). No publication information available; obtained June 2002 from Manjit Singh Bedi in Leeds, England.

Saṅkhep Itihās: Takhat Srī Damdamā Sāhib. Talwandi Sabo, Bathinda: Manager, Takhat Sri Damdama Sahib (Guru Kashi), no date.

Sarkar, Sumit. *Beyond Nationalist Frames: Postmodernism, Hindu Fundamentalism, History*. Bloomington: Indiana University Press, 2002.

Shackle, Christopher. "A Sikh Spiritual Classic: Vīr Singh's *Rāṇā Sūrat Singh*." In *Classics of Modern South Asian Literature*, edited by Rupert Snell and I. M. P. Raeside, 183–209. Wiesbaden: Harrassowitz, 1998.

Shackle, Christopher, Gurharpal Singh, and Arvind-pal Singh Mandair, eds. *Sikh Religion, Culture, and Ethnicity*. Richmond, UK: Curzon Press, 2001.

Sharf, Robert H. "On the Allure of Buddhist Relics." *Representations* 66 (1999): 76–99.

———. "Introduction." In *Living Images: Japanese Buddhist Icons in Context*, edited by Robert H. Sharf and Elizabeth Horton Sharf. Stanford, CA: Stanford University Press, 2001.

Sharma, Radha. *Peasantry and the State: Early Nineteenth Century Punjab*. New Delhi: K. K. Publishers and Distributors, 2000.

———. "The State and Agrarian Society in the Early Nineteenth Century Punjab." In *Precolonial and Colonial Punjab, Society, Economy, Politics, and Culture: Essays for Indu Banga*, edited by Reeta Grewal and Sheena Pall, 143–55. New Delhi: Manohar, 2005.

Schopen, Gregory. *Bones, Stones and Buddhist Monks: Collected Papers on the Archaeology, Epigraphy and Texts of Monastic Buddhism in India*. Honolulu: University of Hawaii Press, 1997.

Scott, David. *Refashioning Futures: Criticism after Postcoloniality*. Princeton, NJ: Princeton University Press, 1999.

Sekhon, Sant Singh and Kartar Singh Duggal. *A History of Punjabi Literature*. Delhi: Sahitya Akedemi, 1992.

Selections from the Records of the Government of India, 1849–1937. IOR v/23/1. India Office Records, British Library, United Kingdom.

Sen, Sudipta. *Empire of Free Trade: The East India Company and Making of the Colonial Marketplace*. Philadelphia: University of Pennsylvania Press, 1998.

———. "Imperial Orders of the Past: The Semantics of History and Time in the Medieval Indo-Persianate Culture of North India." In *Invoking the Past: The Uses of History in South Asia*, edited by Daud Ali, 231–57. New Delhi: Oxford University Press, 1999.

———. *Distant Sovereignty: National Imperialism and the Origins of British India*. New York: Routledge, 2002.

Shani, Giorgio. *Sikh Nationalism and Identity in a Global Age*. London: Routledge, 2008.

Sheehan, James. "The Problem of Sovereignty in European History." *American Historical Review* 111, 1 (2006): 1–15.

Simpson, Moira. *Making Representation: Museums in the Post-Colonial Era*. London: Routledge, 1996.

Singh, Giani Anokh. *Shahīdī Valvale*. Amritsar: Khalsa Pradesi Malwa Press and Sardar Kartar Singh Printer, 1929[?]. IOL Panj B 1128.

Singh, Attar, ed. and trans. "The Travels of Guru Tegh Bahadur and Guru Gobind Singh." In *The Panjab Past and Present*, edited by Ganda Singh. IX, I, 17 (1975): 17–81.

———, ed. and trans. "The Travels of Guru Tegh Bahadur and Guru Gobind Singh." Translated from the original Gurmukhi. Lahore: Indian Public Opinion Press, 1876.

———, trans. Sakhee *Book or The Description of Gooroo Gobind Singh's Religion and Doctrines, Translated from Gooroo Mukhi into Hindi and Afterwards into English*. Benares: Medical Hall Press, 1873.

Singh, Bachan. *Srī Nankāṇā Sāhib dā Sākā tathā Dard Bhare Dukhaṛe Bahut Vadhīā Jisnūṅ Kavī Bacan Siṅgh Siddhamāṅ Nivāsī ne Baiṅtāṅ, Kabitāṅ Surāṅ, te Chaṅdāṅ vic Racke Chapvāyā*. Amritsar: Sri Gurmat Press, Sardar Budh Singh, 1922. IOL Panj F497.

Singh, Bajinder Pal. "Punjab Body to Get Sikh Relics Authenticated." *Indian Express*, July 14, 2000. http://www.indianexpress.com/ie/daily/20000714/ina14015.html. Accessed March 1, 2004.

———. "At Golden Temple, Leap of Faith is Getting Feet Wet, Hands Dirty." *Indian Express*, March 27, 2004. http://www.indianexpress.com/full_story.php?content_id=43838. Accessed April 1, 2004.

Singh, Balwant. *Shrī Damdamā Gurū kī Kāshī* (Punjabi). Kota Guru, Bathinda: Giani Kaur Singh Sahitya Shastri Sadan, 1995[?].

———. *Bhāī Dallā Siṅgh* (Punjabi). No publication information given.

Singh, Bhagat. *A History of the Sikh Misals*. Patiala: Publication Bureau, Punjabi University, 1993.

Singh, Bhai Bhagat. *Shahīdī Nankāṇā Sāhib*. Amritsar: City Press, n.d. IOL Panj F 412 (incomplete).

———. *Sār Amritdhār*. No publication information. IOL Panj D521.

———. *Patibratā Bībī Rajnī Jī*. Amritsar: Bharat Printing Press and Bhai Chatar Singh Jiwan Singh, n.d. [catalog says 1923].

Singh, Chaupa. *The Chaupa Singh Rahit Nama*. Translated and edited by W. H. McLeod. Dunedin, New Zealand: University of Otago Press, 1987.

Singh, Chetan. *Region and Empire: Panjab in the Seventeenth Century*. New Delhi: Oxford University Press, 1991.

Singh, Bhai Dharam. *Sākā Gurū Bāg*. Amritsar: Sri Gurmat Press, 1923. IOL Panj F 1053.

Singh, Fauja, ed. *Historians and Historiography of the Sikhs*. New Delhi: Oriental Publishers and Distributors, 1978.

Singh, Ganda, ed. *Early European Accounts of the Sikhs*. Calcutta: Quality Printers and Binders, 1962.

———. *Some Confidential Papers of the Akali Movement*. Amritsar: Shiromani Gurdwara Parbandhak Committee, Sikh Itihas Research Board, 1965.

———. *Hukamnāme: Gurū Sāhibāṅ, Mātā Sāhibāṅ, Baṅdā Siṅgh and Khālsā Jī de.* 1967[?] Reprint, Patiala: Publication Board, Panjabi University, 1999.

Singh, Ganda, "The Punjab News in the Akhbar-i-Darbar-i-Mualla." *Punjab Past and Present* 2 (October 1970).

———. "Importance of Hair and Turban." In *Sikh Forms and Symbols*, edited by Mohinder Singh, 39–44. New Delhi: Manohar, 2000.

Singh, Gurmukh. *Historical Sikh Shrines.* Amritsar: Singh Brothers, 1995.

Singh, Hari, ed. *Sikh Heritage, Gurdwaras, and Memorials in Pakistan.* New Delhi: Asian Publication Services, 1994.

Singh, Jupinderjit. "Raikot residents wait for 'Ganga Sagar'" *The Tribune*, Monday, December 20, 2004. http://www.tribuneindia.com/2004/20041220/punjab1.htm. Accessed April 23, 2005.

Singh, Kahn. *Mahānkosh: Encyclopedia of Sikh Literature.* New Delhi: National Book Trust, 2000.

Singh, Kavita. "The Museum is National." In *India: A National Culture?* edited by Geeti Sen, 176–96. New Delhi: Sage Publications and India International Centre, 2003.

Singh, Khushwant. "British Loot from India." Originally published in *Hindustan Times*, August 19, 1995, and republished on http://www.sikh-heritage.co.uk/research/british%20loot/br%20loot%20india.htm. Accessed August 23, 2004.

Singh, Kuir. *Gurbilās Pātshāhī Das.* Edited by Shamsher Singh Ashok, introduction by Fauja Singh. Patiala, Punjab: Publications Bureau, Punjabi University, 1999.

Singh, Mahitab. *Nāvāṅ te Thāvāṅ dā Kosh* (Punjabi). Amritsar: Singh Brothers, 1991.

Singh, Bhai Mann. The Damdama Sahib Takhat's Head Granthi or Textual Specialist. Interview, March 2002.

Singh, Bhai Mihar. *Paṅjāb dā Raushan Kisā.* Manuscript, dated 1859. IOL Oriental Manuscript Panjabi B41. India Office Library, British Library, United Kingdom.

Singh, Mohinder. *The Akali Movement.* 1978. Reprint, New Delhi: National Institute of Punjab Studies, 1997. Page references are to the 1997 edition.

———. "The Relics of the Tenth Master." In *The Khalsa: A Saga of Excellence*, 115–27. New Delhi: Media Transasia India Limited, 1999.

———. "Jewels and Relics from Maharaja Ranjit Singh's Toshakhana." *The Tribune*, August 4, 2001. http://www.tribuneindia.com/2001/20010408/spectrum/main8.htm.

———. *Anandpur.* New Delhi: UBS Publishers' Distributors Ltd. in association with National Institute of Panjab Studies, 2002.

———. *The Golden Temple.* New Delhi: UBS Publishers' Distributors Ltd. in association with National Institute of Panjab Studies, 2002.

———. "Sikh Relics Researched, Documented, and Preserved." *The Sikh Times*, January 4, 2003. http://www.sikhtimes.com/analysis_archive_more.html. Accessed February 20, 2005.

———, ed. *Sikh Forms and Symbols.* New Delhi: Manohar, 2000.

Singh, Mohinder and Rishi Singh. *Maharaja Ranjit Singh.* New Delhi: UBS Publishers' Distributors Ltd. in association with National Institute of Panjab Studies, 2002.

Singh, Bhai Nahar. *Dilī Muhabbatāṅ* (Amritsar: Sri Gurmat Press, n.d.; noted by hand 1921). IOL Panj F 709.

———. *Farebī Tiṅṅaṇ arthāt Desh vic Ulaṭ Cālāṅ.* Amritsar: Panjab Khalsa Press, n.d. IOL Panj F 1048.

———. *Kalūkāl dā Puāṛā.* Amritsar: Sri Gurmat Press, 1916. IOL Panj F 391.

———. *Prem de Tīr te Dardāṅ dīāṅ Puṛīāṅ.* Amritsar: Sri Gurmat Press, n.d. [noted by hand 1921]. IOL Panj F 1049.

Singh, Nahar. *Documents Relating to Objects Relating to Guru Gobind Singh's Swords and Sacred Books of the Sikhs in England.* Ludhiana, Punjab: Nangal Khurd, 1967.

Singh, Bhai Nahar and Bhai Kirpal Singh. *Two Swords of Guru Gobind Singh in England (1666–1708 A.D.).* New Delhi: Atlantic Publishers and Distribributors, 1989.

Singh, Nikky-Guninder Kaur. "The Myth of the Founder: The Janamsakhis and Sikh Tradition." *History of Religions* 31 (1992): 329–43.

———. *The Feminine Principle in the Sikh Vision of the Transcendent.* Cambridge: Cambridge University Press, 1993.

———. *The Birth of the Khalsa: A Feminist Re-memory of Sikh Identity.* Albany: State University of New York Press, 2005.

Singh, Nonika. "Restoring Ranjit Singh's Architectural Legacy." http://www.sikhchic.com/architecture/restoring_ranjit_singhs_architectural_legacy. Accessed May 28, 2012.

Singh, Pashaura. "Formulation of the Convention of the Five Ks: A Focus on the Evolution of the Khalsa Rahit." *International Journal of Punjab Studies* 6 (1999): 155–69.

———. *The Guru Granth Sahib: Canon, Meaning and Authority.* New Delhi: Oxford University Press, 2000.

———. *Life and Work of Guru Arjan: History, Memory, and Biography in the Sikh Tradition.* New Delhi: Oxford University Press, 2006.

Singh, Rishi. "State Formation and the Establishment of Non-Muslim Hegemony in the Post Mughal Nineteenth Century Punjab." PhD dissertation, School of Oriental and African Studies, 2009.

Singh, Santokh. *Srī Gur Pratāp Sūraj Graṅth.* Edited by Vir Singh. 1843. Reprint, Amritsar: Khalsa Samachar (For Bhai Vir Singh Sahit Sadan), 1961–65.

Singh, Satbir. *Album of the Central Sikh Museum.* Amritsar: Sri Darbar Sahib, no date.

Singh, Bhayee Sikandar and Roopinder Singh. *Sikh Heritage: Ethos and Relics.* New Delhi: Rupa & Co, 2012.

Singh, Bhai Variam. *Atha Ikk Nek Calaṇ Bībī dī Jabānoṅ Lobhī Māpiāṅ nūṅ Chaṅgī Sikkhyā (Hissā Tīsarā).* Amritsar: Sri Gurmat Press, n.d. IOL Panj F 1223.

———. *Bharatī Nāmā.* Amritsar: Sri Gurmat Press, n.d.

———. *Kuṛī Vecāṇ dā Hāl.* Amritsar: Sri Gurmat Press, n.d.

———. *Guru ke Bāg dā Shāṅt maī Jaṅg ate Bājāṅ Vāle Gurū de Akālī Sūrme.* Amritsar: Gurmat Press, n.d. [marked in IOL catalog as 1923]. IOL Panj F 799.

Singh, Trilochan. "Turban and Sword of the Sikhs." In *Sikh Forms and Symbols*, ed. Mohinder Singh, 45–55. New Delhi: Manohar, 2000.

Smith, Jonathan Z. *To Take Place: Toward Theory in Ritual.* Chicago: University of Chicago Press, 1987.

Smith, Richard Saumarez. *Rule by Records: Land Registration and Village Custom in Early British Panjab.* New Delhi: Oxford University Press, 1996.

Smith, W. C. *The Meaning and End of Religion.* New York: Harper & Row, 1978.

Snell, Rupert. 1994. "Introduction: Themes in Indian Hagiography." In *According to Tradition: Hagiographical Writing in India*, edited by Winand M. Callewaert and Rupert Snell, 1–13. Wiesbaden: Harrassowitz Verlag, 1994.

Sobti, Harcharan Singh. *Studies in Panjabi Fiction.* New Delhi: Eastern Book Linkers, 1987.

"Sodhi Family Asked to Hand Over Kartarpuri Bir to SGPC." *The Tribune.* August 27, 2004. http://www.tribuneindia.com/2004/specials/ggs.htm. Accessed April 23, 2012.

Sri Dasam Granth Sahib Ji Satik (Sri Dasam Granth with Commentary in Modern Punjabi). Commentary by Pandit Narain Singh Ji Giani. Amritsar: Jawahar Singh Kripal Singh and Company, 1992.

Stein, Burton, ed. *The Making of Agrarian Policy in British India: 1770–1900.* New Delhi: Oxford University Press, 1992.

Stoker, Valerie. "Zero Tolerance? Sikh Swords, School Safety, and Secularism in Québec." *Journal of the American Academy of Religion* 75, 4 (December 2007): 814–39.

Stokes, Eric. *The English Utilitarians and India.* Oxford: Clarendon Press, 1959.

Strong, John S. *Relics of the Buddha.* Princeton, NJ: Princeton University Press, 2004.

———. "Buddhist Relics in Comparative Perspective: Beyond the Parralels" in *Embodying the Dharma: Buddhist Relic Veneration in Asia*, eds. David Germano and Kevin Trainor, 27–49. Albany, NY: State University of New York Press, 2004.

Stronge, Susan. *The Arts of the Sikh Kingdoms.* New York: Weatherhill, 1999.

———. "The Sikh Treasury: The Sikh Kingdom and the British Raj." In *Sikh Art and Literature*, edited by Kerry Brown, 72–88. London: Routledge, 1999.

Sundaram, Viji. "Thousands Flock to Fresno to View Guru's Miracle Pitcher." *India-West*, March 1, 1996.

Sweetman, Will. "'Hinduism' and the History of 'Religion': Protestant Presuppositions in the Critique of the Concept of Hinduism." *Method & Theory in the Study of Religion* 15, 4 (2003): 329–53.

Talbot, Cynthia. "Inscribing the Other, Inscribing the Self: Hindu-Muslim Identities in Pre-Colonial India." *Comparative Studies in Society and History* 37, 4 (1995): 692–722.

Tan, Tai Yong. "Assuaging the Sikhs: Government Responses to the Akali Movement, 1920–25." *Modern Asian Studies* 29, 3 (1995): 655–703.

———. *The Garrison State: The Military, Government and Society in Colonial Punjab, 1849–1947.* New Delhi: Sage, 2005.

Tatla, Darshan Singh. "Nurturing the Faithful: The Role of the Sant among Britain's Sikhs." *Religion* 22 (1992): 349–74.

Taussig, Michael. *My Cocaine Museum.* Chicago: University of Chicago Press, 2004.

Terā ek Nemu Tāre Sansār: Sackhaṇḍ Itihās. Publication information not available.

Thapar, Romila. "Society and Historical Consciousness: The *Itihasa-Purana* Tradition." In *Interpreting Early India*, 137–73. New Delhi: Oxford University Press, 1992 [1986].

———. "Time as a Metaphor of History: Early India." In *History and Beyond*. New Delhi: Oxford University Press, 2000.

Todd, Douglas. "B.C. Sikhs Have Had a Long, Hard Road for 100 Years." *Vancouver Sun*, January 11, 2011. http://blogs.vancouversun.com/2011/01/11/b-c-sikhs-have-had-a-long-hard-road-for-100-years/. Accessed May 28, 2012.

Trainor, Kevin. *Relics, Ritual, and Representation in Buddhism: Rematerializing the Sri Lankan Theravada Tradition.* New York: Cambridge University Press, 1997.

———. "Introduction: Beyond Superstition." In *Embodying the Dharma: Buddhist Relic Veneration in Asia*, edited by David Germano and Kevin Trainor, 1–26. Albany: State University of New York Press, 2004.

Tribune, assorted editions. Chandigarh: Tribune Press, 1965–66, 1973.

Uberoi, J. P. S. "The Five Symbols of Sikhism." In *Perspectives on Guru Nanak*, edited by Harbans Singh, 502–13. Patiala: Punjabi University, 1975.

Vahiria, Bhai Avtar Singh. *Shok Pattr.* Lahore: Sri Gurmat Press, n.d. Received by the India Office in 1909. IOL Panj B 1380.

Vaid, Bhai Mohan Singh. *Bhayānak Sākkā.* Amritsar Punjab: Wazir Hind Press, n.d.

———. *Adutī Sākā.* Amritsar: Panth Sevak Press, n.d.

Vatsyayan, Kapila. "Introduction." In *Govindadeva: A Dialogue in Stone*, edited by Margaret H. Case. New Delhi: Indira Gandhi National Centre for the Arts, 1996.

von Stietencron, Heinrich. "Religious Configurations in Pre-Muslim India and the Concept of Hinduism." In *Representing Hinduism: The Construction of Religious Traditions and National Identity*, edited by Vasudha Dalmia and H. von Stietencron, 51–81. Thousand Oaks, CA: Sage Publications, 1995.

Wagoner, Phillip B. "Sultan among Hindu Kings: Dress, Titles, and the Islamicization of Hindu Culture at Vijayanagara." *Journal of Asian Studies* 55, 4 (1996): 851–80.

Warner, Michael. *Publics and Counterpublics.* Brooklyn, NY: Zone Books, 2002.

Wayland, Sarah V. "Religious Expression in Public Schools: *Kirpans* in Canada, *Hijab* in France." *Ethnic & Racial Studies* 20, 3 (July 1997): 544–60.

Weber, Max. *On Charisma and Institution Building: Selected Papers.* Edited by S. N. Eisenstadt. Chicago: University of Chicago Press, 1968.

White, Hayden. *Content of the Form: Narrative Discourse and Historical Representation.* Baltimore, MD: John Hopkins University Press, 1987.

Index

Thapar, Romila, 8
tract/pamphlet literature, 38, 127–34,
    203, 212, 213, 218, 241
Trainor, Kevin, 5, 22, 23n9, 64
"The Travels of Guru Tegh Bahadur and
    Guru Gobind Singh," 109, 111,
    112n7, 115, 116, 120
Trehan family, 95
Trumpp, Ernest, 146, 230, 231

Uberoi, J. P. S., 61, 63
Udasi sect, 106, 168, 169, 206, 211, 216,
    231, 232
(Bhai) Udday Singh, 35
Udday Singh, king of Kaithal, 114,
    115
UK. *See* England
Una, 53n111, 167n63, 180
United States of America (USA), 5n6,
    10, 11, 52, 198, 201, 213n101, 258,
    261–63

Vaid, Mohan Singh. *See* (Bhai) Mohan
    Singh Vaid
Vaisakhi, 4, 86, 245
(Bhai) Variam Singh, 132
Vatsyayan, Kapila, 162
vernacular language and literature,
    72–78, 228. *See also* Braj, Punjabi,
    tract/pamphlet literature
(Bhai) Vir Singh (BVS), 77, 121, 123, 124,
    132, 133, 152. *See also Sundari*

warrior ascetics, 90n85, 91
White, Hayden, 94, 253
Wing Luke Asian Museum, Seattle,
    258

Zafar, Ali J., 231
Zafar Namah of Guru Gobind Singh,
    73
*zamindar*s/*zamindari*, 79, 157n21, 158,
    173, 175, 176